Fabian Wagner

Isomorphism Testing for Restricted Graph Classes

Fabian Wagner

Isomorphism Testing for Restricted Graph Classes

On the complexity of isomorphism testing
and reachability problems for restricted
graph classes

Südwestdeutscher Verlag für Hochschulschriften

Impressum/Imprint (nur für Deutschland/ only for Germany)
Bibliografische Information der Deutschen Nationalbibliothek: Die Deutsche Nationalbibliothek verzeichnet diese Publikation in der Deutschen Nationalbibliografie; detaillierte bibliografische Daten sind im Internet über http://dnb.d-nb.de abrufbar.

Alle in diesem Buch genannten Marken und Produktnamen unterliegen warenzeichen-, markenoder patentrechtlichem Schutz bzw. sind Warenzeichen oder eingetragene Warenzeichen der jeweiligen Inhaber. Die Wiedergabe von Marken, Produktnamen, Gebrauchsnamen, Handelsnamen, Warenbezeichnungen u.s.w. in diesem Werk berechtigt auch ohne besondere Kennzeichnung nicht zu der Annahme, dass solche Namen im Sinne der Warenzeichen- und Markenschutzgesetzgebung als frei zu betrachten wären und daher von jedermann benutzt werden dürften.

Verlag: Südwestdeutscher Verlag für Hochschulschriften Aktiengesellschaft & Co. KG
Dudweiler Landstr. 99, 66123 Saarbrücken, Deutschland
Telefon +49 681 37 20 271-1, Telefax +49 681 37 20 271-0
Email: info@svh-verlag.de
Zugl.: Ulm, Universität, Diss., 2010

Herstellung in Deutschland:
Schaltungsdienst Lange o.H.G., Berlin
Books on Demand GmbH, Norderstedt
Reha GmbH, Saarbrücken
Amazon Distribution GmbH, Leipzig
ISBN: 978-3-8381-1954-0

Imprint (only for USA, GB)
Bibliographic information published by the Deutsche Nationalbibliothek: The Deutsche Nationalbibliothek lists this publication in the Deutsche Nationalbibliografie; detailed bibliographic data are available in the Internet at http://dnb.d-nb.de.

Any brand names and product names mentioned in this book are subject to trademark, brand or patent protection and are trademarks or registered trademarks of their respective holders. The use of brand names, product names, common names, trade names, product descriptions etc. even without a particular marking in this works is in no way to be construed to mean that such names may be regarded as unrestricted in respect of trademark and brand protection legislation and could thus be used by anyone.

Publisher: Südwestdeutscher Verlag für Hochschulschriften Aktiengesellschaft & Co. KG
Dudweiler Landstr. 99, 66123 Saarbrücken, Germany
Phone +49 681 37 20 271-1, Fax +49 681 37 20 271-0
Email: info@svh-verlag.de

Printed in the U.S.A.
Printed in the U.K. by (see last page)
ISBN: 978-3-8381-1954-0

Copyright © 2010 by the author and Südwestdeutscher Verlag für Hochschulschriften Aktiengesellschaft & Co. KG and licensors
All rights reserved. Saarbrücken 2010

Acknowledgments

I would like to thank my supervisor, Prof. Dr. Jacobo Torán. His continuous support and guidance have greatly influenced my research and this work. This thesis arose in the context of the DFG research project: *Die Komplexität des Graphenisomorphieproblems* and the Graduate School: *Mathematical Analysis of Evolution, Information and Complexity*. I am grateful to Prof. Dr. Thomas Thierauf for the close collaboration. I wish to thank Meena Mahajan, Samir Datta, Nutan Limaye and Prajakta Nimbhorkar for intensively working together on isomorphism and reachability problems. Finally, I thank my parents and my family Gudrun and Sebastian for love and patience.

Contents

1 Introduction   **1**
    1.1 Overview of the Thesis 4

2 Preliminaries   **9**
    2.1 Complexity Theory 9
    2.2 Graph Theory 17
    2.3 Group Theory 28
    2.4 Graph Isomorphism and Related Decision Problems 31
    2.5 Graph Reachability and Related Decision Problems 32
    2.6 Proof Techniques 34

3 Tournament Isomorphism   **39**
    3.1 Introduction 39
    3.2 Hardness Results for Tournament Isomorphism 40
    3.3 Hardness Results for Tournament Automorphism 51

4 Isomorphism for Bounded Valence Graphs   **57**
    4.1 Introduction 57
    4.2 Valence-2 Graph Isomorphism 57
    4.3 Coloring and Bounded Valence 59
    4.4 Valence-k Graph Isomorphism 61
    4.5 Isomorphism for Cycles and Lines 63
    4.6 Hardness of Valence-k Graph Automorphism 64
    4.7 An Application, the Complexity of the Poset-Game Problem . . . 67

5 Isomorphism for Planar 3-Connected Graphs   **71**
    5.1 Introduction 71
    5.2 The Complexity of UL ∩ coUL 73
    5.3 Computing Distances in Planar Graphs 73
    5.4 Planar 3-Connected Graph Isomorphism 75
    5.5 Oriented Graph Isomorphism 80

5.6 Hardness of Isomorphism for Planar 3-Connected Graphs and Oriented Trees . . 81
5.7 Label Gadgets for Planar 3-Connected Graphs and Oriented Graphs 84
5.8 Label Gadgets for Planar Biconnected Graphs 88
5.9 Further Work 89

6 Isomorphism for $K_{3,3}$-Minor Free Graphs   91
6.1 Introduction 91
6.2 Canonization of Biconnected $K_{3,3}$-Minor Free Graphs 94
6.3 Canonization of $K_{3,3}$-Minor Free Graphs 104

7 Isomorphism for K_5-Minor Free Graphs   121
7.1 Introduction 121
7.2 Decomposition of K_5-Minor Free Graphs 122
7.3 Isomorphism Order of K_5-Minor Free Graphs 128

8 Isomorphism for Graphs of Bounded Treewidth   153
8.1 Introduction 153
8.2 Graphs of Bounded Tree Distance Width 154
8.3 Graphs of Bounded Treewidth 165

9 Reachability in $K_{3,3}$-Minor Free and K_5-Minor Free Graphs   175
9.1 Introduction 175
9.2 Reachability in $K_{3,3}$-Minor Free Graphs 176
9.3 Reachability in K_5-Minor Free Graphs 183

10 The Quasigroup Isomorphism Problem   195
10.1 Introduction. 195
10.2 On the Complexity of Quasigroup Isomorphism 196
10.3 On the Complexity of Cayley-Group Isomorphism 199
10.4 On the Complexity of Abelian Cayley-Group Isomorphism 201

11 Further Work and Conclusions   203

Index   205

Bibliography   211

Deutsche Zusammenfassung   223

Notation

Symbol	Explanation	Page
1^n	word of length n encoded in unary	9
$\leq_m^{\mathcal{F}}$	many-one reduction	17
$\leq_T^{\mathcal{F}}$	Turing reduction	17
$\leq_{ctt}^{\mathcal{F}}$	conjunctive truth table reduction	17
$\leq_{dtt}^{\mathcal{F}}$	disjunctive truth table reduction	17
$\leq_m^{\mathsf{AC}^0}$	AC^0 many-one reduction	17
$\leq_m^{log}$	logspace many-one reduction	17
$\leq_T^{log}$	logspace Turing reduction	17
$\leq_\mathsf{A}, =_\mathsf{A}$	isomorphism order on augmented trees	158, 159
$\leq_\mathsf{B}, =_\mathsf{B}$	isomorphism order on biconnected component trees	106, 107
$\leq_\mathsf{F}, =_\mathsf{F}$	isomorphism order on four-connected component trees	133
$\leq_\mathsf{T}, =_\mathsf{T}$	isomorphism order on triconnected component trees	99, 128
$\cong$	isomorphism relation, $G \cong H$	18
$\square$	operator, for the Cartesian product of graphs	19
$\times$	operator, for the Cartesian product of sets	19
$\circ, f \circ g$	composition of functions, we define $(f \circ g)(x) = f(g(x))$	16
$\circ, \mathcal{C} \circ \mathcal{C}'$	composition of complexity classes, function $f \circ g \in \mathcal{C} \circ \mathcal{C}'$ if f is computable in $\mathcal{C}$ and g in $\mathcal{C}'$, also see $\mathcal{C}(\mathcal{C}')$	16
(u,v)	directed edge, points from u to v	17
$\{u,v\}$	undirected edge, connects u with v	17
$[k,n]$	set of elements $\{k, k+1, \ldots, n-1, n\}$	28
$\langle S \rangle$	generating set of a group	29
$\overline{L}$	complement of language L	9
$\#\mathsf{L}$	counting complexity class, sharp-L	15
$\#t$	number of children of a node t in a rooted tree	27
$|T|$	size (number of nodes) of a tree T	27
$\oplus, \oplus_k$	operator for modulo addition in $\mathbb{Z}_k$	28
$\oplus\mathsf{L}$	complexity class, parity-L	14
$\beta_i \mathcal{C}$	complexity class, $\mathcal{C}$ with $O(\log^i n)$ bits as additional choice input (i.e. for non-deterministic computations), where $\mathcal{C}$ is one of L, FOLL, SAC^j, NC^j or P	16
$\Gamma(v), \Gamma_G(v)$	set of neighbors of vertex v in graph G	18
Σ	alphabet, a set of symbols	9

NOTATION

Symbol	Explanation	Page
Σ^*	set of all words over alphabet Σ	9
ρ	rotation scheme for a graph G, $\rho = \{\rho_v \mid v \in V(G)\}$	19
ρ_v	rotation function, rotation over all edges around a vertex v in a graph	19
τ, τ_i, σ	separating triple nodes (with index i)	127
$\sigma\phi(\Omega)$	permutations applied to Ω, i.e. $\sigma(\phi(\Omega))$	29
Ω	set of elements, where a group acts on this set	29
$acc_M(x)$	function, computes the number of accepting computation paths of a non-deterministic Turing machine M on input x	11
AC^0	complexity class, contains languages, accepted by families of polynomial size, unbounded fanin, $O(1)$-depth circuits	14
AC^i	complexity class, contains languages accepted by families of polynomial size, unbounded fanin, $O(\log^i(n))$-depth circuits	14
$Aut(G)$	automorphism group of a graph G	30
$Aut_G(H)$	set of automorphisms of subgraph H which can be extended to an automorphism of graph G	30
AuxPDA	auxiliary pushdown automaton	12
$B_G[U, W]$	induced bipartite subgraph of graph G on sets U, W	18
$C_=L$	complexity class, exact-counting logspace	15
$\mathcal{C}(\mathcal{C}')$	composition of complexity classes, a function $f \circ g$ is in $\mathcal{C}$-closure of $\mathcal{C}'$, if f is computable in $\mathcal{C}$ and g in $\mathcal{C}'$	16
$C[w]$	circuit C with word w as input	10
CFL	set of context free languages	15
color-GI	decision problem, color graph isomorphism	31
DAG	directed acyclic graph	19
DET	complexity class, determinant (of integer matrices)	15
$d_G(S, v), d(S, v)$	minimum distance from a vertex in S to v in graph G	19
$d_G(u, v), d(u, v)$	minimum distance from vertex u to v in graph G	19
$d_G(v), d(v)$	maximum distance from v to all vertices in G	19
Distance	decision problem, distance	33
DLOGTIME	complexity class, $\log n$ time bounded computation	13
DTIME($f(n)$)	complexity class, $f(n)$-time bounded computation	13

Symbol	Explanation	Page
DTM	deterministic Turing machine	11
$E(G)$	set of edges of a graph G	17
$\mathsf{FirstChild}(t, \mathsf{order})$	function, computes the first child of node t according to function order in a rooted tree	35
FL	complexity class, functional deterministic logspace	16
FP	complexity class, functional deterministic polynomial time	16
$\mathcal{G}$	set of all graphs	30
$G(C)$	circuit graph for circuit C	41
$G \setminus E'$	graph G with edges $E(G) \setminus E'$	18
$G \setminus H$	induced subgraph on vertex set $V(G) \setminus V(H)$	18
$G \cup H$	disjoint union of graphs	19
G^k	modulo addition graph gadget	41
$G(M, x)$	configuration graph of Turing machine M on input x	33
$G_{[S_1,\ldots,S_k]}$	graph G with S_i setwise stabilized in its automorphism group	30
$G[X]$	induced subgraph of G on vertex set $X \subseteq V(G)$	18
GA	decision problem, graph automorphism	31
Gad_k	oracle graph gadget	49
GI	decision problem, graph isomorphism	31
GI_b	decision problem, graph isomorphism for graphs with n vertices and color classes of size $\leq b(n)$	31
$\mathsf{graph}(T)$	the graph which corresponds to a tree T of a tree decomposition	24
$K_{i,j}$	complete bipartite graph on two sets of i and of j vertices	18
K_n	clique, complete graph on n vertices	17
L	complexity class, deterministic logspace	13
LogCFL	complexity class, contains languages logspace reducible to a context free language	15
LongPath	decision problem, longest simple paths	33
$\mathbb{N}$	infinite set of natural numbers: $\{1, 2, \ldots\}$	28
$\mathbb{N}_0$	infinite set of natural numbers, including $\{0\}$	28
NAuxPDA	non-deterministic auxiliary push down automaton	12

NOTATION

Symbol	Explanation	Page
NC^i	complexity class, contains languages accepted by families of polynomial size, fanin 2, $O(\log^i(n))$-depth circuits	14
NDTM	non-deterministic Turing machine	11
NextSibling(t, order)	function, computes the next sibling of t according to function order in a rooted tree	35
NimGame	decision problem, nim game	69
NL	complexity class, non-deterministic logspace	13
NP	complexity class, non-deterministic polynomial time	13
Ord	decision problem, order between vertices	34
P	complexity class, deterministic polynomial time	13
Parent(t)	function, computes the parent of t in a rooted tree	35
PDA	pushdown automaton	12
PGA	decision problem, promise-GA, set of all tuples $((G,H),(I,J))$ with rigid graphs and $G \cong H \Leftrightarrow I \not\cong J$	32,52
PGI	decision problem, promise-GI, set of all tuples $((G,H),(I,J))$ with $G \cong H \Leftrightarrow I \not\cong J$	32,46
PL	complexity class, probabilistic logspace	15
PosetGame	decision problem, poset game	68
prefix-GA	decision problem, prefix graph automorphism	31
PTA	decision problem, promise-TA, set of all tuples $((G,H),(I,J))$ with rigid tournaments and $G \cong H \Leftrightarrow I \not\cong J$	53
PTI	decision problem, promise-TI, set of all tuples $((G,H),(I,J))$ with tournaments and $G \cong H \Leftrightarrow I \not\cong J$	46
Reachability	decision problem, reachability	33
$rej_M(x)$	function, computes the number of rejecting computation paths of a non-deterministic Turing machine M on input x.	11
SAC^1	complexity class, contains languages accepted by families of polynomial size, semi-unbounded fanin, $O(\log(n))$-depth circuits	15
size($\mathcal{T}$)	function, sum of the sizes of individual components associated to nodes in a component tree $\mathcal{T}$	27

Symbol	Explanation	Page
S_n	symmetric group, group over all permutations of the set of n elements, $\{1, 2, \ldots, n\}$	29
$\mathsf{SPACE}(f(n))$	complexity class, $f(n)$-space bounded computation	13
$Sym(V)$	symmetric group over the set V	29
$T(C)$	circuit graph of circuit C, which is a tournament	45
$T_{(G,D)}$	augmented tree of a tree-distance width graph G and a tree distance decomposition D	155
TA	decision problem, tournament automorphism	40
TC^i	complexity class, contains languages accepted by families of polynomial size, unbounded fanin, $O(\log^i(n))$-depth circuits with threshold gates	14
$\mathcal{T}, \mathcal{T}(G), \mathcal{T}_C$	component tree rooted at node C, nodes are associated to components and separating sets of a graph G	27
$\mathcal{T}^4, \mathcal{T}^4(G), \mathcal{T}_C^4$	tree on 4-connected components of a 3-connected K_5-minor free graph G, respectively rooted at node C	188
$\mathcal{T}^{\mathsf{B}}, \mathcal{T}^{\mathsf{B}}(G), \mathcal{T}_C^{\mathsf{B}}$	biconnected component tree of a connected graph G, respectively rooted at node C	21, 26
$\mathcal{T}^{\mathsf{F}}, \mathcal{T}^{\mathsf{F}}(G), \mathcal{T}_C^{\mathsf{F}}$	four-connected component tree of a triconnected graph G, respectively rooted at node C	127
$\mathcal{T}^{\mathsf{T}}, \mathcal{T}^{\mathsf{T}}(G), \mathcal{T}_C^{\mathsf{T}}$	triconnected component tree of a biconnected graph G, respectively rooted at node C	24, 27
$TGad_k$	oracle tournament gadget	49
TI	decision problem, tournament isomorphism	40
T^k	tournament modulo addition graph gadget	43
T_t	subtree of a (rooted) tree T, rooted at node t	27
UL	complexity class, unambiguous logspace	14
$V(G)$	set of vertices of a graph G	17
$(\{X_i \mid i \in I\}, T = (I, F))$	tree decomposition, tree distance decomposition of a graph G	27
$\mathbb{Z}$	infinite set of integers: $\{\ldots, -1, 0, 1, 2, \ldots\}$	28
$\mathbb{Z}_k$	set of integers modulo k: $\{0, 1, 2, \ldots, k-1\}$	28

1 Introduction

The Graph Isomorphism Problem

Two graphs G and H are *isomorphic* if there is a bijection from the vertices of G onto the vertices of H which preserves the edge relation. Given two graphs, the *graph isomorphism problem* (GI) is the problem of deciding if the two graphs are isomorphic or not.

The wide gap between the known lower and upper bounds for the problem has kept alive the research interest in GI. The problem is clearly in NP. It is known to be in coAM [GS87, Sch88], by a group theoretic proof also in SPP [AK06]. By combining Zemlyachenko's degree reduction technique with Luks' algorithm for graphs of bounded degree, it is possible to solve GI in time $2^{\sqrt{O(n \log n)}}$, see [Bab81, ZKT85, BL83]. This is the current frontier as far as upper bounds go. The inability to find efficient algorithms for GI motivates the conjecture, that the problem is hard. On the other hand, NP-hardness is precluded by a result that states if GI is NP-hard then the polynomial time hierarchy collapses to the second level [BHZ87, Sch88]. Kozen defined a class of graphs of size n^2, where finding a clique of size n is logspace equivalent to GI [Koz78]. What is more surprising is, that not even P-hardness is known for the problem. The best we know is, that GI is hard for DET [Tor04], the class of problems NC^1-reducible to the determinant, defined by Cook [Coo85]. In [Tor07] it is shown that several reducibility notions coincide when applied to GI.

Related to GI are several other decision problems, some graph-theoretic and others group-theoretic in nature. One such problem is the graph automorphism problem (GA): decide whether a graph has a non-trivial automorphism. Mathon [Mat79] proved that GI and GA are equivalent under polynomial time Turing reductions. Lubiw [Lub81] and Lozano and Raghavan [LR98] consider GA with the restriction of the number k of vertices not allowed to be fixed. The problem is NP-complete for $k \in O(n^\epsilon)$ for any fixed $0 < \epsilon < 1$, it becomes equal to GA for $k \in O(\log n / \log \log n)$ and equal to GI for $k \in O(\log n)$. Arvind, Beigel and Lozano [ABL98] define and study the modular graph automorphism problem mod_k-GA, i.e. for $k > 1$ decide whether the number of automorphisms of a graph is divisible by k. These problems turn out to be intermediate in complexity between GA and GI. There are problems which are polynomial time equivalent to GI, for example, the isomorphism problem for semigroups when given as multiplication table as well as for finite automata [Boo78], or computing the number of isomorphisms from one onto another graph, also denoted #GI [Mat79], or the construction problem

1. INTRODUCTION

of an isomorphism from G onto H. In contrast, the counting versions of NP-complete problems are complete for #P [Tod91].

Graph Isomorphism is polynomial time Turing reducible to the permutation group isomorphism problem which is known to be in NP ∩ coAM [Luk93]. It also reduces to the problem: find on input a graph G the generators of its automorphism group $Aut(G)$. The double coset membership problem is a natural generalization of GI, it is complete for NP [Hof82b].

This enormous gap has motivated a study of isomorphism in *general* graphs. It has also induced research in isomorphism restricted to special cases of graphs where this gap can be reduced. For example, isomorphism of strongly regular graphs can be determined in $n^{O(n^{1/3}\log n)}$ time [Spi96]. Tournaments are graphs, where each pair of vertices is connected by one directed edge. Tournament isomorphism is an example where the DET lower bound is preserved [Wag07], while there is a quasi-polynomial time upper bound [BL83], i.e. the algorithm takes $n^{O(\log n)}$ time.

The graph isomorphism problem is polynomial time reducible to the ring isomorphism problem when given in basis representation [KS05]. When given in table representation there is an algorithm that runs in time $n^{O(\log n)}$, c.f. [Agr07]. Related to this, there is also the isomorphism problem on Cayley groups. When two groups are given in table representation, algorithms are known which run in time $n^{O(\log n)}$ by Tarjan (c.f. [Mil78]), or run in space $O(\log^2 n)$ [LSZ76]. Group isomorphism and also quasigroup isomorphism in table representation are reducible to GI [Mil79].

Efficient algorithms are known for isomorphism testing on many classes of graphs. Polynomial time algorithms exist for the isomorphism problem restricted to the graphs of bounded genus [Mil80], bounded degree [Luk82], bounded color classes [Luk86], bounded treewidth [Bod90] or graphs with excluded minors [Pon91].

In some cases problems have been classified in small complexity classes below P. Luks gives a NC algorithm for isomorphism testing for graphs of bounded color classes [Luk86]. Arvind, Kurur and Vijayaraghavan [AKV05] further improved this result by showing that the problem is in $\mathsf{Mod}_k\mathsf{L}$, where the constant k and the level of the hierarchy depend on the size bound b of the color classes. Prior to this result, Torán proved that GI_{b^2}, i.e. isomorphism testing for graphs of color class size b^2, is hard for $\mathsf{Mod}_b\mathsf{L}$ [Tor04]. This lower bound has been extended in [AKV05], where it is shown that for each level in the $\mathsf{Mod}_k\mathsf{L}$ hierarchy there is a constant b such that GI_b is hard for this level. There is also an NC algorithm for isomorphism testing for graphs with bounded eigenvalue multiplicity [BLS87, Bab86, Luk86]. It remains open whether GI for graphs of bounded degree is in NC. Grohe and Verbitsky improved Bodlaender's upper bound by showing that GI for graphs of bounded treewidth is in TC^1 [GV06]. We showed in joint work with Das and Torán that GI for graphs of bounded treewidth is in LogCFL [DTW10]. For the planar graph isomorphism problem, the parallel complexity was first considered by

Miller and Reif [MR91] and Ramachandran and Reif [RR94]. They showed that the upper bound is AC^1, see also [Ver07]. Lindell presented a logspace algorithm for canonization for trees [Lin92]. Logspace-completeness follows from Jenner et.al. [JKMT03].

Some of these upper bounds have been improved with the development of space efficient techniques, most notably Reingold's deterministic logarithmic space algorithm for connectivity in undirected graphs [Rei08].

In joint work with Datta, Limaye, Nimbhorkar and Thierauf, the complexity of canonization for planar graphs could be settled. For planar 3-connected graphs canonization is in logspace [DLN08], completeness follows from [TW08]. The Log-space completeness could be extended to the class of planar graphs [DLN+09], $K_{3,3}$-minor free graphs and K_5-minor free graphs [DNTW09]. In joint work with Das and Torán, we gave a logspace algorithms for the canonization of bounded tree-distance width graphs [DTW10]. Recently, Köbler and Kuhnert prove logspace completeness for canonization of k-trees [KK09]. More recently, Köbler et.al. prove that a canonical representation for interval graphs can be computed in logspace [KKLV10].

If we consider complexity bounds below L, then the encoding of the input graphs becomes important. For example for trees, when encoded in string representation, the canonization problem is in NC^1 [Bus97], which is optimal [JKMT03]. The same holds for isomorphism testing for abelian groups. When abelian groups are given as generating sets, isomorphism testing is hard for ModL and is contained in ZPL^{ModL} [AV04]. But if abelian groups are given as multiplication tables then isomorphism testing is in L, we can prove that it is also in TC^0(FOLL).

The Reachability Problem

Besides the isomorphism problem we also consider in this thesis the complexity of reachability and related decision problems for restricted graph classes. The reachability problem is defined as follows. On input a graph G and vertices s, t, the problem is to decide whether there exists a path connecting s with t. Reachability is a widely studied problem in complexity theory, especially in the space setting. It characterizes complexity classes, for example L or NL when considering edges to be undirected or directed, respectively. It also has its importance in graph theory.

For undirected graphs, the reachability problem is L-complete [Rei08]. For general graphs, reachability is NL-complete. Bourke, Tewari and Vinodchandran [BTV07] prove that reachability on planar graphs is in UL ∩ coUL and is hard for L. They build on the work of Reinhard and Allender [RA00] and Allender, Datta and Roy [ADR05]. A more direct proof is given by Kulkarni [Kul09]. Jakoby and Tantau [JT07] show for series-parallel graphs that reachability is complete for L. They also consider the problems of computing distances (**Distance**) or longest simple paths (**LongPath**) between two vertices. They show that both problems are complete for L. Thierauf and Wagner [TW08] prove that **Distance** for planar graphs is in UL ∩ coUL.

1. INTRODUCTION

For general graphs and even undirected planar graphs, LongPath is complete for NP. It is NL-complete for directed acyclic graphs (DAG). Limaye, Mahajan and Nimbhorkar [LMN09] prove that LongPath for planar DAG's is in UL ∩ coUL. Thierauf and Wagner [TW09] prove that reachability for $K_{3,3}$-minor free graphs and K_5-minor free graphs is reducible to planar reachability. Allender et.al. [ABC+09] showed that reachability for graphs embedded on the torus is logspace reducible to the planar case. Kynčl and Vyskočil [KV10] generalize this result to graphs embedded on a fixed surface of arbitrary genus. More recently, Das, Datta and Nimbhorkar [DDN10] give a logspace algorithm for the reachability problem for directed k-trees, where k is a constant. They also give a logspace algorithm for Distance and LongPath on directed acyclic k-trees. These results are also applicable for acyclic bounded tree width graphs when given together with a tree decomposition.

1.1 Overview of the Thesis

We contribute to find new upper and lower bounds by considering the graph isomorphism problem, the reachability problem and related versions of these problems restricted to many classes of graphs. We list the results presented in this thesis in detail.

Isomorphism testing. For tournament isomorphism, no lower bounds were discussed in the literature before. We prove in Chapter 3 that the known lower bounds for graph isomorphism in general also hold for tournament isomorphism, i.e. tounament isomorphism is hard for DET [Wag07]. We show, that the same lower bounds also hold for the tournament automorphism problem.

For graphs of bounded valence, we prove L-hardness for graphs of valence 2 in Chapter 4 [Wag08]. L-hardness holds even on input of two cycles or two line graphs. The later one is a quite restricted version of the L-complete problem tree isomorphism. We further discuss the situation for bounded valence graphs, i.e. when it becomes hard for the complexity class #L. As an application, in Section 4.7, we prove for a game theoretic problem, the posetgame problem, that it is hard for L. The proof is adapted from the logspace hardness proof of Theorem 4.5.2 for line-GI. As a consequence, the nim-game is L-complete.

In Chapter 5 we improve the upper bounds of isomorphism for planar 3-connected graphs to UL ∩ coUL and for oriented graphs to NL [TW08]. Before, AC^1 was known as upper bound for these problems. We reduce these isomorphism problems to computing the distance between vertices in undirected graphs. We can show that this problem is contained in UL ∩ coUL by modifying the known UL ∩ coUL-algorithm for reachability in planar directed graphs. In the case of oriented graphs we get an NL upper bound with the same algorithm taking oracle queries to distance computation in arbitrary directed graphs, which is complete for NL. We also prove

L-hardness for isomorphism for oriented trees and planar 3-connected graphs. We define label gadgets which proves L-hardness also for the automorphism problem for these graph classes. Recently, isomorphism for planar 3-connected graphs was improved further to L [DLN08]. As a consequence, oriented GI is also complete for L. In Section 5.8, we reduce GA onto GI when restricted to biconnected planar graphs. In the proof, we design new graph gadgets.

For canonization of planar graphs and the more general classes of $K_{3,3}$-minor free and K_5-minor free graphs we give the first logspace algorithm in Chapter 6 and Chapter 7 [DLN+09, DNTW09]. Hence, lower and upper bounds match and we get L-completeness.

In Chapter 8, for graphs of bounded treewidth we improve the known upper bound from TC^1 [GV06] to LogCFL [DTW10]. When for both graphs in the input tree decompositions are given, then we can prove that isomorphism testing is in L. For a sub-class of these graphs, the graphs of bounded tree-distance width, we prove that isomorphism testing is complete for L.

In Chapter 10, we consider the complexity of the quasigroup isomorphism problem where the quasigroups are given as multiplication tables. The best known upper bound is $\beta_2\mathsf{NC}^2$ from Wolf [Wol94] and as a consequence $\mathsf{SPACE}(\log^2 n)$. Let G, H be two quasigroups in table representation together with sequences of $k \leq \lceil \log_2 n \rceil$ generators $(g_1, \ldots, g_k)$ of G and $(h_1, \ldots, h_k)$ of H within $O(k \log n)$ bits. In SAC^1, we can verify whether G and H can be generated by these sequences and we can decide whether there is an isomorphism, which maps g_i onto h_i for all $i \in \{1, \ldots, k\}$. Formally, quasigroup isomorphism testing is in $\beta_2\mathsf{SAC}^1$.

For Cayley groups in table representation, isomorphism testing is in β_2FOLL and in β_2L. We further consider the complexity of isomorphism testing on abelian groups in table representation. The problem is known to be in L, we give an algorithm in $\mathsf{TC}^0(\mathsf{FOLL})$.

In the following table, we summarize the complexity bounds of GI restricted to the graph classes listed in the first row. In the lower part, we state some results for the isomorphism problem on groups and quasigroups when given in table representation. The table shows the known lower and upper bounds followed by the improvements presented in this thesis.

Here, 'Bounded tree (distance) width' is abbreviated with 'B. tree (d.) width' and 'Cayley groups' with 'C. groups'.

1. INTRODUCTION

Graph class	lower bound	upper bound
Valence-2	L [Wag08]	L
Planar 3-connected	L [TW08]	AC^1 [MR91, RR94], UL $\cap$ coUL [TW08], L [DLN08]
Oriented	L [TW08]	AC^1 [MR91], NL [TW08], L [DLN08]
Planar	L [JKMT03]	AC^1 [MR91, RR94], L [DLN+09]
$K_{3,3}$-free	L [JKMT03]	P [Pon91], L [DNTW09]
K_5-free	L [JKMT03]	P [Pon91], L [DNTW09]
B. tree dist. width	L [JKMT03]	TC^1 [GV06], L [DTW10]
B. tree width	L [JKMT03]	TC^1 [GV06], LogCFL [DTW10]
Tournaments	DET [Wag07]	$DTIME(n^{O(\log n)})$ [BL83]
General graphs	DET [Tor04]	$DTIME(2^{\sqrt{O(n \log n)}})$ [BL83]
Abelian C. groups		L, TC^0(FOLL)
Cayley groups		$SPACE(\log^2 n)$[LSZ76], $DTIME(n^{\log n + O(1)})$[Mil78], $\beta_2 NC^2$ [Wol94], $\beta_2 L$, $\beta_2 FOLL$
Quasigroups		$DTIME(n^{\log n + O(1)})$[Mil78], $\beta_2 NC^2$ [Wol94], $\beta_2 SAC^1$

Table 1.1: Lower and upper bounds for isomorphism testing.

Reachability Testing and Related Decision Problems. For $K_{3,3}$-minor free and K_5-minor free graphs we can prove in [TW09] that the reachability problem is reducible to reachability in planar graphs, which is known to be in UL $\cap$ coUL. This is done in Chapter 9. The proof technique can be generalized to **Distance** for these graph classes, which generalizes our result from Chapter 5, that computing distances in planar graphs is in UL $\cap$ coUL [TW08]. It can also be generalized to **LongPath** when considering the same graph classes restricted further to directed acyclic graphs.

We summarize the complexity results of reachability testing for most of the graph classes from Table 1.1. The following table summarizes the known upper bounds. The results from [TW08] and [TW09] are presented in this thesis.

Distance on bounded tree distance width graphs is in L for directed acyclic graphs (DAG's). The results for bounded tree distance width graphs follows from a logspace algorithm for reachability testing in bounded treewidth graphs if a tree decomposition is given for the input graph [DDN10]. It uses the fact that bounded tree distance width graphs can simply be reduced to bounded tree width graphs and that a tree distance decomposition can be computed in logspace [DTW10]. Very recently, the complexity of computing a tree decomposition was improved from LogCFL [Wan94, GLS02] to logspace [EJT10]. When given graphs of bounded tree width which

Graph class	Reachability upper bound	Distance upper bound	Long-Path (DAG's) upper bound
Valence-2	L-complete	L-complete	L-complete
Planar 3-conn.	UL ∩ coUL [BTV07]	UL ∩ coUL [TW08]	UL ∩ coUL [LMN09]
Planar	UL ∩ coUL [BTV07]	UL ∩ coUL [TW08]	UL ∩ coUL [LMN09]
$K_{3,3}$-free	UL ∩ coUL [TW09]	UL ∩ coUL [TW09]	UL ∩ coUL [TW09]
K_5-free	UL ∩ coUL [TW09]	UL ∩ coUL [TW09]	UL ∩ coUL [TW09]
B. tree d. width	L [DDN10, DTW10]	NL, L [DDN10, DTW10][1]	L [DDN10, DTW10]
B. tree width	L [DDN10, EJT10]	NL, L [DDN10, EJT10][1]	L [DDN10, EJT10]
Tournaments	AC^0 [Tan01]	NL-complete [Tan04]	NL

Table 1.2: The complexity of Reachability and related decision problems. Some improvements are restricted to DAG's only[1].

are DAG's, reachability testing is in L and also Distance and LongPath is in L [DDN10, EJT10].

For valence-2 graphs, reachability testing is in L, because each vertex has out-degree at most one [CM87]. For L-hardness, we reduce from the L-complete decision problem *order between vertices* [Ete97]. The problem is: given a directed simple path where all edges point into one direction and two vertices v_i, v_j, accept if v_j is reachable from v_i and reject otherwise. This also generalizes to Distance and LongPath, because vertices have out-degree one, i.e. simply traverse the paths and cycles in logspace.

Since it is not reasonable to consider a rotation scheme for reachability testing, we do not have oriented graphs in the table. We simply get NL-completeness for reachability and the related decision problems.

2 Preliminaries

In the first three sections we present notions and basic definitions in complexity theory, graph theory and group theory which are used in this thesis. In further two sections we define decision problems related to isomorphism testing and reachability testing. Finally, we describe some elementary techniques to prove logspace lower and upper bounds.

2.1 Complexity Theory

The basic notions and standard terminology in complexity theory can be found in standard books in complexity theory, we refer for example to [AB09], [Sav98] and [Lee90].

An *alphabet* is a set of symbols, which is denoted Σ. A *word* (or *string*) is a tuple of symbols of Σ. If $\Sigma = \{1\}$ then for all integers $n > 0$, there is only one word of length n, in short 1^n. We say that this word 1^n is encoded in *unary*. The set of all words over Σ is denoted Σ^*. The basic computational task is to compute a function $f : \Sigma^* \to \Sigma^*$. A special case of functions are *Boolean functions*, whose output is a single bit. We identify such a function f with the set $L_f = \{x \mid f(x) = 1\}$, i.e. $L_f \subseteq \{0,1\}^*$. Clearly, L_f is a set of words over Σ, also denoted *language* or *decision problem*. The *complement language* of L_f is $\overline{L_f} = \Sigma^* \setminus L_f$. Because languages are sets of words, we use the standard set operations ($A \cup B$, $A \cap B$, $A \setminus B$) on languages.

2.1.1 Computational Models

In literature, different computational models are considered. We say that it *decides* or *accepts* a language L_f if it computes a function $f : \Sigma \to \{0,1\}$ where $f(x) = 1 \Leftrightarrow x \in L_f$. Some of these models are described in this section.

Logic Circuits

A *logic gate* is a physical device that computes a Boolean function. A gate has *fanin* k if the function takes k arguments (is k-ary). The *outcome* of a gate is a *Boolean value* $\mathcal{B} = \{0,1\}$, i.e. it is 1 to encode *true*, or 0 to encode *false*. We consider

2. PRELIMINARIES

- *and*-gates: output 1 iff all inputs are 1 and 0 otherwise,
- *or*-gates: output 1 iff at least one input is 1 and 0 otherwise,
- *xor*-gates: output 1 iff an odd number of inputs is 1 and 0 otherwise,
- *negation*-gates: unary function, output 1 iff the single input is 0 and 0 otherwise,
- *threshold*-gates: output 1 iff at least half of the inputs are 1 and 0 otherwise.

A *circuit* is a finite directed acyclic graph, also denoted *circuit graph* where internal vertices (with indegree ≥ 1) carry labels of gates. The *basis* of the circuit is the set of gates which are labeled to at least one vertex in the circuit graph. Here the condition is enforced that the number of ancestors of an internal vertex is equal to the number of arguments of its label. Vertices with indegree 0 are input vertices which carry labels of input variables $x_1, \ldots, x_n$, variables assuming values over the set $\mathcal{B} = \{0, 1\}$. A directed edge (a, b) is a *wire* from the outcome of gate a (or from the input vertex a) to one of the inputs of another gate b. A circuit naturally computes a function of its n input variables. By induction, one defines for every vertex in the circuit a function *represented* by this vertex. For an input x_i, we have the *projection function* $p(x_1, \ldots, x_n) = x_i$. An internal vertex labeled with the function $g(y_1, \ldots, y_k)$, for which the k ancestors represent the functions $y_1 = h_1(x_1, \ldots, x_n), \ldots, y_k = h_k(x_1, \ldots, x_n)$, represents the function $g(h_1(x_1, \ldots, x_n), \ldots, h_k(x_1, \ldots, x_n))$. There is a designated *output gate*. A function $f(x_1, \ldots, x_n)$ is *computed* by the circuit iff it is represented by an output vertex. The *circuit valuation problem (CVP)* decides, on input a circuit given by its circuit graph and the input variables $x_1, \ldots, x_n$, whether the circuit accepts the input $x_1, \ldots, x_n$.

In a *layered* circuit, two gates belong to the same layer if they have the same distance to an input gate. We consider circuits with all inputs at gates in the first layer, i.e. the *input layer*, and the output at the gate in the last layer. Let $C[w]$ be the circuit C where we assign the letters of a word $w = (w_1, \ldots, w_n)$ of length n to the variables $x_1 = w_1, \ldots, x_n = w_n$. We say, w is an *assignment* for variables in C. If the output of $C[w]$ is 1 then C *accepts* w. A circuit C accepts the language $L(C)$ consisting of all words w where the output of $C[w]$ is 1. If the output of a circuit C is 1 on all inputs of a language A and 0 otherwise then C *accepts* A. The *size* of a circuit is the number of its gates. The *depth* of a circuit is the length of the longest path from an input vertex to an output vertex. We are interested in circuits having restricted resources, i.e. restrictions to the size or depth of the circuit or to the fanin of its gates.

We also consider non-Boolean circuits which represent functions over $\mathbb{Z}_k$. The basis of such a circuit consists of the following gate:

- *modulo-k addition*-gates: output the sum of the inputs modulo k.

Turing Machine

A *deterministic Turing machine (DTM)* is a standard model of computation. It consists of a *control unit* and a *tape unit* that has a potentially infinite linear array of cells each containing letters from an alphabet that can be read and written by a tape head directed by the control unit. Formally, it can be described as a six-tuple $M = (\Sigma, \Box, Q, \delta, s, h)$, where Σ is the *tape alphabet* not containing the *blank symbol* $\Box$, Q is the *set of states*, and the *transition function*:

$$\delta : Q \times (\Sigma \cup \{\Box\}) \to (Q \cup \{h\}) \times \{L, N, R\}$$

which is a bijective function. $\{L, N, R\}$ is the set of possible head moves: *left, no move* and *right*, respectively. The state s is the *initial state* and $h \notin Q$ is the *accepting halt state*. A Turing machine cannot exit from h. The control unit performs a transition, i.e. change the state and move the location of the tape head according to δ.

The *configuration* of a Turing machine M at any point of time is $[x_1 x_2 \ldots \mathbf{p}x_j \ldots x_n]$ where p (in bold) is the state of the control unit, indicating that the tape head is over the jth tape cell, and $x = (x_1, x_2, \ldots, x_n)$ is the string that contains all the non-blank symbols on the tape as well as the symbol under the head.

A Turing machine M on an *input string* $x \in \Sigma$ (it contains no blanks) starts with x written on the work-tape, i.e. the configuration at the beginning is $[\mathbf{s}x_1, \ldots, x_n]$. A Turing machine M *accepts* the input string x if, when started in state s with x placed left-adjusted on its otherwise blank tape, the last state entered by M is h. If M has other halting states (states from which it does not exit) these are *rejecting states*. A Turing machine M accepts the language $L(M)$ consisting of all strings accepted by M. That is, M halts and accepts on all inputs of the language and rejects all inputs not in the language. The *running time* is the number of basic operations performed until a halting state is reached.

A *non-deterministic Turing machine (NDTM)* is the extension of the DTM model by the addition of a *choice input* to its control unit. The bits from the choice input can only be read once from left to right. When reading such a bit, a transition is selected based on this bit. The NDTM accepts the input word x if there is some computation (i.e. some choice string $c \in \Sigma^*$) such that the last state entered is the accepting state h. We define the function $acc_M(x)$ as the number of accepting computation paths of M on input x, and $rej_M(x)$ as the number of rejecting computation paths of M on input x.

An *oracle Turing machine* is a Turing machine M augmented with a special write-only *oracle tape* and special states $q_{query}, q_{yes}, q_{no} \in Q$. The *oracle* for M is a language $L_o \in \Sigma^*$. When M starts writing bits onto the oracle-tape it behaves like a deterministic Turing machine. When M enters the state q_{query} then the oracle tape is erased and it moves to the state q_{yes}

2. PRELIMINARIES

if the contents on the oracle-tape belong to L_o and moves to the state q_{no} otherwise. This happens in a single computational step. For an input x and an oracle L_o the output of an oracle Turing machine M is denoted $M^{L_o}(x)$.

Pushdown Automaton

The *pushdown automaton (PDA)* or *auxiliary pushdown automaton (AuxPDA)* is a Turing machine with the following changes to the DTM model. The input is written on a read-only input-tape and the work-tape is used as a pushdown stack. A *stack* (or *pushdown*) is a semi-infinite worktape with the special property that whenever the head makes a left-move, the previous contents of the cell are erased (*popping* the stack). After a write instruction the head can move right (*pushing* a symbol on the stack). The head cannot move left of the origin but it can notice the beginning (the *bottom*) of the stack, e.g. by reading some special symbol. A pushdown automaton is *non-deterministic* if the underlying Turing machine is non-deterministic, i.e. a NAuxPDA.

Parallel Random Access Machine

A *parallel random-access machine (PRAM)* consists of a bounded set of processors (i.e. polynomial in the length of the input) and a common memory containing potentially an unlimited number of words. Processors work in parallel and have a local memory. They can also use the global memory, with restriction for the read and write access to the memory cells. If simultaneous access is allowed then access is *concurrent*. For example, we mention the *Concurrent Read/Concurrent Write PRAM*, (CRCW-PRAM).

2.1.2 Complexity Classes

In complexity theory, we are interested in the resources required during computation to solve a given decision problem. A *complexity class* is a set of decision problems accepted by a machine M of a computational model within given resource bounds. We consider space and time as a resource. The resource bounds are related to the length of the input by a function which fulfills the following properties.

A function is *space constructible* (or *time constructible*) if there is a deterministic Turing machine running in space (or time) $O(f(n))$ that on input 1^n (i.e. n in unary) computes $f(n)$ in binary. In particular, exponents 2^n, polynomials n^2 or logarithms $\lceil \log n \rceil$ are space (and time) constructible.

Complexity classes characterized by Turing machines

Let f be a time constructible function. A language $L \subseteq \{0,1\}^*$ is in DTIME($f(n)$) if there is a deterministic Turing machine M such that M accepts L and for each $w \in \Sigma^*$, M on input w halts in $c \cdot f(|w|)$ steps, for a constant c.

We define $\mathsf{P} = \bigcup_{c \geq 1} \mathsf{DTIME}(n^c)$, the complexity class *deterministic polynomial time*.

We define DLOGTIME = DTIME($\log n$).

A language $L \subseteq \Sigma^*$ is in NP i.e. *non-deterministic polynomial time*, if there exists a time constructible polynomial $p(n)$ and a deterministic polynomial time Turing machine M such that for every $x \in \Sigma^*$,
$$x \in L \Leftrightarrow \exists c \in \{0,1\}^{p(|x|)} \text{ such that } M(x,c) = 1.$$
Here, c is the choice input for M.

Let $g : \mathbb{N}_0 \to \mathbb{N}_0$ be a total time constructible function. We define NP[$g(n)$] as the class of languages which can be characterized by a polynomial time Turing machine making $O(g(n))$ non-deterministic steps on every input of length n. That is, the choice input is $c \in \{0,1\}^{g(|x|)}$.

Let f be a space constructible function. A language $L \subseteq \{0,1\}^*$ is in SPACE($f(n)$) if there is a deterministic Turing machine M which accepts L such that for every $x \in \Sigma^*$, M on input x visits at most $c \cdot f(|x|)$ locations on its work-tape, for a constant c. Similarly, L is in NSPACE($f(n)$), if M is non-deterministic and guarantees the $f(n)$ space bound, regardless of its non-deterministic choices.

L is the class of languages accepted by deterministic Turing machines using a work tape bounded by logarithmic space, i.e. SPACE($\log n$).

NL is the class of languages accepted by non-deterministic Turing machines using a work tape bounded by logarithmic space, i.e. NSPACE($\log n$). We also say PSPACE for SPACE($f(n)$), if function f is bounded by a polynomial.

The known containments are as follows.
$$\mathsf{DLOGTIME} \subseteq \mathsf{L} \subseteq \mathsf{NL} \subseteq \mathsf{P} \subseteq \mathsf{NP} \subseteq \mathsf{PSPACE}$$

Let C be a complexity class characterized by Turing machines (eventually with restricted computational resources) and L_o a language. C^{L_o} is the complexity class characterized by the same Turing machines augmented with an oracle to accept L_o. For example, P^{L_o} is the class of languages accepted by deterministic oracle Turing machines with polynomial time bound and oracle L_o.

Complexity Classes Characterized by Circuits

Uniformity. A *circuit family* $\mathcal{C} = \{C_1, C_2, \dots\}$ is a collection of logic circuits in which C_n has n inputs and $m(n)$ outputs with function $m : \mathbb{N} \to \mathbb{N}$. We consider here the standard basis with *and*-, *or*- and *not*-gates.

2. PRELIMINARIES

A circuit accepts only words of the same length, whereas Turing machines do not have this restriction. Hence, we consider a circuit family $\mathcal{C}$ which characterizes the language $L = \bigcup_n L_n$, where L_n contains words of length n. Therefore, we need a computational device D which on input the length of a word $w \in L$ in unary (i.e. $1^{|w|}$) determines the appropriate circuit $C_{|w|}$ from $\mathcal{C}$. Clearly, D should have low computational complexity such that there is no computational power hidden.

A DLOGTIME *uniform circuit family* is a circuit family for which there is a deterministic Turing machine M such that for each integer $n > 0$ in unary 1^n on its input tape, M produces the description of C_n as output. For this, M runs in time $O(\log n)$ and it has the following properties. $M(1^n, i, c)$ has access to only $O(\log n)$ bits of the input and it accepts if the i-th bit of the output C_n is c, and it rejects otherwise. The *function f is computed by* $\mathcal{C}$ if for each $n \geq 1$, f restricted to inputs of length n is the function computed by C_n.

In particular, the DLOGTIME-uniformity is of interest in the study of constant-depth circuit-classes such as AC^0. On the other hand, non-uniform circuit families can be used to define non-computable languages, (i.e. there is no Turing machine that can accept such a language).

Circuit Complexity Classes. Let n be the length of the input to the circuits considered now.

The class AC^i contains the languages accepted by a DLOGTIME uniform family of Boolean circuits of depth $O(\log^i(n))$ and size polynomial in n, with unbounded fanin *and*-gates and *or*-gates.

The class NC^i contains the languages accepted by a DLOGTIME uniform family of Boolean circuits of depth $O(\log^i n)$ and size polynomial in n, with fanin two *and*-gates and *or*-gates. $\mathsf{NC} = \bigcup_i \mathsf{NC}^i$.

The class TC^i contains the languages accepted by a DLOGTIME uniform family of circuits of depth $O(\log^i n)$ and size polynomial in n, with unbounded fanin *and*-gates, *or*-gates and *threshold*-gates.

The class $\mathsf{Mod}_k\mathsf{L}$ contains the languages accepted by a DLOGTIME uniform family of circuits with *modulo-k addition*-gates and size polynomial in n. The class $\oplus\mathsf{L}$ is the same as $\mathsf{Mod}_2\mathsf{L}$. The following containments are known:

$$\mathsf{DLOGTIME} \subseteq \mathsf{AC}^0 \subseteq \mathsf{NC}^1 \subseteq \mathsf{L} \subseteq \mathsf{AC}^1 \subseteq \mathsf{TC}^1 \subseteq \mathsf{NC}^2 \subseteq \mathsf{AC}^2 \subseteq \cdots \subseteq \mathsf{NC} \subseteq \mathsf{P}$$

Logspace Counting Classes

A non-deterministic Turing machine is *unambiguous*, if it has at most one accepting computation on any input. The class of languages computable by unambiguous logspace bounded Turing machines is denoted UL. NL is known to be closed under complement [Imm88, Sze88], but this is open for UL.

#L [AJ93] (analogously to Valiant's class #P), is the class of functions $acc_M : \Sigma^* \to \mathbb{N}$ where $acc_M(x)$ is the number of accepting computation paths of a NL (NP) machine M on input x. The complexity classes PL (probabilistic logspace, [Gil77] [RST84]), $C_=L$ (exact-counting in logspace, [AO96]), and $Mod_k L$ (modular counting in logspace, $k \geq 2$, [BDHM91]) can be defined in terms of #L functions:

$$PL = \{A \mid \exists p \in Poly, f \in \#L \; \forall x \in \Sigma^* : x \in A \Leftrightarrow f(x) \geq 2^{p(|x|)}\}$$
$$C_=L = \{A \mid \exists p \in Poly, f \in \#L \; \forall x \in \Sigma^* : x \in A \Leftrightarrow f(x) = 2^{p(|x|)}\}$$
$$Mod_k L = \{A \mid \exists f \in \#L \; \forall x \in \Sigma^* : x \in A \Leftrightarrow f(x) \equiv 1 \mod k\}$$

DET(also denoted $NC^1(\#L)$) is the class of functions NC^1 Turing reducible to computing the determinant [Coo85]. That is the class of problems, solvable by NC^1 circuits with additional oracle gates for computing the determinant of an integer matrix.

The known containments among the considered classes are:

$$L \subseteq Mod_k L \subseteq DET$$
$$L \subseteq UL \subseteq NL \subseteq C_=L \subseteq PL \subseteq DET \subseteq TC^1$$

Complexity Class FOLL

Barrington et.al. [BKLM00] introduce the complexity class FOLL, or $FO(\log \log n)$. This is the class of problems solvable by uniform polynomial size circuit families of unbounded fanin and depth $O(\log \log n)$. Since Parity is not in FOLL, no problem in FOLL can be complete for any class containing Parity, such as NC^1, L or NL. But FOLL is not known to be contained in L. The known containments are:

$$AC^0 \subseteq FOLL \subseteq AC^1$$

Complexity Class LogCFL

A language is in the class of *context free languages* (CFL) if it is accepted by non-deterministic pushdown automata in polynomial time and with a pushdown of polynomial size, i.e. polynomial in the length of the input.

Formally, the complexity class LogCFL consists of all decision problems that can be Turing reduced in logarithmic space to a context free language. The notion of reducibility is defined below. LogCFL is known to be closed under complementation [BCD$^+$89]. There are several alternative characterizations of LogCFL.

- Problems in LogCFL are those accepted by families of *semi-unbounded fanin* circuits, i.e. uniform families of polynomial size and logarithmic depth circuits with fanin two *and*-gates and unbounded fanin *or*-gates. This class is also denoted *semi-unbounded-fanin* AC^1, in short SAC^1.

2. PRELIMINARIES

- LogCFL is the class of decision problems computable by non-deterministic auxiliary pushdown machines (NAuxPDA). These are Turing machines with a logarithmic space work tape, an additional pushdown and a polynomial time bound [Sud77].

Analogously, there is a deterministic version, the deterministic auxiliary pushdown machines. LogDCFL is the class of decision problems computable by these machines in polynomial time. The following containments are known:
$$L \subseteq \mathsf{LogDCFL} \subseteq \mathsf{LogCFL} \subseteq \mathsf{AC}^1$$
$$L \subseteq \mathsf{NL} \subseteq \mathsf{LogCFL} \subseteq \mathsf{AC}^1$$

Limited Non-determinism

Let complexity class $\mathcal{C}$ be one of L, NC^j, FOLL, SAC^j or P. For $i \geq 0$, $\beta_i \mathcal{C}$ is defined to be the class of languages L for which there is a language $L' \in \mathcal{C}$ such that for every $x \in \Sigma^*$, $x \in L \Leftrightarrow \exists c \in \{0,1\}^{O(\log^i |x|)}$ such that $(x, c) \in L'$.
Here, c is a choice input of bounded length $|c| \in O(\log^i |x|)$. For integers $i, j \geq 0$, the corresponding classes are denoted $\beta_i \mathsf{L}$, $\beta_i \mathsf{NC}^j$, $\beta_i \mathsf{FOLL}$, $\beta_i \mathsf{SAC}^j$ and $\beta_i \mathsf{P}$, c.f. [GLM96]. Let $\beta \mathcal{C} = \bigcup_{i \geq 0} \beta_i \mathcal{C}$. The known containments for these classes are:
$$\mathcal{C} \subseteq \beta_i \mathcal{C} \subseteq \beta \mathcal{C} \subseteq \mathsf{NP}$$

Functional Complexity Classes

P and NP are defined in terms of decision problems only, i.e. the result of the computations is one bit. This means, that Turing machines accept functions $f : \Sigma^* \to \{0, 1\}$.

The Turing machines are modified to output a sequence of bits. The bits are written on a write-only output tape. This means, they *recognize* functions $f : \Sigma^* \to \Sigma^*$.

For example, FP is the class of functions computed by a deterministic Turing machine in polynomial time in the length of the input. The functional version of L is denoted FL.

A function f can be considered as a sequence of decision problems. Let $f(x, i)$ be the i-th bit of $f(x)$ in binary representation. The decision problem is, on input of some string x and an integer $1 \leq i \leq p(|x|)$ for some polynomial p, accept if $f(x, i) = 1$ and reject otherwise.

Let $f : B \to C$ and $g : A \to B$ for some sets A, B, C. The *composition* of these functions is a function $f \circ g : A \to C$ with $(f \circ g)(x) = f(g(x))$. Let f, g be two functions, where f is computable in complexity class $\mathcal{C}$ and g in $\mathcal{C}'$. Then $f \circ g$ computes a function which is in the complexity class, denoted by $\mathcal{C} \circ \mathcal{C}'$ or $\mathcal{C}(\mathcal{C}')$, i.e. this function is in the $\mathcal{C}$-*closure of* $\mathcal{C}'$. For example, we use the fact that functions in FL are closed under composition, i.e. FL $\circ$ FL $=$ FL.

2.1.3 Reducibility

We are interested in the classification of decision problems within complexity classes. To compare languages, we use the notion of reducibility.

Let $\mathcal{F}$ be a class of functions. The language $L_1 \subseteq \Sigma_1^*$ is $\mathcal{F}$ *many-one reducible* to the language $L_2 \subseteq \Sigma_2^*$ (in short $\leq_m^{\mathcal{F}}$) if there is a total function $f : \Sigma_1^* \to \Sigma_2^*$ in $\mathcal{F}$ so that for all $w \in \Sigma_1^*$, $w \in L_1$ if and only if $f(w) \in L_2$.

Let $\mathcal{F}$ be a class of space (time) constructible functions. The language $L_1 \subseteq \Sigma_1^*$ is $\mathcal{F}$-space ($\mathcal{F}$-time) *Turing reducible* to the language $L_2 \subseteq \Sigma_2^*$ (in short $\leq_T^{\mathcal{F}}$) if there is a $\mathcal{F}$-space ($\mathcal{F}$-time) bounded Turing machine M which accepts an input x if and only if $x \in L_1$ and where M is augmented with an oracle to accept L_2.

Let $\mathcal{F}$ be a class of functions. The language $L_1 \subseteq \Sigma_1^*$ is $\mathcal{F}$ *conjunctive truth table reducible* (in short $\leq_{ctt}^{\mathcal{F}}$) to the language $L_2 \subseteq \Sigma_2^*$ if there are total functions $f_1, \ldots, f_k$, with $f_i : \Sigma_1^* \to \Sigma_2^*$ in $\mathcal{F}$ for all i, which compute, all on input $x \in \Sigma_1^*$, the queries $y_1, \ldots, y_k \subseteq \Sigma_2^*$, respectively such that:

$$x \in L_1 \Leftrightarrow \bigwedge_i y_i \in L_2.$$

The language $L_1 \subseteq \Sigma_1^*$ is $\mathcal{F}$ *disjunctive truth table reducible* (in short $\leq_{dtt}^{\mathcal{F}}$) to the language $L_2 \subseteq \Sigma_2^*$ if there are total functions $f_1, \ldots, f_k$, with $f_i : \Sigma_1^* \to \Sigma_2^*$ in $\mathcal{F}$ for all i, which compute, all on input $x \in \Sigma_1^*$, the queries $y_1, \ldots, y_k \subseteq \Sigma_2^*$, respectively such that:

$$x \in L_1 \Leftrightarrow \bigvee_i y_i \in L_2.$$

In particular, we consider AC^0 *many-one reductions* (in short $\leq_m^{\mathsf{AC}^0}$) i.e. $\mathcal{F}$ is the class of AC^0 computable functions. We consider *logspace many-one reductions* (in short $\leq_m^{log}$) and *logspace Turing reductions* (in short $\leq_T^{log}$) i.e. $\mathcal{F}$ is the class of functions computable by logspace Turing machines.

We say that a language L is *hard* for L' under certain kind of reducibility, iff L' is reducible to L. We say that a language L is *hard* for a complexity class $\mathcal{C}$ under certain kind of reducibility, iff L is hard for all languages in $\mathcal{C}$. We say that L is *complete* for $\mathcal{C}$ iff L is hard for $\mathcal{C}$ and $L \in \mathcal{C}$.

2.2 Graph Theory

A *graph* G is a pair (V, E) with a set of *vertices* $V = V(G)$ and *edges* $E = E(G) \subseteq V \times V$. A *directed* edge or *arc* is denoted (v_1, v_2) and an *undirected* edge $\{v_1, v_2\}$. Two vertices are *adjacent* if they are connected by an edge. A *loop* is an edge that connects a vertex to itself. A *simple* graph is loop-free, has undirected edges and no more than one edge between each pair of vertices. A *digraph* is a graph with directed edges. The *size* of a graph is the number of its vertices.

In a *clique* or *complete graph* of size n, also denoted K_n, each pair of vertices is connected

2. PRELIMINARIES

by an edge. A *bipartite graph* is a graph $G = (U \cup V, E)$ with two disjoint sets of vertices U, V and an edge set $E \subseteq \{\{u, v\} \mid u \in U, v \in V\}$. If $E = \{\{u, v\} \mid u \in U, v \in V\}$ then G is a *complete bipartite graph*, also denoted $K_{i,j}$ if $|U| = i$ and $|V| = j$.

$G[X]$ is a subgraph of G *induced* on vertex set X, i.e. $G[X] = (X, E)$ with edge set $E(G[X]) = (X \times X) \cap E(G)$. Let H be a subgraph of G then $G \setminus H = G[V(G) \setminus V(H)]$. For $E' \subseteq E(G)$ we define $G \setminus E' = (V(G), E(G) \setminus E')$. $\Gamma_G(v)$ denotes the set of neighbors of v in G. If the context is clear, we also write $\Gamma(v)$. For $G = (V, E)$ and two disjoint subsets U, W of V we use the following notion for an *induced bipartite subgraph* $B_G[U, W]$ of G on vertex set $U \cup W$ with edge set $\{\{u, w\} \in E \mid u \in U, w \in W\}$.

An *isomorphism* between graphs $G_1 = (V, E_1)$ and $G_2 = (V, E_2)$ is a bijective mapping $\phi : V \to V$ such that $\{u, v\} \in E_1$ if and only if $\{\phi(u), \phi(v)\} \in E_2$. Both graphs are *isomorphic* ($G_1 \cong G_2$) if such an isomorphism exists. When we say, an isomorphism *respects* a property $\mathcal{P}$, then we mean the following. For two graphs $G_1 = (V, E_1)$ and $G_2 = (V, E_2)$, we define the following: for $j \in \{1, 2\}$ let $\mathcal{P}_j = \{U_1^j, \ldots, U_k^j\}$ with $U_i^j \subseteq V$ for all $1 \leq i \leq k$. An isomorphism ϕ from G_1 onto G_2 respects P_1 and P_2 if the following holds: if $\phi(u) = v$ and $u \in U_i^1$ and $v \in U_h^2$ then for all $u' \in U_i^1 : \phi(u') \in U_h^2$. We use this notion e.g. when considering tree decompositions where vertices are partitioned into bags of constant size or when we arrange the neighbors around vertices in a fixed cyclic order.

An *automorphism* of graph G is a permutation $\phi : V(G) \to V(G)$ preserving the adjacency relation: $\{u, v\} \in E(G) \Leftrightarrow \{\phi(u), \phi(v)\} \in E(G)$. A *rigid* graph has no automorphisms except the identity.

Let $k > 0$ be a fixed integer. A *labeling* for a graph G is a function $f : V(G) \to \{1, \ldots, k\}$ which gives a *label* (i.e. one of the k elements) to each vertex. It is also common to say *coloring* of a graph G, or giving a *color* to a vertex. Do not get confused with the standard definition of coloring, which is to find a labeling of vertices such that adjacent vertices have different colors. An isomorphism or automorphism between colored graphs must preserve the colors, i.e. the set of vertices having the same color are fixed blockwise.

The *degree* or *valence* of a vertex v in a graph G is the number of edges which have v as end vertex. The *valence of a graph* is the maximum valence of its vertices. A graph is d-*regular* if every vertex has valence d. A graph is *regular* if all vertices have the same valence.

In graph $G = (V, E)$, a *walk* is a sequence of vertices $W = (v_1, \ldots, v_k)$ such that for $i = \{1, \ldots, k-1\}$, v_i and v_{i+1} are the endpoints of an edge in G. A *path* is a walk where no edges are repeated. If G is directed and $e_i = (v_i, v_{i+1}) \in E(G)$ for $i \in \{1, \ldots, k-1\}$, then W is a *directed path*. If all vertices in P are pairwise distinct then P is a *simple path*. A *line-graph* $G = (V, E)$ is a directed simple path, with vertices $V(G) = \{v_1, \ldots, v_n\}$ and edges $E(G) = \{(v_1, v_2), \ldots, (v_{n-1}, v_n)\}$. A *(simple) cycle* $C = (v_1, \ldots, v_k, v_1)$ is a walk where $(v_1, \ldots, v_k)$ is a (simple) path. In $G = (V, E)$, a *Hamiltonian cycle* is a simple cycle of length $|V|$. A *directed acyclic graph* (DAG) is a simple graph with directed edges which has no directed cycle as a subgraph.

A graph is *connected* if there is a path between any two vertices. A graph is a *tree* if it is connected and does not have a simple cycle. A *root* of a tree is a designated vertex. A *rooted tree* is a tree with a root. Let $(u, v, \ldots, r)$ be a simple path from u to the root r in a rooted tree. Then v is the *parent* of u and u is a *child* of v. A *forest* is a graph with a disjoint union of trees.

A *Cartesian product of graphs* $G \square H$ is a graph with the Cartesian product $V(G) \times V(H)$ as vertices, i.e. $V(G \square H) = \{v_{i,j} \mid v_i \in G, v_j \in H\}$, and edges $E(G \square H) = \{\{v_{ij}, v_{kl}\} \mid i = k \wedge \{v_j, v_l\} \in E(H)$ or $j = l \wedge \{v_i, v_k\} \in E(G)\}$. The *disjoint union* of two graphs $G = (V_1, E_1), H = (V_2, E_2)$ with $V_1 \cap V_2 = \emptyset$ is the graph $G \cup H = (V_1 \cup V_2, E_1 \cup E_2)$.

Let E_v be the set of edges with v as end vertex. A permutation ρ_v on E_v that has only one cycle is called a *rotation*. A *rotation scheme* for a graph G is a set ρ of rotations,
$$\rho = \{\rho_v \mid v \in V \text{ and } \rho_v \text{ is a rotation on } E_v\}.$$
Let ρ^{-1} be the set of inverse rotations, $\rho^{-1} = \{\rho_v^{-1} \mid v \in V\}$. A rotation scheme ρ describes an embedding of graph G in the plane. We call G together with ρ an *oriented graph*.

A graph is *planar* if it can be embedded in the plane without crossing of edges. A planar graph G, along with its planar embedding (given by ρ) is called a *plane graph* $\widehat{G} = (G, \rho)$ with ρ a *planar rotation scheme*. Allender and Mahajan [AM00] showed that a planar rotation scheme for a planar graph can be computed in logspace. A *reflection* of an embedding is a mirror image of the embedded graph. Note that in this case ρ^{-1} is a planar rotation scheme as well. A planar graph divides the plane into regions. Each such region is called a *face*.

If a planar graph is in addition 3-connected, then there exist precisely two planar rotation schemes [Whi33], namely some planar rotation scheme ρ and its inverse ρ^{-1}. We say, an isomorphism ϕ from (G, ρ^G) onto (H, ρ^H) *respects* the rotation schemes if the neighbors of every vertex v in G are arranged in the same cyclic order (given by ρ_v^G) as the neighbors of $\phi(v)$ in H (given by $\rho_{\phi(v)}^H$). Not every isomorphism has this property.

The *distance* between two vertices u, v in a graph G is the length of the shortest path between u and v. Let $d_G(u, v)$ denote the distance from u to v. For a set $S \subseteq V$, and a vertex $v \in V$, $d_G(S, v) = \min\{d_G(u, v) \mid u \in S\}$. The *eccentricity* of a vertex v in a graph G is the longest distance to another vertex, i.e. $d_G(v) = \max\{d_G(u, v) \mid u \in V(G)\}$. We also write $d(u, v), d(v), d(S, v)$ if the graph G is clear from the context. The *center* of G consists of all vertices with minimal eccentricity in G. Note that if G is a tree such that every simple path from a leaf to a leaf has even length, then the center consists of only one node, namely the node at the midpoint on a longest simple path in the tree.

A graph H is a *minor* of a graph G if and only if H can be obtained from G by a finite sequence of edge-removal and edge-contraction operations. For example, a $K_{3,3}$-*minor free*

2. PRELIMINARIES

graph (or a K_5-*minor free graph*) is an undirected graph which does not contain a $K_{3,3}$ (or K_5) as a minor. We also say in short $K_{3,3}$-free graph.

A *tournament* is a directed graph with one arc between each pair of distinct vertices.

A *series parallel graph* has two distinguished vertices called *terminals*, one being the *source* and the other the *sink*. Its construction is done recursively by two simple composition operations:

Series operation: take the disjoint union of two series parallel graphs and identify the source of the one graph with the sink of the other. The other two terminals form now source and sink.

Parallel operation: take the disjoint union and identify both sources forming the new source, and identify both sinks forming the new sink.

A two terminal series parallel graph has no K_4 as minor. It is a subclass of the planar graphs and has tree width at most 2.

2.2.1 Decomposition of Graphs into k-Connected Components

In a *connected* simple graph, there are paths between all pairs of vertices. This notion is well known. Here we define further connectivity notions which are used in different kinds of graph decompositions.

A connected graph G is k-*connected* if k vertices are required to disconnect the graph. In a k-connected graph G there are k vertex-disjoint paths between any pair of vertices in G. A 1-connected graph is simply called *connected* and a 2-connected graph *biconnected*.

Let $S \subseteq V$ with $|S| = k$. S is a k-*separating set* if $G \setminus S$ has more connected components than G. If not explicitly stated then we consider k-separating sets in k-connected graphs. S is called *articulation point (or cut vertex)* for $k = 1$, *separating pair* for $k = 2$, and *separating triple* for $k = 3$.

Let C be a connected component in $G \setminus S$ and let $S' \subseteq S$ be those vertices from S connected to $V(C)$ in G. A *split component* of S in G is the induced subgraph of G on vertices $V(C)$ where we add vertices of S', and edges connecting C with S', and *virtual edges* between all pairs of S'. More formally, the edges of the split component are

$$E(C) \cup \{\{u,v\} \mid u \in V(C),\ v \in S'\} \cup \{\{u,v\} \mid u,v \in S'\}.$$

The last set of edges might not have been edges in G and form a complete subgraph on S'. For $u, v \in V$, the set S *separates* u from v if $u, v \notin S$ and u and v are in different split components of $G \setminus S$.

2.2.2 Decomposition of Graphs into Biconnected Components

A vertex $v \in V$ is an *articulation point* if $G[V \setminus \{v\}]$ is not connected. A *biconnected graph* is a connected graph which contains no articulation points.

The decomposition of graphs into their biconnected components is used in many applications. For example, for computing the number of perfect matchings of $K_{3,3}$-free graphs [Vaz89] or for the isomorphism testing of two planar graphs [KHC04]. We use the decomposition besides isomorphism testing [DLN+09, DNTW09] also in the context of reachability testing [TW09]. The first step is to decompose the connected graph G into biconnected components, also see Hopcroft and Tarjan [HT73].

For each pair of adjacent articulation points u, v there is a biconnected component B which consists of one edge. Every induced subgraph B of G with the following properties is also a biconnected component. For all $u, v \in V(B)$ there are two vertex disjoint paths from u to v. B is maximal, meaning for all $u \in V(B)$ there is no $v \in V(G) \setminus V(B)$ such that there are two vertex disjoint paths from u to v. Note, an articulation point can be contained in more than one biconnected component. We define nodes for these components and the articulation points for a new graph as follows. An *articulation point node* is connected to a *biconnected component node* if this articulation point is contained as vertex in the corresponding component. The resulting graph is a tree, the *biconnected component tree* of G, also denoted $T^B(G)$.

Lemma 2.2.1 *The biconnected component tree of an undirected graph can be computed in logspace.*

Proof. We can find all the articulation points of G in logspace: a vertex a is an articulation point if we can find two further vertices u and v such that there is no path from u to v in $G \setminus \{a\}$.

Similarly, we can compute all biconnected components of G: two vertices u and v are in the same biconnected component, if there is a path from u to v in $G \setminus \{a\}$, for every articulation point $a \notin \{u, v\}$ of G.

The biconnected component tree has an arbitrary articulation point as root, say a_0. To walk on the tree, we have to identify the *parent articulation point node* and distinguish it from the *child articulation point nodes*. These nodes correspond to biconnected components with respect to the root a_0 in the tree. Let B be a biconnected component with articulation points $a_1, \ldots, a_k$. Then a_i is the parent articulation point of B, if there is a path from a_i to a_0 in $G \setminus \{a_j\}$, for all $j \neq i$. Also the children can be distinguished by their labels in increasing lexicographical order, in logspace we can compute the next sibling according to this order. Hence, the biconnected component tree can be traversed in depth first manner in logspace, keeping the labels of the root a_0 and the node at the current position on the work-tape, see for example [Lin92]. □

2.2.3 Decomposition of Graphs into Triconnected Components

In a biconnected graph $G = (V, E)$, a pair of vertices $u, v \in V$ is a *separating pair* if $G[V \setminus \{u, v\}]$ is not connected. A *3-connected graph* is biconnected and contains no separating pairs. A

2. PRELIMINARIES

triconnected graph is either a 3-connected graph or a cycle or a 3-bond. A *k-bond* is a graph consisting of two vertices joined by k edges. A pair of vertices $\{a,b\}$ is said to be *3-connected* if there are three or more vertex-disjoint paths between them. In particular, we consider *3-connected separating pairs*.

Hopcroft and Tarjan [HT73] presented a sequential algorithm for the decomposition of a biconnected planar graph into its triconnected components. Their algorithm recursively removes separating pairs from the graph and puts a copy of the separating pair in each of the components so formed. The nodes of the separating pair are connected by a virtual edge. If simple cycles are split at any intermediate steps then they are combined later. This gives a decomposition which is unique [Mac37]. Datta et.al. [DLN+09] describe a logspace algorithm for such a decomposition of a biconnected planar graph.

Miller and Ramachandran [MR87] showed that the triconnected components of a $K_{3,3}$-free graph can be computed in NC^2. Thierauf and Wagner [TW09] describe a construction that works in logspace. They showed, that it suffices to compute the triconnected components and recognize the K_5 components by running through all 5-sets and checking for each pair whether it is an edge or a 3-connected separating pair. In [DNTW09], a logspace algorithm for the decomposition of arbitrary biconnected graphs into triconnected components is presented. They use the fact, that 3-connected separating pairs can be removed simultaneously. Hence, two vertices belong to the same 3-connected component iff they cannot be separated by 3-connected separating pairs. We state here this result, which is used in our decompositions.

If a separating pair $\{a,b\}$ is connected by only two vertex-disjoint paths, then a and b lie on a cycle. As we will see below, it is not necessary to decompose cycles further. Therefore we decompose a biconnected graph only along 3-connected separating pairs. This decomposition is described next.

Two vertices u,v belong to a *3-connected component* or a *cycle component* if there is no 3-connected separating pair which separates u from v. The components so formed are the induced subgraphs of G, where we introduce in addition a special edge, called *virtual edge*, that connects the 3-connected separating pair $\{u,v\}$. Furthermore, we add a *3-bond component* for $\{u,v\}$. A 3-bond is a pair of vertices connected by 3 edges. A *triconnected component* is a 3-connected component, a cycle component or a 3-bond component.

Similar to the tree based on biconnected components, in Section 2.2.4 we define a tree based on triconnected components. We prove now that these triconnected components are unique and can be computed in logspace.

Lemma 2.2.2 *In a simple undirected biconnected graph G, the removal of 3-connected separating pairs gives a unique decomposition into triconnected components, irrespective of the order in which they are removed. This decomposition can be computed in logspace.*

Proof. Let G be a biconnected graph and let $s_1 = \{u_1, v_1\}$ and $s_2 = \{u_2, v_2\}$ be 3-connected separating pairs in G. It suffices to show that the decomposition of G after the removal of s_1 and s_2 does not depend on the order of their removal.

Claim 2.2.3 *s_2 is a 3-connected separating pair in a split component of s_1.*

Proof. Suppose, u_2 and v_2 are in two different split components of s_1. Then every path from u_2 to v_2 must pass the pair u_1 and v_1. Hence, there can be at most two vertex-disjoint paths. Assume now, u_2 and v_2 are in the same split component of s_1.

Consider three paths between u_2 and v_2 which are pairwise vertex-disjoint except for their endpoints. If a path contains at most one of u_1 or v_1, then the path remains intact in a split component of s_1, because in the split components we have copies of u_1 and v_1.

If a path contains both of u_1 and v_1 then the part between u_1 and v_1 is split off when it leaves the current split component. However, since we introduce a virtual edge $\{u_1, v_1\}$, we still have a path between u_2 and v_2 which is disjoint from the other two paths in one split component of s_1. This proves the claim. □

Clearly, the claim holds as well when interchanging the roles of s_1 and s_2.

Two vertices end up in different split components only if they are separated by a 3-connected separating pair. Hence, removing split components from s_1 before or after removing those from s_2 has no effect on the resulting components. This shows that 3-connected separating pairs uniquely partition the graph into triconnected components. Thus they can be removed in parallel.

It remains to argue that the decomposition can be computed in log-space.

Claim 2.2.4 *In a biconnected graph G, 3-connected separating pairs can be computed in log-space.*

Proof. Separating pairs in G can be computed easily in log-space: find all pairs of vertices such that their removal from G disconnects the graph. This can be done with queries to the reachability testing problem which is in L [Rei08]. Among those separating pairs we identify the 3-connected ones as follows. A separating pair $\{u, v\}$ in G is *not* 3-connected if either

- there are exactly two split components of $\{u, v\}$ (without attaching virtual edges) and both are not biconnected, or

- there is an edge $\{u, v\}$ and one such split component which is not biconnected.

To see this, a split component which is not biconnected has an articulation point a. All paths from u to v through this split component must go through a. Hence there is only one vertex disjoint path from u to v. It suffices, to find articulation points in split components of $\{u, v\}$,

2. PRELIMINARIES

which is in log-space, again with oracle queries to reachability testing. This proves the claim.
□

With the 3-connected separating pairs in hand the decomposition of a biconnected graph into its triconnected components can be done in logspace with appropriate reachability tests. This proves Lemma 2.2.2.
□

Separating pairs in a tree decomposition and separating pair nodes are always considered to be 3-connected.

2.2.4 The Triconnected Component Tree

Construct a graph T such that its nodes correspond to triconnected components and 3-connected separating pairs, see Figure 2.1. There is an edge between a *triconnected component node* and a *separating pair node* if the vertices of the separating pair are contained in the triconnected component. Two triconnected component nodes or two separating pair nodes do not share an edge.

It is easy to see that T is a tree, referred to as the *triconnected component tree* of G, also denoted $\mathcal{T}^\mathsf{T}(G)$.

Conversely, given T, we define $\mathsf{graph}(T) = G$, the graph which corresponds to the triconnected component tree T. We list some properties of T.

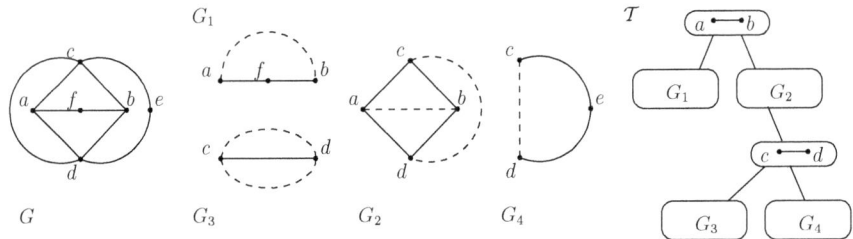

Figure 2.1: The decomposition of a biconnected planar graph G. Its triconnected components are $G_1, \ldots, G_4$ and the corresponding decomposition into the tree $\mathcal{T}$ of triconnected components. The separating pairs are $\{a, b\}$ and $\{c, d\}$. Since the 3-connected separating pair $\{c, d\}$ is connected by an edge in G, we also get $\{c, d\}$ as 3-bond G_3. The virtual edges corresponding to the 3-connected separating pairs are drawn with dashed lines.

Lemma 2.2.5 *The graph T defined above has the following properties:*

1. *T is a tree and all the leafs of T are triconnected components.*

2. *Each path in T is an alternating path of separating pairs and triconnected components. Hence, a path between two leafs always contains an odd number of nodes and therefore T has a unique center node which has even eccentricity.*

3. *With an arbitrary separating pair node as root, T has odd depth.*

4. *A 3-bond is introduced as a child of a separating pair only as an indicator that the vertices of the separating pair have an edge between them in G. Hence a 3-bond is always a leaf node. In [HT73] it is a k-bond, where k is the number of components formed by the removal of the separating pair. Observe, k is the number of children of its parent separating pair and can be computed easily.*

Proof. We only show the first claim, because the others follow directly from the fact that along a path in the tree the type of nodes alternate and nodes for 3-bonds are adjacent to one separating pair node only.

Suppose T has a cycle C. By definition it is an alternating cycle of separating pairs and triconnected components, i.e. $C = (s_1, G_1, s_2, G_2, \ldots, s_r, G_r, s_1)$. Remove any separating pair s_i from C. Then the triconnected components G_{i-1} and G_i remain connected along a path through the other components from the cycle, contradicting the assumption that s_i separates them. □

Lemma 2.2.6 *The triconnected component tree $\mathcal{T}$ of a biconnected graph G can be computed in logspace.*

Proof. In Lemma 2.2.2 we showed that the 3-connected separating pairs in G can be computed in logspace. We have nodes for them in $\mathcal{T}$.

Let $\{a_0, b_0\}$ be a 3-connected separating pair in G. Let S be a split component of $G \setminus \{a_0, b_0\}$. We define a triconnected component C with respect to S which has the following properties. For C there is a node in $\mathcal{T}$. The node for C is adjacent to the separating pair node for $\{a_0, b_0\}$. Intuitively, C is obtained from S by collapsing split components at separating pairs in S to virtual edges. More precisely, we distinguish whether C is a cycle or a 3-connected component as follows (cf. Battista and Tamassia [BT89], [BT96]).

- If $S \setminus \{a_0, b_0\}$ contains articulation points then C is a *cycle*. Let $c_1, \ldots, c_l$ be this set of articulation points. Then, $a_0, c_1, c_2, \ldots, c_l, b_0$ is the cycle C. Two consecutive vertices c_i, c_{i+1} are connected by an edge as in C or form a separating pair. In the latter case we connect this pair in C by a virtual edge which replaces the original edge, if there is one in S.

25

2. PRELIMINARIES

- If $S \setminus \{a_0, b_0\}$ does not contain articulation points, then C is a *3-connected component* which is defined as follows. Two vertices u and v of S are in C if for all separating pairs $\{a, b\}$ different from $\{a_0, b_0\}$ in G there are simple paths from u and v to a_0 (or b_0) and from u to v in $S \setminus \{a, b\}$. The pair $\{a_0, b_0\}$ also belongs to C. Connect each separating pair of S in C by a virtual edge which replaces the original edge if it is present in S. Then C is a 3-connected component, because it does not contain separating pairs by construction.

- If there is an edge between a_0 and b_0 in G then this edge is maintained in an extra component called a *3-bond*, i.e. the directed edge and two virtual edges. This is also a triconnected component.

All the tasks, in particular the detection of separating pairs and articulation points or finding paths in undirected graphs, where some vertices are deleted can be done in logspace via queries to reachability testing [Rei08]. The construction of the triconnected component tree can be done in logspace, since we operate on a tree structure.

The navigation on the triconnected component tree can be done in logspace because there are logspace computable functions to compute the parent, first child and next sibling for each node in the tree. We recompute the triconnected components and 3-connected separating pairs if required. It suffices to locally store information of the current separating pair a_0, b_0 the current child (i.e. the label of one vertex of a split component which identifies it) and for finding the unique parent we store the root node of the tree if it is a separating pair and if the root is a triconnected component node then we store a vertex of the corresponding component.

We consider later in Section 2.6.2 a depth first tree traversal algorithm which runs in logspace, in more detail. □

2.2.5 Component Trees for Individual (k)-Connected Components

Besides triconnected component trees we define a more general version.

Let G be a $(k-1)$-connected graph together with a complete set of $(k-1)$-*separating sets* and *individual (k)-connected components* (here we leave open how the set of components is defined in detail). We define nodes for them, the *component nodes* and the $(k-1)$-*separating set nodes*. There is an edge between a component node and a separating set node iff the separating set is entirely contained in the component node. The resulting graph is a tree, the (k)-*connected component tree*.

- In case $k = 2$, $\mathcal{T}^B(G)$ denotes the *biconnected component tree* of a connected graph G which exactly fits this definition.

- In case $k = 3$, $\mathcal{T}^{\mathsf{T}}(B)$ denotes the *triconnected component tree* of a biconnected graph B, this was defined earlier. Besides 3-connected components, cycles and 3-bonds are a special type of components.

- We also consider the case $k = 4$. We introduce two versions which are defined in the context of isomorphism and reachability testing. We define for a triconnected component G_0, the *four-connected component tree* $\mathcal{T}^{\mathsf{F}}(G_0)$ on Page 127 and the *4-connected component tree* $\mathcal{T}^4(G_0)$ on Page 188.

Parameters for Trees and Component Trees. A *component tree* of a graph G is a tree where nodes are associated to components, i.e. induced subgraphs of the graph G, and separating sets. We consider separating sets being of constant size. The component tree is denoted $\mathcal{T}$ or $\mathcal{T}(G)$. If $\mathcal{T}$ is rooted at a node C then we also write $\mathcal{T}_C$.

For a component tree $\mathcal{T}$, the *size of an individual component node* t of $\mathcal{T}$ is the number of vertices in the component which is associated to t. The size of a $(k-1)$-separating set node is $k-1$. The vertices of the separating sets are counted in every component where they occur.

The *size of a tree* T, denoted $|T|$, is the number of nodes in the tree. For component trees, we rather use the following definition. The *size of the component tree* $\mathcal{T}$, denoted by $\mathsf{size}(\mathcal{T})$, is the sum of the sizes of its individual component nodes. The size of $\mathcal{T}$ is at least as large as the number of vertices in $\mathsf{graph}(\mathcal{T})$. This is the induced subgraph on vertex set $\{v \mid v$ belongs to a component which corresponds to a node in $T\}$.

The following definitions are used for trees and component trees. Let T_t be T when rooted at node t. A child t_0 of t is called a *large child* if $|T_{t_0}| > |T_t|/2$ ($\mathsf{size}(\mathcal{T}_{t_0}) > \mathsf{size}(\mathcal{T}_t)/2$ respectively), i.e. the immediate subtree of T_t rooted at child t_0 has more than half the size than the subtree T_t. There can be at most one such subtree for T_t. $\#t$ denotes the number of children of node t.

2.2.6 Tree Decomposition and Tree Distance Decomposition

A *tree decomposition* of a graph $G = (V, E)$ is a pair $(\{X_i \mid i \in I\}, T = (I, F))$, where $\{X_i \mid i \in I\}$ is a collection of subsets of V called bags, and T is a tree with node set I and edge set F, satisfying the following properties:

i) $\bigcup_{i \in I} X_i = V$,

ii) for each $\{u, v\} \in E$, there is an $i \in I$ with $u, v \in X_i$ and

iii) for each $v \in V$, the set of nodes $\{i \mid v \in X_i\}$ forms a subtree of T.

The *width* of a tree decomposition $(\{X_i \mid i \in I\}, T = (I, F))$ of G is defined as $\max\{|X_i| \mid i \in I\} - 1$. The *treewidth* of a graph G is the minimum width over all possible

2. PRELIMINARIES

tree decompositions of G.

A *tree distance decomposition* of a graph $G = (V, E)$ is a triple $(\{X_i \mid i \in I\}, T = (I, F), r)$, where $\{X_i \mid i \in I\}$ is a collection of subsets of V called *bags*, T is a tree with node set I, edge set F and root r, and $S = X_r$ the *root set*, satisfying the following properties:

i) $\bigcup_{i \in I} X_i = V$ and for all $i \neq j$, $X_i \cap X_j = \emptyset$ (i.e. the bags partition the set of vertices in G),

ii) for each $v \in V$, if $v \in X_i$ then $d_G(X_r, v) = d_T(r, i)$ (i.e. the distance from i to r in T is equal the distance from the elements in bag X_i to S in G)

iii) for each $\{u, v\} \in E(G)$, there are $i, j \in I$ with $u \in X_i, v \in X_j$ and $i = j$ or $\{i, j\} \in F$ (i.e. for every edge in G its two endpoints belong to the same or to adjacent bags in T).

Let $D = (\{X_i \mid i \in I\}, T = (I, F), r)$ be a tree distance decomposition of G. X_r is the *root bag* of D. The *width* of D is the maximum number of elements of a bag X_i. The *tree distance width* of a graph G is the minimum width over all possible tree distance decompositions of G.

The tree distance decomposition D is *minimal* if for each $i \in I$, the set of vertices in the bags with labels in the subtree rooted at i in T induce a connected subgraph in G. In [YBdFT99] it is shown that for every root set $S \subseteq V$ there is a unique minimal tree distance decomposition of G with root set S. The width of such a decomposition is minimal among the tree distance decompositions of G with root set S.

The following notions will be used for both, tree decomposition and tree distance decomposition. A nice consequence is, that the bags are separating sets in the corresponding graphs. In contrast to the decompositions into k-connected components, we consider here separating sets of size k, even if the underlying graph is not k-connected. In tree (distance) decompositions we say a bag X_i *separates* a bag X_a from another bag X_b if the vertices in $X_a \setminus X_i$ are separated from vertices in $X_b \setminus X_i$ in graph $G \setminus X_i$.

An isomorphism from G onto H *respects* their tree (distance) decompositions D, D' if vertices in a bag of D in G are mapped blockwise onto vertices in a bag of D' in H. Not every isomorphism has this property.

2.3 Group Theory

We start with some basic notions. Let $\mathbb{N} = \{1, 2, 3, \dots\}$ be the infinite set of *natural numbers* and let $\mathbb{N}_0 = \mathbb{N} \cup \{0\}$. Let $\mathbb{Z} = \{0, 1, -1, 2, -2, \dots\}$ be the infinite set of *integers*. $\mathbb{Z}_k = \{0, 1, \dots, k-1\}$ is the set of integers modulo k with $k \geq 2$.

We use the notion of an *interval* for sets over $\mathbb{Z}$. Let $[k, n] = \{k, k+1, \dots, n-1, n\}$ for integers $k \leq n$. Let $\oplus_k$ be the modulo addition in $\mathbb{Z}_k$ for some integer $k \geq 2$. We also write $\oplus$ if k is clear from the context.

A *multiplication table* or *Cayley table* of a 2-ary function f over a set $\{1,\ldots,n\}$ is a table of size $n \times n$ with entries $f(i,j)$ located in line i and row j in the table.

Groups. A *group* $G = (\Omega, \circ)$ is a set Ω together with an operation $\circ$, i.e. a 2-ary function, which satisfy the following axioms:

- *closure*: for all $a, b \in \Omega$: $a \circ b \in \Omega$
- *associativity*: for all $a, b, c \in \Omega$: $(a \circ b) \circ c = a \circ (b \circ c)$
- *identity element*: there exists $e \in \Omega$ such that for all $a \in \Omega$: $e \circ a = e$
- *inverse element*: for all $a \in \Omega$ there exists $b \in \Omega$: $a \circ b = e$

A group is *commutative* or *abelian* if for all $a, b \in \Omega$: $a \circ b = b \circ a$ holds. We consider *finite* groups, i.e. Ω is a finite set of size n.

The *order* of a group G, also denoted $|G|$ is the number of elements in G. For an integer i, g^i is the element g multiplied i times with itself. If $g^i = e$ for the smallest $i \geq 0$, then i is the *order* of g in the group. The element g^{-1} denotes the *inverse* element of g, it satisfies the equation $g^{-1} \circ g = e$.

Let Ω be a finite set. A *permutation* on Ω is a bijective function $\phi : \Omega \to \Omega$. For two permutations σ, ϕ, the notation $\sigma\phi(\Omega)$ means that the permutations are applied to Ω from right to left, this is $\sigma(\phi(\Omega))$. The *symmetric group* $Sym(\Omega)$ is the group over all permutations on Ω. We write $S_n = Sym(\{1,\ldots,n\})$. A *permutation group* on Ω is a subgroup of $Sym(\Omega)$.

A *generating set* of a group $(\Omega, \circ)$ is a subset $S \subseteq \Omega$ such that every element of the group can be expressed as the product of finitely many elements of S and their inverses, i.e. a *word*. The group is denoted by
$$\langle S \rangle = \{g \in \Omega \mid \exists s_1, \ldots, s_k \in S : g = s_1^{i_1} \circ \cdots \circ s_k^{i_k}\}.$$
Clearly, $i_1, \ldots, i_k$ are integers with $0 \leq i_j \leq order(s_j)$.

In a group $(\Omega, \circ)$, an *orbit* of an element $x \in \Omega$ is the set of elements $\Omega x = \{g \circ x \mid g \in \Omega\}$.

Let G be a group and H a subgroup of G and g an element in G. Then $gH = \{gh \mid h \text{ an element of } H\}$ is a *left coset* of H in G, and $Hg = \{hg \mid h \text{ an element of } H\}$ is a *right coset* of H in G.

A group given in *table representation* or *Cayley representation* consists of a multiplication table of size n by n filled with numbers in the range from 1 to n, such that the total size is $n^2 \log n$ bits.

Quasigroups. A *quasigroup* is a set Ω together with an operation $\circ$, i.e. a 2-ary function, which satisfies from the group axioms the following: closure, unique identity element and unique inverse elements. The associativity is not required. Therefore, we have unique left and unique right inverse elements. We consider *finite* quasigroups, i.e. Ω is a finite set.

29

2. PRELIMINARIES

We consider quasigroups given in table representation, i.e. a multiplication table of size n by n, filled with numbers in the range from 1 to n. It has the property, that each line and each row is a permutation of the n elements.

Automorphism Groups. The *automorphism group* $Aut(G)$ is the set of automorphisms of G. It is a permutation group. The *orbit* of a vertex $v \in V(G)$ is the set of vertices $\{u \mid \phi(v) = u, \phi \in Aut(G)\}$. That is, a vertex u belongs to the orbit of v if there exists an automorphism which maps v onto u.

Let H be an induced subgraph of G. Define $Aut_G(H) \subseteq Aut(G)$ as the set of automorphisms of H, which can be extended to an automorphism in $Aut(G)$. Clearly, $Aut_G(H) \subseteq Aut(H)$. We say that an automorphism $\phi \in Sym(V)$ *acts cyclically* on a vertex set $V = \{v_0, \ldots, v_{n-1}\}$, if there exists $a \in \{0, \ldots, n-1\}$ such that $\phi(v_i) = v_{i \oplus a}$ for all $i \in \{0, \ldots, n-1\}$. We further say $\phi \in Sym(V(G))$ acts cyclically on subgraphs $G[V_0], \ldots, G[V_{k-1}]$, if there exists $a \in \{0, \ldots, k-1\}$ such that $\phi(v) \in V_{i \oplus a}$ for all $v \in V_i$ and $i \in \{0, \ldots, k-1\}$.

Let $S_1, \ldots, S_k \subseteq V(G)$ be sets of distinct vertices of graph G. The set of automorphisms, mapping for all $i \in \{1, \ldots, k\}$ vertices in S_i onto vertices in S_i in any order, are called *setwise stabilizer*. These automorphisms *fix* $S_1, \ldots, S_k$ *blockwise*. If $|S_1| = \cdots = |S_k| = 1$ then these automorphisms *fix* $S_1, \ldots, S_k$ *pointwise*. $G_{[S_1, \ldots, S_k]}$ denotes graph G with $S_1, \ldots, S_k$ *setwise stabilized* in the automorphism group of G.

Canons and Codes. Let $\mathcal{G}$ be a class of graphs. Let $f : \mathcal{G} \to \{0,1\}^*$ be a function such that for all $G, H \in \mathcal{G}$ we have $G \cong H \Leftrightarrow f(G) = f(H)$. Then f computes a *complete invariant* for $\mathcal{G}$. Moreover, if f computes for G a graph $f(G)$ such that $G \cong f(G)$ then f computes *canonical forms* for $\mathcal{G}$. We call $f(G)$ the *canon* for G. If f depends on parameters, say $p_1, \ldots, p_k$, then $f(G, p_1, \ldots, p_k)$ is a *code* for G. A parameter is for example the choice of one edge in G or an embedding of G in the plane. For example, the minimum code (e.g. the lexicographical smallest code for G) can be used as a canon for G.

Let $\mathcal{G}$ be a class of graphs, where each graph $G \in \mathcal{G}$ has a unique tree decomposition $\mathcal{T}(G)$ (unique up to isomorphism, i.e. every automorphism fixes blockwise the unique components associated with the nodes of $\mathcal{T}(G)$). Let $\mathcal{TG} = \{\mathcal{T}(G) \mid G \in \mathcal{G}\}$. Let $f' : \mathcal{TG} \to \{0,1\}^*$ be a function such that for all $G, H \in \mathcal{G}$ we have $G \cong H \Leftrightarrow f'(\mathcal{T}(G)) = f'(\mathcal{T}(H))$. Then f' computes a complete invariant for $\mathcal{G}$, we call $f'(\mathcal{T}(G))$ the *tree-canon* for $\mathcal{T}(G)$. If this canonization procedure depends on some parameters (e.g. the choice of a root for the tree decomposition) then it is denoted a *tree-code* for $\mathcal{T}(G)$. For example, the minimum tree-code (depending on f', e.g. the lexicographical smallest tree-code for $\mathcal{T}(G)$) can be used as a tree-canon for $\mathcal{T}(G)$.

2.4 Graph Isomorphism and Related Decision Problems

Graph Isomorphism and Graph Automorphism. The *graph isomorphism problem* is defined as the problem

$\text{GI} = \{(G, H) \mid G \text{ and } H \text{ are isomorphic graphs }\}$.

The *graph automorphism problem* is defined as

$\text{GA} = \{G \mid \text{graph } G \text{ has an automorphism different to the identity }\}$.

Color Graph Isomorphism and Prefix Graph Automorphism. Given two colored graphs, for an isomorphism between them, the color relations have to be preserved. The *isomorphism problem for colored graphs* is defined as

$\text{color-GI} = \{((G, f_G), (H, f_H)) \mid \text{for graphs } G, H \text{ there exists a color}$
$\quad\text{preserving isomorphism } (G, f_G) \cong (H, f_H)\}$.

Here, f_G and f_H are labeling functions which assign colors to vertices of G and H, respectively. Observe that color-GI $\leq_m^{\mathsf{AC}^0}$ GI (c.f. [KST93]).

The *automorphism problem for colored graphs* is defined as

$\text{color-GA} = \{(G, f_G) \mid \text{graph } G \text{ has color preserving automorphisms different to the identity}\}$.

GI_b denotes the restriction of graph isomorphism to graphs with n vertices where the number of vertices with the same color is bounded by function $b(n)$. The *bounded color class graph isomorphism problem* (BCGI) is the union of GI_b for all $b \in O(1)$.

Let $(x_1, \ldots, x_k), (y_1, \ldots, y_k) \subseteq V(G)$ be two ordered sets of vertices of graph G. The *prefix graph automorphism problem* as denoted in [KST93] is

$\text{prefix-GA} = \{(G, (x_1, \ldots, x_k), (y_1, \ldots, y_k)) \mid \exists \phi \in Aut(G) \text{ such that}$
$\quad \phi(x_i) = y_i \text{ for all } 1 \leq i \leq k\}$.

The sequences of vertices are the prefixes for the graph G which define a *partial automorphism*. The question is whether this partial automorphism can be extended to an automorphism in $Aut(G)$ which is different to the identity. Observe that prefix-GA $\leq_m^{\mathsf{AC}^0}$ GI (c.f. [KST93, Tor04]).

Graph isomorphism restricted to graph classes. Let $\mathcal{G}$ be a class of graphs. Then $\mathcal{G}$-GI is the graph isomorphism problem but with the input graphs restricted to graphs from $\mathcal{G}$.

In this thesis we consider for example the complexity of the isomorphism problem restricted to valence-k graphs, planar graphs, $K_{3,3}$-minor free graphs, K_5-minor free graphs, tournaments and graphs of bounded tree-width.

2. PRELIMINARIES

Promise-Graph Isomorphism and Promise-Graph Automorphism. The *promise-graph isomorphism problem* is defined as

$$\mathsf{PGI} = \{((G,H)(I,J)) \mid G \cong H \Leftrightarrow I \not\cong J\}.$$

PGI will be used as a promise problem [Sel88] in the sense, that we will work in settings in which two given pairs of graphs will be known to be in PGI and the question will be to find which of the pairs is isomorphic, the first or the second one. It is a tool for the simulation of an *and*-function or an *or*-function with GI [Tor04]. For more details on this, see Definition 3.2.12.

The *promise-graph automorphism problem* (PGA) is defined the same way as PGI but with the condition that the graphs in the tuples are rigid graphs. The use of PGA is the same as of PGI, it is a tool for the simulation of boolean functions with GA [Tor04], see Definition 3.3.3 for more details.

Isomorphism Testing on Groups and Quasigroups. We define the isomorphism problem on quasigroups and groups given in table representation.

Quasigroup isomorphism problem

Input: Two finite quasigroups $G = (\Omega, \cdot), G' = (\Omega, \circ)$ of order n given as multiplication tables of size n by n, stored within $O(n^2 \log n)$ bits.
Computation: accept, if G and G' are quasigroups and there exists an isomorphism $\phi \in Sym(\Omega)$ from G onto G'. This means, for all $i, j \in \Omega : \phi(i \cdot j) = \phi(i) \circ \phi(j)$.

Clearly, the group isomorphism problem, when groups are given in table representation, reduces to the quasigroup isomorphism problem, because groups are associative quasigroups.

Cayley-group isomorphism problem

Input: Two finite groups $G = (\Omega, \cdot), G' = (\Omega, \circ)$ of order n given as multiplication tables of size n by n, stored within $O(n^2 \log n)$ bits.
Computation: accept, if G and G' are groups and there exists an isomorphism $\phi \in Sym(\Omega)$ from G onto G'. This means, for all $i, j \in \Omega : \phi(i \cdot j) = \phi(i) \circ \phi(j)$.

Accordingly, we define the *abelian Cayley-group isomorphism problem*, where the input, the groups G and G' will be accepted, iff they are abelian groups and isomorphic.

2.5 Graph Reachability and Related Decision Problems

Given a graph G and two designated vertices s, t. The *reachability problem* is to decide whether there is a path from s to t in G. If G is directed, the path is considered to be directed from s to t.

There is a close connection between the reachability problem for directed graphs and the Turing machine model. A *configuration graph* $G(M, x)$ associated with Turing machine M is a graph whose vertices are configurations of M. There is a directed edge between two vertices if M can move from the first configuration to the second one in one computation step. There is one configuration corresponding to the initial state of the machine and one corresponding to the final state. Let s and t be these vertices, respectively. Hence, there is a path from s to t if M accepts the input x. If M is a non-deterministic logarithmic space bounded Turing machine then $G(M, x)$ is of size polynomial in $|x|$. If M is symmetric (i.e. for each transition there is an inverse transition), then in $G(M, x)$, for an edge (u, v) there also is an edge (v, u). Reingold proved that SL= L [Rei08].

In complexity theory it is a fundamental question to understand the relationship between L and NL. Therefore there is a natural interest in considering the reachability problem restricted to certain classes of directed graphs.

For some particular classes of graphs reachability is known to be in L. Jakoby and Tantau [JT07] proved L-completeness for directed series-parallel graphs. This also holds for several sub-classes of grid graphs [ABC+09].

Bourke, Tewari and Vinodchandran [BTV07] proved that reachability on planar graphs is in UL ∩ coUL and is hard for L. They built on work of Reinhard and Allender [RA00] and Allender, Datta and Roy [ADR05]. A planar graph is transformed into a grid graph maintaining the reachability properties between the vertices s and t. With a weight function on the horizontal and vertical edges, every closed circle has positive weight. As a consequence there exists a unique minimum weight path from s to t. A more direct proof is given by Kulkarni [Kul09].

Recently, the study of reachability on certain classes of directed graphs gained much interest. Thierauf and Wagner [TW09] reduce reachability on $K_{3,3}$-minor free and K_5-minor free graphs onto planar reachability. This result is presented in Chapter 9. Allender et.al. [ABC+09] showed that reachability for graphs embedded on the torus is logspace reducible to the planar case. Kynčl and Vyskočil [KV10] generalize this result to graphs embedded on a fixed surface of arbitrary genus.

From an algorithmical point of view it is also of interest to know the complexity of variants of the reachability problem, also when considering restricted classes of graphs.

Let $\mathcal{G}$ be a class of directed graphs. We define the following problems on input graphs restricted to $\mathcal{G}$.

$\mathcal{G}$-Reachability $=\{(G, s, t) \mid G \in \mathcal{G}$ has a path from s to $t\}$
$\mathcal{G}$-Distance $=\{(G, s, t, k) \mid G \in \mathcal{G}$ has a path from s to t of length $\leq k\}$
$\mathcal{G}$-LongPath $=\{(G, s, t, k) \mid G \in \mathcal{G}$ has a simple path from s to t of length $\geq k\}$

2. PRELIMINARIES

For example, in Section 5.3 we prove that Planar-Distance is in UL ∩ coUL and reduce the isomorphism problem on planar 3-connected graphs to Planar-Distance.

Limaye, Mahajan and Nimbhorkar [LMN09] prove that longest paths in planar DAGs can be computed in UL ∩ coUL. Recently, Das, Datta and Nimbhorkar [DDN10] give a logspace algorithm for the reachability problem on directed k-trees, where k is a constant. They also give a logspace algorithm for Distance and LongPath on directed acyclic k-trees. These results are also applicable for bounded tree width graphs when a tree decomposition is given. More recently, Elberfeld, Jakoby and Tantau [EJT10] showed, that a tree decomposition can be computed in logspace.

2.6 Proof Techniques

2.6.1 Proof Techniques for Logspace Hardness

We prove that the isomorphism problem for some restricted classes of graphs are hard for logspace. For this we reduce from the following logspace complete problem.

> **Order between Vertices (Ord)** [Ete97, JKMT03]
> *Input:* A digraph $G = (V, E)$ with $|V| = n$ that is a line and two designated vertices $v_i, v_j \in V(G)$.
> *Computation:* accept, if $v_i \prec v_j$ in the total order induced by G.

Etessami proved that Ord is complete for logspace under quantifier-free projections (in short $\leq_{qfp}$). For a detailed definition of this kind of reducibility, we refer to e.g. [Ete97]. Projection means in the sense of Valiant [Val82] that each bit of the output depends on at most one bit of the input. This kind of reduction needs less computational resources than AC^0 many-one reductions.

We use this technique to prove L-hardness for the following decision problems: valence-2 GI, see Theorem 4.2.1, cycle-GI, see Theorem 4.5.1, line-GI, see Theorem 4.5.2, the poset game problem, see Theorem 4.7.1 and planar 3-connected GI, see Theorem 5.6.1.

2.6.2 A Logspace Algorithm for the Depth First Traversal of Trees

Lindell [Lin92] described a simple logspace algorithm for a depth first traversal of trees. Let t be a tree with a designated root node t_0. The algorithm is based on three functions which compute the parent and the children of a node t in some fixed order, given by a function order:

- Parent(t) returns the neighbor of t which separates t from t_0, or it returns t_0 itself if it is a neighbor of t. If $t = t_0$ then it returns 0. This task can be queried to a reachability test.

- FirstChild(t, order) returns the first child of t (with respect to function order) if it exists and 0 if t is a leaf. Search among all neighbors the smallest node according to function order which is not the parent.

- NextSibling(t, order) returns the next sibling of t (with respect to function order) if it exists and 0 otherwise. Search among all neighbors of Parent(t) the smallest node t' larger than t according to order such that $t' \neq$ Parent(Parent(t)).

The function order can be an arbitrary function computable in logspace. A *depth first traversal* in a tree is based on three procedures using the according functions described above:

- down: go down to the *first child* if it exists, and proceed with down. Otherwise, t is a leaf and we move over.

- over: move over to the *next sibling* if it exists, and proceed with down. Otherwise, t is the last child and we go up in the tree.

- up: return back up to the *parent* if it exists, and proceed with over. Otherwise, $t = t_0$ and we traversed the whole tree.

For a depth first traversal, we just remember the root t_0 and the current position t.

Theorem 2.6.1 *(Lindell [Lin92]) There is a logspace computable algorithm for the depth first traversal of trees.*

With these functions, we can also compute the size $|T|$ of a tree and $\#t$ the number of children of node t. For the size of a tree, we initialize a global counter with 1 and perform a tree traversal. We increment the global counter when going up in the tree. For $\#t$ we start at node t and perform FirstChild(t, order) once. Then we perform NextSibling(t, order) until this function returns 0. Thereby, we count the number of calls to these functions.

2.6.3 A Logspace Algorithm for Tree Canonization

The following algorithm is an important tool for the design of new logspace canonization algorithms for new classes of graphs.

Lindell [Lin92] gave a logspace algorithm for tree canonization. The algorithm is based on an order relation $\leq$ on trees defined below. The order relation has the property that two trees S and T are isomorphic if and only if $S = T$. Clearly, an algorithm that decides the order can

2. PRELIMINARIES

be used as an isomorphism test. Lindell showed how to extend such an algorithm to compute a canon for a tree in logspace. Let S and T be two trees with root s and t, respectively. The *isomorphism order* is defined $S < T$ if:

1. $|S| < |T|$, or

2. $|S| = |T|$ but $\#s < \#t$, where $\#s$ and $\#t$ are the number of children of s and t, respectively, or

3. $|S| = |T|$ and $\#s = \#t = k$, but $(S_1, \ldots, S_k) < (T_1, \ldots, T_k)$ lexicographically, where it is inductively assumed that $S_1 \leq \ldots \leq S_k$ and $T_1 \leq \cdots \leq T_k$ are the ordered subtrees of S and T rooted at the k children of s and t, respectively.

In Step 3, the notation $(S_1, \ldots, S_k) < (T_1, \ldots, T_k)$ with respect to the isomorphism order means, that there exists $i \in \{1, \ldots, k\}$ such that $S_1 = T_1 \leq S_2 = T_2 \leq \cdots \leq S_{i-1} = T_{i-1}$ and $S_i < T_i$. We will generalize the isomorphism order for component trees, which we obtain from tree-like decompositions of graphs.

The comparisons in Steps 1 and 2 can be done in logspace. Lindell proved that even the third step can be performed in logspace with a *two-pronged* depth-first search and *cross-comparing* children of S with children of T. This is briefly described below:

- Find the number of minimal sized children of s and t. If these numbers are different then the tree with a larger number of minimal children is declared to be smaller. If equality is found then remember the minimal size and check for the next size. This process is continued till an inequality in the sizes is detected or all the children of s and t are exhausted.

- If s and t have the same number of children of each size then assume that the children of s and t are partitioned into *size-classes* (referred to as *blocks* in [Lin92]) in the increasing order of the the sizes of the subtrees rooted at them. Blocks are pairwise disjoint and each child belongs to one block. The i-th block has cardinality k_i and the subtrees in that block have size N_i, where $N_1 < N_2 < \cdots$. It follows that $\sum_i k_i = k$ and $\sum_i k_i N_i = n - 1$. Then compare the children in each size-class recursively as follows:

Case 1, $k = 0$. Hence s and t have no children. They are isomorphic as all one-node trees are isomorphic. We conclude that $S = T$.

Case 2, $k = 1$. Recursively consider the grand-children of s and t. No space is needed when going into recursion.

Case 3, $k \geq 2$. For each of the subtrees S_j compute its order profile. The order profile consists of three counters, $c_<$, $c_>$ and $c_=$. These counters indicate the number of subtrees in the size-class of S_j that are respectively smaller than, greater than, or equal to S_j. The counters are computed by making cross-comparisons.

Note, that isomorphic subtrees in the same size-class have the same order profile. Therefore, it suffices to check that each such order profile occurs the same number of times in each size-class in S and T. To perform this check, compare the different order profiles of every size class in lexicographical order. The subtrees in the size-class i of S and T, which is currently being considered, with a count $c_< = 0$ form the first isomorphism class. The size of this isomorphism class is compared across the trees by comparing the values of the $c_=$ variables. If these values match then both trees have the same number of minimal children. Note that the lexicographical next larger order profile has the current value of $c_< + c_=$ as its value for the $c_<$-counter.

This way, one can loop through all the order profiles. If a difference in the order profiles of the subtrees of S and T is found then the lexicographical smaller order profile defines the smaller tree.

The last order profile considered is the one with $c_< + c_= = k$ for the current counters. If this point is passed without finding an inequality then the trees must be isomorphic and it follows that $S = T$.

Since $\sum_i k_i N_i \leq n$, the following recursion equation for the space complexity holds. For each new size class, the work-tape allocated for the former computations can be reused.

$$\mathcal{S}(n) = \max_i \{\mathcal{S}(N_i) + O(\log k_i)\} \leq \max_i \left\{ \mathcal{S}\left(\frac{n}{k_i}\right) + O(\log k_i) \right\},$$

where $k_i \geq 2$ for all i. It follows that $\mathcal{S}(n) = O(\log n)$.

The *tree-canon* is obtained as follows. We start a depth first traversal of the tree at the root s of the tree. When going down one level in the tree, the algorithm writes '(' on the output-tape and when going up one level then the algorithm writes ')'. We invoke the isomorphism order algorithm as subroutine and traverse the immediate subtrees of s in isomorphism order. Among isomorphic subtrees, the order is decided by comparing the labels of the children of s. Since logspace is closed under composition, we get:

Theorem 2.6.2 *(Lindell [Lin92]) Trees can be canonized in logspace.*

3 Tournament Isomorphism

3.1 Introduction

A *tournament* is a directed graph with one arc between each pair of distinct vertices. Tournaments comprise a large and important class of directed graphs and can be found in many applications. Tournament theory was intensively examined the past 35 years. Many results up to 1968 have been summarized in Moon's monograph [Moo68]. For further results and links, we refer to [GY04].

The tournament isomorphism problem (TI) is GI restricted to tournaments. For TI, no polynomial-time algorithm is known. The best known algorithm takes $n^{\log(n)}$ time [BL83]. Luks and Zemlyachenko (cf. [BL83]) give an upper bound for GI of $\exp(\sqrt{cn\log(n)})$ but there is no evidence of this bound being optimal. TI seems to be an easier computational problem than GI. Ponomarenko [Pon94] give a polynomial time algorithm for recognition and isomorphism testing of cyclic tournaments. Arvind et al. [ABL98] reduced TI onto Mod_2GA, an intermediate problem between GA and GI. Mod_2GA is the class of graphs with an even number of automorphisms. This follows, because the automorphism group of any tournament is of odd size [KST93], which in turn implies, that two tournaments are isomorphic, iff the automorphism group of their disjoint union contains an order two permutation (switching the tournaments). Arvind, Das and Mukhopadhyay [ADM06] extend Babai-Luks tournament canonization algorithm and give an $n^{O(k+\log n)}$ algorithm for canonization and isomorphism testing of k-hypertournaments, with n the number of vertices and k the size of the hyperedges.

Since the relation between GI and TI is not clear, we contribute to analyze the complexity status of tournament isomorphism. In this chapter we show, that TI and the tournament automorphism problem (TA) is hard for NC^1, L, NL, Mod_kL with $k \geq 3$ odd integer, #L and DET under AC^0 many-one reductions.

In the proof showing GI hard for DET, some graph gadgets were defined [Tor04]. The main idea of our proof is, to transform these graph gadgets into tournaments. For obtaining a tournament, we also need to connect the graph gadgets with directed edges. After closer consideration, this task is complex. To prove that GI is hard for Mod_kL, we need one of these graph gadgets. This gadget contains subgraphs, where vertices have orbits of size k in order to encode an integer in $\mathbb{Z}_k$. Since the order of automorphism groups of tournaments always

3. TOURNAMENT ISOMORPHISM

are odd [KST93], we cannot directly encode an integer in $\mathbb{Z}_k$ with $k \geq 2$ an even integer. Furthermore, we need the representation of Boolean values. For this, we use a graph gadget, consisting of a tuple of graphs. To encode Boolean values, we encode value 0 in an isomorphism as the identical mapping of two subgraphs and the value 1 by switching them. The difficulty is, that vertices in these tuples again have orbits of even size. Therefore, value 1 is encoded in new graph gadgets still with a non-trivial mapping, i.e. a cyclic rotation of its vertices which have orbits of odd size. We prove, that TI is hard for DET. It follows, that TI is hard for Mod_kL with $k \geq 2$ any integer under logspace Turing reductions. Observe, since TA $\leq_m^{\text{AC}^0}$ TI (see Corollary 3.1.1, TA is prefix-TA without prefix) and the converse direction is unknown, it is a stronger result to show DET $\leq_m^{\text{AC}^0}$ TA. Indeed, we can prove that the same lower bounds which hold for TI, also hold for TA.

Definitions. We begin with some specific definitions used throughout the chapter. To keep notation short, we write $[1, n]$ instead of $\{1, \ldots, n\}$.

A *cyclic tournament* T is a tournament on n vertices $x_0, \ldots, x_{n-1}$ such that $(x_i, x_{i \oplus j}) \in E(T)$ for all $i \in [0, n-1], j \in [1, \lfloor \frac{n}{2} \rfloor]$. For tournaments as input-graphs, we define similar to GI the *tournament isomorphism problem* (TI). An isomorphism must respect the direction of the edges.

The *tournament automorphism problem* (TA) is given a tournament, decide whether it has a non-trivial automorphism which respects the direction of the arcs. Then we also write color-TI, TA, prefix-TA corresponding to color-GI, GA, prefix-GA. Arvind et.al. [ADM06] showed that color-TI is polynomial-time many-one reducible to TI without coloring. By verifying the proof, we observe that it is an AC^0 many-one reduction. Adapting the proof of prefix-GA $\leq_m^{\text{AC}^0}$ GI in [Tor04], we obtain the following chain of reductions. We conclude, that it suffices to prove lower bounds for prefix-TA.

Corollary 3.1.1 *prefix-TA* $\leq_m^{\text{AC}^0}$ *color-TI* $\leq_m^{\text{AC}^0}$ *TI.*

3.2 Hardness Results for Tournament Isomorphism

In this section we show that TI is hard for the complexity classes Mod_kL, NL, #L, C$_=$L, PL and DET under DLOGTIME uniform AC^0 many-one reductions.

3.2.1 Hardness of TI for Modular Counting Classes

GI is hard for the logarithmic space modular counting classes Mod_kL for all $k \geq 2$ [Tor04]. Since the circuit value problem restricted to *modulo addition*-gates over $\mathbb{Z}_k$ for $k \geq 2$ is complete for Mod_kL and with Corollary 3.1.1, we prove that TI is hard for Mod_kL with odd $k \geq 3$.

With the following graph gadget, we can simulate a *modulo addition*-gate.

Definition 3.2.1 [Tor04] *Fix $k \geq 2$. The* modulo addition graph gadget G^k *is defined by the following sets of vertices and edges:*

$$V(G^k) = \{x_a, y_a, z_a, u_{a,b} \mid a, b \in [0, k-1]\},$$

$$E(G^k) = \{\{x_a, u_{a,b}\}, \{y_b, u_{a,b}\}, \{u_{a,b}, z_{a \oplus b}\} \mid a, b \in [0, k-1]\}.$$

Let $U, X, Y, Z \subseteq V$ be vertex sets containing the $k^2 + 3k$ vertices denoted by indexed lower case letters each, e.g. $X = \{x_1, \ldots, x_{k-1}\}$. Denote vertex sets X as *left input-*, Y as *right input-* and Z as *output-vertices*. Figure 3.1 shows an example for $k = 3$.

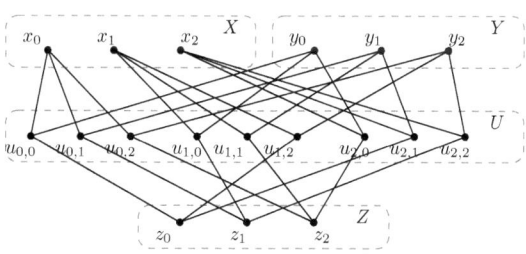

Figure 3.1: Modulo addition graph gadget G^3.

Lemma 3.2.2 describes automorphism properties of this graph gadget. It has only automorphisms which fix the vertex sets U, X, Y, Z blockwise.

Lemma 3.2.2 [Tor04] *Fix $k \geq 2$. For any $a, b \in [0, k-1]$ there is a unique automorphism $\phi_{a,b} \in Aut(G^k)$ with $\phi_{a,b}(x_i) = x_{a \oplus i}$ and $\phi_{a,b}(y_i) = y_{b \oplus i}$ for $i \in [0, k-1]$ and with $\phi_{a,b}(u_i) = u_{a \oplus i, b \oplus j}$ and $\phi_{a,b}(z_i) = z_{a \oplus b \oplus i}$.*

Every automorphism acts cyclically on each block X, Y or Z. With this graph gadget we construct a graph $G(C)$ which simulates a circuit C. For each gate C_i in C there is a copy of G^k in $G(C)$. There are edges connecting vertices in gadget $G(C_i)$ to vertices in $G(C_j)$ iff C_i and C_j are wired in C. Moreover, we use the notation $v(C) \in U(C) \subseteq V(G(C))$ also for vertices and vertex sets. If the context is clear then (C) will be omitted.

Definition 3.2.3 [Tor04] *Let C be a circuit of m modulo addition gates $C_1, \ldots, C_m$ and $k \geq 2$. We define $G(C)$ with*

$$V(G(C)) = \bigcup_{p \in [1,m]} V(G^k(C_p)),$$

$$E(G(C)) = \bigcup_{p \in [1,m]} E(G^k(C_p)) \cup \bigcup_{1 \leq p < q \leq m} E_{p,q} \text{ with}$$

41

3. TOURNAMENT ISOMORPHISM

$$E_{p,q} = \begin{cases} \{z_i(C_p), x_i(C_q)\} & \text{if } C_p \text{ and left input of } C_q \text{ are wired,} \\ \{z_i(C_p), y_i(C_q)\} & \text{if } C_p \text{ and right input of } C_q \text{ are wired,} \\ \emptyset & \text{if } C_p, C_q \text{ are not wired directly.} \end{cases}$$

Color vertices in $U(C_j), X(C_j), Y(C_j), Z(C_j)$ with colors $(u,j), (x,j), (y,j), (z,j)$ in this order for all $j \in [1, m]$.

The colors ensure the vertex sets X, Y, Z of each gadget are fixed blockwise in the automorphisms. The reduction of this decision problem for circuit C to prefix-GA is as follows: compute a graph $G(C)$ and define prefixes for input- and output values. We conclude that $\mathsf{Mod}_k\mathsf{L} \leq_m^{\mathsf{AC}^0}$ GI. Example 3.2.4 shows how prefixes can be set up for C.

Example 3.2.4 *Assume C has $2n$ inputs at gates in the first layer only. We define prefixes*
$$(x_0(C_1), y_0(C_1), x_0(C_2), y_0(C_2), \ldots, y_0(C_n), z_0(C_m)) \to$$
$$(x_{i_1}(C_1), y_{i_2}(C_1), x_{i_3}(C_2), y_{i_4}(C_2), \ldots, y_{i_{2n}}(C_n), z_1(C_m))$$
in $G(C)$ where $i_1, \ldots, i_{2n} \in [0, k-1]$ fix the left and the right inputs to the input gates in the first layer, i.e. values in $\mathbb{Z}_k$. The prefix $z_0(C_m) \to z_1(C_m)$ forces that the output of the circuit is 1.

We will show, that hardness for $\mathsf{Mod}_k\mathsf{L}$ also holds for TI, if k is odd.

Theorem 3.2.5 $\mathsf{Mod}_k\mathsf{L} \leq_m^{\mathsf{AC}^0}$ *TI with $k \geq 3$ an odd integer.*

The main proof idea is to transform the graph gadgets G^k and the circuit $G(C)$ (containing graph gadgets G^k as subgraphs) into tournaments. For this task, we first state in two lemmas that graphs can be modified while keeping the automorphism group unchanged. The following lemma says that if a subgraph H is fixed blockwise in the automorphism group of a graph G then we can replace H by another subgraph H' if $Aut(H)$ is a subgroup of $Aut(H')$.

Lemma 3.2.6 *Let H be an induced subgraph of a graph G with $Aut(G)$ setwise stabilizing vertices in H. Let H' be a graph with $V(H') = V(H)$ and let G' be G after replacing the induced subgraph H by subgraph H', setwise stabilizing vertices in H'. If $Aut_G(H) \subseteq Aut(H') \subseteq Aut(H)$ then $Aut(G) = Aut(G')$.*

Proof. In this prove, we assume familiarity with the prefix-GA problem. Fix $\phi \in Aut(H') \subseteq Aut(H)$. Construct $G_\phi = (G \setminus E(H), \phi)$, an instance for the prefix-GA problem. Observe that ϕ can be extended to an automorphism $\psi \in Aut(G)$, iff ψ solves prefix-GA with G_ϕ. Since $\phi \in Aut(H')$ let $G'_\phi = (G' \setminus E(H'), \phi)$ be another instance of the prefix-GA problem and then it follows, that $G_\phi = G'_\phi$. Observe that $G \setminus E(H)$ and $G' \setminus E(H')$ are identical graphs. Thus, by definition ϕ can be extended to an automorphism in G and G'. Any $\psi \in Aut(H) \setminus Aut(H')$ cannot be extended to an automorphism in $Aut(G)$, because $\psi \notin Aut_G(H)$. Thus, $Aut(G) = Aut(G')$. □

The next lemma shows, how to connect two subgraphs with arcs, such that each vertex in the first graph is connected to every vertex in the second graph, without changing the automorphism group.

Lemma 3.2.7 *Let $G[X], G[Y]$ be vertex-disjoint and setwise stabilized subgraphs of G. Suppose that in G all the edges with one endpoint in X and one endpoint in Y point from X to Y. There is an AC^0 computable function that transforms G into a graph G' over the same vertex set such that $Aut(G'_{[X,Y]}) = Aut(G_{[X,Y]})$. If $G[X], G[Y]$ are tournaments then G' is a tournament.*

Proof. Let $X = \{x_1, \ldots, x_m\}$, $Y = \{y_1, \ldots, y_n\}$ and let E_{XY} be the set of arcs, pointing from X to Y. Let $E_{YX} = \{(y,x) \mid (x,y) \notin E_{XY}\}$, i.e. $E_{XY} \cup E_{YX}$ is a complete bipartite edge set. Let $E(G') = E(G[X]) \cup E(G[Y]) \cup E_{XY} \cup E_{YX}$. Clearly, if $G[X], G[Y]$ are tournaments then G' as well. Fix any $\phi \in Aut(G_{[X,Y]})$, $e \in E_{XY}$, $e' \notin E_{XY}$. Verify, that any isomorphism maps edges onto edges and non-edges onto non-edges: $e, \phi(e) \in E(G)$ and $e, \phi(e) \in E_{XY} \subseteq E(G'_{[X,Y]})$ and $e', \phi(e') \notin E(G)$, and $e', \phi(e') \in E_{YX}$. The other direction is similar. Thus, $Aut(G_{[X,Y]}) = Aut(G'_{[X,Y]})$. □

With Lemmas 3.2.6 and 3.2.7, we can transform graph gadgets into tournaments and prove that they obey the same automorphism properties as the modulo addition graph gadget. We define a tournament with the same automorphism properties as G^k.

Definition 3.2.8 *Fix an odd integer $k \geq 3$. The* tournament modulo addition graph gadget T^k *is defined by vertex set*
$$V(T^k) = \{x_a, y_a, z_a, u_{a,b} \mid a, b \in [0, k-1]\}.$$
Let $U, X, Y, Z \subseteq V(T^k)$ contain vertices denoted by indexed lower case letters each. Let $U_a = \{u_{a,b} \mid b \in [0, k-1]\}$ for any $a \in [0, k-1]$. $E(T^k)$ unifies

1. $\{(x_a, x_{a \oplus i}), (y_a, y_{a \oplus i}), (z_a, z_{a \oplus i}) \mid a \in [0, k-1], i \in [1, \lfloor \frac{k}{2} \rfloor]\}$,

2. $\{(u_{a,b}, u_{a,b \oplus i}) \mid a, b \in [0, k-1], i \in [1, \lfloor \frac{k}{2} \rfloor]\}$,

3. $\{(u_{a,b}, u_{a \oplus i, b \oplus b'}) \mid a, b, b' \in [0, k-1], i \in [1, \lfloor \frac{k}{2} \rfloor]\}$,

4. $\{(x_a, u_{a,b}), (u_{i,b}, x_a) \mid a, b \in [0, k-1], i \in [0, k-1] \setminus \{a\}\}$,

5. $\{(y_b, u_{a,b}), (u_{a,i}, y_b) \mid a, b \in [0, k-1], i \in [0, k-1] \setminus \{b\}\}$,

6. $\{(u_{a,b}, z_{a \oplus b}), (z_i, u_{a,b}) \mid a, b \in [0, k-1], i \in [0, k-1] \setminus \{a \oplus b\}\}$,

7. $\{(x_a, y_b), (x_a, z_b), (y_a, z_b) \mid a, b \in [0, k-1]\}$.

Remark that $V(T^k) = V(G^k)$. In Item 1 we define cyclic tournaments for induced subgraphs on vertex sets X, Y and Z. In Item 2 we define cyclic tournaments $T^k[U_a]$ induced on vertices $U_a = \{u_{a,b} \mid b \in [0, k-1]\}$ for any fixed $a \in [0, k-1]$. In Item 3 we describe the connection

43

3. TOURNAMENT ISOMORPHISM

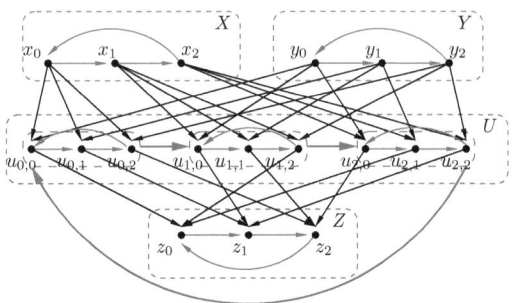

Figure 3.2: Sketch of tournament modulo addition graph gadget T^3.

between subgraphs $T^k[U_a]$, such that automorphisms in $Aut(T^k)$ act cyclically on subgraphs $T^k[U_a]$ for all $a \in [0, k-1]$. Items 4 to 7 describe complete bipartite edge sets among pairs of the vertex sets U, X, Y, Z. Figure 3.2 shows T^3 and contains edge sets of items 4 to 7 partially.

Lemma 3.2.9 *There is an* AC^0 *computable function that transforms G^k with odd $k \geq 3$ into the tournament modulo addition graph gadget T^k containing unique automorphisms as described in Lemma 3.2.2.*

Proof. In Lemma 3.2.2 the unique automorphisms act cyclically on vertex sets of the induced subgraphs $G^k[X]$, $G^k[Y]$ and $G^k[Z]$. First, consider $G^k[X]$; $Aut(G^k[X]) = Sym(G^k[X])$ and $Aut_{G^k}(G^k[X])$ is generated by permutation $(x_0 \ldots x_{k-1})$. Clearly, $Aut(T^k[X]) \subseteq Aut(G^k[X])$ and because of $T^k[X]$ being a cyclic tournament, it contains cyclic automorphisms such that $Aut_{G^k}(G^k[X]) \subseteq Aut(T^k[X])$. Apply Lemma 3.2.6 and replace $G^k[X]$ by $T^k[X]$ in G^k, without changing the automorphism group. The same holds for $G^k[Y]$ and $G^k[Z]$.
Second, consider $G^k[U]$. $Aut(G^k[U]) = Sym(G^k[U])$ and $Aut_{G^k}(G^k[U])$ is generated by ϕ, ψ, which are defined as follows: $\phi(u_{i,j}) = u_{i,j\oplus 1}$ and $\psi(u_{i,j}) = u_{i\oplus 1, j}$ for all $i, j \in [0, k-1]$. It follows that $Aut_{G^k}(G^k[U]) \subseteq Aut(T^k[U])$. Apply Lemma 3.2.6 and replace $G^k[U]$ by $T^k[U]$ in G^k, without changing the automorphism group.
Third, consider the edge sets of Item 4 to Item 7 in the definition of $E(T^k)$. Exchange undirected edges between stabilized vertex sets X, Y, Z, U by arcs. By Lemma 3.2.7, this also keeps the automorphism group unchanged.
Hence T^k is the union of all these modifications on G^k which can be computed in AC^0. □

With Lemma 3.2.9 we can prove that the replacement of gadgets G^k in $G(C)$ by tournament gadgets T^k does not change the automorphism group of $G(C)$. With Lemma 3.2.10, we describe how to obtain a tournament for the circuit C. This completes the proof of Theorem 3.2.5.

Lemma 3.2.10 *Let C be a circuit of modulo addition gates in $\mathbb{Z}_k$, with odd $k \geq 3$ and output value $s \in [0, k-1]$. Construct under AC^0 many-one reductions a tournament $T(C)$ containing non-trivial prefix automorphisms, iff C outputs s.*

Proof. Transform $G(C)$ (of Definition 3.2.3) into a tournament $T(C)$, such that $Aut(G(C)) = Aut(T(C))$ and $T(C)$ contains a non-trivial prefix automorphism, iff $G(C)$ does. First, apply Lemma 3.2.6 and 3.2.9. Exchange the subgraphs $G^k(C_i)$ by tournament gadgets $T^k(C_i)$ for all $i \in [1,m]$ under AC^0 many-one reductions. Since $Aut_{G(C)}(G^k(C_i)) \subseteq Aut(T^k(C_i)) = Aut(G^k(C_i))$, this does not change the automorphism group of $G(C)$.

Second, let $p, q \in [1,m]$ with $p < q$. Assume, that the gate C_p comes at least one layer before C_q in circuit C. Let $E_{p,q}$ be the edge set with one vertex in $G^k(C_p)$ and the other one in $G^k(C_q)$ and replace them by arcs which point from vertices in $G^k(C_q)$ to $G^k(C_p)$. Applying Lemma 3.2.7, we amend the edge set between subgraphs $G^k(C_p)$ and $G^k(C_q)$ by a complete bipartite edge set, denoted $E'_{p,q}$. Thus, we get $T(C)$ defined as follows:

$$V(T(C)) = \bigcup_{p \in [1,m]} V(T^k(C_p)) = V(G(C)),$$

$$E(T(C)) = \bigcup_{p \in [1,m]} E(T^k(C_p)) \cup \bigcup_{p,q \in [1,m], p<q} E'_{p,q},$$

$$E'_{p,q} = \{(v,u) \mid \{u,v\} \in E_{p,q}, u \in V(G^k(C_p)), v \in V(G^k(C_q))\} \cup$$

$$\{(u,v) \mid \{u,v\} \notin E_{p,q}, u \in V(G^k(C_p)), v \in V(G^k(C_q))\}.$$

Take the same prefixes and coloring to vertices in $T(C)$ as for $G(C)$, such that $T(C)$ contains non-trivial automorphisms obeying the prefixes, iff $G(C)$ does. Finally, we examine that this construction can be done in AC^0. Since $V(T^k) = V(G^k)$, we just have to compute the new edge set $E(T^k)$. This needs local information, since the decision, whether two vertices are connected by an edge, can be decided by knowing their indices and to which vertex sets U, X, Y, Z they belong. The same holds for the construction of $E'_{p,q}$ and taking the prefixes from $G(C)$ for $T(C)$. □

3.2.2 Hardness of TI for NL, #L, $C_=L$ and PL

We introduce graph gadgets for the simulation of *and*- and *or*-gates in circuits. For this, we need a special representation of a circuit in NC^1. A NC^1-circuit can be simulated by a balanced DLOGTIME uniform family of circuits with fanout 1, logarithmic depth, polynomial size and alternating layers of *and*-gates and *or*-gates [BIS90]. A circuit with fanout one is a formula. Hence, in the reduction we replace sub-circuits by sub-graphs recursively.

Lemma 3.2.11 [Tor04] *Given a uniform family of circuits C_n with logarithmic depth and polynomial size and given n tuples of pairs of graphs $((G_i, H_i), (I_i, J_i)) \in$ PGI. There is an AC^0*

3. TOURNAMENT ISOMORPHISM

computable function, constructing a tuple $((G,H),(I,J)) \in$ PGI with the property that $G \cong H$, iff C_n outputs 1, and $I \cong J$, iff C_n outputs 0. The i-th input to C_n consists of the bit of the Boolean value of the statement $G_i \cong H_i$.

With the isomorphism properties of the graph tuples in PGI, the circuit value problem of an NC^1 circuit is simulated. We transform these graphs in the tuples into tournaments, to get the same hardness results for TI which hold for GI.

Definition 3.2.12 A PGI-graph tuple *is a tuple of pairs of graphs* $((G,H),(I,J))$ *with* $G \cong H \Leftrightarrow I \not\cong J$. *Let* PGI *be the set of all such tuples.*

Let $((G_\wedge, H_\wedge),(I_\wedge, J_\wedge)) \in$ PGI *be the graph tuple for the simulation of conjunction and* $((G_\vee, H_\vee),(I_\vee, J_\vee)) \in$ PGI *for disjunction, containing* $((G_0, H_0),(I_0, J_0))$ *and* $((G_1, H_1),(I_1, J_1))$ $\in$ PGI *as in proof of Theorem 4.3 in [Tor04].*

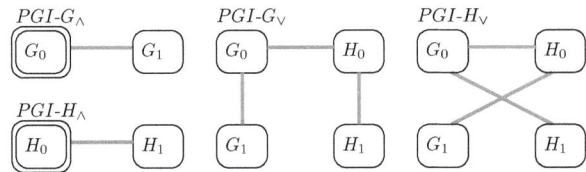

Figure 3.3: PGI-graph tuple simulating *and*- and *or*-gates [Tor04].

The graph tuples for conjunction have the following properties:
$G_\wedge \cong H_\wedge$ iff $G_0 \cong H_0$ and $G_1 \cong H_1$; $I_\wedge \cong J_\wedge$ iff $G_0 \not\cong H_0$ or $G_1 \not\cong H_1$ (in this case $I_0 \cong J_0$ or $I_1 \cong J_1$). Similarly, the graph tuples for disjunction:
$G_\vee \cong H_\vee$ iff $G_0 \cong H_0$ or $G_1 \cong H_1$; $I_\vee \cong J_\vee$ iff $G_0 \not\cong H_0$ and $G_1 \not\cong H_1$ (in this case $I_0 \cong J_0$ and $I_1 \cong J_1$).

Note, the gadgets PGI-$I_\wedge$, PGI-$J_\wedge$ are defined similarly as PGI-$G_\vee$, PGI-$H_\vee$, just exchange G_i with I_i and H_i with J_i for $i \in \{0,1\}$. PGI-$I_\vee$, PGI-$J_\vee$ are defined similarly as PGI-$G_\wedge$, PGI-$H_\wedge$ by doing the same changes.

For clear notation, we apply prefixes e.g. PGI-$G_\wedge$, PGI-$G_\vee$. If the context is clear, we omit these prefixes. We show how PGI-graph tuples can be transformed into tuples of tournaments maintaining the isomorphism properties.

Definition 3.2.13 A PTI-graph tuple *is a tuple of pairs of tournaments* $((G,H),(I,J))$ *with* $G \cong H$, *iff* $I \not\cong J$. *Let* PTI *be the set of all such tuples. We define for the simulation of conjunction* $((G_\wedge, H_\wedge),(I_\wedge, J_\wedge)) \in$ PTI *(write e.g. PTI-$G_\wedge$) and for disjunction* $((G_\vee, H_\vee),(I_\vee, J_\vee)) \in$ PTI *(write e.g. PTI-$G_\vee$) as follows:*

First, PTI-$G_\wedge$ contains tournaments G_0, G_1 and a set of arcs, pointing from every vertex in G_0 to every vertex in G_1. Replace G_0, G_1 in PTI-$G_\wedge$ by H_0, H_1 for obtaining PTI-$H_\wedge$, by I_0, I_1 for PTI-$I_\vee$ and by J_0, J_1 for PTI-$J_\vee$.

Second, let $i \in [0,1]$ and $j \in [0,2]$. Let X be a graph as in Figure 3.4. PTI-$G_\vee$ contains subgraphs $X, G_0, G_0', G_1, G_1', H_0$ and H_1 with G_0', G_1' copies of G_0, G_1. Let $E(PTI$-$G_\vee) = E_1 \cup \ldots \cup E_4$. E_1 unifies edges of all subgraphs. E_2 contains edges $(x_{i,0}, v)$ for all $v \in G_i$ (call G_i associated to $x_{i,0}$), and similar edge sets with $x_{i,1}$ associated to G_i' and $x_{i,2}$ to H_i. E_3 contains the following arcs: If $(x, x') \in E(X)$ then $(u, v) \in E_3$ if u belongs to a subgraph associated to x and v belongs to a subgraph associated to x'. E_4 contains (u, v) for all $u \in V(PTI$-$G_\vee \setminus X)$, $v \in V(X)$, iff $(v, u) \notin E_2$.

Construct PTI-$H_\vee$ with minor changes: Associate $x_{1,1}$ with H_1 and $x_{1,2}$ with G_1'. The rest of the construction is the same. Now replace subgraphs G_0, G_1, H_0, H_1 in PTI-$G_\vee$ (and PTI-$H_\vee$) by I_0, I_1, J_0, J_1 in this order and obtain PTI-$I_\wedge$ (and PTI-$J_\wedge$).

The tuples PTI-$G_\vee$ and PTI-$H_\vee$ have the property that X blockwise fixes the sub-graphs, i.e. the copies of G_0, G_1, H_0, H_1. An isomorphism simulates an or-function. An isomorphism maps either a copy of G_0 onto H_0 or a copy of G_1 onto H_1 or both.

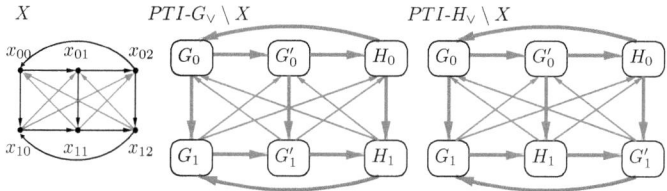

Figure 3.4: Construction of tournaments simulating and- and or-gates.

Lemma 3.2.14 *There is an AC^0 computable function, such that any of the PGI-tuples simulating and-gates and or-gates can be transformed into PTI-tuples maintaining the isomorphism properties.*

Proof. First, the construction of PTI-$G_\wedge$ can be obtained from PGI-$G_\wedge$, if coloring and undirected edges with both ends in different subgraphs G_0, G_1 and H_0, H_1 are replaced by arcs. The same holds for PTI-$H_\wedge$, PTI-$I_\vee$, PTI-$J_\vee$.

Second, we transform PGI-$G_\vee$ to PTI-$G_\vee$. Let $i \in [0,1]$, $j \in [0,2]$. Any automorphism $\phi \in Aut(X)$ acts cyclically on the vertices $x_{i,0}, x_{i,1}, x_{i,2}$. Every vertex in X has one associated subgraph in PTI-$G_\vee \setminus X$ via E_2. E_3 transfers the edge-connections of $E(X)$ onto the connections among the associated subgraphs in $E(PTI$-$G_\vee \setminus X)$. Intuitively, when collapsing subgraphs to

3. TOURNAMENT ISOMORPHISM

single vertices so far, then X can be considered as a minor of $PTI\text{-}G_\vee \setminus E_4$ and $Aut(X)$ would be a sub-group of $Aut_{PTI\text{-}G_\vee \setminus E_4}(X)$.

Apply E_4 to $E(PTI\text{-}G_\vee)$, as in Lemma 3.2.7 this does not change the automorphism group. Hence, associated subgraphs to $x_{i,j}$ must be mapped via $\phi \in Aut(PTI\text{-}G_\vee)$ onto the associated subgraph of $\phi(x_{i,j})$. The same holds for X and $PTI\text{-}H_\vee$. Observe, that this can be done in AC^0. Now to the isomorphism properties. Observe, that any isomorphism ϕ mapping $PTI\text{-}G_\vee$ onto $PTI\text{-}H_\vee$ satisfies:

1. $\phi(x_{i,j}) = x_{i,j\oplus 0}$ if $G'_1 \cong H_1 \cong G'_1$,

2. $\phi(x_{i,j}) = x_{i,j\oplus 1}$ if $G'_0 \cong H_0 \cong G_0$ and $G_1 \cong H_1 \cong G_1$,

3. $\phi(x_{i,j}) = x_{i,j\oplus 2}$ if $G_0 \cong H_0 \cong G'_0$ (and $G_1 \cong G'_1$).

Either $G'_1 \cong H_1$ (Item 1) or $G_0 \cong H_0$ (Item 3) or both are isomorphic (Item 2). We conclude, this encodes an *or*-function. We get $PTI\text{-}I_\wedge$ and $PTI\text{-}J_\wedge$, if we exchange in $PTI\text{-}G_\vee$ and $PTI\text{-}H_\vee$ the subgraphs G_0, G_1, H_0, H_1 by I_0, I_1, J_0, J_1 in this order, respectively. □

With all the graph gadgets $(G^k, PGI\text{-}G_\wedge, PGI\text{-}G_\vee, \dots)$ as defined so far, Torán proved that GI is hard for NL, #L, C$_=$L and PL under AC^0 many-one reductions [Tor04]. We prove that the same lower bounds hold for TI.

Theorem 3.2.15 *Tournament isomorphism is hard for* NL, #L, C$_=$L *and* PL *under* AC^0 *many-one reductions.*

Proof. To prove all the hardness bounds, graph gadgets are needed as described above. We refer to Theorems 4.1, 4.4 and Corollaries 4.5, 4.6 in [Tor04] for details. First, Mod$_k$L circuits are needed to compute the result of a #L function $f(x)$ mod k. These gadgets encode $f(x)$ mod k for a set of r different primes $k \in \{k_1, \dots, k_r \mid 3 \leq k_1 < \cdots < k_r\}$ (in Chinese remainder representation). The results are inputs to a NC^1-circuit, which compute bits of $f(x)$. Since tournament modulo addition gadgets for even k are not defined, the prime 2 cannot be chosen. In every step, the graph gadgets serve as subgraphs in new PGI-tuples. Applying Lemma 3.2.10 and 3.2.14, the graph gadgets can be transformed into tournaments under AC^0 many-one reductions. □

3.2.3 Hardness of TI for DET

Observe that DET $\leq_m^{AC^0}$ GI (Theorem 4.9 in [Tor04]) and that the complexity class DET coincides with $NC^1(\#L)$. We already described, how NC^1-circuits and #L-functions can be reduced to graph gadgets. For the implementation of oracle questions, with another graph gadget every #L-function f can be transformed in AC^0 into a sequence of PGI-tuples, encoding the bits of $f(x)$. The input $x \in \Sigma^n$ is also encoded as PGI-tuples. For details see the proof of Lemma 4.7 in [Tor04].

Definition 3.2.16 [Tor04] *The oracle graph gadget Gad_k contains subgraphs $G_a, H_a^h, I_a^i, J_a^{i,j}$ with $h \in [1, k-1]$, $i, j \in [0, k-1]$, which are copies of graphs in $((G_a, H_a), (I_a, J_a)) \in$ PGI, encoding bit x_a of $f(x)$ mod k. Let $W = \{w_0, \ldots, w_{k-1}\}$, $Z = \{z_0, \ldots, z_{k-1}\} \subseteq V(Gad_k)$. Henceforth, for simplifying notations, let $W^0 = G_a$ and $W^h = H_a^h$. We also denote $Z[i,j] = J_a^{i,j}$ for $j \neq i$ and $Z[i,i] = I_a^i$ for $i, j \in [0, k-1]$. Let $Z^i = \bigcup_{j \in [0,k-1]} Z[i,j]$. We define the edge set $E(Gad_k)$ as the union of the following edge sets*

1. $E(G_a), E(H_a^h), E(I_a^i), E(J_a^{i,j})$,
2. $\{\{u,v\} \mid u = z_i, v \in Z^i \text{ or } u \in W^i, v = w_i\}$,
3. $\{\{u,v\} \mid u \in Z[i,j], v \in W^j\}$,
4. $\{(u,v) \mid u = w_i, v = w_{i \oplus 1} \text{ or } u = z_i, v = z_{i \oplus 1}\}$.

This gate has the property, that if $G_a \cong H_a$ then for $c \in [0, k-1]$, any automorphism mapping z_i to $z_{i \oplus c}$ also maps w_i onto $w_{i \oplus c}$. But, if $I_a \cong J_a$ then any automorphism mapping z_i to $z_{i \oplus c}$ fixes all vertices w_i pointwise.

In the proofs of the hardness results for GI, the graphs have PGI tuples as subgraphs (Lemma 4.8 in [Tor04]). With the assumption, that the subgraphs of Item 1 are PGI tuples and that any automorphism acts cyclically on vertex sets W and Z, then any automorphism of Gad_k acts cyclically on subgraphs $\{Z[i,j] \mid j \in [0, k-1]\}$ for each $i \in [0, k-1]$, and on subgraphs Z^i for all $i \in [0, k-1]$. Therefore, we can introduce arcs as in Item 4, to restrict the automorphism group of Gad_k and for simplifying proofs.

All graph gadgets are necessary which were described so far to prove that GI is hard for DET. We want to show the same result for TI.

Theorem 3.2.17 DET $\leq_m^{\mathsf{AC}^0}$ TI.

More precisely, we show hardness of TI for $\mathsf{NC}^1(\#\mathsf{L})$. Oracle questions will be implemented, using oracle graph gadgets like Gad_k. We transform Gad_k into a tournament and consider its automorphism properties.

Definition 3.2.18 *Let $k \geq 3$ be an odd integer and $i, j \in [0, k-1]$. The oracle tournament gadget $TGad_k$ has vertex set $V(TGad_k) = V(Gad_k)$ and edge set $E(TGad_k)$ as the union of the following edge sets (see also Figure 3.5):*

1 $E(Gad_k)$ but write '(u,v)' for Items 2, 3 in Definition 3.2.16 of $E(Gad_k)$,
2 $E(W) \cup E(Z) = \{(w_i, w_{i \oplus h}), (z_i, z_{i \oplus h}) \mid h \in [1, \lfloor \frac{k}{2} \rfloor]\}$,

3. TOURNAMENT ISOMORPHISM

3 $\{(u,v) \mid u \in W^i, v \in W^j, \text{ iff } (w^i, w^j) \in E(W)\}$,

4 $\{(u,v) \mid u \in Z^i, v \in Z^j, \text{ iff } (z_i, z_j) \in E(Z)\}$,

5 $\{(u,v) \mid u \in Z[i,j], v \in Z[i, j \oplus h] \text{ with } h \in [1, \lfloor \frac{k}{2} \rfloor] \}$,

6 $\{(u,v) \mid u \in Z^i, v = z_j \text{ with } j \neq i\}$,

7 $\{(u,v) \mid u \in W^i, v \in Z[j,k] \text{ with } i \neq k\}$,

8 $\{(u,v) \mid u = w_i, v \in W^j \text{ with } j \neq i\}$.

Lemma 3.2.19 *If Gad_k contains tournaments (*PTI*-tuples) as subgraphs of Item 1 in Definition 3.2.16, then Gad_k with odd $k \geq 3$ can be transformed into a tournament $TGad_k$ under* AC^0 *many-one reductions, without changing the automorphism group.*

Proof. Item 1 in Definition 3.2.18 of $TGad_k$ can be done in AC^0 giving a direction to the edges. Since in Gad_k automorphisms are considered, acting cyclically on vertex set W, Apply Lemma 3.2.6 and replace the edge set of $Gad_k[W]$ by that of a cyclic tournament as described in Item 2 for $TGad_k$. The same is done for vertex set Z, for both in AC^0.

The edge set of Item 3 describes, how the subgraphs W^i are transformed into tournaments. If an automorphism ϕ maps w_i onto $w_{i \oplus c}$ with $c \in [0, k-1]$ then by Item 1 the subgraph W^i must be mapped onto $W^{i \oplus c}$ and hence, ϕ acts cyclically on vertex set W and ϕ also acts cyclically on the subgraphs W^i. Since the formulation 'iff $(w^i, w^j) \in E(W)$' is the same as 'iff $j = i \oplus h, h \in [1, \lfloor \frac{k}{2} \rfloor]$', only local information is needed for adjoining edges, this can be done in AC^0. The same is done for Item 4 with subgraphs Z^i instead of W^i and vertex set Z instead of W.

Keep $i \in [0, k-1]$ fixed from now on. Item 5 describes the edge sets inside of Z^i. Any automorphism ϕ in Gad_k acts cyclically on subgraphs $Z[i, 0], \ldots, Z[i, k-1]$. Because of Item 1 there is an edge-connection between subgraphs $Z[i,j]$ and W_j and by Item 3 there are the connections among all subgraphs in W. This directly leads to conditions for connecting subgraphs in Z_i. That is, $Z[i,j]$ is connected to $Z[i, j \oplus c]$, iff W_j is connected to $W_{j \oplus c}$ for any $c \in [0, k-1]$. This is a generalization of Lemma 3.2.6, because here we do not have just a single cyclic permutation, we rather have an automorphism group generated by two cyclic permutations, moving subgraphs $Z[i,j]$ blockwise.

Now, Z^i forms a tournament if contained subgraphs $Z[i,j]$ (i.e. I_a^i if $i = j$ and $J_a^{i,j}$ otherwise) are tournaments. Figure 3.5 shows the current construction up to Item 5.

Items 6 to 9 follow immediately by Lemma 3.2.7 since the automorphism group is maintained. This also can be done in AC^0. Consider thereby, that the layers with vertices Z, $V(Z^i)$, $V(W^i)$ and W are setwise stabilized.

Finally, with $E(TGad_k)$ the graph $TGad_k$ is a tournament and has the desired automorphism properties from oracle graph gadget Gad_k. □

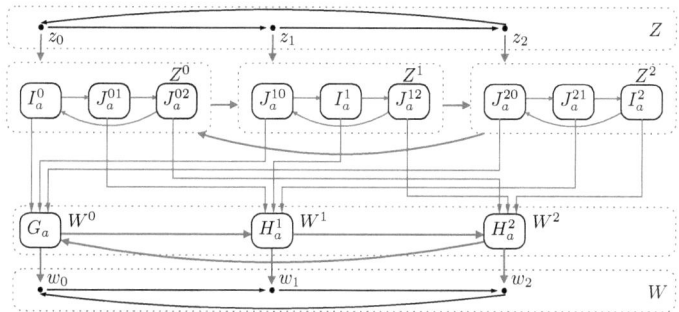

Figure 3.5: Graph gadget $TGad_3$ with edge sets of Items 1 to 5.

Let C be an NC^1 circuit and $w \in \{0,1\}^n$ an assignment to the input variables of C. We aim to construct a graph $G(C, w)$ together with prefixes on $V(G(C, w))$ according to w, which contains non-trivial prefix automorphisms, iff C on input of w and queries to an oracle in #L, outputs $true$. The oracle queries must have the same size. This makes it possible to use one fixed type of oracle graph gadget Gad_k (for exactly one value of k). For more details we refer to [Tor04]. Any subgraph like Gad_k inside of $G(C, w)$ is setwise stabilized in $Aut(G(C, w))$. By Lemma 3.2.6 and 3.2.19, transform any subgraph in $G(C, w)$ isomorphic to Gad_k into a tournament $TGad_k$ without changing the automorphism group of $G(C, w)$. Then apply Lemma 3.2.7 in order to connect this graph gadget with any other graph gadget. Since $G(C, w)$ contains only graph gadgets as described in this chapter and every graph gadget is setwise stabilized in the automorphism group of $G(C, w)$, replace them all by tournaments and connect them with each other as intended by Lemma 3.2.7. Hence, we can transform $G(C, w)$ into a tournament $T(C, w)$ under AC^0 many-one reductions. It follows that TI is hard for $\mathsf{NC}^1(\#\mathsf{L})$ and thus for DET. Corollary 3.2.20 follows by the fact that $\mathsf{Mod}_k\mathsf{L}$ is logspace Turing reducible to DET for all $k \geq 2$.

Corollary 3.2.20 $\mathsf{Mod}_k\mathsf{L} \leq_T^{log}$ TI for all $k \geq 2$.

3.3 Hardness Results for Tournament Automorphism

The graph automorphism problem (GA) is hard for the $\mathsf{Mod}_k\mathsf{L}$ hierarchy (Theorem 5.1 [Tor04]) under DLOGTIME uniform AC^0 many-one reductions. To see this, transform a circuit C into a rigid graph $G(C)$ as in Definition 3.2.3. Rigidity follows when applying prefixes to the inputs and the output of $G(C)$. Take two copies G_1 and G_2 of graph $G(C)$ and apply colors $Col(G_1), Col(G_2)$ to the vertices which represent the input and output values of the circuit

3. TOURNAMENT ISOMORPHISM

in order to encode the prefixes the same way as for prefix-GA (c.f. Example 3.2.4). Then, the graph $G_1 \cup G_2$ has a unique non-trivial automorphism (i.e. switching both graphs), iff the output value of the circuit C is 1. We show that this result also holds for TA.

Theorem 3.3.1 $\mathsf{Mod}_k\mathsf{L} \leq_m^{\mathsf{AC}^0}$ TA with $k \geq 3$ odd integer.

Proof. First, transform $G(C)$ into a tournament $T(C)$ as described in the proof of Lemma 3.2.10. Instead of taking two copies we need three copies T_0, T_1, T_2 of $T(C)$ and apply the colors $Col(G_1)$ to T_0 and $Col(G_2)$ to T_1 and T_2. Then include complete bipartite edge sets $\{(u,v) \mid u \in V(T_i), v \in V(T_{i\oplus 1}), i \in [0,2]\}$. Thus, $T(C)$ is a tournament and contains two non-trivial automorphisms (i.e. mapping T_0 onto T_1 or T_2), iff $G(C)$ contains one non-trivial automorphism. □

We want to prove that TA is also hard for DET.

Theorem 3.3.2 DET $\leq_m^{\mathsf{AC}^0}$ TA.

To prove the theorem, we define the graph tuples which correspond to PGI- and PTI-tuples for the tournament isomorphism problem.

Definition 3.3.3 [Tor04] *A* PGA-*graph tuple is a tuple of pairs of rigid graphs* $((G,H),(I,J))$ *with* $G \cong H \Leftrightarrow I \not\cong J$. *Let* PGA *be the set of all such tuples. The graph tuple* $((G_\wedge, H_\wedge), (I_\wedge, J_\wedge)) \in$ PGA *(write e.g. PGA-$G_\wedge$) for the simulation of conjunction and* $((G_\vee, H_\vee), (I_\vee, J_\vee)) \in$ PGA *(write e.g. PGA-$G_\vee$) for disjunction is defined as follows:*

PGA-$G_\wedge$ = PGI-$G_\wedge$, PGA-$H_\wedge$ = PGI-$H_\wedge$ and we define the same for PGA-$I_\wedge$, PGA-$J_\wedge$. For PGA-$G_\vee$, PGA-$H_\vee$ see Figure 3.6. PGA-$I_\wedge$ can be obtained from PGA-$G_\vee$ and PGA-$J_\wedge$ from PGA-$H_\vee$ when subgraphs G_i, H_i, I_i, J_i are replaced by I_i, J_i, G_i, H_i for $i \in [0,1]$ in this order.

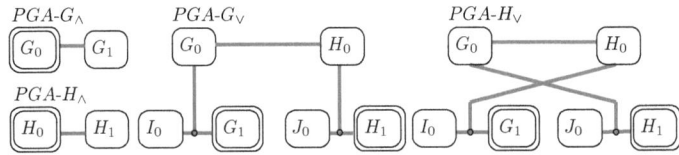

Figure 3.6: PGA-tuples simulating *and-* and *or-*functions [Tor04].

These tuples have the property, that $G_\wedge \cong H_\wedge \Leftrightarrow (G_0 \cong H_0$ and $G_1 \cong H_1)$, and that $G_\vee \cong H_\vee \Leftrightarrow (G_0 \cong H_0$ or $(G_1 \cong H_1 \wedge I_0 \cong J_0))$. If all the subgraphs are rigid then the new graphs in the tuples $G_\wedge, G_\vee, \ldots$ are rigid as well. The rigidity is not ensured by the construction

52

of PGI-tuples and PTI-tuples. For example, $PGI\text{-}G_\vee$ has a non-trivial automorphism iff $G_0 \cong H_0$ and $G_1 \cong H_1$. We transform now these PGA-tuples into tuples of pairs of tournaments.

Lemma 3.3.4 *There is an AC^0 computable function, such that the PGA-graph tuples can be transformed into tournaments, having the same isomorphism properties and rigidity properties as in Definition 3.3.3.*

Definition 3.3.5 *A PTA-graph tuple is a tuple of pairs of rigid tournaments $((G,H),(I,J))$ with $G \cong H \Leftrightarrow I \not\cong J$. Let PTA be the set of all such tuples.*
The graph tuple $((G_\wedge, H_\wedge), (I_\wedge, J_\wedge)) \in$ PTA *(write e.g. $PTA\text{-}G_\wedge$) for the simulation of conjunction and $((G_\vee, H_\vee), (I_\vee, J_\vee)) \in$ PTA (write e.g. $PTA\text{-}G_\vee$) for disjunction is defined as follows:*
The graph $PTA\text{-}G_\vee$ contains subgraphs $X, G_0, G'_0, H_0, A_0, A_1, A_2$. Let subgraphs G'_0, G'_1, I'_0 be copies of G_0, G_1, I_0. Let X be defined as shown in Figure 3.7. A_0 contains subgraphs I_0 and G_1, with vertices in I_0 pointing to all vertices in G_1. A_1 is a copy of A_0. A_2 is constructed like A_0, containing J_0 instead of I_0 and H_1 instead of G_1. Let G_0 be associated to $x_{0,0}$, G'_0 to $x_{0,1}$ and H_0 to $x_{0,2}$ and let the A_i be associated to $x_{1,i}$ for $i \in [0,2]$. Concerning the edge sets, the rest of the construction is similar to that of $PTI\text{-}G_\vee$.
The subgraph $H_\vee$, is constructed like $G_\vee$ but A_1 exchanged with A_2, i.e. A_1 is associated to $x_{1,2}$ and A_2 to $x_{1,1}$. Obtain $I_\wedge$ from $G_\vee$ and $J_\wedge$ from $H_\vee$, if subgraphs G_i, H_i, I_i, J_i will be replaced by I_i, J_i, G_i, H_i for $i \in [0,1]$ in this order.

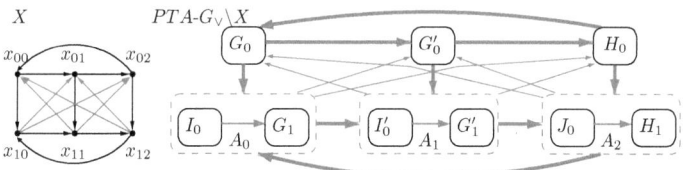

Figure 3.7: PTA-tuples simulating ∧- and ∨-functions.

Proof. The proof is like that of Lemma 3.2.14, simulate the alternating layers of *and*-gates and *or*-gates of an NC^1 circuit with recursively nesting the PTA-tuples. It is crucial to preserve the rigidity of the graphs in the tuples.

First, the gadgets for an *and* in PTA are equal to the gadgets for an *and* in PTI. Hence, we can argue as in the proof of Lemma 3.2.14. With the directed edge set between vertices of G_0 pointing to G_1 and Lemma 3.2.7 it follows, that $Aut(PTA\text{-}G_\wedge) = Aut(G_0) \times Aut(G_1)$. Thus, if both subgraphs are rigid, then $PTA\text{-}G_\wedge$ is rigid. For the other graph tuples $PTA\text{-}H_\wedge$, $PTA\text{-}I_\vee$ and $PTA\text{-}J_\vee$, the proof is similar.

3. TOURNAMENT ISOMORPHISM

Second, the automorphism properties for gadgets for an *or* in PTA are similar to that for gadgets for an *or* for PTI as in Lemma 3.2.14. Recall, that any automorphism must map $x_{i,j}$ onto $x_{i,j\oplus k}$ for $i \in [0,1]$, $j,k \in [0,2]$. PTA-$G_\vee$ is rigid, since the mapping of $x_{i,j}$ onto $x_{i,j\oplus 1}$ will map associated subgraphs G'_0 onto H_0 and I'_0 onto J_0. Since $G_0 \cong H_0 \Leftrightarrow I_0 \not\cong J_0$, this mapping is no automorphism of PTA-$G_\vee$. The same holds for mapping $x_{i,j}$ onto $x_{i,j\oplus 2}$. The automorphism properties of PTA-$G_\vee$ are the same as that for PTI-$G_\vee$. For the other graphs PTA-$H_\vee$, PTA-$I_\wedge$ and PTA-$J_\wedge$, the proof is similar. □

An immediate consequence of this result is, that TA is hard for NC^1 under AC^0 many-one reductions. By applying Theorem 3.3.1, it is possible to prove hardness of TA for complexity class DET. The proof of this result follows (similar to that in [Tor04]) exactly the same lines as that for Theorem 3.2.17 taking in consideration that the tournament gadgets in the reduction from Theorem 3.2.5 are rigid and that the gadgets in the proof of Theorem 3.2.17 also preserve rigidity. Similar to the Corollary 3.2.20 we get:

Corollary 3.3.6 $Mod_k L \leq_T^{log}$ TA for any $k \geq 2$.

Further Observations.

Recent work shows that several reducibility notions coincide when applied to GI [Tor07]. In particular, if a set is many-one logspace reducible to GI, then it is in fact many-one AC^0 reducible to GI. Intuitively, this result can be understood as a version of the fact NP (NP ∩ coNP) = NP scaled down from NP to GI. In the proof, the following lemma is crucial.

Lemma 3.3.7 *[Tor07] Given two undirected graphs A and B with n vertices each, given in* PGI*-representation. There is an* AC^0 *circuit that on input these representations produces the adjacency matrices of two graphs A', B' such that $A \cong B$ if and only if $A' \cong B'$.*

The PGI-*representation* of a graph is a sequence of $\binom{n}{2}$ tuples of PGI graphs (given by their adjacency matrices) $((G_{i,j}^A, H_{i,j}^A), (I_{i,j}^A, J_{i,j}^A))$, $1 \leq i, j \leq n$ such that for every i, j:

$$(i,j) \in E(A) \Rightarrow G_{i,j}^A \cong H_{i,j}^A \text{ and } I_{i,j}^A \not\cong J_{i,j}^A$$
$$(i,j) \notin E(A) \Rightarrow G_{i,j}^A \not\cong H_{i,j}^A \text{ and } I_{i,j}^A \cong J_{i,j}^A$$

In the proof, a new graph is constructed where for each edge a graph gadget is constructed. The isomorphism properties of the graphs in the tuples indicate in the graph gadgets the presence of an edge in A.

It is not clear whether this lemma can be restricted to tournaments, i.e. how to give a PTI-representation of a tournament, such that there is an AC^0 circuit that produces the adjacency matrix of a tournament. The problem is, that every pair of vertices is connected by a directed edge. For the gadget construction in the proof of Lemma 3.3.7, it is not clear how to give orientations between pairs of vertices from different gadgets.

This lemma seems to be the critical part. The other tasks, e.g. a parity check construction can be replaced by $O(\log n)$ different $\mathsf{Mod}_k\mathsf{L}$ circuits for different values of k (i.e. odd prime numbers) with use of the Chinese remainder theorem.

Another aspect is remarkable. Assume, Lemma 3.3.7 can be modified such that A' and B' are tournaments. If the given graphs A and B in PTI-representation are arbitrary graphs and no tournaments, then GI would be many-one AC^0 reducible to TI.

Open Question 3.3.8 *Is there a representation of tournaments A, B via PTI-graph tuples such that there is an AC^0 circuit which produces the adjacency matrices of two tournaments A', B' such that $A \cong B$ if and only if $A' \cong B'$.*

If this question can be answered with yes then the following holds.

Corollary 3.3.9 *If open Question 3.3.8 holds then for any set A, if A is many-one logarithmic space reducible to TI then A is man-one AC^0 reducible to TI.*

Proof. The proof is similar as the proof for Theorem 3.4 in [Tor07]. If A is many-one logarithmic space reducible to TI via a function f, then the language $L_f = \{(x, i, b) \mid x \in \{0,1\}^*, b \in \{0,1\}$ and the i-th bit of $f(x)$ is $b\}$ is in L. It suffices to note that every set in L is *strongly many-one AC^0 reducible* to PTI, i.e. there is a total function f computable in AC^0 such that for every $x \in \{0,1\}^*$ $f(x) = ((G, H), (I, J)) \in \mathsf{PTI}$ and $x \in A \Leftrightarrow G \cong H$. □

4 Isomorphism for Bounded Valence Graphs

4.1 Introduction

In a bounded valence graph every vertex has $O(1)$ neighbors. It is open whether bounded valence GI is as hard as GI [Mil79], [Hof82a]. Tutte proved that the automorphism group of a trivalent graph which stabilizes some edge e is a 2-group (cf. [Hof82a]). Luks gives for bounded valence GI a polynomial time algorithm [Luk82] something that is not clear to hold for the graph isomorphism problem in general.

The motivation for studying the complexity status of bounded valence GI is that there is a huge gap between the best known upper and lower bounds. We prove that isomorphism for undirected, directed and colored valence-2 graphs is complete for logspace. A special version of prefix-GA is introduced. We say that the prefix-GA problem has the fixed vertex property if automorphisms of the given graph, which satisfy the prefixes, are required to map at least one vertex to itself.

We also consider the current known complexity lower bounds. If a special version of bounded valence GI is hard for $\mathsf{Mod}_k\mathsf{L}$ then it is also hard for #L. We prove the results with respect to DLOGTIME uniform AC^0 many-one reductions.

4.2 Valence-2 Graph Isomorphism

We discuss the complexity of valence-2 GI and prove that Valence-2 GI of directed, undirected and colored graphs is complete for logspace.

Theorem 4.2.1 *Valence-2 GI is* L*-complete under* AC^0 *many-one reductions.*

Proof. For hardness we reduce the logspace complete problem Ord to valence-2 GI. Etessami proved that this problem is L-complete via quantifier-free projections. Recall the following definition.

4. BOUNDED VALENCE GI

Order between vertices (Ord) [Ete97, JKMT03]
Input: A digraph $G = (V, E)$ with $|V| = n$ that is a line and two designated vertices $v_i, v_j \in V(G)$.
Computation: accept, if $v_i \prec v_j$ in the total order induced by G.

For the reduction we construct two graphs X, Y such that $X \cong Y$ if and only if $v_i \prec v_j$ in the order given by G, also see Figure 4.1.

- X is the undirected version of G (replace arcs by undirected edges) but with an exception: $\{v_j, v_{j+1}\} \notin E(X)$.
- Y is the undirected version of G but with the following changes: $\{v_i, v_{i+1}\}, \{v_j, v_{j+1}\} \notin E(Y)$, whereas $\{v_j, 1\} \in E(Y)$.
- If $i \prec j$ then $Y = Y_1$ is isomorphic to X. But if $j \prec i$ then $Y = Y_2$ contains a cycle and is not isomorphic to X.

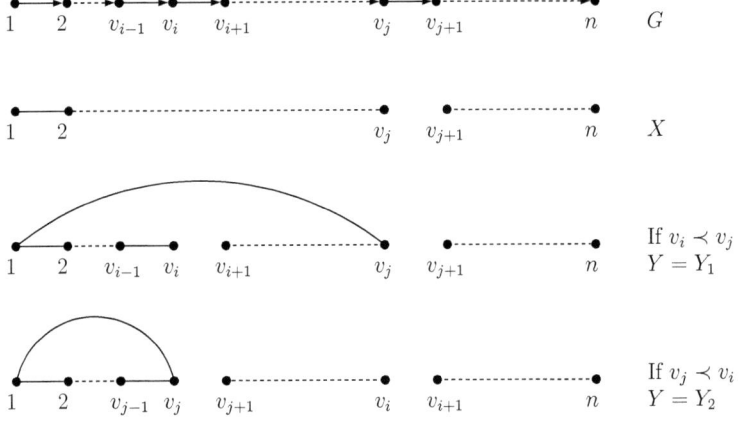

Figure 4.1: Graph gadgets for simulation of Ord.

This reduction is an AC^0 many-one reduction, because all the modifications can be done locally. Since Ord is L-complete via quantifier-free projections, valence-2 GI is hard for L under AC^0 many-one reductions.

For completeness we give a logspace Turing machine which decides isomorphism between valence-2 graphs G and H. The machine works as follows:

- Count and compare the number of isolated vertices in G and H. If the numbers differ then reject and say non-isomorphic.

- For each $k \in \{1, \ldots, n\}$ compare the number of paths of length k in G and H. To compute the length of a path it starts at a vertex with a single neighbor and then it traverses the path with a counter for the length of the path and the current vertex with its predecessor stored on the work-tape. Additionally we have a counter for the number of paths of length k. To do not count paths twice, we ignore the path if the label of the end vertex is smaller than the label of the starting vertex from the current path.

- For each $k \in \{1, \ldots, n\}$ compare the number of cycles of length k in G and H. This task is similar to comparing paths. We start at vertices of valence 2 and follow the neighbors. If we reach an end then this is no cycle and we proceed with the next vertex. If we reach the starting vertex then we know this is a cycle. We additionally have a counter for the length of the cycle and the number of cycles of length k.

- We do not have to remember explicitly which components have been visited yet. Instead, we run through all vertices sorted by their labels. Thereby, we ignore the components where the starting vertex is not the one with the minimum label of the component. This is done while traversing the component. In paths it suffices to consider both of its ends. Thus, we reach every component and consider it exactly once.

□

4.3 Coloring and Bounded Valence

GI and color-GI have the same complexity. To replace a color of a vertex v, a special tree-gadget is connected to v. Vertices with different colors are connected then to non-isomorphic tree-gadgets instead (cf. [KST93]). As a side-effect the valency of colored vertices is increased by 1.

First we consider the complexity of colored and directed valence-2 graphs. The situation here is different since the standard techniques can not be adapted for valence less than three. With minor changes to the standard techniques we also prove that valence-k color-GI is reducible to valence-k GI for $k \geq 3$ under AC^0 many-one reductions.

Theorem 4.3.1 *Valence-2 color-GI is complete for* L.

Proof. Hardness for L follows since valence-2 GI without coloring is hard for L.

For completeness we give a logspace Turing machine which decides isomorphism between colored valence-2 graphs. Let G, H be two such graphs.

4. BOUNDED VALENCE GI

- For each color c count and compare the number of isolated vertices with color c in G and H.

- For each value $k \in \{1, \ldots, n\}$ compare the number of paths of length k with the same sequence of colors in G and H. The length of the paths can be computed in logspace, see for example proof of Theorem 4.2.1. Let P_1, P_2 be two paths of length k. Find one end v in P_1 and both ends w, w' in P_2. Start with v and test whether $color(v) = color(w)$. If so then compare the color of the neighbors at distance i for all $i \in \{1, \ldots, n\}$ until we reach the other end of the paths. If we distinguished the paths then do the same with vertices v and w', that is we run through the reverse of P_2. If we cannot distinguish the sequences of colors in one of both tests then both colored paths are isomorphic.

- For each value $k \in \{1, \ldots, n\}$ compare the number of cycles of length k with the same sequence of colors in G and H. The length of cycles can be computed in logspace, see for example proof of Theorem 4.2.1. In G we run through all cycles of length k as follows. Run through all vertices which belong to cycles of length k and have the minimum label in the cycle. In H we run through all cycles of length k the same way.

  One comparison is done as follows. Let C_1 be in G with vertex v and let C_2 in H with vertex w. Let v and w have the minimum label in C_1 and C_2, respectively. In C_1 let $v', v'' \in \Gamma(v)$ with v' the neighbor with the smaller label. In C_2 let $w', w'' \in \Gamma(w)$ with w' the neighbor with the smaller label. Start with $v, v', \ldots, v'', v$ and $w, w', \ldots, w'', w$ and pairwise compare the colors of the corresponding vertices v with w and v' with w' and so on. If we distinguish the sequence of colors then do the same with $v, v', \ldots, v'', v$ and $w, w'', \ldots, w', w$. If we cannot distinguish them then both cycles are isomorphic. Now, we count the number of isomorphic cycles in G which are isomorphic to C_2. Clearly, there is at least one isomorphic cycle, i.e. C_1. If both counters match then there are the same number of isomorphic cycles to C_1 in G and H.

- Space requirements and the technique to traverse the components in both graphs follow similar arguments as in the proof of Theorem 4.2.1.

$\square$

We can derive from Theorem 4.3.1 that considering directed graphs keeps the complexity of valence-2 GI unchanged.

Corollary 4.3.2 *Valence-2 GI $\leq_m^{\mathsf{AC}^0}$ Valence-2 directed GI $\leq_m^{\mathsf{AC}^0}$ Valence-2 color-GI.*

Proof. First, valence-2 GI $\leq_m^{\mathsf{AC}^0}$ valence-2 directed GI. Let $\{u, v\}$ be a undirected edge. Replace it and insert a vertex w in between and arcs $(u, w), (v, w)$. Second, valence-2 directed GI $\leq_m^{\mathsf{AC}^0}$ Valence-2 color-GI. Let (u, v) be a directed edge. Replace it by a path of length three, that is $\{u, w_1\}, \{w_1, w_2\}, \{w_2, v\}$. Apply special colors c_1 to w_1 and c_2 to w_2. $\square$

We have shown that the following problems are complete for L under AC^0 many-one reductions: Valence-2 undirected GI, valence-2 directed GI, valence-2 color GI. For graphs of higher valence, standard techniques as in [KST93] suffice to proof valence-k directed GI $\equiv_m^{AC^0}$ valence-k undirected GI for $k \geq 3$. Now, we discuss coloring for graphs of higher valence.

Lemma 4.3.3 *Valence-k color-GI $\leq_m^{AC^0}$ Valence-k GI for all $k \geq 3$.*

Proof. When considering the proof in [KST93], the valence of vertices increases, namely from k to $k+1$. Let G be a valence-k graph for some $k \geq 3$. We construct now a valence-k graph H as follows. Replace each edge by a path of length three. Let vertex $v \in V(G)$ be labeled with color $c_i \in \{c_1, \ldots, c_k\}$. Connect each vertex $v' \in \Gamma(v)$ in H with a path $u_1, \ldots, u_{2n+3}$ such that u_j is at distance j to v' and connect to u_{n+2} another path of length i (cf. [KST93]). Observe, that the neighbors of vertex v are of degree two and thus, we can connect them with copies of the new graph gadget. Thus, H is also of valence k. □

Let $\{x_1, \ldots, x_k\}, \{y_1, \ldots, y_k\} \subseteq V(G)$ be vertex sets of graph G. Let ϕ be a mapping with $\phi(x_i) = y_i, i \in \{1, \ldots, k\}$ such that (G, ϕ) is an instance for prefix-GA. Adapting the proof of prefix-GA $\leq_m^{AC^0}$ GI [KST93], we obtain the following chain of reductions.

Corollary 4.3.4 *For $k \geq 2$,*
valence-k prefix-GA $\leq_m^{AC^0}$ valence-k color-GI $\leq_m^{AC^0}$ valence-k GI.

4.4 Valence-k Graph Isomorphism

GI is known to be hard for $Mod_k L$ under AC^0 many-one reductions, for all $k \geq 2$ [Tor04]. In the proof, graphs of valence $k+1$ are considered.

An NC^1 circuit can be simulated by a balanced DLOGTIME uniform family of circuits with fanout 1, logarithmic depth, polynomial size and alternating layers of and-gates and or-gates [BIS90]. For simulation of NC^1 circuits graph gadgets were used as shown in proof of Lemma 3.1 in [JKMT03] for simulation of *and*- and *or*-gates in circuits. These graph gadgets have designated root vertices and are recursively connected again to root vertices of other graph gadgets. Before we present the main result of this section, we define a special version of the prefix-GA problem.

Prefix-GA with fixed vertex property
Input: $G = (V, E)$ a connected graph and $U \subseteq V$ and let $\phi : U \to U$ be a mapping which fixes at least one vertex.
Computation: accept, if ϕ can be extended to an automorphism of G

4. BOUNDED VALENCE GI

This version of prefix-GA also reduces to GI, even if we consider bounded valence graphs. Let C be a Mod_k circuit with input values x. In Theorem 3.3 in [Tor04] Torán proved that there is an AC^0 computable function which computes for C a valence-$(k+1)$ graph $G(C)$ and prefixes ϕ such that $(G(C),\phi)$ can be extended to an automorphism iff C outputs 1. Note, $G(C)$ is connected and can be modified such that ϕ contains fixed vertices. For example, transform C into a circuit C' that adds 0 to the output value. Then some of the input vertices according to the new output-gate are fixed in ϕ and are of valence at most k. Thus, $(G(C'),\phi')$ is in prefix-GA with fixed vertex property iff C (and C') outputs 1.

The valence of $G(C')$ depends on parameter k. If there would be a different construction such that $(H(C'),\psi')$ with the same properties as $(G(C'),\phi')$ but with valence of $H(C')$ bounded by a constant $c \geq 3$, then valence-c GI would be hard for Mod_kL (for all values of k). Then the following theorem says that valence-c GI would also be hard for $\#\text{L}$.

Theorem 4.4.1 *If there exists a constant $c \geq 3$ such that for every $k \geq 2$ every instance of the Mod_k circuit value problem can be AC^0 reduced to an instance of valence-c prefix-GA with the fixed vertex property, which is of size polynomial in the circuit size then valence-c GI is hard for $\text{NL}, \#\text{L}, \text{C}_=\text{L}$ and PL under AC^0 many-one reductions.*

Proof. We give a sketch of the important proof steps. Observe that $G(C')$ is a connected valence-$(k+1)$ graph which simulates circuit C' from the discussion before. Take two copies of this graph, say G_1, G_2 and apply prefixes to these graphs (i.e. colors to the vertices) as in [Tor04] (also see Example 3.2.4) and obtain H_1, H_2. By Lemma 4.3.3 valence-k color-GI reduces to valence-k-GI. Because of fixed vertex property of ϕ there is at least one designated vertex v in H_1 and H_2 which has its own unique color in both graphs and is of valence k. Such graph pairs H_1, H_2 can be connected as input to the graph gadgets, encoding an NC^1 circuit in a similar way as in Theorem 4.4 in [Tor04]. In this theorem different graph tuples are needed to simulate *and*- and *or*-functions. We can replace these graph gadgets by those in proof of Lemma 3.1 in [JKMT03] in order to keep the degrees of vertices bounded by a constant. □

The next lemma states that the fixed vertex property does not change the complexity of the prefix-GA problem for bounded valence graphs.

Lemma 4.4.2 *For $c \geq 3$, valence-c prefix-GA $\equiv_m^{\text{AC}^0}$ valence-c prefix-GA with fixed vertex property.*

Proof. The direction $\geq$ is trivial, because GA with fixed vertex property is a sub-problem of GA. Accept if the prefixes keep one vertex fixed and the corresponding partial automorphism can be extended to an automorphism for the whole graph, and reject otherwise. Now to the other direction. We assume that G is a connected graph. Let (G,ϕ) be an instance of valence-c prefix-GA where G is a graph with n vertices. Fix a pair of edges $e_1, e_2 \in E(G)$. Replace e_i by path P_i of length 2. The middle vertex of P_i is connected to a path P_i' of length $n+2$. The other end vertices of the paths P_1', P_2' are connected to a new vertex u. Add u as a fixed vertex to ϕ and we obtain ϕ'. Let G' be the resulting graph. Note, G' still has valence c. If G has non-trivial automorphisms respecting the prefixes in ϕ, which map e_1 onto e_2 then also (G', ϕ') has non-trivial automorphisms.

We run through all edges e_2 and accept the input if at least one of the tests detects non-trivial automorphisms. So far, we have a $\leq_{dtt}^{\mathsf{AC}^0}$ reduction.

To see that we get a many-one reduction we do the following. For each test make a copy of the graph and the prefixes and define a new graph (G^*, ϕ^*) which is the disjoint union of all the copies of graphs and prefixes. With the prefixes in every automorphism a copy is mapped onto itself. □

4.5 Isomorphism for Cycles and Lines

In this section we further restrict the graph classes considered in Theorem 4.2.1 where we proved logspace hardness of valence-2 GI. Let *cycle-GI* be the graph isomorphism problem where the input graphs are cycles only.

Theorem 4.5.1 *Cycle-GI is* L*-complete under* AC^0 *many-one reductions.*

Proof. We reduce from Ord, which is logspace-complete via first-order projections [Ete97]. Given a graph that is a directed line of size n and two designated vertices v_i, v_j. The problem is to decide whether v_i comes before v_j in the line graph. For the reduction we construct two graphs X, Y such that $X \cong Y$ if and only if $v_i \prec v_j$ in the order induced by G.

- X is an undirected cycle of size n.
- Y is the undirected version of G but with the following changes:
  $\{v_i, v_{i+1}\}, \{v_j, v_{j+1}\} \notin E(Y)$, but $\{v_1, v_j\}, \{v_{j+1}, v_i\}, \{v_{i+1}, v_n\} \in E(Y)$.
- If $v_i \prec v_j$ then Y consists of one cycle of size n and is isomorphic to X. But if $v_j \prec v_i$ then Y consists of three cycles and is not isomorphic to X.

This reduction is an AC^0 many-one reduction. Since Ord is L-complete via quantifier-free projections, cycle-GI is hard for L under AC^0 many-one reductions. Completeness follows since cycle-GI is a special case of the logspace-complete problem valence-2 GI. □

Let *line-GI* be graph isomorphism where the input graphs are lines only. We prove now that this result also generalizes to line-GI.

Theorem 4.5.2 *Line-GI is* L*-complete under* AC^0 *many-one reductions.*

4. BOUNDED VALENCE GI

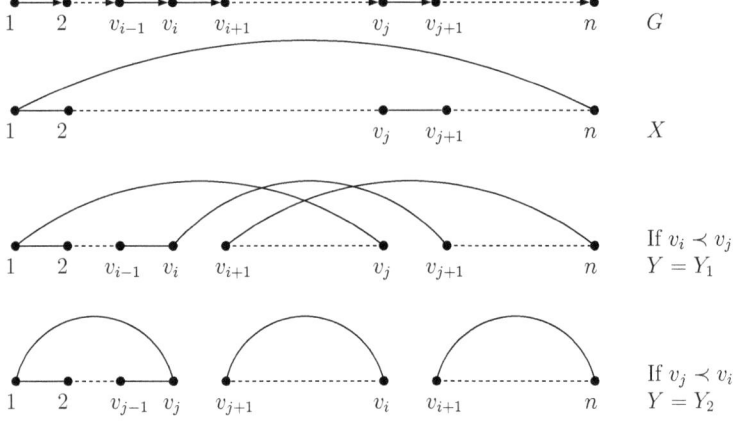

Figure 4.2: Cycle-Graph gadgets for simulation of Ord.

Proof. Consider the same situation as before in the proof of Theorem 4.5.1 but with the following changes:

- X is an undirected path of size n but with the following changes: $\{v_j, v_{j+1}\} \notin E(X)$. Connect a copy of a path of length $2n$ to the vertices v_j and v_n. Hence, X consists of two paths, one of length $2n + j$ and one of length $2n + (n-1) - j$.
- Y is an undirected path of size n but with the following changes: $\{v_i, v_{i+1}\}$, $\{v_j, v_{j+1}\} \notin E(Y)$, but $\{1, v_{i+1}\} \in E(Y)$. Connect a copy of a path of length $2n$ to the vertices v_j and v_n.
- If $v_i \prec v_j$ then Y has two paths, one of length $2n + (j-1)$ and the other of length $2n + (n-1) - j$. Hence, $X \cong Y$. But if $j \prec i$ then Y contains a path of length $2n + (i-1) - j + 2n > 4n$ and it follows that $X \not\cong Y$.

This reduction is an AC^0 many-one reduction. Since Ord is L-complete via quantifier-free projections, line-GI is hard for L under AC^0 many-one reductions. Completeness follows since line-GI is a special case of the logspace-complete problem valence-2 GI. □

4.6 Hardness of Valence-k Graph Automorphism

Valence-2 GA is a trivial task, because each path and cycle has non-trivial automorphisms. The only graph of valence 2 which does not have non-trivial automorphisms has only one isolated

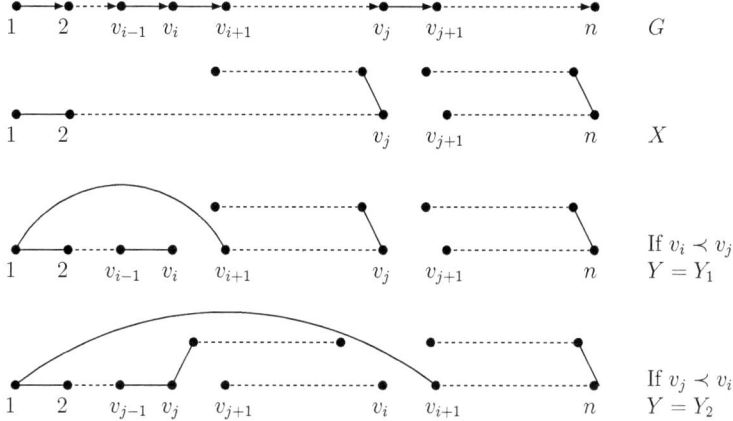

Figure 4.3: Line-Graph gadgets for simulation of Ord.

vertex. Hence, it is sufficient to read a constant number of bits from the input to decide valence-2 GA. The situation is different for valence-k GA for $k \geq 3$. In this section we discuss hardness results for this problem.

GA is many-one hard for the $\mathsf{Mod_k L}$ hierarchy (Theorem 5.1 [Tor04]). In this proof the same circuit graph $G(C)$ is used as in Theorem 3.3 [Tor04]. In detail, prefixes were defined, i.e. two subsets of vertices in $G(C)$. Take two copies G_1 and G_2 of graph $G(C)$ and apply colorings $Col(G_1), Col(G_2)$ to the vertices which represent the input and output values of the circuit in order to encode these prefixes. Thus the graph $G_1 \cup G_2$ has a non-trivial automorphism, iff the output of the original circuit is 1.

The proof uses similar graph-gadgets as in the proof of GI being hard for $\mathsf{Mod_k L}$. Hence, the valence of the graphs is bounded the same way. Since valence-k color GI reduces to valence-k GI, we obtain the following corollary.

Corollary 4.6.1 *Valence-$k+1$ GA is hard for $\mathsf{Mod_k L}$, $k \geq 2$, under AC^0 many-one reductions.*

An important property of $G(C)$ is that this graph is rigid and coloring does not change rigidity. We will formulate Theorem 4.4.1 for bounded valence GA. In the following Theorem, by *GA with the fixed vertex property* we mean GA restricted to graphs which contain fixed vertices in their automorphisms.

Theorem 4.6.2 *If there exists a constant $c \geq 3$ such that for every $k \geq 2$ every instance of the $\mathrm{Mod_k}$ circuit value problem can be AC^0 reduced to an instance of valence-c GA with fixed*

65

4. BOUNDED VALENCE GI

vertex property, which is of size polynomial in the circuit size then valence-c GA with fixed vertex property is hard for NL, #L, C$_=$L and PL under AC^0 many-one reductions.

Proof. Basically, we construct similar graphs as in Theorem 4.4.1. The graphs encoding a circuit with modulo addition gates can be connected as input to the graph gadgets, encoding an NC^1 circuit in a similar way as in Theorem 4.4 in [Tor04]. In this theorem graph tuples are needed simulating *and*- and *or*-functions but the vertices in the construction do not have bounded degree. We can replace the graphs simulating an *and* by those in proof of Lemma 3.1 in [JKMT03] in order to keep the degrees of vertices bounded by a constant. For a rigid graph gadget simulating an *or*-function, we need a different construction, see Figure 4.4. The graph gadget G^2 is the same as defined in Definition 3.1 in [Tor04]. G^2 simulates a parity gate, that is an automorphism which maps x_i onto $x_{i \oplus a}$ and y_i onto $y_{i \oplus b}$, such that then it maps z_i onto $z_{i \oplus a \oplus b}$ for all $i, a, b \in \{0, 1\}$. This graph gadget preserves the rigidity conditions as desired.

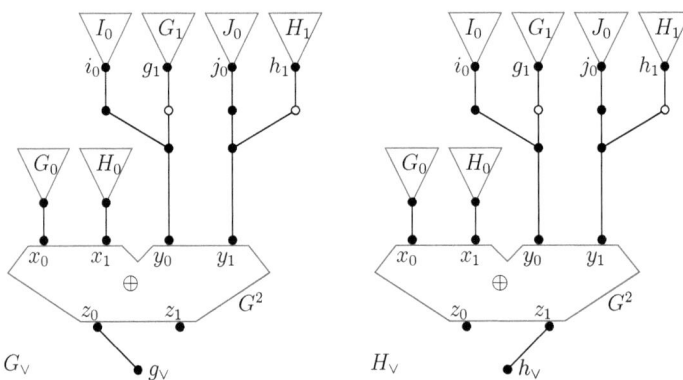

Figure 4.4: Rigid graph gadgets for simulation of an *or*-function.

□

Also for GA, we can show that the fixed vertex property does not change the complexity of the problem.

Lemma 4.6.3 *For $c \geq 3$,*

valence-c GA $\equiv_m^{\mathsf{AC}^0}$ valence-c GA with fixed vertex property.

Proof. The direction $\geq$ is trivial, because GA with fixed vertex property is a sub-problem of GA. Accept if the prefixes keep one vertex fixed and the corresponding partial automorphism can be extended to an automorphism for the whole graph, and reject otherwise. Now to the other direction. We assume that G is a connected graph. The proof follows the same lines as in Lemma 4.4.2 in order to obtain a $\leq_{dtt}^{AC^0}$ reduction. The argument for the many-one reduction does not work here, because we do not have prefixes.

We still can get a many-one reduction. To see this, for each copy of G we said that we added paths P_1' and P_2' of length $n + 2$. For each copy of G we add paths P_1' and P_2' but they are of different lengths, such that each copy of G has a different number of vertices. □

4.7 An Application, the Complexity of the Poset-Game Problem

We describe a nice application of the proof techniques from Theorem 4.5.2, where we show that line-GI is hard for L. We can prove new lower bounds for a game-theoretic decision problem.

The poset-game problem is given a partial ordered set as a directed acyclic graph. Two players play in rounds, selecting an element x from the poset and deleting all the elements y with $x \leq y$. The player who has to play an empty set loses. The decision problem is to find out whether player 1 has a winning strategy. Poset-game problems were already studied in 1902 by [Bou02].

Winning strategies for many game problems can be determined by evaluating a quantified boolean formula. This gives an upper bound of **PSPACE** for **PosetGame**. Soltys and Wilson [SW08] give a simple proof of this fact and reduce **PosetGame** to **Geography**, which is known to be a **PSPACE** complete problem [Sch78]. Curiously, nothing is known about the upper and lower bound of the poset-game problem. We consider the decision problem **PosetGame** and proof that it is hard for **L**.

The proof is derived from Theorem 4.5.2 in Section 4.5 where we show that Line-GI is hard for **L**. We slightly modify in the proof technique the graph construction, computing an instance of the poset game problem.

The Poset Game Problem. We start with some definitions. A *partially ordered set* (a *poset*) is a set U together with an ordering relation $\prec$, which is a subset of $U \times U$. It satisfies the conditions *anti-symmetry* ($a \prec b \Rightarrow b \not\prec a$) and *transitivity* ($a \prec b \wedge b \prec c \Rightarrow a \prec c$). Some elements a, b might be not comparable, i.e. $a \neq b$, where $a \not\prec b \wedge b \not\prec a$. We write $a \preceq b \Leftrightarrow [a \prec b \vee a = b]$.

Given a poset $(U, \preceq)$, a *poset game* $(A, \preceq)$ on $(U, \preceq)$ is played as follows. At first, $A = U$. Two players take turns making moves. On each move, a player picks an element $x \in A$ and removes all $y \in A$ with $x \preceq y$. Let S_x be these elements. Hence, we reduce the universe to be $A \setminus S_x$. The player loses, who is unable to move because A becomes the empty set.

The poset can be interpreted as a directed acyclic graph, with the universe U as vertices and

67

4. BOUNDED VALENCE GI

the relation $\preceq$ interpreted as a set of directed edges, i.e. $(x,y) \in E$ iff $x \preceq y$. The poset game problem is defined as follows.

PosetGame
Input: Poset $(A, \preceq)$ as directed graph $G = (V, E)$ and two players.
Computation: accept, if player 1 has a winning strategy.

PosetGame is Hard for Logspace. We prove that ORD reduces to PosetGame under AC^0 many-one reductions.

Theorem 4.7.1 PosetGame *is hard for* L.

Proof. We construct a directed acyclic graph H which can be interpreted as a poset game. Player 1 has a winning strategy on H if and only if $v_i \prec v_j$ in G.

The construction of H is as follows, also see Figure 4.5.

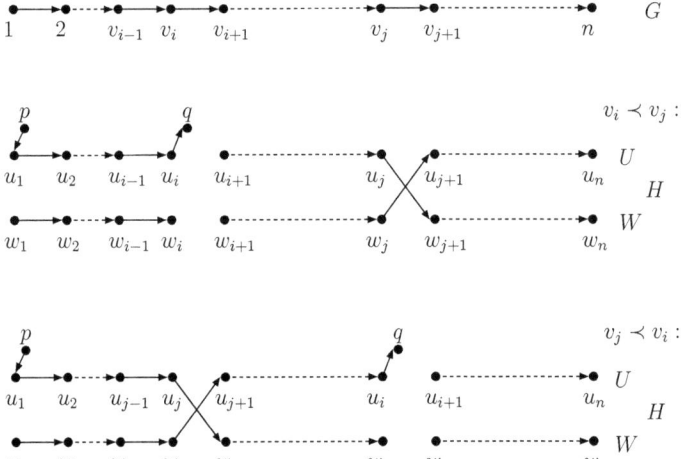

Figure 4.5: Graph G induces $v_i \prec v_j$. For graph H, both situations are shown, i.e. $v_i \prec v_j$ and $v_j \prec v_i$ in G.

- H contains two copies of G, say U, W where we label vertices in U with u and in W with w, but we additionally make the following changes:
- remove edges $(u_i, u_{i+1}), (u_j, u_{j+1}) \notin E(U)$ and $(w_i, w_{i+1}), (w_j, w_{j+1}) \notin E(W)$,
- add *crossing edges* $(u_j, w_{j+1}), (w_j, u_{j+1}) \in E(H)$,

- add two vertices p, q to H,
- add *connecting edges* $(p, u_1), (u_i, q) \in E(H)$.

The resulting graph H has the following properties:

1. $v_i \prec v_j$ in G: in H, there is one path of length $i - 1$, one path of length $i + 1$ and two paths of length $n - i - 1$.
2. $v_j \prec v_i$ in G: in H, there are two paths of length i and two paths of length $n - i - 1$.

In Case 1, player one has a winning strategy. He takes u_i such that after his move there are two paths of length $i - 1$ and two paths of length $n - i - 1$. Whatever strategy player two plays, from now on player one mimics the same move but on the other path, restoring the situation of having pairs of equal sized graphs. We say, that he makes a *winning situation*.

In Case 2, the situation is the other way round. Whatever strategy player one plays, here player two mimics the same move on the other path which was of the same length. Hence, player 2 makes a *winning situation*.

In both cases the player wins who makes a winning situation, because when his opponent removes one path completely then he removes the other path. At the end, no paths remain and his opponent cannot move.

This reduction is an AC^0 many-one reduction. Since ORD is L-complete via quantifier free projections, PosetGame is hard for L. □

In fact, here we have a rather restricted instance of the poset game. If the input consists of directed paths only then the game is also known as the *nim-game*. Here the input is a set of directed paths. A logspace machine can compute their length and output the input as numbers in unary. When the input is given in unary or binary, in both cases the nim-game is in logspace [Cal06]. To see this, consider the binary representation of the numbers, where a numbers equals the sizes of the directed paths. Compute the binary sum (modulo 2) of all the numbers, neglecting all the carries. For example, $011 + 100 + 101 = 010$. In normal play, the winning strategy is to finish every move with a Nim-sum of 0, which is always possible if the Nim-sum is not zero before the move. This is known as the *Misère winning condition*. It is easy to see, that on input of n numbers, a move can be decided in logspace, which produces the Nim-sum of 0.

Corollary 4.7.2 NimGame *is complete for* L.

5 Isomorphism for Planar 3-Connected Graphs

5.1 Introduction

The isomorphism problem for planar graphs is known to be efficiently solvable. For planar 3-connected graphs, the isomorphism problem can be solved by efficient parallel algorithms, it is in the class AC^1 [MR91, RR94]. In this paper we improve the upper bound for isomorphism testing for planar 3-connected graphs to unambiguous logspace, in fact to $UL \cap coUL$. As a consequence of our method we get that the isomorphism problem for oriented graphs is in NL. We also show that the problems are hard for L. Furthermore, we give an $UL \cap coUL$ algorithm for computing distances (i.e. the length of the shortest path between two vertices) in planar graphs.

In 1966, Weinberg [Wei66] presented an $O(n^2)$-algorithm for testing isomorphism for planar 3-connected graphs. This algorithm was improved and extended by Hopcroft and Tarjan [HT74] to an $O(n \log n)$-algorithm for the planar graph isomorphism problem (planar-GI). Then Hopcroft and Wong [HW74] showed that it is solvable in linear time. Since the constant hidden in the linear time bound is very large, the problem has been reconsidered with a more practical approach [KHC04]. The parallel complexity of planar-GI has been studied by Miller and Reif [MR91]. They reduced planar-GI to the 3-connected case in $O(\log n)$ time on a CRCW-PRAM, i.e. an AC^1-reduction. They further proved that when given an embedding in the plane, planar-GI is in AC^1. Ramachandran and Reif [RR94] gave a CRCW-PRAM algorithm which runs in $O(\log n)$ time for the construction of an embedding of planar graphs in the plane. Hence, planar GI is in AC^1. Grohe and Verbitsky [GV06] gave an alternative way to show that planar-GI is in AC^1. They proved for a class $\mathcal{G}$ of graphs, that if every graph in $\mathcal{G}$ is definable in a finite-variable first order logic within logarithmic quantifier depth, then the isomorphism problem for $\mathcal{G}$ is in AC^1. Later Verbitsky [Ver07] showed that planar 3-connected graphs are definable with 15 variables and quantifier depth $O(\log n)$ which leads to a 14-dimensional Weisfeiler-Lehman algorithm. With the reduction of [MR91] one obtains a new AC^1-algorithm for planar-GI.

In the above papers on planar-GI, the authors consider first 3-connected graphs. The reason

5. 3-CONNECTED PLANAR GI

is a result due to Whitney [Whi33] that every planar 3-connected graph has precisely two embeddings on a sphere, where one embedding is the reflection (i.e. a mirror image) of the other. Moreover, one can efficiently compute these embeddings. Weinberg [Wei66] used these embeddings to compute a code (i.e. a string) for a graph, (which depends on the selection of a starting edge) such that isomorphic graphs will have the same code, i.e. there exist edges when chosen as starting edges, which lead to the same codes. Clearly, non-isomorphic graphs never have the same codes.

Some of the subroutines in the above algorithms have complexity below AC^1. Allender and Mahajan [AM00] showed that planarity testing is hard for L and in symmetric logspace, SL. Since SL= L [Rei08], planarity testing is complete for logspace. Allender and Mahajan [AM00] showed that a planar embedding can be computed in logspace. Also the connectivity structure of a (undirected) graph can be computed in logspace [NTS95]. Hence a natural question is whether planar-GI is in logspace.

This work is a first step towards an answer for this question. We considerably improve the upper bound for planar-GI for 3-connected graphs in Section 5.4, namely from AC^1 to unambiguous logspace, UL, in fact to UL ∩ coUL. Recently, Datta, Limaye and Nimbhorkar [DLN08] strengthened the complexity bound to L.

Like Weinberg, we construct codes for the given graphs. In order to use only logarithmic space, our code is constructed via a spanning tree, which depends on the planar embedding of the graph. A crucial tool in the construction of the spanning tree is based on a recent result by Bourke, Tewari and Vinodchandran [BTV07] that the reachability problem for planar directed graphs is in UL ∩ coUL. They built on work of Reinhard and Allender [RA00] and Allender, Datta and Roy [ADR05]. We argue in Section 5.3 that their algorithm can be modified to not just solve reachability questions but to compute distances between vertices in UL ∩ coUL.

The embedding of a planar graph can be represented as a *rotation scheme*. Intuitively this gives the edges in clockwise or counter clockwise order around each vertex such that it leads to a planar drawing of the graph. Rotation schemes have also been considered for non-planar graphs. We talk of *oriented graphs* in this case. We extend our results to the isomorphism problem for oriented graphs. The input to this problem is a pair of graphs G and H and a rotation scheme for each of the graphs. One has to decide whether there is an isomorphism between G and H that respects the rotation schemes. In Section 5.5 we show that the problem is in NL.

We show in Section 5.6 that the isomorphism problem for planar 3-connected graphs and oriented trees is hard for logspace. In Section 5.7 we introduce label gadgets for planar 3-connected graphs, oriented graphs and trees, to encode labels of vertices. In Section 5.8 we introduce label gadgets for planar biconnected graphs.

5.2 The Complexity of UL ∩ coUL

The functional version of L is denoted FL. FL-functions are closed under composition, i.e. FL ∘ FL = FL. The proof goes by recomputing bits of the function value of the first function at each time when such a bit is needed by the second function. The same argument works when we consider functions that are computed by unambiguous logspace bounded Turing machines. If we call the class FUL, then this says that FUL ∘ FUL = FUL. We need a further property of UL.

Lemma 5.2.1 $L^{UL \cap coUL} = UL \cap coUL$.

Proof. Let M be a logspace oracle Turing machine with oracle $A \in UL \cap coUL$. Let M_0, M_1 be (non-deterministic) unambiguous logspace Turing machines such that $L(M_0) = \overline{A}$ and $L(M_1) = A$. We construct an unambiguous logspace Turing machine M' for $L(M, A)$ that replaces the oracle as follows on input x:

Simulate M on input x. If M queries an oracle question y, then non-deterministically guess whether the answer is 0 or 1.

- If the guess is answer 0, then simulate M_0 on input y. If M_0 accepts, then continue the simulation of M with oracle answer 0. If M_0 rejects then reject and halt.
- If the guess is answer 1, then simulate M_1 on input y. If M_1 accepts, then continue the simulation of M with oracle answer 1. If M_1 rejects then reject and halt.

Finally accept iff M accepts.

Note that M' is unambiguous, because M_0 and M_1 are unambiguous and of the two guessed oracle answers always exactly one guess is correct. □

5.3 Computing Distances in Planar Graphs

An important tool in our isomorphism test is to compute distances in planar graphs. We show that this can be computed in unambiguous logspace.

Theorem 5.3.1 *The distance between any two vertices in a planar graph can be computed in* UL ∩ coUL.

Bourke, Tewari and Vinodchandran [BTV07] showed that the reachability problem for planar directed graphs is in UL ∩ coUL. Their algorithm is essentially based on two results:

5. 3-CONNECTED PLANAR GI

1. Allender, Datta and Roy [ADR05] showed that the reachability problem for planar directed graphs can be reduced to grid graph reachability. A *grid graph* is a graph whose vertices can be identified with the grid points in a 2-dimensional grid with the edges connecting only the direct horizontal or vertical neighbors.

2. Reinhard and Allender [RA00] showed that the NL-complete reachability problem for directed graphs is in UL ∩ coUL if there is a logspace computable weight function for the edges such that for every pair of vertices u and v, if there is a path from u to v, then there is a unique minimum weight shortest path between u and v.

Bourke, Tewari and Vinodchandran [BTV07] provide such a weight function for grid graphs. Therefore the reachability problem for planar directed graphs is in UL ∩ coUL.

We modify this algorithm in order to determine distances between vertices in the given planar graph G. This is adapted from the Reinhard-Allender algorithm applied to the weighted grid graph computed from G. Here, we only describe the changes that have to be made in the cited references.

We start by considering the reduction from reachability for a planar graph G to a grid graph G_{Grid} [ADR05]. The reduction from G to G_{Grid} is a special combinatorial embedding that introduces only degree 2 vertices. Thereby it preserves the exact number of paths between any two original vertices. Vertices in G are replaced by directed cycles and edges in G are replaced by paths such that they can be embedded into a grid. For our purpose it suffices to note that one can modify the construction and *mark the original edges of G* in G_{Grid}. Hence if we consider paths in G_{Grid} and count only the marked edges, we get distances in G.

The next step is to define a weight function such that shortest paths in G_{Grid} with respect to marked edges are unique. Bourke, Tewari and Vinodchandran [BTV07] defined the following weight function. For an edge e let

$$w_0(e) = \begin{cases} n^4, & \text{if } e \text{ is an } \textit{east}\text{- or } \textit{west}\text{-edge,} \\ n^4 + i, & \text{if } e \text{ is a } \textit{north}\text{-edge in column } i, \\ n^4 - i, & \text{if } e \text{ is a } \textit{south}\text{-edge in column } i. \end{cases}$$

Let p be a path in G_{Grid}. The weight $w_0(p)$ is the sum of the weights of the edges on p and can be written as $a + bn^4$. Clearly, b is the number of edges on p. Also, it is easy to see that if another path p' of weight $w_0(p') = a' + b'n^4$ has the same weight as p, i.e. $w_0(p) = w_0(p')$, then $a = a'$ and $b = b'$. This enforces that shortest paths between two vertices must have the same number of edges. The crucial part now is the value of a. Let p and p' be different simple paths connecting the same two vertices. Then Bourke, Tewari and Vinodchandran [BTV07] showed that $a \neq a'$. It follows that the minimum weight path with respect to w_0 is always unique.

Now we modify the weight function in order to give priority to the marked edges. That is, we define

$$w(e) = \begin{cases} w_0(e) + n^8, & \text{if } e \text{ is marked,} \\ w_0(e), & \text{otherwise.} \end{cases}$$

Clearly, minimum weight paths must minimize the number of marked edges. The next parameter to minimize is the number of all edges on a path. Finally, by the same argument as above, the a-values of different simple paths that connect the same two vertices will be different. It follows that the minimum weight path with respect to w is always unique.

Reinhard and Allender [RA00] extended the counting technique of Immerman [Imm88] and Szelepcsényi [Sze88]. In addition to the number of vertices within distance k from some start vertex s, they also sum up the length of the shortest paths to these vertices. The input of the algorithm is a grid graph G_{Grid} where all vertices from G and new vertices are arranged along grid points. If the shortest paths in G_{Grid} are unique then they show that the predicate $d_{G_{Grid}}(s,v) \leq k$ is in UL $\cap$ coUL. By augmenting the algorithm with a counter for marked edges we also can refer to distances in G by construction of the weight function w. This suffices for our purpose, because by several invocations of this procedure with different k's we can determine $d_G(s,v)$ for any s and v in UL $\cap$ coUL.

5.4 Planar 3-Connected Graph Isomorphism

We use Theorem 5.3.1 to prove the following.

Theorem 5.4.1 *The isomorphism problem for planar, 3-connected graphs is in* UL $\cap$ coUL.

In 1966, Weinberg [Wei66] presented an $O(n^2)$ algorithm for testing isomorphism for planar 3-connected graphs. The algorithm computes a *canonical form* for each of the two graphs. This is a coding of graphs such that these codings are equal iff the two graphs are isomorphic. For a 3-connected graph G, the algorithm starts by constructing a code for every edge of G and both rotation schemes. Among all these codes, the lexicographical smallest one is the canon for G.

For a designated edge (s,t) and a rotation scheme ρ for G, the code is constructed roughly as follows. Every undirected edge is considered as two directed edges. Now one can define an Euler tour based on some rules for selecting the next edge. Basically, the rules distinguish between the case whether a vertex or edge was already visited or not. The next edge to consider is chosen to the left or right of the active edge according to ρ. Define edge (s,t) to be the start of the tour. The code consists of the vertices as they appear on the tour, where the names are replaced by the order of their first appearance on the tour. That is, the code starts with $(1,2)$ for the edge (s,t) and every later occurrence of s or t on the tour is replaced by 1 or 2, respectively.

5. 3-CONNECTED PLANAR GI

Weinberg's algorithm does not work in logspace, because one has to store the vertices and edges already visited. Thierauf and Wagner give in [TW08] a construction of a different code in UL. Their high level description works in three steps. Here, a similar but simpler version is described. Let (s,t) be a designated edge and ρ be a rotation scheme for G. The construction has three steps.

1. First compute a canonical spanning tree T for G. This is a spanning tree which depends on (s,t), ρ and G, but not on the way these inputs are represented.
2. Next invoke a depth-first traversal on the tree and rename the vertices depending on the position of their first occurrence in the tree traversal.
3. Finally, order all the edges lexicographically according to the new vertex labels.

We will see that the spanning tree in Step 1 can be computed in (the functional version of) UL ∩ coUL. The renaming and the lexicographical arrangement of the edges in Step 2 and Step 3 can be computed in logspace. Therefore, the composition of the three steps is in UL ∩ coUL.

The overall algorithm has to decide whether two given graphs G and H are isomorphic. To do so, we fix (s,t) and ρ for G and cycle through all edges of H as designated edge and the two possible rotation schemes of H. Then G and H are isomorphic iff we find a code for H that matches the code for G. It is not hard to see that this outer loop is in logspace. Therefore, the isomorphism problem for planar, 3-connected graphs is in UL ∩ coUL.

Step 1: Construction of a Canonical Spanning Tree.

We show that the following problem can be solved in unambiguous logspace.

Input: An undirected graph $G = (V, E)$, a rotation scheme ρ for G, and a designated edge $(s,t) \in E$.
Output: A canonical spanning tree $T \subseteq E$ of G.

Recall that by a canonical spanning tree we mean that T does not depend on the input representation of ρ or G, any representation will result in the same spanning tree T.

The idea to construct the spanning tree is to traverse G with a breadth-first search starting at vertex s. The neighbors of a vertex are visited in the order given by the rotation scheme ρ. Since the algorithm should work in logspace, we cannot afford to store all the vertices which we already visited, as in a standard breadth-first search. We get around this problem by working with distances between vertices.

We start with the vertices at distance 1 from s. That is, write (s,v) on the output tape, for all $v \in \Gamma(s)$. Now let $d \geq 2$ and assume that we have already constructed T up to vertices at distance $\leq d-1$ to s. Then we consider the vertices at distance d from s. Let w be a vertex with $d_G(s,w) = d$. We have to connect w to the tree constructed so far. We do so by computing a shortest path from s to w. Ambiguities are resolved by using the first feasible edge according to ρ. We start with (s,t) as the active edge (u,v).

- If $d_G(u,w) > d_G(v,w)$, then (u,v) is the first edge encountered that is on a shortest path from u to w. Therefore we go from u to v and start searching the next edge from v. As starting edge we take the successor of (v,u). That is, $\rho_v(v,u)$ is the new active edge.

- If $d_G(u,w) \leq d_G(v,w)$, then (u,v) is not on a shortest path from u to w. Then we proceed with $\rho_u(u,v)$ as the new active edge.

After $d-1$ steps in direction of w, the vertex v of the active edge (u,v) is a predecessor of w on a shortest path from s to w. Then we write (v,w) on the output tape. The following pseudocode summarizes the algorithm.

for all $v \in \Gamma(s)$ **do** **output** (s,v)
for $d \leftarrow 2$ **to** $n-1$ **do**
    for all $w \in V$ such that $d_G(s,w) = d$ **do**
        $(u,v) \leftarrow (s,t)$
        for $k \leftarrow 1$ **to** $d-1$ **do**
            while $d_G(u,w) \leq d_G(v,w)$ **do** $(u,v) \leftarrow \rho_u(u,v)$
            $(u,v) \leftarrow \rho_v(v,u)$
        output (v,w)

The spanning tree T is canonical, because its construction depends only on ρ, edge (s,t) and edge set E. Figure 5.1 shows an example of a spanning tree T for a graph G with rotation function ρ which arranges the edges in clockwise order around each vertex.

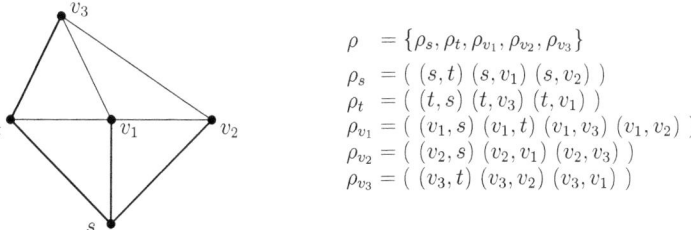

Figure 5.1: A planar 3-connected graph and its rotation scheme ρ. The canonical spanning tree according to (s,t) and ρ contains the edges from s to its neighbors and $\{t,v_3\}$.

5. 3-CONNECTED PLANAR GI

Except for the computation of the distances, the algorithm works in logspace. We have to store the values of d, k, u and v and the position of w, plus some extra space for doing calculations. By Theorem 5.3.1 above, the distances can be computed in UL ∩ coUL. By Lemma 5.2.1 the canonical spanning tree can be computed in UL ∩ coUL.

Step 2: Rename Vertices.

From here, the description of the algorithm deviates from the description of the Steps 2 and 3 of [TW08]. Both algorithms use the traversal of the spanning tree of Step 1. The new version is an application of the tree traversal algorithm from Section 2.6.2. It computes the following function in logspace.

Input: An undirected graph $G = (V, E)$, a rotation scheme ρ for G, a spanning tree $T \subseteq E$ of G and a designated edge $(s, t) \in T$.
Output: A function ϕ mapping vertices to their new labels.

By Theorem 2.6.1 a tree can be traversed in depth first manner in logspace. We use this algorithm and ρ to have a unique traversal of the spanning tree. We describe this now in more detail. Let t be a node in the tree. We refine the functions Parent(t), FirstChild(t, order) and NextSibling(t, order) of the tree traversal algorithm from Section 2.6.2.

- Parent(t) computes the neighbor of t which is the parent in the spanning tree. Here, we have no changes to the algorithm.

- FirstChild(t, order) computes the first child of t in the spanning tree. For the function order we use the rotation scheme ρ of graph G. Among the neighbors of t we search the one which comes next according to the rotation function ρ_t. We return 0 if we reach the parent of t. The following pseudocode summarizes this.

  $u \leftarrow t$, $v \leftarrow$ Parent(t)
  repeat
    $v \leftarrow \rho_u(v)$
  until $(u, v) \in T$
  if $v \neq$ Parent(u) **then return** v **else return** 0

- NextSibling(t, order) computes the next sibling of t in the spanning tree. Again, for the function order we use the rotation scheme ρ of graph G. Among the neighbors of Parent(t) we search the one which comes next according to the rotation function $\rho_{\text{Parent}(t)}$ if it exists and we return 0 otherwise. We change the first line in the algorithm for FirstChild and obtain the algorithm for NextSibling.

  $u \leftarrow$ Parent(t), $v \leftarrow t$

Let $(v_1, v_2, \ldots, v_{\mathsf{poly}(n)})$ be the list of vertices in the tree traversal. In this list, all vertices occur several times. The following procedure gives new labels to them according to their first occurrences in the traversal.

$c \leftarrow 0$ {counter for new vertex labels}
for all $v_i \in (v_1, v_2, \ldots, v_{\mathsf{poly}(n)})$ **do**
    $b \leftarrow \mathit{false}$
    for all $w \in (v_1, v_2, \ldots, v_{i-1})$ **do**   {the part before reaching v_i}
        if $w = v_i$ **then** $b \leftarrow \mathit{true}$
    if $b = \mathit{false}$ **then** $c \leftarrow c + 1$, **output** $\phi(v_i) \leftarrow c$

In the example of Figure 5.1 when starting with edge (s, t), we get the following labeling of vertices: $\phi(s) = 1$, $\phi(t) = 2$, $\phi(v_3) = 3$, $\phi(v_1) = 4$ and $\phi(v_2) = 5$.

Step 3: Order Edges Lexicographically.

We order all the edges lexicographically according to the new vertex labels as in [DLN08]. This is done by the following procedure, where n is the number of vertices in G and ϕ the function which maps vertices to their new labels.

for $(a, b) \in \{(1, 2)(1, 3) \ldots, (n, n-1)\}$ {all pairs in lexicographical order}
    for $(u, v) \in E(G)$
        if $(\phi(u), \phi(v)) = (a, b)$ **then output** (a, b)

In the example of Figure 5.1 when starting with edge (s, t), we get the following: $\mathsf{code}(s, t, \rho) = (1,2)\ (1,4)\ (1,5)\ (2,1)\ (2,3)\ (2,4)\ (3,2)\ (3,4)\ (3,5)\ (4,1)\ (4,2)\ (4,3)\ (4,5)\ (5,1)\ (5,3)\ (5,4)$.

It remains to argue that the new names of the vertices are independent of their names in G. Let H be a graph which is isomorphic to G, and let φ be an isomorphism between G and H. Note that $\varphi(\rho)$ is a rotation scheme for H. In particular, $\varphi(\rho) = \{\varphi(\rho_v) \mid v \in V(G)\}$ where $\varphi(\rho_v) = \rho_{\varphi(v)}$ such that for all $u, v, w \in V(G)$: $\rho_v(v, u) = (v, w)$ iff $\rho_{\varphi(v)}(\varphi(v), \varphi(u)) = (\varphi(v), \varphi(w))$. Consider the computation of the code for graph H with rotation scheme $\varphi(\rho)$ and designated edge $(\varphi(s), \varphi(t))$. The spanning tree computed in Step 1 will be $\varphi(T)$ and the list computed in Step 2 will be $\varphi(L)$. Now the above renaming procedure will give the same number to vertex v in L and to vertex $\varphi(v)$ in $\varphi(L)$. For example, the vertices $\varphi(s)$ and $\varphi(t)$ will get number 1 and 2, respectively. It follows that $\mathsf{code}(G, \rho, s, t) = \mathsf{code}(H, \varphi(\rho), \varphi(s), \varphi(t))$. We summarize:

5. 3-CONNECTED PLANAR GI

Theorem 5.4.2 *Let G and H be connected, undirected graphs, let ρ^G be a rotation scheme for G and (s,t) be an edge in G. Then G and H are isomorphic iff there exists a rotation scheme ρ^H for H and an edge (u,v) in H such that $\mathsf{code}(G, \rho^G, s, t) = \mathsf{code}(H, \rho^H, u, v)$.*

This completes the proof of Theorem 5.4.1. Next, we show some extensions of it.

The isomorphism test can easily be extended to count the number of isomorphisms between G and H. We simply have to count the number of edges (u,v) from H and rotation schemes ρ^H such that $\mathsf{code}(G, \rho^G, s, t) = \mathsf{code}(H, \rho^H, u, v)$. Note the number of isomorphisms between two planar 3-connected graphs with m edges is bounded by $4m$, because this is the number of triples (ρ^H, u, v) as above. Therefore we can afford to implement a standard counter on the work tape.

Corollary 5.4.3 *The number of isomorphisms between two planar 3-connected graphs can be computed in $\mathsf{FL}^{\mathsf{UL} \cap \mathsf{coUL}}$.*

Based on the above decision procedure, we can actually construct an isomorphism for two isomorphic graphs: suppose we have already verified that G and H are isomorphic. Moreover, we modify the decision procedure at the end and store the vertices and the (index of the) rotation schemes for both graphs that led to the same code. For these values we repeat Step 1 and 2 of the decision procedure and compute new labels for the vertices of the graphs. Now, we do not sort the edges as in Step 3. Instead, we output the pair of vertices (u,v) with u from G and v from H which get the same label k in Step 2, for all $k \in \{1, \ldots, n\}$. This can be done in logspace. The output constitutes an isomorphism between G and H.

Corollary 5.4.4 *An isomorphism between two planar 3-connected graphs can be constructed in $\mathsf{FL}^{\mathsf{UL} \cap \mathsf{coUL}}$.*

5.5 Oriented Graph Isomorphism

In the previous sections we considered planar 3-connected graphs, where the planar embedding is provided by a rotation scheme. It is also interesting to consider *arbitrary* (undirected) graphs with a rotation scheme that induces some orientation, i.e. cyclic order, on the edges. In the *isomorphism problem for oriented graphs*, two graphs are given, each with a rotation scheme. One has to decide whether there is an isomorphism between the graphs that *respects the orientation*. That is, for oriented graphs (G, ρ^G) and (H, ρ^H) an isomorphism φ from G to H it holds that for all $v \in V(G)$ and all $u \in \Gamma_G(v)$:

$$\rho_v^G(v, u) = (v, w) \Leftrightarrow \rho_{\varphi(v)}^H(\varphi(v), \varphi(u)) = (\varphi(v), \varphi(w)).$$

Miller and Reif [MR91] proved that the isomorphism problem for oriented graphs is in AC^1. We improve the complexity bound to NL. The proof goes along the same lines as for isomorphism for planar 3-connected graphs: compute a canonical form for each of the graphs according to the given rotation schemes such that precisely in the isomorphic case, these canonical forms are equal.

Theorem 5.5.1 *The oriented graph isomorphism problem is in* NL.

It suffices to analyze the complexity of computing a canonical form for a graph G and a rotation scheme ρ. If G is not connected then we determine the connected components in logspace [NTS95, Rei08] and compute canonical forms for each of them. Then we sort these canonical forms lexicographically and write them onto the output tape. Thus, we may assume that G is connected.

The three steps to compute a canonical form for a planar graph were all in logspace, except for the subroutine to compute distances, which is in UL ∩ coUL. Without planarity, the best upper bound for computing distances in a graph G is NL: to determine if $d_G(u, v) \leq k$, simply guess a path of length $\leq k$ from u to v. This proves Theorem 5.5.1.

5.6 Hardness of Isomorphism for Planar 3-Connected Graphs and Oriented Trees

Lindell [Lin92] proved that tree isomorphism is in L. In fact, tree isomorphism is complete for L [JKMT03]. Since trees are planar graphs, planar-GI is hard for L. We show that the problem remains hard for L even when restricted to planar 3-connected graphs. All the hardness and completeness results in this section are with respect to AC^0-many-one reductions.

Theorem 5.6.1 *Planar 3-connected graph isomorphism is hard for* L.

We reduce from the known L-complete problem Ord which was defined by Etessami [Ete97] as follows.

Order between vertices (Ord)
Input: a directed line-graph $G = (V, E)$ (given as a list of vertices and edges) and two designated vertices $s, t \in V$.
Computation: accept, if $s \prec t$ in the total order induced by G.

We first describe the reduction from Ord to tree isomorphism [JKMT03]. Let $v_1, \ldots, v_n$ be the vertices of G in the order induced by G. In particular, v_1 is the unique vertex with in-degree 0 and v_n is the unique vertex with out-degree 0. Let $s = v_i$ and $t = v_j$. W.l.o.g. assume that $i \neq n$ (otherwise map the instance to a non-isomorphic pair of trees). The (undirected) tree T constructed from G has two copies $u_1, \ldots, u_n$ and $w_1, \ldots, w_n$ of G, and there is an additional node r that is connected to u_1 and w_1. Up to this point, we have constructed one line-graph of

5. 3-CONNECTED PLANAR GI

length $2n$. Now the trick is to interrupt this line: take out the edge $\{u_i, u_{i+1}\}$ and instead put the edge $\{w_i, u_{i+1}\}$. Let T be the resulting tree.

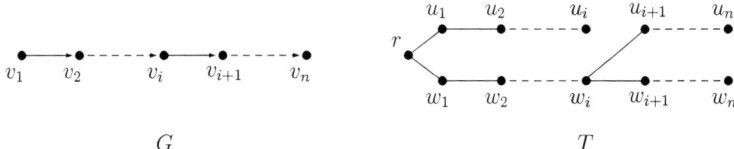

G T

Note that there is a unique non-trivial automorphism for T: exchange u_{i+1} with w_{i+1}, ..., u_n with w_n, and fix the other vertices pointwise. We construct two trees T_1 and T_2 from T. With respect to T, tree T_1 has two extra nodes x_0, x_1 which are connected with node u_j, and T_2 has extra nodes y_0, y_1 which are connected with node w_j. The extra edges enforce that an isomorphism between T_1 and T_2 has to map u_j to w_j, because these are the only vertices of degree 4 (for $j < n$). Now, if $v_i \prec v_j$, then the above automorphism of T yields an isomorphism between T_1 and T_2. On the other hand, if $v_j \prec v_i$, then there is no isomorphism between T_1 and T_2.

We modify T to a graph H that is no longer a tree, but planar and 3-connected. Split each node v of degree 1 or 2 in T into three vertices v^0, v^1, v^2. Connect these vertices via edges $\{v^0, v^1\}$ and $\{v^1, v^2\}$. If v has degree 1, then additionally put the edge $\{v^0, v^2\}$. Now, if $\{u, v\}$ is an edge in T, where u and v have degree 1 or 2, then we have edges $\{u^0, v^0\}$, $\{u^1, v^1\}$ and $\{u^2, v^2\}$ in H. The following picture illustrates the situation. In (a) node v has degree 2, in (b) node v has degree 1.

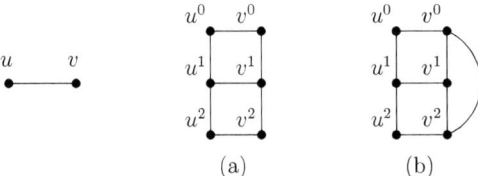

(a) (b)

A special case is node w_i which has degree 3. For w_i we need a gadget with 9 vertices which are connected as a 3×3 grid. The connections from this graph gadget (bold lines) to the other vertices are shown in the following picture.

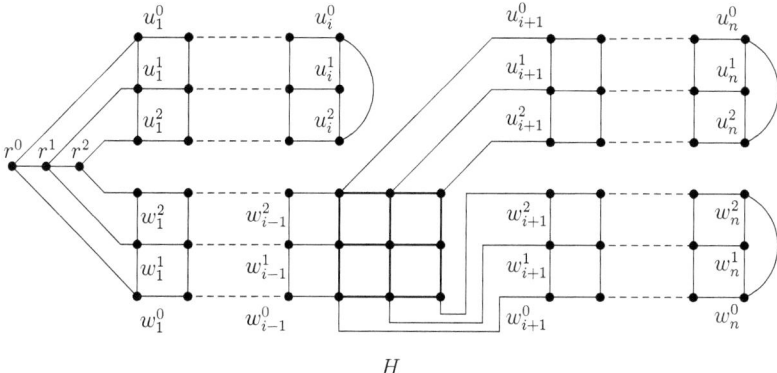

H

Now it suffices again to mark the vertices corresponding to v_j. That is, define graph H_1 as graph H plus the edge $\{u_j^0, u_j^2\}$, and H_2 as H plus the edge $\{w_j^0, w_j^2\}$. Note that H_1 and H_2 are planar and 3-connected. Furthermore, any isomorphism between H_1 and H_2 has to map u_j^0 to w_j^0, u_j^1 to w_j^1 and u_j^2 to w_j^2. Again, this is only possible iff $v_i \prec v_j$. This completes the proof of Theorem 5.6.1.

A final observation is about oriented trees. An *oriented tree* is a tree with a planar rotation scheme. It is not hard to see that one can adapt Lindell's algorithm to work for oriented trees, so that the corresponding isomorphism problem is in L. We show that it is also hard for L.

Theorem 5.6.2 *Oriented tree isomorphism is complete for* L.

Proof. We reduce Ord to the oriented tree isomorphism problem. Let G be the given linegraph and consider again the trees T_1 and T_2 from above constructed from G in the proof of Theorem 5.6.1. For vertices of degree 1 or 2 there is only one rotation scheme. Therefore we only have to take care of the vertices of degree 3 and 4, i.e. w_i, w_j and u_j.

- The rotation scheme for w_i is easy to handle: output the edges around w_i for T_1 in an arbitrary order, and choose the opposite order for w_i in T_2. This definition fits together with the only possible isomorphism that should exchange u_{i+1} and w_{i+1}.

- In the rotation function for w_j the order of edges to its neighbors can be chosen: $(w_{j-1}, y_0, w_{j+1}, y_1)$, and around u_j in order $u_{j-1}, x_0, u_{j+1}, x_1$. Because of the symmetry of the parts (u_j, x_0) and (u_j, x_1) in T_1 and of (w_j, y_0) and (w_j, y_1) in T_2 an isomorphism mapping w_j to u_j can be defined respecting the rotation functions for these nodes.

Now the same argument as for Theorem 5.6.1 shows that the oriented trees T_1 and T_2 are isomorphic iff $v_i \prec v_j$. This proves the theorem. □

5.7 Label Gadgets for Planar 3-Connected Graphs and Oriented Graphs

In many of the standard reductions between various GI related problems it is important to have a *labeling function* for the vertices. Given graphs G and H, we can attach the same label to vertex v from G and to vertex u from H. The effect is that all isomorphisms between the labeled graphs have to map v to u. The label usually can be replaced by some special subgraph $L_{n,j}$ which is connected to v (and to u in H, cf. [KST93]).

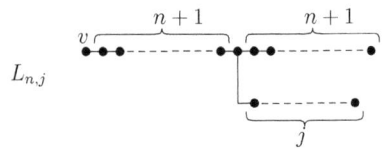

The figure to the right shows an example of a *label gadget*.
Since we want to maintain the property that a graph is 3-connected, we cannot use such label gadgets, e.g. if v has already valence 3. We provide a different construction. The idea is based on the label gadget shown in the above figure.

Let G be a planar 3-connected graph with n vertices and let ρ be a planar rotation scheme for G. Suppose we want to put label j at vertex v of degree d, where $1 \leq j \leq n$. Note that $d \geq 3$, because G is 3-connected. First, we define a special graph gadget $G_{d,h}$ that serves as a building block to construct the label. $G_{d,h}$ consists of h nested cycles C_d of size d each. Call these cycles $C_d^1, \ldots, C_d^h$ such that C_d^1 is the outermost cycle. Then the d vertices of a cycle are connected with the d vertices of a neighboring cycle by d edges in a clockwise manner, such that there emerge d faces between any two cycles. Each face is bounded by four edges. Figure 5.2 shows the construction for $d = 4$. The gadget can formally be described as a Cartesian product of graphs $C_d \square P_h$, where C_d is a cycle of size d and P_h is a path of length h.

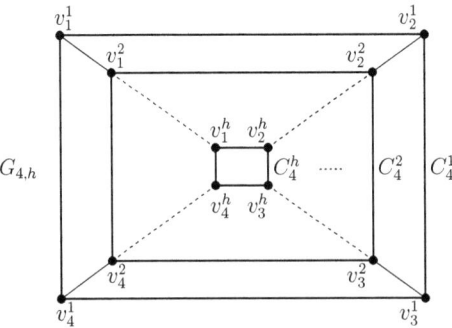

Figure 5.2: Gadgets $G_{d,h}$ are the building blocks of our label gadgets.

Next, we construct the gadget $L_{n,d,j}$ that serves as label j. Take gadget $G_{d,2n+2}$ which consists of $2n + 2$ cycles $C_d^1, \ldots, C_d^{2n+2}$ of size d. Recall that C_d^1 is the outermost cycle in $G_{d,2n+2}$, and C_d^{2n+2} is the innermost cycle. Hence the two neighboring cycles in the middle are C_d^{n+1} and C_d^{n+2}. Recall that there are d faces between any two neighboring cycles, each bounded by four edges. Next we take d copies of gadget $G_{4,j}$ and place them between C_d^{n+1} and C_d^{n+2}. These copies are placed one-to-one in the d faces between C_d^{n+1} and C_d^{n+2}. Then we connect the four vertices at the boundary of such a face with the four vertices of the outermost cycle of $G_{4,j}$ in that face with one edge each. Figure 5.3 shows the construction of $L_{n,d,j}$ for $d = 4$. Note that the gadget is planar and 3-connected.

Finally, to encode the label, replace vertex v by gadget $L_{n,d,j}$. The neighbors of v are connected to the outermost cycle of the gadget in an order according to the planar rotation scheme ρ of G. Figure 5.3 below shows the construction for $d = 4$. The resulting graph G_v is still planar and 3-connected.

Now let u be a vertex of a second graph H of the same degree d. Encode the same label with the gadget $L_{n,d,j}$ also at vertex u. Let H_u be the resulting graph. Then any isomorphism φ between G_v and H_u maps the label gadget in G_v onto the label gadget in H_u. Therefore, φ corresponds to an isomorphism between G and H that maps v to u. More general, if we label vertices $v_1, \ldots, v_k$ of G, all of degree d, with the same label gadget $L_{n,d,j}$ and do the same with $u_1, \ldots, u_k$ of H, again all of degree d, then any isomorphism φ between the labeled graphs maps the label gadgets onto each other. Therefore φ corresponds to an isomorphism between G and H that maps $\{v_1, \ldots, v_k\}$ onto $\{u_1, \ldots, u_k\}$.

We mention some applications of the labeling technique.

Replace Colors by Label Gadgets. We can reduce the problem color-GI back to the standard problem by putting label gadgets. Namely, for any vertex v of degree d and color c in G or H, replace v by the gadget $L_{n,d,c}$, where n is the number of vertices of G (and H). Then, by the properties of the labels explained above, the resulting graphs are isomorphic iff G and H are isomorphic under a color preserving isomorphism.

Theorem 5.7.1 *Planar 3-connected color-GI $\leq_m^{log}$ planar 3-connected GI.*

Graph Automorphism. We adapt the known reduction from GA to GI (see [KST93]) to the case of planar 3-connected graphs. This works in logspace as follows: take any two vertices $u \neq v$ of the same degree d. Let G_u and G_v be the graphs obtained from G by replacing u and v by label gadget $L_{n,d,1}$, respectively. Then $G \in$ GA iff $(G_u, G_v) \in$ GI for some pair of vertices u, v.

5. 3-CONNECTED PLANAR GI

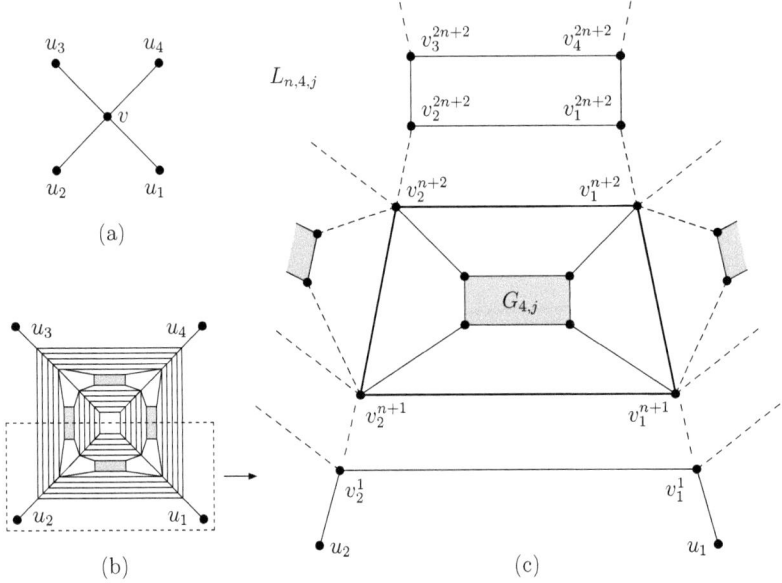

Figure 5.3: An example of a label gadget for a vertex of degree $d = 4$.
(a) Vertex v in graph G with its four neighbors $u_1, \ldots, u_4$.
(b) A schematic drawing when vertex v is replaced by the label gadget $L_{n,4,j}$. The part enclosed by the dashed rectangle is shown in more detail in (c).

Theorem 5.7.2 *Planar 3-connected GA $\leq_T^{log}$ planar 3-connected GI.*

Counting Isomorphisms. In Corollary 5.4.3 we have already seen that we can count the number of isomorphisms. In the polynomial time setting, counting the number of isomorphisms Turing reduces to GI for general graphs (see [KST93]). The same construction works also for planar 3-connected graphs in logspace.

Instead of isomorphisms we count automorphisms, which is essentially the same task. Given a graph G with n vertices, $G^{(k)}$ is the graph obtained from G by putting pairwise different labels at vertices $v_1, \ldots, v_k$. For $k = 1, \ldots, n-1$ we determine the size of the orbit of vertex v_k in the automorphism group of the graph $G^{(k)}$. This is done by putting the same label for vertex v_k and vertex v_j, for $j > k$. Then the resulting graphs $G_k^{(k-1)}$ and $G_j^{(k-1)}$ are isomorphic iff v_j is in the orbit of v_k in the automorphism group of $G^{(k-1)}$. The product of these orbit sizes gives the number of automorphisms of G. Since there are $\leq 2n^2$ automorphisms, the product of the orbit sizes can be computed in logspace.

Theorem 5.7.3 *Planar 3-connected* $\#GA \leq_T^{log}$ *planar 3-connected GI*

Oriented Graphs and Trees. As a final observation we note, that the Theorems 5.7.1, 5.7.2 and 5.7.3 can be generalized from planar 3-connected graphs to oriented graphs with the same proof techniques. It suffices to note that we can still encode labels at vertices in a graph: one can extend in logspace a given rotation scheme ρ for a graph G to the vertices of a label gadget. By the construction of our gadgets, it is trivial to construct a planar rotation scheme, say ρ' for the gadget itself. Then it remains to combine ρ and ρ'. If the gadget replaces a vertex v of G, then the vertices of the outermost cycle of the gadget are connected to the neighbors of v. Hence we only have to add one edge to the rotation function of each of these vertices. This requires only local changes at $\rho \cup \rho'$ and can easily be accomplished in logspace.

Corollary 5.7.4 *It holds, that*
1. *Oriented color-GI* $\leq_T^{log}$ *Oriented GI*
2. *Oriented GA* $\leq_T^{log}$ *Oriented GI*
3. *Oriented* $\#GA \leq_T^{log}$ *Oriented GI*

In the case of oriented trees we cannot use the above label gadget, because it is not a tree. Instead, we describe a modified version of the standard labeling technique. Let (T, ρ) be an oriented tree and v be a node of T. We mark v with label j. Recall that with standard techniques we would construct the label gadget $L_{n,j}$ and connect it to v. The problem is that we have many possibilities to update the rotation function ρ_v such that the different resulting graphs would not be pairwise isomorphic. Therefore we change the label gadget slightly.

- Let x be the middle vertex in $L_{n,j}$ (the one with degree 3). The new label gadget $L'_{n,j}$ is constructed like $L_{n,j}$ but with a second path of length j connected to x. Figure (1) below shows the label. The new rotation function ρ'_x arranges the edges in such a way that the edges to both paths of length j are not neighbors.

- Let d be the degree of v. Take d copies of $L'_{n,j}$ and connect them to v. The new rotation function ρ'_v of v puts a copy of $L'_{n,j}$ between any two original edges which are neighbors in the rotation function ρ_v as shown in Figure (2) below. This construction respects the automorphism properties of the oriented tree.

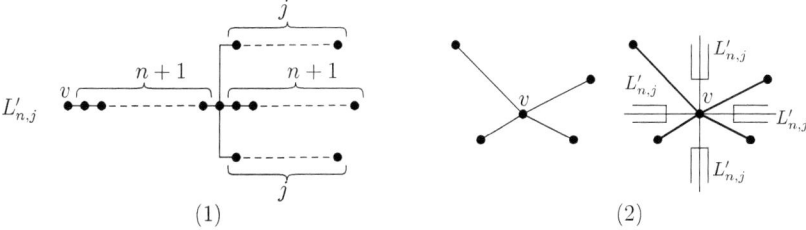

5. 3-CONNECTED PLANAR GI

Note that the reductions mentioned in Theorems 5.7.1, 5.7.2 and 5.7.3 are in fact in NC^1 when considering oriented trees. Hence, with this labeling technique these theorems hold for oriented trees under NC^1-reductions by the same proof techniques.

Corollary 5.7.5 *It holds, that*
1. *Oriented color-TreeIso $\leq_T^{\mathsf{NC}^1}$ Oriented GI*
2. *Oriented TreeAut $\leq_T^{\mathsf{NC}^1}$ Oriented GI*
3. *Oriented #TreeAut $\leq_T^{\mathsf{NC}^1}$ Oriented GI*

5.8 Label Gadgets for Planar Biconnected Graphs

In Section 5.7 we defined new label gadgets for planar 3-connected graphs. Also in the case of biconnected planar graphs it is reasonable to define label gadgets.

Here we have the same problem. In the standard proof techniques from [KST93] where GA is reduced to GI, labeling vertices plays an important role. To remove colors from vertices, a graph gadget is connected to the vertex. If the colored graph is biconnected then the resulting graph does not remain biconnected. We go around this problem by defining new label gadgets without violating the biconnected property. In this section we prove the following theorem.

Theorem 5.8.1 *Biconnected planar GA $\leq_{dtt}^{\mathsf{AC}^0}$ biconnected planar color-GI $\leq_m^{\mathsf{AC}^0}$ biconnected planar GI*

We adapt the proof of GA $\leq_{dtt}^{\mathsf{AC}^0}$ GI [Tor04]. Given a graph G, make a copy, say G'. Label an arbitrary vertex u in G. For every vertex v in G' we do the following. Label u and v and query both colored graphs G, G' to color-GI. If one of the tests states isomorphic, then G contains a non-trivial automorphism which maps u onto v.

We describe now the labeling function. Let $G = (V, E)$ be a planar biconnected colored graph. We construct a new graph $f(G)$ that contains no colored vertices with the desired properties. Let $j \in \{1, \ldots, n\}$ be the label of $v \in V$. We do the following.

- Construct a label gadget G_j as in Figure 5.4 which is a 3-connected planar graph G_j with $(3n + 2) + j$ vertices. G_j has a non-trivial automorphism which maps s onto t and vice versa.

- Let $u_1, \ldots, u_d \in \Gamma(v)$ be the set of neighbors of v in G. Make d copies of G_j.

- Connect vertices s of all these copies (from G_j) to vertex v.

- Connect vertex t of the i-th copy (from G_j) to vertex u_i.

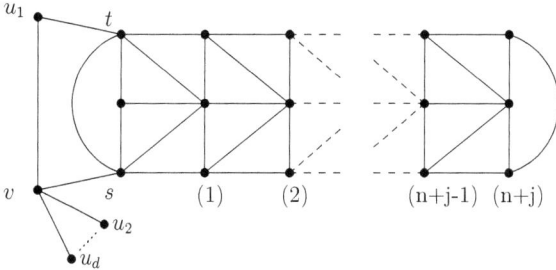

Figure 5.4: Label gadget G_j.

Note, the replacement of colors by introducing gadgets is not sequential. We connect the new gadgets to all neighbors of the original graph G, this is made in parallel. It is easy to see, that this gives a planar biconnected graph without colors and that, in an automorphism, a label gadget is mapped onto a gadget of the same size. Also the number of vertices in the resulting graph is polynomial in n, the size of G.

With this labeling technique adapted from standard proof techniques (see eg. [KST93]) we can conclude that computing orbits and #GA restricted to planar biconnected graphs is reducible to GI under logspace Turing reductions.

5.9 Further Work

All the steps except one of our isomorphism algorithm for 3-connected planar graphs can be implemented in logspace as well. Just for the task to compute distances in planar graphs we have an upper bound of UL ∩ coUL. This is in turn based on the reachability problem in planar graphs [BTV07]. Maybe we can take this as an indication that the reachability problem for planar graphs is in fact in logspace.

As already mentioned, Datta, Limaye and Nimbhorkar [DLN08] strengthened the complexity bound for 3-connected planar GI to L. They use a result of Reingold [Rei08] that one can compute *universal exploration sequences* [Kou02] for regular graphs in logspace.

Universal Exploration Sequences. The celebrated result from Reingold [Rei08] showing that the reachability problem in undirected graphs can be computed in L, has an important consequence for the construction of universal exploration sequences in logarithmic space. This fact is used in some of the isomorphism algorithms.

For a d-regular graph G and a numbering of the edges and a starting edge e_0, a se-

5. 3-CONNECTED PLANAR GI

quence $(\tau_1, \tau_2, \ldots, \tau_l) \in \{0, \ldots, d-1\}^l$ defines a *walk* $v_{-1}, v_0, \ldots, v_k$ in G in the following way: starting at $e_0 = (v_{-1}, v_0)$, for each i if (v_{i-1}, v_i) is the k-th edge of v_i then (v_i, v_{i+1}) is the $(k \oplus \tau_i)$-th edge of v_i modulo d. With a logspace computable function order the edges of each vertex are arranged uniquely.

A sequence $(\tau_1, \tau_2, \ldots, \tau_l) \in \{0, \ldots, d-1\}^l$ is called an (n, d) *universal exploration sequence* if for every connected d-regular graph with at most n vertices, any numbering of its edges and any starting edge, the walk obtained from the sequence explores all the vertices in the graph.

Theorem 5.9.1 *[Rei08] There exists a logspace algorithm that on input $(1^n, 1^d)$ in unary produces an (n, d)-universal exploration sequence of polynomial size in n.*

A Logspace Algorithm for 3-Connected Planar GI. Datta, Limaye and Nimbhorkar [DLN08] use the fact that such universal exploration sequences exist and can be computed in logarithmic space. As function order we use the rotation scheme for the graph G which describes one of two possible planar embeddings. Another logspace machine runs through the sequence of edges and records the first occurrences of vertices in this sequence. This is similar to Step 2 of the isomorphism order algorithm on Page 78. Another logspace machine arranges the edges according to these new vertex names in lexicographical order and computes a canon for the 3-connected planar graph, also see Step 3 of the isomorphism order algorithm on Page 79.

Theorem 5.9.2 *[DLN08] Isomorphism and canonization of 3-connected planar graphs is in* L.

Logspace completeness also carries over to oriented GI. We summarize the consequences of this result.

Corollary 5.9.3 *The following improvements of corollaries hold.*

- *Improvement of Corollary 5.4.3: The number of isomorphisms between two planar 3-connected graphs can be computed in* FL.

- *Improvement of Corollary 5.4.4: An isomorphism between two planar 3-connected graphs can be constructed in* FL.

- *Improvement of Theorem 5.5.1: Isomorphism and canonization of oriented graphs is in* L.

6 Isomorphism for $K_{3,3}$-Minor Free Graphs

6.1 Introduction

In this chapter we consider planar graph isomorphism and settle its complexity by significantly improving the known upper bound of AC^1. The result is particularly satisfying because Planar Graph Isomorphism turns out to be complete for a well-known and natural complexity class, namely logspace.

We even handle the graph isomorphism problem for a more general class of graphs, $K_{3,3}$-minor free graphs. Planar graphs can be characterized as graphs which are $K_{3,3}$ minor free and in addition K_5-minor free. There is a nice characterization of $K_{3,3}$-minor free graphs. The 3-connected components are either planar or isomorphic to the complete graph on 5 vertices i.e. the clique K_5 [Vaz89].

Trees are an example of graphs where the lower and upper bounds match and where isomorphism testing is complete for L [Lin92, JKMT03]. The complexity crucially depends on the encoding of the input: if the trees are presented as strings then the lower and upper bound is NC^1 [MJT98, Bus97]. Lindell's logspace result has been extended to partial 2-trees, also known as generalized series-parallel graphs [ADK08]. This class also contains all outer-planar graphs. Trees and partial 2-trees are special cases of planar graphs. In the proof of this result Arvind, Das and Köbler represent a partial 2-tree as a tree of cycles. Similar to Lindell's algorithm [Lin92] they compare trees of cycles up to isomorphism, defining a canonical ordering procedure, which finally gives a canonization algorithm.

Planar Graph Isomorphism has been studied in its own right since the early days of computer science. Weinberg [Wei66] presented an $O(n^2)$ algorithm for testing isomorphism of 3-connected planar graphs. Hopcroft and Tarjan [HT74] extended this to general planar graphs, improving the time complexity to $O(n \log n)$. Hopcroft and Wong [HW74] further improved it to $O(n)$. Recently Kukluk, Holder and Cook [KHC04] gave an $O(n^2)$ algorithm for planar graph isomorphism, which is suitable for practical applications. The parallel complexity of planar GI was first considered by Miller and Reif [MR91] and by Ramachandran and Reif [RR94]. They showed that the upper bound is AC^1, see also [Ver07].

Recent work further improved the complexity bounds of planar 3-connected graphs. Thierauf and Wagner [TW08] presented a new upper bound of UL ∩ coUL, making use of the machinery

6. $K_{3,3}$-MINOR FREE GI

developed for the reachability problem [RA00] and specifically for planar reachability [ADR05, BTV07]. They also show that the problem is L-hard. Further progress, in the form of a logspace algorithm is made by Datta, Limaye and Nimbhorkar [DLN08] where the planar 3-connected case is settled, by building on ideas from [TW08] and using Reingold's construction of universal exploration sequences [Rei08]. We summarize the known results for planar and $K_{3,3}$-minor free graphs and their restrictions as follows:

Graph class	Lower bound	Upper bound
Trees	L [MJT98]	L [Lin92]
Partial 2-trees	L	L [ADK08]
Planar 3-connected graphs	L [TW08]	L [DLN08]
Planar graphs	L	AC^1 [RR94]
$K_{3,3}$-minor free graphs	L	P[Pon91]

The current work is a natural culmination of this series where we settle the complexity question for planar and $K_{3,3}$-minor free graph isomorphism by presenting the first logspace algorithm for the problem. In fact, we give a logspace algorithm for the *graph canonization problem*, to which graph isomorphism reduces. The canonization involves assigning to each graph an isomorphism invariant, polynomial length string.

We consider $K_{3,3}$-minor free undirected graphs without parallel edges and loops, also called *simple* graphs. For $K_{3,3}$-minor free graphs which are not simple there are logspace many-one reductions to simple $K_{3,3}$-minor free graphs (cf. [KST93]).

Our algorithm decomposes graphs into their 3-connected components. For $K_{3,3}$ minor free graphs, we obtain a decomposition into components which have nice properties. After doing this we summarize the algorithm in more detail.

The Structure of Triconnected Components. We consider the decomposition of biconnected $K_{3,3}$-free graphs into triconnected components. Tutte [Tut66] proved that the decomposition is unique. Moreover, Asano [Asa85] proved that it has the following form.

Lemma 6.1.1 [Asa85] *Each triconnected component of a $K_{3,3}$-minor free graph is either planar or isomorphic to the complete graph K_5.*

We use Lemma 2.2.2 which is more general, saying that 3-connected components and separating pairs can be computed in logspace for an arbitrary biconnected graph. We get the following corollary.

Corollary 6.1.2 *For a biconnected $K_{3,3}$-free graph, the triconnected planar components and K_5 components can be computed in logspace.*

The Algorithm. Our algorithm consists of the following steps.

1. Decompose the $K_{3,3}$-minor free graph into its biconnected components and construct a *biconnected component tree* in logspace ([ADK08], cf. [TW09] and Section 2.2.2).

2. Decompose biconnected components into their triconnected components to obtain a *triconnected component tree* in logspace. This is essentially a parallel implementation of the sequential algorithm of [HT73] (Section 2.2.3).

3. Invoke the algorithm of Datta, Limaye and Nimbhorkar [DLN08] to canonize the triconnected planar components of the graph. Also the non-planar 3-connected components, i.e. the K_5 components, can be canonized in logspace. As this component is of constant size, we can test all possibilities to canonize a K_5 (Section 6.2.1).

4. Canonize biconnected graphs using their triconnected component trees. Lindell's algorithm ([Lin92] and Section 2.6.3) for tree canonization and its complexity analysis had to be modified in a non-trivial way for this step to work in logspace (Section 6.2).

5. Canonize $K_{3,3}$-minor free graphs using their biconnected component trees, by substituting the biconnected components with their triconnected component trees (Section 6.3).

Notice, that in Step 4, pairwise isomorphism of two triconnected component trees labelled with the canons of their components does not imply isomorphism of the corresponding graphs. Figure 6.1 illustrates this fact. So, a naive combination of [Lin92] and [DLN08] does not work. We need to introduce the concept of *orientations of separating pairs* (see Section 6.2.1 for details) to ensure the extendibility of isomorphism of individual 3-connected components to the entire biconnected planar graph.

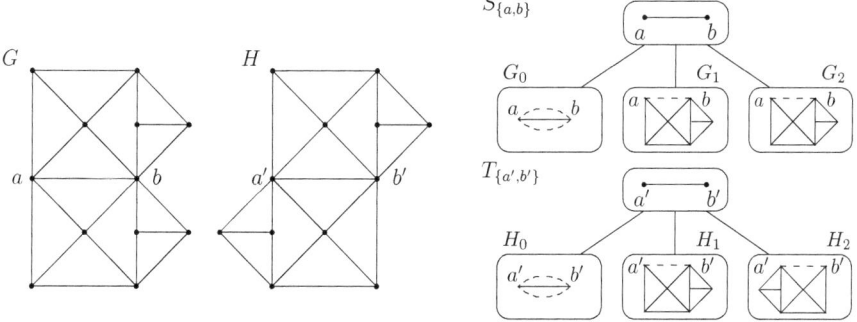

Figure 6.1: The graphs G and H have the same triconnected component trees but are not isomorphic.

6. $K_{3,3}$-MINOR FREE GI

Planar 3-connected components have at most two embeddings on the sphere (cf. [Whi33]). This property helps to perform Step 4 in L. Biconnected components do not have this property. Hence, the naïve approach for Step 5 would need to keep track of an exponential number of cases. We solve this problem by resorting to an intricate case analysis and a group theoretic lemma (Lemma 6.3.3) to bound the number of automorphisms of a colored planar 3-connected graph. We emphasize that Step 5 does not use Step 4 as a black-box but as a co-routine. In fact, we maintain two (logarithmically bounded) work-tapes for the two steps.

6.2 Canonization of Biconnected $K_{3,3}$-Minor Free Graphs

We give a logspace algorithm to canonize biconnected $K_{3,3}$-free graphs. For this, we extend the isomorphism order procedure on trees (Section 2.6.3). to work with triconnected component trees.

6.2.1 Isomorphism Order of Triconnected Component Trees

We describe now an isomorphism order procedure for two triconnected component trees S and T, corresponding to two biconnected planar graphs G and H, respectively. We root S and T at separating pair nodes $s = \{a, b\}$ and $t = \{a', b'\}$, respectively, which are chosen arbitrarily. Note, an isomorphism test can easily run through all possibilities of choosing these roots. The rooted trees are denoted $S_{\{a,b\}}$ and $T_{\{a',b'\}}$. They have separating pair nodes at odd levels and triconnected component nodes at even levels. Figure 6.2 shows two trees to be compared.

Our isomorphism order procedure is more complex than Lindell's algorithm, because each node of the tree is a separating pair or a triconnected component. Thus, two leafs in a triconnected component tree are not always isomorphic, in a tree they are.

In [DLN08], a logspace canonization algorithm for planar 3-connected graphs is described. An obvious way to canonize a triconnected component tree would be to invoke the algorithm of [DLN08] along with Lindell's algorithm. However, the situation is more complex. See for example, Figure 6.1 on Page 93.

We define the isomorphism order $<_T$ for $S_{\{a,b\}}$ and $T_{\{a',b'\}}$ by first comparing their sizes, then the number of children of s and t. These two steps are exactly the same as in Lindell's algorithm, i.e. first, comparing the size of the trees and second, the number of children of the root nodes. If equality is found in these two steps, then in the third step we make recursive comparisons of the subtrees of $S_{\{a,b\}}$ and $T_{\{a',b'\}}$. We deviate now from the tree canonization algorithm and introduce a further comparison step to ensure that G and H are indeed isomorphic.

To see this we refer to the example of Figure 6.1 on Page 93. Assume that s has children G_1, G_2 and t the children H_1, H_2, such that $G_1 \cong H_1$ and $G_2 \cong H_2$. It is possible now

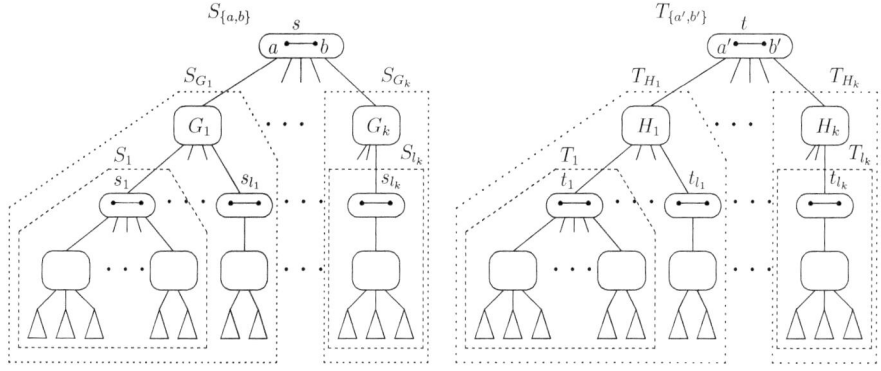

Figure 6.2: Triconnected component trees.

that the isomorphism between G_1 and H_1 maps a to a' and b to b', but the isomorphism between G_2 and H_2 maps a to b' and b to a'. Both partial isomorphisms cannot be extended to an isomorphism between G and H.

To handle this, we introduce the notion of an *orientation of a separating pair*. A separating pair gets an orientation from subtrees rooted at its children. Also, every subtree rooted at a triconnected component node gives an orientation to its parent separating pair. If the orientation is consistent, then we define $S_{\{a,b\}} =_T T_{\{a',b'\}}$ and we will show that G and H are isomorphic in this case.

Isomorphism Order of two Subtrees Rooted at Triconnected Component Nodes. We consider the isomorphism order of subtrees S_{G_i} and T_{H_j} rooted at the component nodes G_i and H_j, respectively. We distinguish the following cases.

Case 1, G_i *and* H_j *are of different types.* To detect an inequality, it suffices to check whether each of them is a K_5 or a cycle or a 3-bond or a 3-connected component. For example, cycles can be distinguished from 3-connected components by simply comparing their number of edges. We define an isomorphism order among subtrees based on their roots in this ascending order:

3-bond component $\leq_T$ cycle component $\leq_T$ 3-connected component $\leq_T$ K_5-component.

For example, $S_{G_i} <_T T_{H_j}$ if G_i is a 3-bond and H_j is a cycle.

Case 2, G_i *and* H_j *are 3-bonds.* clearly $S_{G_i} =_T T_{H_j}$ because S_{G_i} and T_{H_j} are leafs and 3-bonds are always isomorphic.

Case 3, G_i *and* H_j *are cycles or planar* 3-*connected components.* We construct the codes of G_i and H_j and compare them bit-by-bit. To canonize a cycle, we traverse it starting from the

6. $K_{3,3}$-MINOR FREE GI

virtual edge that corresponds to its parent and then traversing the entire cycle along the edges encountered. There are two possible traversals depending on which direction of the starting edge is chosen. There are two possible ways to canonize a cycle, i.e. two codes for a cycle.

To canonize a planar 3-connected component G_i, we use the logspace algorithm from Datta, Limaye and Nimbhorkar [DLN08]. Besides G_i, the algorithm gets as input a starting edge and a combinatorial embedding ρ of G_i. We always take the virtual edge $\{a, b\}$ corresponding to G_i's parent to be the starting edge. Then there are two choices for the direction of this edge, (a, b) or (b, a). Further, a planar 3-connected graph has two planar combinatorial embeddings [Whi33]. Hence, there are four possible ways to canonize G_i, i.e. four codes for G_i.

Case 4, G_i and H_j are K_5-components. There are 5! ways of labeling the vertices of a K_5, but the first two vertices will always be the vertices from the parent separating pair. There remain $2 \cdot 3! = 12$ ways of labelling the vertices. For example, $a = 1, b = 2, c = 3, d = 4, e = 5$ is one possibility to label the vertices a, b, c, d, e of a K_5. The canonical description of the graph with this labeling is then $(1, 2)(1, 3), (1, 4), (1, 5), (2, 1), (2, 3), \dots, (5, 4)$. All of them are possible ways to canonize the K_5, i.e. twelve codes for G_i.

In Case 3 and Case 4, we start the canonization of G_i and H_j in all the possible ways (two if they are cycle components, four if they are planar 3-connected components and twelve if they are K_5 components) and compare these codes bit-by-bit. Let C_g and C_h be two codes to be compared. The base case is that G_i and H_j are leaf nodes and therefore contain no further virtual edges. In this case we use the lexicographic order between C_g and C_h. If G_i and H_j contain further virtual edges then these edges are specially treated in the bitwise comparison of C_g and C_h:

1. If a virtual edge is traversed in the construction of one of the codes C_g or C_h but not in the other, then we define the one without the virtual edge to be the *smaller code*.

2. If C_g and C_h encounter virtual edges $\{u, v\}$ and $\{u', v'\}$ corresponding to a child of G_i and H_j, respectively, we need to recursively compare the subtrees rooted at $\{u, v\}$ and $\{u', v'\}$. If we find in the recursion that one of the subtrees is smaller than the other, then the code with the smaller subtree is defined to be the *smaller code*.

3. If we find that the subtrees rooted at $\{u, v\}$ and $\{u', v'\}$ are equal then we look at the orientations given to $\{u, v\}$ and $\{u', v'\}$ by their children. This orientation, called the *reference orientation*, is defined below. If one of the codes traverses the virtual edge in the direction of its reference orientation but the other one does not, then the one with the same direction is defined to be the *smaller code*.

We eliminate the codes which were found to be the larger codes in at least one of the comparisons. In the end, the codes that are not eliminated are the *minimum codes*. If we have the same minimum code for both G_i and H_j then we define $S_{G_i} =_T T_{H_j}$. The construction of the codes also defines an isomorphism between the subgraphs described by S_{G_i} and T_{H_j}, i.e. graph(S_{G_i}) $\cong$ graph(T_{H_j}). This holds for a single planar 3-connected component [DLN08]. If the trees contain several components, then our definition of $S_{G_i} =_T T_{H_j}$ guarantees that we can combine the isomorphisms of the components to an isomorphism between graph(S_{G_i}) and graph(T_{H_j}).

Finally, we define the *orientation given to the parent separating pair of G_i and H_j* to be the direction in which the minimum code traverses this edge. If the minimum codes are obtained for both choices of directions of the edge, we say that S_{G_i} and T_{H_j} are *symmetric about their parent separating pair*, and thus do not give an orientation. The following claim shows that also for K_5 components we get orientations the same way.

Claim 6.2.1 *Let G_0 be a K_5 component node which is the root in a triconnected component tree T_{G_0} and let $V(G_0) = \{a, b, c, d, e\}$ and $\{a, b\}$ be the parent separating pair of G_0. Either all minimum codes start with (a, b) (or (b, a)) or there is an equal number of codes starting with (a, b) and (b, a).*

Proof. We consider labelings of a, b, c, d, e (i.e. automorphisms in $Aut(G_0)$) where the parent separating pair $\{a, b\}$ and the other vertices $\{c, d, e\}$ are fixed blockwise. We can pair up $(i_1, i_2, i_3) \in Aut(G_0)$ with another permutation of the form $(b, a)(i_1, i_2, i_3) \in Aut(G_0)$ where each of the i_j's are either c or d or e. In other words, for each code that keeps a and b fixed, there is a corresponding code that swaps a and b, the other vertices being at the same positions in both of them.

Fix the permutations $\sigma_1 = (i_1, i_2, i_3)$ and $\sigma_2 = (b, a)(i_1, i_2, i_3)$. Consider the corresponding codes to σ_1 and σ_2. For example, when comparing (a, i_1) with (b, i_1) and both are separating pairs, then we also compare the isomorphism order of the trees of $T_{(a,i_1)}$ with $T_{(b,i_1)}$. If we have the situation that both codes are found to be not equal, then we have the following situation:

$$(T_{(a,i_1)} \leq_T T_{(a,i_2)} \leq_T T_{(a,i_3)}) \quad < \quad (T_{(b,i_1)} \leq_T T_{(b,i_2)} \leq_T T_{(b,i_3)}).$$

Also when considering other permutations than σ_1 and σ_2, which permute i_1, i_2, i_3, equality cannot be obtained. Hence, each automorphism that fixes a and b pointwise, leads to a strictly smaller code than its corresponding permutation that swaps a with b. □

This finishes the description of the order for the case of subtrees rooted at planar triconnected components.

When comparing S_{G_i} with T_{H_j} we directly went into recursion, without comparing the sizes and the degree of the root nodes in an intermediate step (i.e. Step 1 and Step 2 in the comparison algorithm in Section 2.6.2 on Page 34). That is, because the degree of the root node G_i is encoded implicitly by number of virtual edges in G_i. The size of S_{G_i} is checked by the length of

6. $K_{3,3}$-MINOR FREE GI

the minimal canons for G_i and when we compare the sizes of the children of the root node G_i with those of H_j.

Isomorphism Order of two Subtrees Rooted at Separating Pair Nodes. The first three steps of the isomorphism ordering are performed similar to that of [Lin92] maintaining the order profiles. Now we assume that the subtrees are partitioned into isomorphism classes. The additional step involves comparison of *orientations* given by the corresponding isomorphism classes defined as follows:

Let $(G_1, \ldots, G_k)$ be the children of the root $\{a, b\}$ of $S_{\{a,b\}}$, and $(S_{G_1}, \ldots, S_{G_k})$ be the subtrees rooted at $(G_1, \ldots, G_k)$. Similarly let $(H_1, \ldots, H_k)$ be the children of the root $\{a', b'\}$ of $T_{\{a',b'\}}$ and $(T_{H_1}, \ldots, T_{H_k})$ be the subtrees rooted at $(H_1, \ldots, H_k)$. We first order the subtrees, say $S_{G_1} \leq_T \cdots \leq_T S_{G_k}$ and $T_{H_1} \leq_T \cdots \leq_T T_{H_k}$, and verify that $S_{G_i} =_T T_{H_i}$ for all i. If we find an inequality then the one with the smallest index i defines the order between $S_{\{a,b\}}$ and $T_{\{a',b'\}}$. Now assume that $S_{G_i} =_T T_{H_i}$ for all i. Inductively, the corresponding split components are isomorphic, i.e. $\mathsf{graph}(S_{G_i}) \cong \mathsf{graph}(T_{H_i})$ for all i.

The next comparison concerns the orientation of $\{a, b\}$ and $\{a', b'\}$. We already explained above the orientation given by each of the S_{G_i}'s to $\{a, b\}$. We define a *reference orientation* for the root nodes $\{a, b\}$ and $\{a', b'\}$ which is given by their children. This is done as follows. We partition $(S_{G_1}, \ldots, S_{G_k})$ into classes of isomorphic subtrees, say $I_1 <_T \cdots <_T I_p$ for some $p \leq k$, and similar $(T_{H_1}, \ldots, T_{H_k})$ into $I'_1 <_T \cdots <_T I'_p$. It follows that I_j and I'_j contain the same number of subtrees for every j.

- Consider the orientation given to $\{a, b\}$ by an isomorphism class I_j: For each isomorphism class I_j we compute an *orientation counter*, which is a pair $O_j = (c_j^{\rightarrow}, c_j^{\leftarrow})$, where $c_j^{\rightarrow}$ is the number of subtrees of I_j which give one orientation, say (a, b), and $c_j^{\leftarrow}$ is the number of subtrees from I_j which give the other orientation (b, a). The larger number decides the orientation given to $\{a, b\}$. If these numbers are equal, or if each component in this class is symmetric about $\{a, b\}$ then no orientation is given to $\{a, b\}$ by this class, and the class is said to be *symmetric about* $\{a, b\}$. Note that in an isomorphism class, either all or none of the components are symmetric about the parent.

- The *reference orientation of* $\{a, b\}$ is defined to be the orientation given to $\{a, b\}$ by the smallest non-symmetric isomorphism class. If all isomorphism classes are symmetric about $\{a, b\}$, then we say that $\{a, b\}$ has *no reference orientation*.

We order all the orientation counters $O_j = (c_j^{\rightarrow}, c_j^{\leftarrow})$ such that the first component $c_j^{\rightarrow}$ is the counter for the reference orientation of $\{a, b\}$.

Let $O'_j = (d_j^{\rightarrow}, d_j^{\leftarrow})$ be the corresponding orientation counters for the isomorphism classes I'_j. Now we compare the orientation counters O_j and O'_j for $j = 1, \ldots, p$. If they are all pairwise equal, then the graphs G and H are isomorphic and we define $S_{\{a,b\}} =_T T_{\{a',b'\}}$. Otherwise, let j be the smallest index such that $O_j \neq O'_j$. Then we define $S_{\{a,b\}} <_T T_{\{a',b'\}}$ if O_j is lexicographically smaller than O'_j, and $T_{\{a',b'\}} <_T S_{\{a,b\}}$ otherwise. This finishes the definition of the order.

For an example, see Figure 6.1. The graphs G and H have the same triconnected component trees but are not isomorphic. In $S_{\{a,b\}}$, the 3-bonds form one isomorphism class I_1 and the other two components form the second isomorphism class I_2, as they all are pairwise isomorphic. The non-isomorphism is detected by comparing the directions given to the parent separating pair. We have $p = 2$ isomorphism classes and for the orientation counters we have $O_1 = O'_1 = (0,0)$, whereas $O_2 = (2,0)$ and $O'_2 = (1,1)$ and hence O'_2 is lexicographically smaller than O_2. Therefore we have $T_{\{a',b'\}} <_T S_{\{a,b\}}$.

Summary of the Steps in the Isomorphism Order. The isomorphism order of two triconnected component trees S and T rooted at separating pairs $s = \{a,b\}$ and $t = \{a',b'\}$ is defined $S_{\{a,b\}} <_T T_{\{a',b'\}}$ if:

1. $\mathsf{size}(S_{\{a,b\}}) < \mathsf{size}(T_{\{a',b'\}})$ or

2. $\mathsf{size}(S_{\{a,b\}}) = \mathsf{size}(T_{\{a',b'\}})$ but $\#s < \#t$ or

3. $\mathsf{size}(S_{\{a,b\}}) = \mathsf{size}(T_{\{a',b'\}})$, $\#s = \#t = k$, but $(S_{G_1}, \ldots, S_{G_k}) <_T (T_{H_1}, \ldots, T_{H_k})$ lexicographically, where we assume that $S_{G_1} \leq_T \cdots \leq_T S_{G_k}$ and $T_{H_1} \leq_T \cdots \leq_T T_{H_k}$ are the ordered subtrees of $S_{\{a,b\}}$ and $T_{\{a',b'\}}$, respectively. To compute the order between the subtrees S_{G_i} and T_{H_i} we compare the types and lexicographically the canons of G_i and H_i and *recursively* the subtrees rooted at the children of G_i and H_i. Note, that these children are again separating pair nodes.

4. $\mathsf{size}(S_{\{a,b\}}) = \mathsf{size}(T_{\{a',b'\}})$, $\#s = \#t = k$, $(S_{G_1}, \ldots, S_{G_k}) =_T (T_{H_1}, \ldots, T_{H_k})$, but $(O_1, \ldots, O_p) < (O'_1, \ldots, O'_p)$ lexicographically, where O_j and O'_j are the orientation counters of the jth isomorphism classes I_j and I'_j of all the S_{G_i}'s and the T_{H_i}'s.

We say that two triconnected component trees S_e and $T_{e'}$ are *equal according to the isomorphism order*, denoted by $S_e =_T T_{e'}$, if neither $S_e <_T T_{e'}$ nor $T_{e'} <_T S_e$ holds. The following theorem states that two trees are $=_T$-equal, precisely when the underlying graphs are isomorphic.

Theorem 6.2.2 *The biconnected $K_{3,3}$-free graphs G and H are isomorphic if and only if there is a choice of separating pairs e, e' in G and H such that $S_e =_T T_{e'}$ when rooted at e and e', respectively.*

Proof. Assume that $S_e =_T T_{e'}$. The argument is an induction on the depth of the trees that follows the inductive definition of the isomorphism order. The induction goes from depth d

6. $K_{3,3}$-MINOR FREE GI

to $d+2$. If the grandchildren of separating pairs, say s and t, are $=_T$-equal up to step 4, then we compare the children of s and t. If they are equal then we can extend the $=_T$-equality to the separating pairs s and t.

When subtrees are rooted at separating pair nodes, the comparison describes an order on the subtrees which correspond to split components of the separating pairs. The order describes an isomorphism among the split components.

When subtrees are rooted at triconnected component nodes, say G_i and H_j, the comparison states equality if the components have the same canon, i.e. are isomorphic. By the induction hypothesis we know that the children rooted at virtual edges of G_i and H_j are isomorphic. The equality in the comparisons inductively describes an isomorphism between the vertices in the children of the root nodes.

Hence, the isomorphism between the children at any level can be extended to an isomorphism between the corresponding subgraphs in G and H and therefore to G and H itself.

The reverse direction holds obviously as well. Namely, if G and H are isomorphic and there is an isomorphism that maps the separating pair $\{a,b\}$ of G to the separating pair $\{a',b'\}$ of H, then the triconnected component trees $S_{\{a,b\}}$ of G and $T_{\{a',b'\}}$ of H rooted respectively at $\{a,b\}$ and $\{a',b'\}$ will clearly be equal. Hence, such an isomorphism maps separating pairs of G onto separating pairs of H. This isomorphism describes a permutation on the split components of separating pairs, which means we have a permutation on triconnected components, the children of the separating pairs. By induction hypothesis, the children (at depth $d+2$) of two such triconnected components are isomorphic and equal according to $=_T$. More formally, one can argue inductively on the depth of $S_{\{a,b\}}$ and $T_{\{a',b'\}}$. □

6.2.2 Complexity of the Isomorphism Order Algorithm

We analyze the space complexity of the isomorphism order algorithm. The first two steps of the isomorphism order algorithm can be computed in logspace as in Lindell's algorithm [Lin92]. We show that Step 3 and Step 4 can also be performed in logspace. We use the algorithm of Datta, Limaye and Nimbhorkar [DLN08] to canonize a planar 3-connected component G_i of size n_{G_i} in space $O(\log n_{G_i})$. K_5-components can be canonized with constant effort.

Comparing two Subtrees Rooted at Triconnected Component Nodes. Consider two subtrees S_{G_i} and T_{H_j} with $\text{size}(S_{G_i}) = \text{size}(T_{H_j}) = N$ rooted at triconnected component nodes G_i and H_j, respectively. The cases that G_i and H_j are of different types or are both 3-bonds are easy to handle. Assume now that both are cycle components, planar 3-connected components or K_5 components. Then we start constructing and comparing all the possible codes of G_i

and H_j. We eliminate the larger ones and make recursive comparisons whenever the codes encounter virtual edges simultaneously. We can keep track of the codes, which are not eliminated, in constant space.

Suppose we construct and compare two codes C_g and C_h and consider the moment when we encounter virtual edges $\{a,b\}$ and $\{a',b'\}$ in C_g and C_h, respectively. Now we recursively compare the subtrees rooted at the separating pair nodes $\{a,b\}$ and $\{a',b'\}$. Note, that we cannot afford to store the entire work-tape content. It suffices to store the information of

- the codes which are not eliminated,
- which codes which encountered the virtual edges corresponding to $\{a,b\}$ and $\{a',b'\}$ and
- the direction in which the virtual edges $\{a,b\}$ and $\{a',b'\}$ were encountered.

This takes altogether $O(1)$ space.

When a recursive call is completed, we look at the work-tape and compute the codes C_g and C_h. Therefore, recompute the parent separating pair of the component, where the virtual edge $\{a,b\}$ is contained. Looking at the bits stored on the work-tape, we can recompute the codes C_g and C_h. Recompute for them, where $\{a,b\}$ and $\{a',b'\}$ are encountered in the correct direction of the edges and resume the computation from that point.

Although we only need $O(1)$ space per recursion level, we cannot guarantee yet, that the implementation of the algorithm described so far works in logspace. The problem is, that the immediate subtrees where we go into recursion might be of size $> N/2$ and in this case the recursion depth can become too large. To get around this problem, we check whether G_i and H_j have a large child, before starting the construction and comparison of their canons. A *large child* is an immediate child whose subtree is of size $> N/2$. If we find a large child of G_i and H_j then we compare them a priori and store the result of their recursive comparison. Because G_i and H_j have at most one large child each, this needs only $O(1)$ additional bits. Now, whenever the virtual edges corresponding to the large children from S_{G_i} and T_{H_j} are encountered simultaneously in a canon of G_i and H_j, the stored result can be used, thus avoiding a recursive call.

Comparing two Subtrees Rooted at Separating Pair Nodes. Consider two subtrees $S_{\{a,b\}}$ and $T_{\{a',b'\}}$ of size N, rooted at separating pair nodes $\{a,b\}$ and $\{a',b'\}$, respectively. We start comparing all the subtrees S_{G_i} and T_{H_j} of $S_{\{a,b\}}$ and $T_{\{a',b'\}}$, respectively. These subtrees are rooted at triconnected components and we can use the implementation described above. Therefore, we store on the work-tape the counters $c_<, c_=, c_>$. If they are pairwise equal, we compute the orientation counters O_j and O'_j of the isomorphism classes I_j and I'_j, for all j. The isomorphism classes are computed via the order profiles of the subtrees, as in Lindell's algorithm.

6. $K_{3,3}$-MINOR FREE GI

When we return from recursion, it is an easy task to find $\{a,b\}$ and $\{a',b'\}$ again, since a triconnected component has a unique parent, which is a separating pair node. Since we have the counters $c_<, c_=, c_>$ and the orientation counters on the work-tape, we can proceed with the next comparison.

Let k_j be the number of subtrees in I_j. The counters $c_<, c_=, c_>$ and the orientation counters need altogether at most $O(\log k_j)$ space. From the orientation counters we also get the reference orientation of $\{a,b\}$. Let N_j be the size of the subtrees in I_j. Then we have $N_j \leq N/k_j$. This would lead to a logspace implementation as in Lindell's algorithm except for the case that $N_j > N/2$, i.e. it corresponds to a large child.

We handle the case of large children as above: we recurse on them a priori and store the result in $O(1)$ bits. Then we process the other subtrees of $S_{\{a,b\}}$ and $T_{\{a',b'\}}$. When we reach the size-class of the large child, we know the reference orientation, if any. Now we use the stored result to compare the orientations given by the large children to their respective parent and return the result accordingly.

As seen above, while comparing two trees of size N, the algorithm uses no space for making a recursive call for a subtree of size $\geq N/2$ and it uses $O(\log k_j)$ space if the subtrees are of size at most N/k_j, where $k_j \geq 2$. Hence we get the same recurrence for the required space $\mathcal{S}(N)$ on the work-tape as Lindell:

$$\mathcal{S}(N) \leq \max_j \left\{ \mathcal{S}\left(\frac{N}{k_j}\right) + O(\log k_j) \right\},$$

where $k_j \geq 2$ for all j. Thus $\mathcal{S}(N) \in O(\log N)$. Note that the number n of vertices of G is in general smaller than N, because the separating pair nodes occur in all components split off by this pair. But we certainly have $n < N \leq O(n^2)$ [HT73]. This proves the following theorem.

Theorem 6.2.3 *The isomorphism order between the triconnected component trees of two biconnected $K_{3,3}$-free graphs can be computed in logspace.*

6.2.3 The Canon of Biconnected $K_{3,3}$-Minor Free Graphs

Once we know the ordering among the subtrees, it is straight forward to output the tree-canon of the triconnected component tree S. We traverse S in the tree isomorphism order as in Lindell [Lin92], writing the canon of each of the vertices along with virtual edges and delimiters onto the output-tape. That is, we output a '[' while going down and ']' while going up a subtree.

We need to choose a separating pair as root for the tree. Since there is no distinguished separating pair, we simply cycle through all of them. Since there are less than n^2 many separating pairs, a logspace transducer can cycle through all of them and can determine the separating pair which, when chosen to be the root, leads to the lexicographical minimum tree-code of S which is the tree-canon of S. We describe the canonization procedure for a fixed

root, say $\{a,b\}$.
The canonization procedure has two steps. In the first step we compute what we call a *tree-code* for $S_{\{a,b\}}$. This is a list of the edges of G, also including virtual edges. In the second step we compute the canon for G from the minimum tree-code.

Tree-Code of a Subtree Rooted at a Separating Pair Node. Consider a subtree $S_{\{a,b\}}$ rooted at the separating pair node $\{a,b\}$. We start with computing the reference orientation of $\{a,b\}$ and output the edge in this direction. This can be done by comparing the children of the separating pair node $\{a,b\}$ according to their isomorphism order with the help of the oracle. Then we recursively output the tree-codes of the subtrees of $\{a,b\}$ according to the increasing isomorphism order. Among isomorphic siblings, those which give the reference orientation to the parent are considered before those which give the reverse orientation. We denote this tree-code $l(S,a,b)$. If the subtree rooted at $\{a,b\}$ does not give any orientation to $\{a,b\}$, then take that orientation for $\{a,b\}$, in which it is encountered during the construction of the tree-code of its parent.

Assume now, the parent of $S_{\{a,b\}}$ is a triconnected component. In the symmetric case, $S_{\{a,b\}}$ does not give an orientation of $\{a,b\}$ to its parent. Then take the reference orientation which is given to the parent of all siblings.

Tree-Code of a Subtree Rooted at a Triconnected Component Node. Consider the subtree S_{G_i} rooted at the triconnected component node G_i. Let $\{a,b\}$ be the parent separating pair of S_{G_i} with reference orientation (a,b). If G_i is a 3-bond then output its code $l(G_i,a,b) = [(a,b)]$. If G_i is a cycle then it has a unique code with respect to the orientation (a,b), that is $l(G_i,a,b)$.

Now we consider the case that G_i is a planar 3-connected component or a K_5. Then G_i has two possible codes with respect to the orientation (a,b), one for each of the two embeddings. Query the oracle for the embedding that leads to the lexicographically smaller code and output it, i.e. $l(G_i,a,b)$. If we encounter a virtual edge $\{c,d\}$ during the construction, we determine its reference orientation with the help of the oracle and output it in this direction. If the children of the virtual edge do not give an orientation, we output $\{c,d\}$ in the direction in which it is encountered during the construction of the code for G_i. Finally, the children rooted at separating pair node $\{c,d\}$ are ordered with the isomorphism order procedure.

We give now an example. We consider the tree-code $l(S,a,b)$, i.e. the list of edges for the tree $S_{\{a,b\}}$ of Figure 6.2 together with the delimiters for the tree structure. Let s_i be the edge connecting the vertices a_i with b_i. We also write for short $l'(S_i,s_i)$ which is one of $l(S_i,a_i,b_i)$

103

6. $K_{3,3}$-MINOR FREE GI

or $l(S_i, b_i, a_i)$. The direction of s_i is as described above.

$$\begin{aligned} l(S,a,b) &= [\,(a,b)\,l(S_{G_1},a,b)\,\ldots\,l(S_{G_k},a,b)\,], \text{ where} \\ l(S_{G_1},a,b) &= [\,l(G_1,a,b)\,l'(S_1,s_1)\,\ldots\,l'(S_{l_1},s_{l_1})\,] \\ &\vdots \\ l(S_{G_k},a,b) &= [\,l(G_k,a,b)\,l'(S_{l_k},s_{l_k})\,] \end{aligned}$$

Canon for the Biconnected Planar Graph. Suppose, the starting edge $\{a,b\}$ leads to the minimum tree-code, such that we have the tree-canon. This is now almost the canon, except that the names of the vertices are still the ones they have in G. Clearly, a canon must be independent of the original vertex names. The final canon for $S_{\{a,b\}}$ can be obtained by a logspace transducer which relabels the vertices in the order of their first occurrence in this tree-code and outputs the list using these new labels, also see the routine on Page 79.

Note that the tree-canon contains virtual edges as well, which are not a part of G. However, this is not a problem since the virtual edges can be distinguished from real edges because of the presence of 3-bonds. To get the canon for G, remove these virtual edges and the delimiters '[' and ']' in the tree-canon for $S_{\{a,b\}}$. This is sufficient, because we describe here a bijective function f which transforms an automorphism ϕ of $S_{\{a,b\}}$ into an automorphism $f(\phi)$ for G with $\{a,b\}$ fixed. We get the following result.

Theorem 6.2.4 *A biconnected $K_{3,3}$-free graph can be canonized in logspace.*

6.3 Canonization of $K_{3,3}$-Minor Free Graphs

In this section, we give a logspace algorithm for the canonization of $K_{3,3}$-free graphs. The main part is to show how to canonize *connected* $K_{3,3}$-free graphs. Then, if a given graph is not connected, we compute its connected components in logspace and canonize each of these components. The canons of the connected components are output in lexicographical increasing order. Hence, from now on we assume that the given $K_{3,3}$-free graph is connected.

We decompose a $K_{3,3}$-free graph into its biconnected components and then construct a tree on these biconnected components and articulation points. We refer to this tree as the *biconnected component tree*. We also refer to the components as *biconnected component nodes* and *articulation point nodes*. This tree is unique and can be constructed in logspace, see Lemma 2.2.1.

Similar to triconnected component trees, we put a copy of an articulation point a into each of the components formed by the removal of a. Thus, an articulation point a has a copy in each of the biconnected components obtained by its removal.

Note that a naive approach is to color all copies of an articulation point with a particular color and check the isomorphism of these colored biconnected components separately. However, this approach does not work as we do not know a priori which articulation points from the two graphs will be mapped to each other. Also, using this method, we can not ensure in logspace that all the copies of an articulation are mapped to the copies of another articulation point.

In the discussion below, we refer to a copy of an articulation point in a biconnected component B as an *articulation point in B*. Although an articulation point has at most one copy in each of the biconnected components, the corresponding triconnected component trees can have many copies of the same articulation point (if it belongs to a separating pair in the biconnected component).

Given a $K_{3,3}$-free graph G, we root its biconnected component tree at an articulation point. During the isomorphism ordering of two such trees S and T, we can fix the root of S arbitrarily and make an equality test for all choices of roots for T. As there are $\leq n$ articulation points, a logspace transducer can cycle through all of them for the choice of the root for T. We state some properties of articulation points which directly follow from the definition of the triconnected and biconnected component trees.

Claim 6.3.1 *Let B be a biconnected component in S and $\mathcal{T}^\tau(B)$ be its triconnected component tree. Then the following holds.*

1. *S has a unique center, similar to a triconnected component tree.*

2. *If an articulation point a of S appears in a separating pair node s in $\mathcal{T}^\tau(B)$, then it appears in all the triconnected component nodes which are adjacent to s in $\mathcal{T}^\tau(B)$.*

3. *If an articulation point a appears in two nodes C and D in $\mathcal{T}^\tau(B)$, it appears in all the nodes that lie on the path between C and D in $\mathcal{T}^\tau(B)$. Hence, there is a unique node A in $\mathcal{T}^\tau(B)$ which contains a copy of vertex a which is nearest to the center of $\mathcal{T}^\tau(B)$. We say that this copy of vertex a is associated with the triconnected component A. Thus, we can uniquely associate each articulation point contained in B with a triconnected component in $\mathcal{T}^\tau(B)$.*

6.3.1 Isomorphism Order for Biconnected Component Trees

The isomorphism order for biconnected component trees is defined in three steps which correspond to the first three steps of the isomorphism order for triconnected component trees in Section 6.2.1 on Page 99. We mention the main differences in the isomorphism ordering for biconnected component trees from that of triconnected component trees.

1. The biconnected component nodes are connected by articulation point nodes. The resulting graph is a tree similar to the tree of triconnected component nodes and separating pair nodes. For articulation points, we do not need the notion of orientation. Instead,

6. $K_{3,3}$-MINOR FREE GI

we color the copy of the parent articulation point in a biconnected component with a distinct color and then the pairwise isomorphism among the subtrees of S and T can be extended to the isomorphism between the corresponding $K_{3,3}$-free graphs G and H in a straight forward way.

2. When comparing biconnected components B and B', then we do not have an obvious, uniquely defined edge as root for the corresponding triconnected component trees $\mathcal{T}^\tau(B)$ and $\mathcal{T}^\tau(B')$. The naive approach would be to cycle through all separating pairs and finally define the one as root that leads to a minimum canon. However, that way we cannot guarantee that the algorithm works in logspace. Let n_B be the size of B. Note that there can be up to $O(n_B)$ separating pairs. When we go into a recursion at some point, we need to store the edge that is currently the root. That is, we need $O(\log n_B)$ space at one level of recursion and this is too much for an overall logspace bound. Hence, our major task will be to limit the number of possible choices of roots appropriately so that the algorithm runs in logspace.

3. There are some more non-trivial tasks, to guarantee the logspace bound. It is not obvious, what to store on the work-tape when we go into recursion at some node in S or some node in $\mathcal{T}^\tau(B)$ and, what can be recomputed. We also need a new definition of the size of a subtree, for the isomorphism ordering to work correctly in logspace.

The size of a triconnected component tree is defined as on Page 27 i.e. the sum of the number of vertices in the components associated with the tree nodes. Here we extend the definition to biconnected component trees.

Definition 6.3.2 *Let B be a biconnected component node in a biconnected component tree S, and let $\mathcal{T}^\tau(B)$ be the triconnected component tree of B. The size of B, denoted $\mathsf{size}(\mathcal{T}^\tau(B))$ is defined as on Page 27. The size of an articulation point node in S is defined to be 1. Note, articulation points may be counted several times, namely in every component where they occur. The size of S, denoted $\mathsf{size}(S)$, is the sum of the sizes of its components.*

We define the isomorphism order for two biconnected component trees S_a and $T_{a'}$ rooted at the nodes s and t corresponding to the articulation points a and a', respectively (see Figure 6.3). Define $S_a <_\mathsf{B} T_{a'}$ if:

1. $\mathsf{size}(S_a) < \mathsf{size}(T_{a'})$ or

2. $\mathsf{size}(S_a) = \mathsf{size}(T_{a'})$ but $\#s < \#t$ or

3. $\mathsf{size}(S_a) = \mathsf{size}(T_{a'})$, $\#s = \#t = k$, but $(S_{B_1}, \ldots, S_{B_k}) <_\mathsf{B} (T_{B'_1}, \ldots, T_{B'_k})$ lexicographically, where we assume that $S_{B_1} \leq_\mathsf{B} \cdots \leq_\mathsf{B} S_{B_k}$ and $T_{B'_1} \leq_\mathsf{B} \cdots \leq_\mathsf{B} T_{B'_k}$ are the ordered subtrees of S_a and $T_{a'}$, respectively. To compare the order between the subtrees S_{B_i} and $T_{B'_j}$ we

compare the triconnected component trees $\mathcal{T}^\mathsf{T}(B_i)$ of B_i and $\mathcal{T}^\mathsf{T}(B'_j)$ of B'_j. When we reach the first occurrences of some articulation points in $\mathcal{T}^\mathsf{T}(B_i)$ and $\mathcal{T}^\mathsf{T}(B_{j'})$ (i.e. the *reference copies* of these articulation points as described later) then we compare *recursively* the corresponding subtrees rooted at the children of B_i and B'_j. Note that these children are again articulation point nodes.

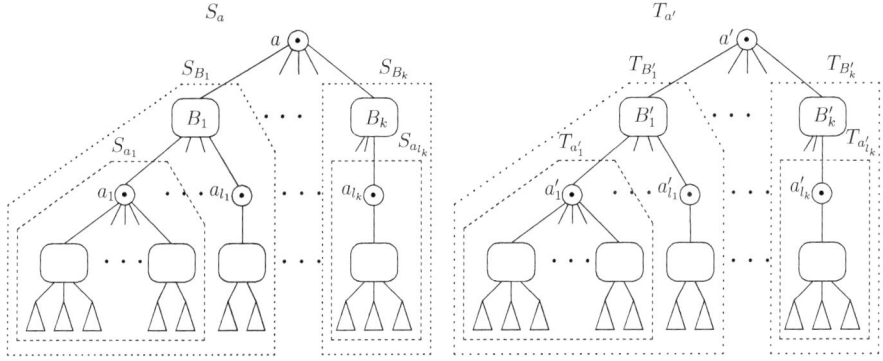

Figure 6.3: Biconnected component trees.

We say that two biconnected component trees are *equal*, denoted by $S_a =_\mathsf{B} T_{a'}$, if neither of $S_a <_\mathsf{B} T_{a'}$ and $T_{a'} <_\mathsf{B} S_a$ holds. The inductive ordering of the subtrees of S_a and $T_{a'}$ proceeds exactly as in Lindell's algorithm, by partitioning them into size-classes and comparing the children in the same size-class recursively. The book-keeping required (e.g. the order profile of a node, the number of nodes in a size-class that have been compared so far) is similar to that in Lindell's algorithm. We discuss now how to compare two such subtrees S_B and $T_{B'}$, rooted at biconnected component nodes B and B', respectively.

Isomorphism Order of two Subtrees Rooted at Biconnected Component Nodes. We consider the isomorphism order of two subtrees S_{B_i} and $T_{B'_j}$ rooted at biconnected component nodes B_i and B'_j, and let a and a' be their parent articulation point nodes, respectively. We start by constructing and comparing the tree-codes of the triconnected component trees $\mathcal{T}^\mathsf{T}(B_i)$ of B_i and $\mathcal{T}^\mathsf{T}(B'_j)$ of B'_j. To do so, we choose a separating pair node as root for each of them. The minimum among the tree-codes is then called the tree-canon. As explained above, we cannot afford to simply try all possible choices as root. We will show below that we can compute in logspace a sufficiently small number of separating pair nodes as roots for $\mathcal{T}^\mathsf{T}(B_i)$ and $\mathcal{T}^\mathsf{T}(B'_j)$ which suffices for our purpose. That is, we make pairwise cross-comparisons of the tree-codes obtained for these separating pair nodes as roots and determine the minimum tree-codes.

107

6. $K_{3,3}$-MINOR FREE GI

The base case is that B_i and B'_j are leaf nodes and therefore contain no articulation points other than the parent articulation point. In this case, we can cycle through all the separating pair nodes as roots and find the lexicographically smallest canon. If B_i does not contain separating pairs, i.e. B_i is just triconnected, then we cycle through all the edges as starting edges in the canonization of the single triconnected component in B_i.

If B_i and B'_j contain articulation points, we go into recursion. If an articulation point is part of a separating pair, it can occur several times in the triconnected component tree. To avoid recursion on the same pair of articulation points multiple times, we need to additionally keep track of whether a pair of articulation points is encountered for the first time in the comparison.

Also, while canonizing $\mathcal{T}^\tau(B_i)$ and $\mathcal{T}^\tau(B'_j)$, we give a separate color to the copy of a and a' in these trees, to ensure that the parent articulation points are always mapped to each other.

Limiting the Number of Possible Choices for the Root. Let S_a be a biconnected component tree rooted at articulation point node a. Let B be a child of a in S_a and $\mathcal{T}^\tau(B)$ be the triconnected component tree of the biconnected component B. We show how to limit the number of potential root nodes for $\mathcal{T}^\tau(B)$. This is a crucial part to obtain a logspace bound.

Besides the parent a, let B have articulation points $a_1, \ldots, a_l$ for some integer $l \geq 0$, such that a_j is the root node of the subtree S_{a_j} of S_a (see Figure 6.3 on Page 107). We partition the subtrees $S_{a_1}, \ldots, S_{a_l}$ into classes $E_1, \ldots, E_p$ of equal size subtrees (i.e. size according to Definition 6.3.2). Let k_j be the number of subtrees in E_j. Let the order of the size classes be such that $k_1 \leq k_2 \leq \cdots \leq k_p$. In the case of equality, e.g. $k_1 = k_2$, as a secondary criterion the class E_1 comes before E_2 if E_1 contains subtrees of larger size than those in E_2. This uniquely specifies an order among the size classes. All articulation points with their subtrees in size class E_j are colored with color j.

To limit the number of potential root nodes for $\mathcal{T}^\tau(B)$, we distinguish several cases below. The center of $\mathcal{T}^\tau(B)$, denoted by C, will play an important role thereby. In some of the cases we will show that the number of automorphisms of the center C is small. This already suffices for our purpose: in this case, for every edge as starting edge, we canonize the component C separately and construct a set of the edges A that lead to the minimum code. Though the possible codes are polynomially many, the minimum ones are bounded by the number of automorphisms of C, which are small. Note that, in this process, we do not recurse on the separating pairs or articulation points.

Now we take the first separating pair encountered in each of the codes obtained from edges in A as starting edges. This set of separating pairs forms the potential root nodes for $\mathcal{T}^\tau(B)$, and hence its cardinality is bounded by the number of automorphisms of C.

If B contains no separating pairs (i.e. $B=C$), we take the edges in A to compute the canon of B, recursively.

Otherwise, we start our case analysis by considering properties of the center C of $\mathcal{T}^{\mathrm{T}}(B)$.

- **The center C of $\mathcal{T}^{\mathrm{T}}(B)$ is a separating pair.** We choose this separating pair as the root of $\mathcal{T}^{\mathrm{T}}(B)$. Thus, we have only one choice for the root and the subtree rooted at B can be canonized in a unique way.

- **C is a triconnected component or a K_5 and a is not associated with C.** Let a be associated with a triconnected component R. We find the path from R to C in $\mathcal{T}^{\mathrm{T}}(B)$ and find the separating pair closest to C on this path. This serves as the unique choice for the root of $\mathcal{T}^{\mathrm{T}}(B)$.

- **a is associated with C and C is a cycle component.** We canonize C for the two edges with endpoint a as starting edges and a as the starting vertex. We construct these codes till a virtual edge is encountered in one or both of them. We choose the separating pairs corresponding to the first virtual edges encountered in these codes as the roots of $\mathcal{T}^{\mathrm{T}}(B)$. Thus, we get at most two choices for the root of $\mathcal{T}^{\mathrm{T}}(B)$.

- **a is associated with C and C is a K_5 component.** If one vertex is fixed in a K_5 then there remain $4! = 24$ codes. We construct these codes till a virtual edge is encountered in at least one of the codes. We choose the separating pairs corresponding to the first virtual edges encountered in these codes as the roots of $\mathcal{T}^{\mathrm{T}}(B)$. Because there are 4 edges with endpoint a and 6 edges not having endpoint a, we get at most 6 choices for the root of $\mathcal{T}^{\mathrm{T}}(B)$.

For the following cases, we assume that the center C is a planar 3-connected component and a is associated with C. We proceed with the case analysis according to the number l of articulation points in B besides a.

Case I: $l = 0$. B is a leaf node in S_a, it contains no articulation points besides a. We color a with a distinct color. In this case we can cycle through all separating pairs as root for $\mathcal{T}^{\mathrm{T}}(B)$.

Case II: $l = 1$. If B has exactly one articulation point besides a, then we process this child a priori and store the result. We color a and a_1 with distinct colors and proceed with B as in case of a leaf node.

Case III: $l \geq 2$. We distinguish several sub-cases.

1. **Some articulation point a_j in E_1 is not associated with C.** Let a_j be associated with a triconnected component $D \neq C$. Find the path from D to C in $\mathcal{T}^{\mathrm{T}}(B)$ and select the separating pair node closest to C on this path. Thus a_j uniquely defines a separating pair. In the worst case, this may happen for every a_j in E_1. Therefore, we get up to k_1 separating pairs as candidates for the root.

6. $K_{3,3}$-MINOR FREE GI

2. **All articulation points in E_1 are associated with C.** We distinguish sub-cases according to the size of E_1.

   a) If $k_1 \geq 2$, then by Lemma 6.3.3 below, C can have at most $4k_1$ automorphisms. Thus, we have at most $4k_1$ ways of choosing the root of $\mathcal{T}^\tau(B)$.

   b) If $k_1 = 1$, then we consider the next larger class of subtrees, E_2. We handle the cases for E_2 exactly as for E_1. However, we do not need to proceed to E_3, because we can handle the case $k_1 = k_2 = 1$ directly.

      i. **Some articulation point a_j in E_2 is not associated with C.** We do the same as in sub-Case 1 with a_j in E_2. We get up to k_2 separating pairs as candidates for the root.

      ii. **All articulation points in E_2 are associated with C.**

      If $k_2 \geq 2$, then we process the child in E_1 a priori and store the result. By Lemma 6.3.3 below, C can have at most $4k_2$ automorphisms in this case. Thus, we have at most $4k_2$ ways of choosing the root of $\mathcal{T}^\tau(B)$.

      If $k_2 = 1$, then C has at least three vertices that are fixed by all its automorphisms (i.e. a and the articulation point with its subtree in E_1 and that in E_2). We will show in Corollary 6.3.7 below that C has at most one non-trivial automorphism in this case. Thus, we have at most two ways of choosing the root of $\mathcal{T}^\tau(B)$.

Let $N = \mathsf{size}(S_B)$. The subtrees in the size class E_m have size $\leq N/k_m$. Since the size classes are ordered according to increasing k_j's, the subtrees in E_j also have size $\leq N/k_m$ for all $j \geq m$. We may assume that all subtrees are of size $\leq N/2$ because otherwise such a subtree is considered as *large* and treated as a special case by the algorithm (see Page 116).

In all of the cases, the number of ways for choosing the root is constant, or bounded by k_1 or k_2, but the latter only if $k_1 = 1$. Then we use constant space or $O(\log k_1)$, (respectively $O(\log k_2)$) space to keep track of which of the potential root edges is currently being used, and all subtrees are of size $\leq N/k_1$, (respectively size $\leq N/k_2$). This will suffice to bound the total space used for the subtree rooted at B by $O(\log N)$.

The following lemma gives a relation between the size of the smallest color class and the number of automorphisms for a planar 3-connected graph with one distinctly colored vertex.

Lemma 6.3.3 *Let G be a 3-connected planar graph with colors on its vertices such that one vertex a is colored distinctly and let $k \geq 2$ be the size of the smallest color class apart from the one which contains a. G has $\leq 4k$ automorphisms.*

To prove Lemma 6.3.3, we refer to the following results.

Lemma 6.3.4 [Bab95](P. Mani) *Every triconnected planar graph G can be embedded on the 2-sphere as a convex polytope P such that the automorphism group of G coincides with the automorphism group of the convex polytope P formed by the embedding.*

Lemma 6.3.5 [AD04, Bab95, Art96] *For any convex polytope other than tetrahedron, octahedron, cube, icosahedron, dodecahedron, the automorphism group is the product of its rotation group and $(1,\tau)$, where τ is a reflection. The rotation group is either C_k or D_k, where C_k is the cyclic group of order k and D_k is the dihedral group of order $2k$.*

Proof of Lemma 6.3.3. Let H be the subgroup of the rotation group, which permutes the vertices of the smallest color class among themselves. Then H is cyclic since the rotation group is cyclic. Let H be generated by a permutation π.

Notice that a non-trivial rotation of the sphere fixes exactly two points of the sphere viz. the end-points of the axis of rotation. Then, the following claim holds.

Claim 6.3.6 *In the cycle decomposition of π each non-trivial cycle has the same length.*

Proof of Claim 6.3.6. Suppose π_1, π_2 are two non-trivial cycles of lengths $p_1 < p_2$ respectively in the cycle decomposition of π. Then π^{p_1} fixes all elements of π_1 but not all elements of π_2. Thus $\pi^{p_1} \in H$ cannot be a rotation of the sphere which contradicts the definition of H. □

As a consequence, the order of H is bounded by k, since the length of any cycle containing one of the k colored points is at most k. □

Now we can justify subcase 2(b)ii of case III, where $k_1 = k_2 = 1$.

Corollary 6.3.7 *Let G be a 3-connected planar graph with at least 3 colored vertices, each having a distinct color. Then G has at most one non-trivial automorphism.*

Proof. An automorphism of G has to fix all the colored vertices. Consider the embedding of G on a 2-sphere. The only possible symmetry is a reflection about the plane containing the colored vertices, which leads to exactly one non-trivial automorphism. □

Note that if the planar triconnected component C is one of the exceptions stated in Lemma 6.3.5, it implies that C has $O(1)$ size. Thus, we do not have to limit its number of possible minimum codes. The preceding discussion implies that if two biconnected component trees are equal for the isomorphism order for some choice of the root, then the corresponding graphs are isomorphic. The reverse direction clearly holds as well.

Theorem 6.3.8 *Given two connected $K_{3,3}$-free graphs G and H and their biconnected component trees S and T, then $G \cong H$ if and only if there is a choice of articulation points a, a' in G and H such that $S_a =_B T_{a'}$.*

6. $K_{3,3}$-MINOR FREE GI

Proof. Assume that $S_a =_B T_{a'}$. The argument is an induction on the depth of the trees that follows the inductive definition of the isomorphism order. The induction goes from depth d to $d + 2$. If the grandchildren of articulation points, say s and t, are $=_B$-equal up to step 3, then we compare the children of s and t. If they are equal, we can extend the $=_B$-equality to the articulation points s and t.

When subtrees are rooted at articulation point nodes, the comparison describes an order on the subgraphs which correspond to split components of the articulation points. The order describes an isomorphism among the split components.

When subtrees are rooted at biconnected component nodes, say B_i and B'_j, the comparison states equality if the components have the same canon, i.e. are isomorphic (cf. Theorem 6.2.2) and by induction hypothesis we know that the children rooted at articulation points of B_i and B'_j are isomorphic. The equality in the comparisons inductively describes an isomorphism between the vertices in the children of the root nodes.

Hence, the isomorphism between the children at any level can be extended to an isomorphism between the corresponding subgraphs in G and H and therefore to G and H itself.

The reverse direction holds obviously as well. Namely, if G and H are isomorphic and there is an isomorphism between G and H that maps the articulation point a of G to the articulation point a' of H, then the biconnected component trees S_a of G and $T_{a'}$ of H rooted respectively at a and a' will clearly be equal. Hence, such an isomorphism maps articulation points of G to articulation points of H. This isomorphism describes a permutation of the split components of the articulation points. By induction hypothesis, the children at depth $d + 2$ of two such biconnected components are isomorphic and equal according to $=_B$. More formally, one can argue inductively on the depth of S_a and $T_{a'}$. □

The space analysis of the isomorphism order algorithm is similar to that of Lindell's algorithm. We highlight the differences needed in the analysis first.

When we compare biconnected components B and B' in the biconnected component tree then a typical query is of the form (s, r), where s is the chosen root of the triconnected component tree and r is the index of the edge in the code, which is to be retrieved. If there are k choices for the root of $\mathcal{T}^\mathsf{T}(B)$ and $\mathcal{T}^\mathsf{T}(B')$, the base machine cycles through all of them one by one, keeping track of the minimum code. This takes $O(\log k)$ space. From the discussion above, we know that the possible choices for the root can be restricted to $O(k)$, and that the subtrees rooted at the children of B have size $\leq \mathsf{size}(S_B)/k$, when $k \geq 2$. Hence the comparison of B and B' can be done in logspace in this case.

When we compare triconnected components in $\mathcal{T}^\mathsf{T}(B)$ and $\mathcal{T}^\mathsf{T}(B')$ then the algorithm asks oracle queries to the triconnected planar graph canonization algorithm. The base machine retrieves edges in these canons one by one from the oracle and compares them. Two edges (a, b)

and (a', b') are compared by first comparing a and a'. If both are articulation points, we check whether we reach them for the first time. In this case, we compare the biconnected subtrees S_a and $S_{a'}$ rooted at a and a'. If these are equal then we look, whether (a, b) and (a', b') are separating pairs. If so, then we compare their triconnected subtrees. If these are equal then we proceed with the next edge, e.g. (b, c), and continue the same way.

We now describe in more detail, how to find out whether articulation points a and a' occur for the first time in our traversal, and what is stored on the work-tape when going into recursion.

Limiting the Number of Recursive Calls for Articulation Point Nodes. When comparing $T^\tau(B)$ with $T^\tau(B')$ (see Figure 6.4) then we might find several copies of articulation points a and a'. That is, a may occur in several components in $T^\tau(B)$, because a can be part of a separating pair. We want to go into recursion on a to the subtree S_a only once. This will be either directly when we reach $T^\tau(B)$, in the case that S_a is a large child of B, or at a uniquely defined point in $T^\tau(B)$. The first case will be described in detail below on Page 116.

Otherwise we will define a unique component node A of $T^\tau(B)$ that contains a, and we go into recursion on a only in this component. Note that a can occur several times in the code of the triconnected component A, once for every edge connected to a. We go into recursion at the first edge where a occurs in the examination of A. We call this occurrence of a the *reference copy of* a, and similar for a' in A' which is a node in $T^\tau(B')$. Note that the reference copy of a depends on the chosen root for $T^\tau(B)$. We will show that the position of the reference copy (i.e. the component A and the position in the code for A) can be found again after recursion without storing any extra information on the work-tape.

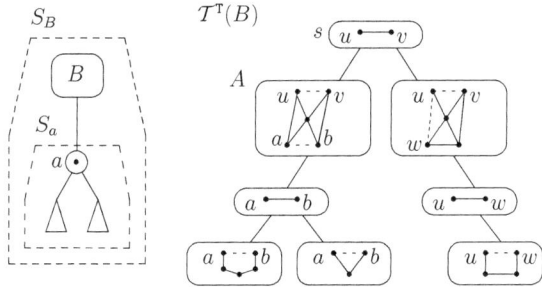

Figure 6.4: A biconnected component tree S_B rooted at biconnected component B which has an articulation point a as child, which occurs in the triconnected component tree $T^\tau(B)$ of B. In A and the other triconnected components the dashed edges are separating pairs.

6. $K_{3,3}$-MINOR FREE GI

Lemma 6.3.9 *The reference copy of an articulation point a in $\mathcal{T}^{\mathtt{T}}(B)$ and a' in $\mathcal{T}^{\mathtt{T}}(B')$ for the comparison of triconnected component trees $\mathcal{T}^{\mathtt{T}}(B)$ with $\mathcal{T}^{\mathtt{T}}(B')$ can be found in logspace.*

Proof. To prove the lemma, we distinguish three cases for a in $\mathcal{T}^{\mathtt{T}}(B)$. Assume, that we have the same situation for a' in $\mathcal{T}^{\mathtt{T}}(B')$. If not, then we found an inequality. We define now a unique component A, where a is contained. We distinguish the following cases.

- Articulation point a occurs in the root separating pair of $\mathcal{T}^{\mathtt{T}}(B)$. That is, a occurs already at the beginning of the comparisons for $\mathcal{T}^{\mathtt{T}}(B)$. Then we define A as the root separating pair.

- Articulation point a occurs in separating pairs other than the root of $\mathcal{T}^{\mathtt{T}}(B)$. Then a occurs in all the component nodes, which contain such a separating pair. By Lemma 2.2.5 these nodes form a connected subtree of $\mathcal{T}^{\mathtt{T}}(B)$. Hence, one of these component nodes is the closest to the root of $\mathcal{T}^{\mathtt{T}}(B)$. This component is always a triconnected component node. Let A be this component. Note that the comparison first compares a with a' before comparing the biconnected or triconnected subtrees, so we reach these copies first in the comparison.

- Articulation point a does not occur in a separating pair. Then, a occurs in only one triconnected component node in $\mathcal{T}^{\mathtt{T}}(B)$. Let A be this component.

In all except the first case, we find a in a triconnected component node A first. Let a' be found first in component node A', accordingly. Assume, we start the comparison of A and A'. More precisely, we start to compare the codes C of A and C' of A' bit for bit. We go into recursion if and only if we reach the first edge in the codes which contain a and a'. Note that C can contain more than one edge with endpoint a. On all the other edges in C and C' we do not go again into recursion. It is easy to see, that we can recompute the first occurrence of A and A'. □

Comparing two Subtrees Rooted at Separating Pair Nodes or Triconnected Component Nodes. We go into recursion at separating pair nodes and triconnected component nodes in $\mathcal{T}^{\mathtt{T}}(B)$ and $\mathcal{T}^{\mathtt{T}}(B')$. When we reach a reference copy of an articulation point in both trees, then we interrupt the comparison of B with B' and go into recursion as described before, i.e. we compare the corresponding articulation point nodes, the children of B and B'. When we return from recursion, we proceed with the comparison of $\mathcal{T}^{\mathtt{T}}(B)$ and $\mathcal{T}^{\mathtt{T}}(B')$.

In this part we concentrate on the comparison of $\mathcal{T}^{\mathtt{T}}(B)$ and $\mathcal{T}^{\mathtt{T}}(B')$. We give an overview of what is stored on the work-tape when we go into recursion at separating pair nodes and triconnected component nodes. Basically, the comparison is similar to that in Section 6.2.2. We summarize the changes.

- We use the size function according to Definition 6.3.2. That is, the size of a triconnected subtree rooted at a node C in $\mathcal{T}^\tau(B)$ also includes the sizes of the biconnected subtrees rooted at the reference articulation points which appear in the subtree of $\mathcal{T}^\tau(B)$ rooted at C.

- For a root separating pair node, we store at most $O(\log k)$ bits on the work-tape, when we have k candidates as root separating pairs for $\mathcal{T}^\tau(B)$. Hence, whenever we make recomputations in $\mathcal{T}^\tau(B)$, we have to find the root separating pair node first. For this, we compute $\mathcal{T}^\tau(B)$ in logspace and with the rules described above, we find the candidate edges in logspace. With the bits on the work-tape, we know which of these candidate edges is the current root separating pair. We proceed as in the case of non-root separating pair nodes described next.

- For a non-root separating pair node and triconnected component nodes, we store the same on the work-tape as described in Section 6.2.2, i.e. the counters $c_<, c_=, c_>$, orientation counters for separating pair nodes, and the information of the current code for triconnected component nodes. First, recompute the root separating pair node, then we can determine the parent component node. With the information on the work-tape, we can proceed with the computations as described in Section 6.2.2.

For the triconnected component trees $\mathcal{T}^\tau(B)$ and $\mathcal{T}^\tau(B')$, we get the same space-bounds as in the previous section on Page 102. That is, for the cross-comparison of the children of separating pair nodes s of $\mathcal{T}^\tau(B)$ and t of $\mathcal{T}^\tau(B')$ we use $O(\log k_j)$ space when we go into recursion on subtrees of size $\leq N/k_j$, where N is the size of the subtree rooted at s and k_j is the cardinality of the j-th isomorphism class. For each such child (a triconnected component node), we use $O(1)$ bits, when we go into recursion. In the case we have large children (of size $\geq N/2$), we treat them a priori. We will discuss this below.

Comparing two Subtrees Rooted at Articulation Point Nodes. When we consider the trees S_a and $S_{a'}$ rooted at articulation points a and a' then we have for the cross comparison of their children, say $B_1, \ldots, B_k$ and $B'_1, \ldots, B'_k$ respectively, a similar space analysis as in the case of separating pair nodes. We use $O(\log k_j)$ space when going into recursion on subtrees of size $\leq N/k_j$, where $N = \mathsf{size}(S_a)$ and k_j is the cardinality of the j-th isomorphism class. Large children (of size $\geq N/2$) are treated a priori. We will discuss this below.

When we compare biconnected components B_i and B'_i, then we compute $\mathcal{T}^\tau(B_i)$ and $\mathcal{T}^\tau(B'_i)$. We have a set of separating pairs as candidates for the root of $\mathcal{T}^\tau(B_i)$. Recall, that for B_i, its children are partitioned into size classes. Let k_i be the number of elements of the smallest size class with $k_i \geq 2$, there are $O(k_i)$ separating pairs as roots for $\mathcal{T}^\tau(B_i)$. Except for the trivial cases, the algorithm uses $O(\log k_i)$ space when it starts to compare the trees $\mathcal{T}^\tau(B_i)$

6. $K_{3,3}$-MINOR FREE GI

and $\mathcal{T}^{\tau}(B_i')$.

Assume now that we compare $\mathcal{T}^{\tau}(B_i)$ and $\mathcal{T}^{\tau}(B_i')$. In particular, assume we compare triconnected components A and A' of these trees. We follow the codes of A and A' as described above, until we reach articulation points, say a and a'. First, we recompute whether a and a' already occured in the parent node. If not, then we recompute the codes of A and A' and check, whether a and a' occur for the first time. If so, then we store nothing and go into recursion.

When we return from recursion, we recompute the components A and A' in $\mathcal{T}^{\tau}(B)$ and $\mathcal{T}^{\tau}(B')$. On the work-tape there is information about which are the current among the unerased codes. We run through the current codes and find the first occurrence of a and a'.

Large Children. As in the case of biconnected graphs we deviate from the algorithm described so far in the case that the recursion would lead to a large child. Large subtrees are again treated a priori.

However, the notion of a large child is somewhat subtle here. We already defined the size of biconnected component trees S_a and S_B with an articulation point a or a biconnected component B as root. A *large child* of such a tree of size N is a child of size $\geq N/2$.

Now consider $\mathcal{T}^{\tau}(B)$, the triconnected component tree of B. Let A be a triconnected component and $\{u, v\}$ be a separating pair in $\mathcal{T}^{\tau}(B)$. We have not yet defined the subtrees S_A and $S_{\{u,v\}}$ rooted at A and $\{u, v\}$, respectively, and this has to be done quite carefully.

Definition 6.3.10 *Let B be a biconnected component and let C be a node in $\mathcal{T}^{\tau}(B)$, i.e. a triconnected component node or a separating pair node. The tree S_C^* rooted at C consists of the subtree of $\mathcal{T}^{\tau}(B)$ rooted at C (with respect to the root of $\mathcal{T}^{\tau}(B)$) and of the subtrees S_a for all articulation points a that have a reference copy in the subtree of $\mathcal{T}^{\tau}(B)$ rooted at C, except those S_a that are a large child of S_B. The size of S_C^* is the sum of the sizes of its components. Let N be the size of S_C^*. A large child of S_C^* is a subtree of C of size $\geq N/2$.*

We already described above that an articulation point a may occur in several components of a triconnected component tree. We said that we go into recursion to the biconnected component tree S_a only once, namely either when we reach the reference copy of a (as defined on Page 113) or even before in the following case: let a be an articulation point in the biconnected component B and let C be the node in $\mathcal{T}^{\tau}(B)$ that contains the reference copy of a. Then it might be the case that S_a is a large child of S_B *and* of S_C^*:

In this case we visit S_a when we reach B, i.e. before we start to compute the root for $\mathcal{T}^{\tau}(B)$. Then, when we reach the reference copy of a in C, we first check whether we already visited S_a. In this case the comparison result (from the comparison with some large child $S_{a'}$ of B') is already stored on the work-tape and we do not visit S_a for a second time. If we would, then we could not guarantee the logspace bound, because we already would have written bits on the work-tape for B when traversing S_a a second time.

On the other hand, if S_a is not a large child of S_B then we recurse on S_a at the reference copy of a.

Consequently, we consider S_a as a subtree only at the place where we go into recursion to S_a. Recall, that this is not a static property, because for example the position of the reference copy depends on the chosen root of the tree, and we try several possibilities for the root. Figure 6.5 shows an example.

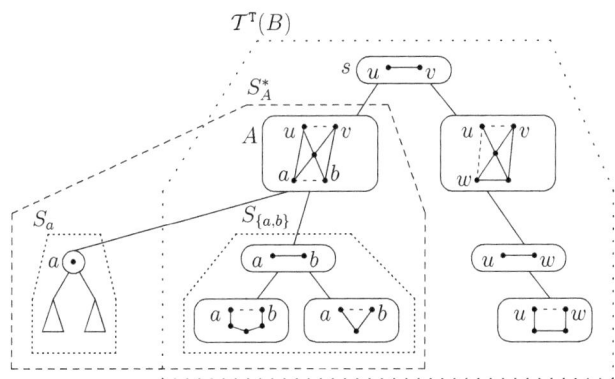

Figure 6.5: The triconnected component tree $\mathcal{T}^\intercal(B)$ of the biconnected component B. The triconnected component A contains the reference copy of articulation point a. If S_a is not a large child of B, then the subtree S_A^* consists of the subtree of $\mathcal{T}^\intercal(B)$ rooted at A and the subtree S_a. In contrast, S_a is not part of the subtree $S_{\{a,b\}}^*$ because it does not contain the reference copy of a.

We summarize, whenever the algorithm reaches a component a, B or C as above, it first checks whether the corresponding tree S_a, S_B or S_C^* has a large child and treats it a priori. The result is stored in $O(1)$ bits. In the case of triconnected components, we also store the orientation. We distinguish large children as follows.

- Large children with respect to the biconnected component tree. These are children of node a in S_a or B in S_B. These children are biconnected component nodes or articulation point nodes. When comparing S_B with $S_{B'}$, then we go for large children into recursion before computing the trees $\mathcal{T}^\intercal(B)$ and $\mathcal{T}^\intercal(B')$.

- Large children with respect to the triconnected component tree. These are children of node C in S_C^*. These children are separating pair nodes or triconnected component nodes.

6. $K_{3,3}$-MINOR FREE GI

- Large children with respect to S_C^*, where C is a node in $\mathcal{T}^\tau(B)$. These are children of node B in S_B which are not large children of B. These children are articulation point nodes which have a reference copy in C.

Analysis of the space requirement. We analyze the comparison algorithm when it compares subtrees rooted at separating pairs and subtrees rooted at articulation points. For the analysis, the recursion goes here from depth d to $d+2$ of the trees. Observe, that large children are handled a priori at any level of the trees. We set up the following recursion equation for the space requirement of our algorithm.

$$\mathcal{S}(N) = \max_j \left\{ \mathcal{S}\left(\frac{N}{k_j}\right) + O(\log k_j) \right\},$$

where $k_j \geq 2$ (for all j) are the values mentioned above in the corresponding cases. Hence, $\mathcal{S}(N) = O(\log N)$.

For the explanation of the recursion equation it is helpful to imagine that we have two work-tapes. We use the first work-tape when we go into recursion at articulation point nodes, and the second work-tape when we go into recursion at separating pair nodes. The total space needed is the sum of the space of the two work-tapes.

- At an articulation point node, the value k_j is the number of elements in the j-th size class among the children $B_1, \ldots, B_k$ of the articulation point node. We store $O(\log k_j)$ bits and recursively consider subtrees of size $\leq N/k_j$.

- At a separating pair node the value k_j is the number of elements in the j-th isomorphism class among the children $G_1, \ldots, G_k$ of the separating pair node. We store $O(\log k_j)$ bits and recursively consider subtrees of size $\leq N/k_j$.

This finishes the complexity analysis. We get the following theorem.

Theorem 6.3.11 *The isomorphism order between two $K_{3,3}$-free graphs can be computed in logspace.*

6.3.2 The Canon of a $K_{3,3}$ minor-free Graph

From Theorem 6.3.11, we know that the isomorphism order of biconnected component trees can be computed in logspace. Using this algorithm, we show that the canon of a $K_{3,3}$-free graph can be output in logspace.

The canonization of $K_{3,3}$-free graphs proceeds exactly as in the case of biconnected $K_{3,3}$-free graphs. With a logspace procedure we traverse the biconnected component tree and make oracle queries to the isomorphism order algorithm and output a tree-code, that is a canonically sorted list of edges along with delimiters to separate the tree-codes for the subtrees rooted at siblings.

For an example, consider the tree-code $l(S, a)$ for the tree S_a of Figure 6.3. Let $l(B_i, a)$ be the tree-code of the biconnected component B_i (i.e. the tree-code of $\mathcal{T}^\tau(B_i)$ with a the parent articulation point). Let $a_1, \ldots, a_{l_1}$ be the order of the reference copies of articulation points as they occur in the tree-code of $\mathcal{T}^\tau(B_i)$ rooted at a. Then we get the following tree-code for S_a.

$$
\begin{aligned}
l(S, a) &= [\,(a)\, l(S_{B_1}, a)\, \ldots\, l(S_{B_k}, a)\,], \text{ where} \\
l(S_{B_1}, a) &= [\,l(B_1, a)\, l(S_{a_1}, a_1)\, \ldots\, l(S_{a_{l_1}}, a_{l_1})\,] \\
&\vdots \\
l(S_{B_k}, a) &= [\,l(B_k, a)\, l(S_{a_{l_k}}, a_{l_k})\,]
\end{aligned}
$$

A logspace transducer then renames the vertices according to their first occurrence in this tree-code for the biconnected component tree. Further logspace transducers cycle through all the articulation points as roots to find the minimum tree-code among them, i.e. the tree-canon, and remove the virtual edges and delimiters to obtain a canon for the $K_{3,3}$-free graph. We proved the following theorem.

Theorem 6.3.12 *A $K_{3,3}$-free graph can be canonized in logspace.*

Conclusion. We improved the known upper bound for isomorphism and canonization of planar graphs from AC^1 to L and of $K_{3,3}$-minor free graphs from P to L. This implies L-completeness for these problems, thereby settling their complexity. An interesting question is to extend it to other important classes of graphs.

7 Isomorphism for K_5-Minor Free Graphs

7.1 Introduction

The complexity of isomorphism is settled for trees [Lin92, MJT98], partial 2-trees [ADK08], and for planar graphs [DLN+09]. For all these graph classes, isomorphism testing is in L. We extend the result of [DLN+09] to isomorphism of K_5-minor free graphs. The previously known upper bound for these graph class is P due to Ponomarenko [Pon91]. K_5-minor free graphs are considerably larger than the class of planar graphs.

We consider undirected graphs without parallel edges and loops, also known as *simple* graphs. For directed graphs or graphs with loops and parallel edges, there are logspace many-one reductions to simple undirected graphs (cf. [KST93]). Our logspace algorithm relies on the following properties of K_5-minor free graphs [Khu88]. The 3-connected components of K_5-minor free graphs are either planar or V_8's (where V_8 is a four-rung möbius ladder on 8 vertices) or the following holds. The 4-connected components of the remaining non-planar 3-connected components are planar.

3-connected components have two embeddings on the sphere (cf. [Whi33]). The embedding is given roughly as follows: For each vertex, its neighbors are ordered by a cyclic permutation. The second embedding for the 3-connected component is obtained by the mirror image, (i.e. consider the reverse permutations for all vertices). Allender and Mahajan [AM00] showed that an embedding of a planar graph can be computed in log-space. This facts are used in [TW08] and [DLN08] (also see Chapter 5) to bring the complexity of canonization on 3-connected planar graphs from AC^1 to L. If one edge is fixed, then there are at most four possibilities (i.e. two embeddings and two orientations of the starting edge) to traverse a triconnected component in L. Such a traversal gives a unique order of the vertices. For a cycle we have two possibilities to canonize, i.e. traverse the cycle from the fixed edge in both directions.

There is a related result where reachability in $K_{3,3}$ and K_5-minor free graphs are reduced to reachability in planar graphs under logspace many-one reductions [TW09]. The basic idea is that the non-planar components are transformed into new planar components, carefully copying subgraphs in a recursive manner, such that the graph remains polynomial in size of the input graph. This technique is designed to keep the reachability conditions unchanged but it is not applicable for isomorphism testing.

7. K_5-MINOR FREE GI

We give a logspace algorithm to get these decompositions in a *canonical* way. The isomorphism of K_5-minor free graphs is more complex, as in addition to biconnected and triconnected component trees, it also has four-connected component trees. This needs considerable modifications and new ideas. We also give logspace algorithms for the canonization of K_5-minor free graphs.

7.2 Decomposition of K_5-Minor Free Graphs

We decompose K_5-minor free graphs into biconnected components. According to Lemma 2.2.1 this can be done in logspace. For an example see Figure 7.1.

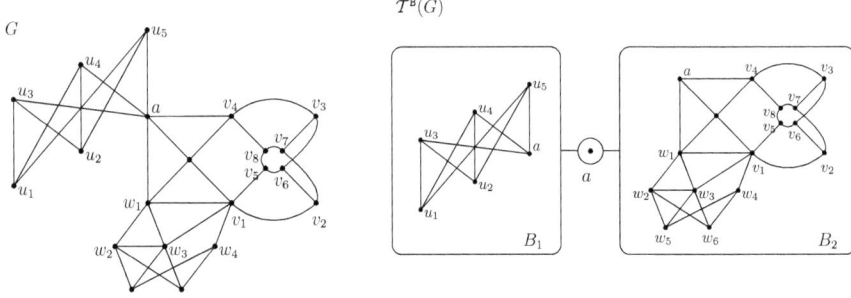

Figure 7.1: Decomposition of a K_5-free graph G into biconnected components B_1 and B_2 and the corresponding biconnected component tree $\mathcal{T}^\mathsf{B}(G)$.

We further decompose a biconnected components into 3-connected and 4-connected components.

Decomposition into 3-Connected Components

Wagner [Wag37] showed that the 3-connected K_5-free graphs can be constructed with a clique-sum operation from planar graphs and the four-rung Möbius ladder, also called V_8 a 3-connected graph on 8 vertices, which is non-planar because it contains a $K_{3,3}$.

Definition 7.2.1 *Let G_1 and G_2 be two graphs each containing cliques of equal size. The clique-sum of G_1 and G_2 is a graph G formed from their disjoint union by identifying pairs of vertices in these two cliques to form a single shared clique, and then possibly deleting some of the clique edges. A k-clique-sum is a clique-sum in which both cliques have at most k vertices.*

122

Let $\mathcal{G}$ be some class of graphs. We define $\langle \mathcal{G} \rangle_k$ as the set of graphs that can be constructed by repeatedly taking k-clique-sums starting from graphs in $\mathcal{G}$.

The class of K_5-free graphs can be decomposed as follows.

Theorem 7.2.2 [Wag37] *Let $\mathcal{C}$ be the class of all planar graphs together with the four-rung Möbius ladder V_8. Then $\langle \mathcal{C} \rangle_3$ is the class of all graphs with no K_5-minor.*

We make the following observations, also see Figure 7.2.

- If we build the 3-clique-sum of two planar graphs, then the three vertices of the joint clique are a separating triple in the resulting graph. Hence, the 4-connected components of a graph cannot be built by 3-clique sums of planar graphs and must all be planar.

- The V_8 is not planar, 3-connected and cannot be part of a 3-clique sum, because it does not contain a triangle as subgraph.

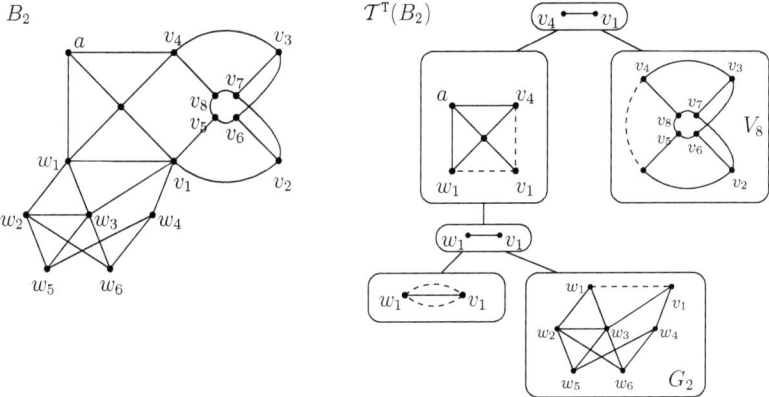

Figure 7.2: Decomposition of the biconnected component B_2 and the corresponding biconnected component tree $\mathcal{T}^\tau(B_2)$. Virtual edges are indicated with dashed lines.

By Theorem 7.2.2 and these observations we have the following situation.

Corollary 7.2.3 (cf. [Khu88]) *A non-planar 3-connected component of a K_5-free undirected graph is either the V_8 or its 4-connected components are all planar.*

7. K_5-MINOR FREE GI

Decomposition into 4-Connected Components

Similar to the decomposition algorithm of Vazirani [Vaz89], we decompose the K_5-free graph into triconnected components. That is, we first decompose it into biconnected components and then the biconnected components further into triconnected components.

Let $G \neq V_8$ be a non-planar 3-connected graph. Thierauf and Wagner [TW09] further decomposed such components into 4-connected components, also see Chapter 9. But the decomposition there is not unique up to isomorphism. We describe here a different way of decomposition. We just decompose G at those separating triples which cause the non-planarity: let τ be a separating triple such that $G \setminus \tau$ splits into at least three connected components. Collapse these connected components into single vertices, and it is easy to see that G has a $K_{3,3}$ as minor.

Definition 7.2.4 *Let τ be a separating triple of a component G' of graph G. Then τ is called 3-divisive if in $G \setminus \tau$ the component G' is split into ≥ 3 connected components.*

Consider a $K_{3,3}$ and let τ be the three vertices of one side and σ be the vertices of the other side. Then τ and σ are 3-divisive separating triples. If we remove σ then the remaining graph $K_{3,3} \setminus \sigma$ consists of three single vertices, namely τ. Each split component of σ is a K_4 which consists of the vertices of σ and one vertex of τ. Hence, τ is not a separating triple anymore in any of the split components of σ. We show next that the $K_{3,3}$ is an exception: if G is a K_5-free 3-connected graph different from $K_{3,3}$ and V_8, and τ and σ are two 3-divisive separating triples, then τ is still a 3-divisive separating triple in a split component of σ.

Definition 7.2.5 *Let G be an undirected and 3-connected graph. Two 3-divisive separating triples $\tau \neq \sigma$ are conflicting if one of them, say τ, is not a 3-divisive separating triple in a split component of σ.*

Lemma 7.2.6 *Let G be an undirected and 3-connected graph. There is a conflicting pair of 3-divisive separating triples in G if and only if G is the $K_{3,3}$.*

Proof. Let $\tau = \{v_1, v_2, v_3\}$ and $\sigma = \{v'_1, v'_2, v'_3\}$ be two 3-divisive separating triples in G. The proof is based on the following claims.

Claim 7.2.7 *If all vertices of $\sigma \setminus \tau$ are contained in one split component of τ and vice versa (i.e. all vertices of $\tau \setminus \sigma$ are contained in one split component of σ) then τ and σ are not conflicting.*

This claim is clearly true because by the assumption, σ will be in one split component of τ, and conversely τ will be in one split component of σ. See also Figure 7.3 and Figure 7.4 (a). G_1, G_2, G_3 indicate split components of τ and G'_1, G'_2, G'_3 of σ. The split components G_i are

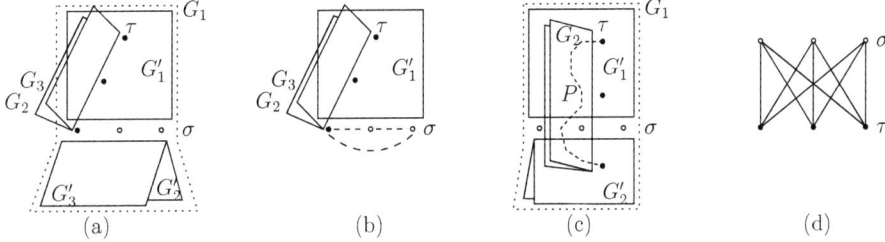

Figure 7.3: (a) Two 3-divisive separating triples σ (shown as circles) and τ (shown as filled circles) which have one vertex in common, and their split components G'_1, G'_2, G'_3 and G_1, G_2, G_3, respectively.
(b) The split component of σ where G'_2 and G'_3 are replaced by virtual edges (indicated with dashed lines).
(c) The situation is shown where σ and τ seem to be conflicting. But this situation cannot occur: σ would not be a separating triple because of path P.
(d) In a $K_{3,3}$, the triples σ and τ are conflicting.

obtained by attaching a copy of τ where each pair of vertices of τ is connected by a virtual edge. The resulting component is 3-connected.

The next claim shows that we can weaken the assumption of Claim 7.2.7.

Claim 7.2.8 *If all vertices of $\sigma \setminus \tau$ are contained in one split component of τ (or vice versa) then τ and σ are not conflicting.*

Proof. If all vertices of σ are contained in split component G_1 of τ, then there is another split component of τ, say G_2, that does not contain any vertices of $\sigma \setminus \tau$. Therefore G_2 is contained in one split component of σ, and τ is in the same split component of σ as G_2. In particular, τ must be in one split component of σ. Now the claim follows from Claim 7.2.7. □

From the proof of Claim 7.2.8 we deduce:

Claim 7.2.9 *If there is a split component of τ that contains no vertices of $\sigma \setminus \tau$ (or vice versa) then τ and σ are not conflicting.*

The assumption of Claim 7.2.9 is fulfilled in the following cases:

- τ or σ has ≥ 4 split components,
- there is a split component of σ that contains ≥ 2 vertices of τ (or vice versa), or
- $\tau \cap \sigma \neq \emptyset$.

7. K_5-MINOR FREE GI

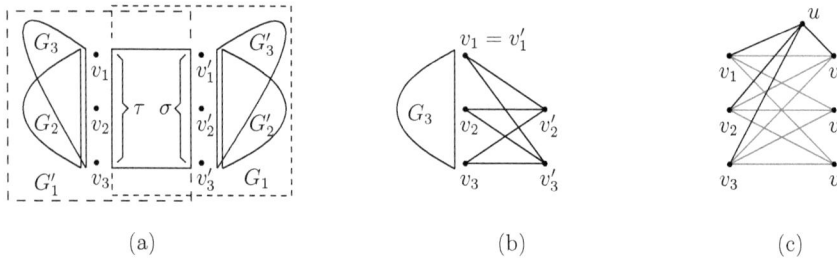

(a) (b) (c)

Figure 7.4: (a) The 3-divisive separating triples τ, σ are shown schematically, as well as the split components G_i of τ and the G'_i of σ, indicated by dashed and solid shapes.
(b) Separating triples τ, σ share the vertex $v_1 = v'_1$ and are pairwise connected.
(c) The split component G_1 of τ collapsed to one vertex u, except vertex v'_1.

The first two items are obvious. For the last item note that if τ and σ have a vertex in common, then the ≤ 2 vertices of $\sigma \setminus \tau$ cannot be in all split components of τ, for an example see Figure 7.4(b).

Hence the only case that remains where τ and σ might be conflicting is when τ and σ are disjoint, τ has precisely 3 split components and each component contains a vertex of σ, and vice versa. Consider this case.

If all the split components of τ and σ are K_4's then G must be a $K_{3,3}$ and τ and σ are conflicting. Hence we consider the case that there is a split component that is not a K_4, say component G_1 of τ. Component G_1 has ≥ 5 vertices: the 3 vertices of τ, a vertex of σ, say v'_1, and at least one more vertex, say u, because G_1 is not a K_4 (w.l.o.g. we can assume, that all the remaining vertices are collapsed to u, also see Figure 7.4(c)). Because G_1 is 3-connected, there are paths from u to at least two vertices of τ that do not go through v'_1. Therefore u and these vertices from τ will be in one split component of σ in G. Hence, because σ is 3-divisive, there is at least one split component which does not contain vertices from τ. By Claim 7.2.9 τ and σ are not conflicting. This finishes the proof of Lemma 7.2.6. $\square$

The Four-Connected Component Tree. If we fix one 3-divisive separating triple as root then we get a unique decomposition for G up to isomorphism, even if G is the $K_{3,3}$. Hence, a logspace transducer cycles then through all possible triples τ of G and counts the number of split components in $G \setminus \tau$. If this number is ≥ 3 then τ is a 3-divisive separating triple.

We decompose the given graph G at 3-divisive separating triples and obtain split components which are free of 3-divisive separating triples. We denote such components as *four-connected*.

Two vertices u, v belong to a *four-connected component* if for all 3-divisive separating triples τ

the following is true:

- at least one of u, v belongs to τ or
- there is a path from u to v in $G \setminus \tau$.

Note, a four-connected component is planar and 3-connected. We define a graph on these components and 3-divisive separating triples.

We define nodes for the four-connected components and 3-divisive separating triples. A *four-connected component node* is connected to a *3-divisive separating triple node* τ if the vertices of τ are also contained in the corresponding four-connected component. The resulting graph is a tree, the *four-connected component tree* $T^F(G)$. For an example see Figure 7.5. The node τ is adjacent to ≥ 3 four-connected component nodes. There is a 3-bond connected to τ_2, because the edge $\{w_2, w_3\}$ is present in T_2.

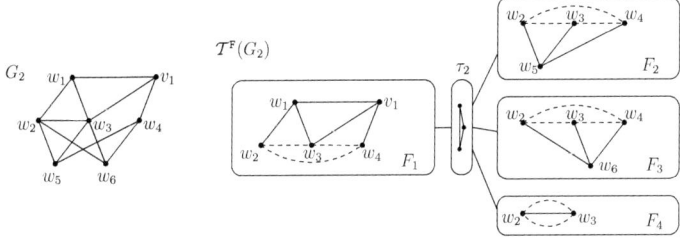

Figure 7.5: The decomposition of G_2 into four-connected components $F_1, \ldots, F_4$ is shown, together with the four-connected component tree $T^F(G_2)$. The edges with both ends in the 3-divisive separating triple $\tau_2 = \{w_2, w_3, w_4\}$ are virtual edges indicated by dashed lines. There is a 3-bond connected to τ_2, because the edge $\{w_2, w_3\}$ is present in G_2.

A unique decomposition of G into four-connected components can be computed in logspace with similar arguments as used in the proof of Lemma 2.2.1 and Lemma 2.2.2. The computation of the 3-divisive separating triples and the four-connected components can be queried to the reachability problem in undirected graphs which is in logspace [Rei08].

Theorem 7.2.10 *A unique decomposition of a 3-connected non-planar K_5-free graph (not the V_8) into four-connected components can be computed in logspace.*

The Triconnected Component Tree of K_5-Free Graphs Datta et. al. [DLN+09] gave a unique decomposition of planar graphs into biconnected and these further into triconnected

7. K_5-MINOR FREE GI

components witch can be computed in logspace. Thierauf and Wagner proved that such decompositions can also be computed for K_5-free graphs in logspace. We also refer to Lemma 2.2.2.

Lemma 7.2.11 *[TW09] The triconnected component tree for a K_5-free biconnected graph can be computed in logspace.*

7.3 Isomorphism Order of K_5-Minor Free Graphs

The difference to the planar case comes with the non-planar triconnected components. Therefore we mainly show how to compute an isomorphism order for these components. We start with an overview of the isomorphism order algorithm.

7.3.1 Isomorphism Order of K_5-Minor Free 3-Connected Graphs

Overview of the Isomorphism Order Algorithm

We extend the isomorphism order for planar graphs in [DLN+09]. We define a total order $<_T$ on triconnected component trees $S_{\{a,b\}}$ and $T_{\{a',b'\}}$ (also see Lemma 7.2.11) which are rooted at separating pairs $s = \{a,b\}$ and $t = \{a',b'\}$. We define $S_{\{a,b\}} <_T T_{\{a',b'\}}$ if one of the following holds:

1. $\mathsf{size}(S_{\{a,b\}}) < \mathsf{size}(T_{\{a',b'\}})$ or

2. $\mathsf{size}(S_{\{a,b\}}) = \mathsf{size}(T_{\{a',b'\}})$ but $\#s < \#t$ or

3. $\mathsf{size}(S_{\{a,b\}}) = \mathsf{size}(T_{\{a',b'\}})$, $\#s = \#t = k$, but $(S_{G_1},\ldots,S_{G_k}) < (T_{H_1},\ldots,T_{H_k})$ lexicographically (with respect to $<_T$), where we assume that $S_{G_1} \leq_T \cdots \leq_T S_{G_k}$ and $T_{H_1} \leq_T \cdots \leq_T T_{H_k}$ are the ordered subtrees of $S_{\{a,b\}}$ and $T_{\{a',b'\}}$, respectively. For the isomorphism order between the subtrees S_{G_i} and T_{H_i} we compare the types of the nodes first and then we compare lexicographically the codes of G_i and H_i and *recursively* the subtrees rooted at the children of G_i and H_i. Note that these children are again separating pair nodes.

4. $\mathsf{size}(S_{\{a,b\}}) = \mathsf{size}(T_{\{a',b'\}})$, $\#s = \#t = k$, $(S_{G_1},\ldots,S_{G_k}) = (T_{H_1},\ldots,T_{H_k})$ lexicographically (with respect to $<_T$), but $(O_1,\ldots,O_p) < (O'_1,\ldots,O'_p)$ lexicographically, where O_j and O'_j are the orientation counters of the jth isomorphism classes I_j and I'_j of all the S_{G_i}'s and the T_{H_i}'s.

For the notion of orientation counters see Section 6.2.1. They define a direction for the edge $\{a,b\}$ for each isomorphism class. The orientation counters compute how often the edge $\{a,b\}$ is traversed in direction (a,b) resp. (b,a) in each isomorphism class. We adapt the notion also for the non-planar components. This is straight forward in the case of V_8-components. The other non-planar 3-connected components are further decomposed into four-connected component trees. In the minimum codes for these trees we take the direction of the first occurrence of $\{a, b\}$ in these codes for the orientation counters.

We say that two triconnected component trees S_e and $T_{e'}$ are *equal according to the isomorphism order*, denoted by $S_e =_T T_{e'}$, if neither $S_e <_T T_{e'}$ nor $T_{e'} <_T S_e$ holds.

In Step 3, the types of components are distinguished: planar triconnected components $<_T$ V_8-components $<_T$ non-planar 3-connected components. For the isomorphism order of subtrees rooted at planar triconnected components we refer to Section 6.2.1. In the following we refine the isomorphism order for the new types of non-planar components.

Isomorphism Order of Subtrees Rooted at V_8-Components

Consider the subtree S_{G_i} rooted at a V_8-component node G_i. The isomorphism order algorithm makes comparisons with T_{H_j} rooted at H_j, accordingly.

To canonize G_i with the parent separating pair $\{a, b\}$, we could proceed as in the case of a K_5 on Page 96: there are $2 \cdot 6!$ way of labelling the vertices of G_i when one of (a, b) or (b, a) is fixed. Because this is a constant, we can try all of them. We obtain the codes by arranging the edges in lexicographical order, according to the new vertex names. The minimum code gives the isomorphism order. If the minimum code occurs in G_i and H_j then they are found to be equal. In the rest of this subsection we take a closer look and show that we can do even better: we have to check at most four possibilities.

To rename the vertices, we use a Hamiltonian cycle in G_i starting at the parent separating pair $\{a, b\}$ of G_i. We rename the vertices in the order of their first occurrence on the Hamiltonian cycle. The code then starts with one of (a, b) or (b, a). It is defined as the list of all edges of G_i in lexicographical order with the new names.

The V_8 has 5 *undirected* Hamiltonian cycles (each corresponding to two directed Hamiltonian cycles). Consider the V_8 in Figure 7.6. Let $E' = \{\{v_1, v_5\}, \{v_2, v_6\}, \{v_3, v_7\}, \{v_4, v_8\}\}$. The edges in E' are contained in two simple cycles of length 4, whereas all the other edges are in only 1 such cycle.

- There is one Hamiltonian cycle which contains no edge from E':

$$C_0 = (v_1, v_2, v_3, v_4, v_5, v_6, v_7, v_8).$$

7. K_5-MINOR FREE GI

- There are 4 Hamiltonian cycles which have two edges from E':

$$C_2[\{v_2, v_6\}, \{v_3, v_7\}] = (v_1, v_2, v_6, v_5, v_4, v_3, v_7, v_8),$$
$$C_2[\{v_3, v_7\}, \{v_4, v_8\}] = (v_1, v_2, v_3, v_7, v_6, v_5, v_4, v_8),$$
$$C_2[\{v_4, v_8\}, \{v_5, v_1\}] = (v_1, v_2, v_3, v_4, v_8, v_7, v_6, v_5),$$
$$C_2[\{v_1, v_5\}, \{v_2, v_6\}] = (v_1, v_5, v_4, v_3, v_2, v_6, v_7, v_8).$$

- There are no further Hamiltonian cycles.

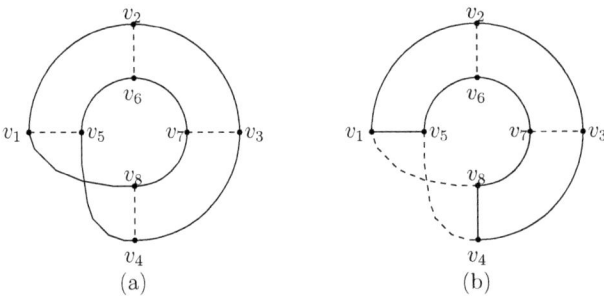

Figure 7.6: (a) A V_8 component where solid edges indicate the Hamiltonian cycle C_0.
(b) A V_8 component where solid edges indicate the Hamiltonian cycle $C_2[\{v_1, v_5\}, \{v_4, v_8\}]$.

We distinguish the situation whether $\{a, b\} \in E'$ or not.

- **Case $\{a, b\} \notin E'$:** We use cycle C_0 to define the codes. We get two codes, one for each direction of $\{a, b\}$ we start with. For example, let $\{a, b\} = \{v_1, v_2\}$ and consider direction (v_1, v_2). Then the new names for the vertices are

vertex	v_1	v_2	v_3	v_4	v_5	v_6	v_7	v_8
new name	1	2	3	4	5	6	7	8

The code is the enumeration of all edges in lexicographic order:
($\{1,2\}$, $\{1,5\}$, $\{1,8\}$, $\{2,3\}$, $\{2,6\}$, $\{3,4\}$, $\{3,7\}$, $\{4,5\}$, $\{4,8\}$, $\{5,6\}$, $\{6,7\}$, $\{7,8\}$).

- **Case $\{a, b\} \in E'$:** Observe that each edge of E' occurs in exactly 2 of the 4 Hamiltonian cycles. Since we have two directions for each cycle, we get 4 codes. The direction of $\{a, b\}$ together with the subsequent edge determines exactly one Hamiltonian cycle. For example, let $\{a,b\} = \{v_1, v_5\}$ and consider the direction (v_1, v_5). Now we have two choices to proceed. If we choose (v_5, v_6) this determines the cycle $C_2[\{v_4, v_8\}, \{v_5, v_1\}]$ and we get the following new names for the vertices:

vertex	v_1	v_5	v_6	v_7	v_8	v_4	v_3	v_2
new name	1	2	3	4	5	6	7	8

The code we obtain is ($\{1,2\}$, $\{1,5\}$, $\{1,8\}$, $\{2,3\}$, $\{2,6\}$, $\{3,4\}$, $\{3,8\}$, $\{4,5\}$, $\{4,7\}$, $\{5,6\}$, $\{6,7\}$, $\{7,8\}$).

Isomorphism Order of the 3-Connected No-Planar Components $\neq V_8$

Let S_{G_i} and T_{H_j} be two triconnected component trees rooted at 3-connected non-planar component nodes G_i and H_j which are different to the V_8. Let $s = \{a,b\}$ and $t = \{a', b'\}$ be the parent separating pairs of G_i and H_j. The isomorphism order algorithm computes the isomorphism order between G_i and H_j and returns an orientation of the parent separating pairs s and t as described after the overview on Page 128.

We partition G_i and H_j into their four-connected component trees $T^F(G_i)$ and $T^F(H_j)$. The isomorphism order algorithm invokes other algorithms as subroutines which we describe below. One algorithm computes a sufficiently small set of candidates for the root separating triples. Another algorithm handles the situations when we go into recursion at biconnected and triconnected subtrees. This is crucial in particular for large children with respect to the different kinds of subtrees.

In summary, we have two possible orientations of the parent separating pair, we have a sufficiently small number of root separating triples and for each root 6! possibilities to arrange the six directed edges of it. Hence, the number of tests depends up to a constant factor on the number of root separating triples. These tests are done via cross comparisons. The choice that leads to the minimum code is used for the isomorphism order.

We give an overview of the differences between the isomorphism order on tri-connected and four-connected component trees. Then we start with the main algorithm, the isomorphism order algorithm on four-connected component trees.

Differences to the Isomorphism Order of Planar Graphs. We summarize the differences to the isomorphism order algorithm for triconnected component trees in Section 7.3.1 (see also [DLN+09]). Figure 7.7 shows two trees to be compared.

- Instead of separating pairs we have 3-divisive separating triples. Therefore, we have to generalize the notion of orientations.

7. K_5-MINOR FREE GI

Remark 7.3.1 *In the isomorphism order algorithm for two triconnected component trees, an orientation of a separating pair $\{a,b\}$ is computed, c.f. Page 6.2.1. The orientation is one of (a,b) or (b,a) or no orientation is given from a child component, also called the* symmetric case. *An orientation can be seen as an automorphism from $T_{\{a,b\}}$ onto the tree-canon of $T_{\{a,b\}}$, keeping the pair $\{a,b\}$ blockwise fixed. Observe, the three mentioned possibilities describe a set of partial automorphisms restricted to the pair $\{a,b\}$ in $T_{\{a,b\}}$. Each partial automorphism can be extended to an automorphism ϕ which brings $T_{\{a,b\}}$ to its tree-canon. We say, ϕ computes a* canonical form *for $T_{\{a,b\}}$. Let A be this set, it forms a coset, i.e. a group where each element is multiplied with a permutation. We give examples, where we use the cycle notation for permutations.*
(a,b)-*orientation:* $A = \{id\}$, *the coset is* $\langle id \rangle \circ id$,
reverse orientation: $A = \{(a,b)\}$, *the coset is* $\langle id \rangle \circ (a,b)$,
symmetric case: $A = \{id, (a,b)\}$, *the coset is* $Sym(\{a,b\}) \circ id$.

For a four-connected component tree S_τ with $\tau = \{a,b,c\}$, we describe now the analogon of orientations: *Accordingly, we have a set of partial automorphisms, each mapping $\{a,b,c\}$ onto $\{a,b,c\}$ which can be extended to an automorphism which computes a canonical form for S_τ. Let A be this set, it forms a coset. The analogon of the* symmetric case *is different here. We give some examples:*
$A = \{(a,b,c)\}$, *the coset is* $\langle id \rangle \circ (a,b,c)$.
$A = \{id, (a,b,c), (a,c,b)\}$, *the coset is* $\langle (a,b,c) \rangle \circ id$.
$A = \{id, (a,b)\}$, *the coset is* $Sym(\{a,b\}) \circ id$, *here c is pointwise fixed.*
$A = \{(a,b), (a,b,c)\}$, *the coset is the group* $Sym(\{b,c\}) \circ (a,b)$.
The analogon to the symmetric case here is, to consider all the cosets where A has more than one element.

- Instead of 3-connected planar components we have four-connected planar components in S_τ and $T_{\tau'}$. We can canonize these components with the canonization algorithm for 3-connected planar components from [DLN08].

Overview of the Isomorphism Order Algorithm

We define a total order $<_F$ on four-connected component trees S_τ and $T_{\tau'}$ which are rooted at 3-divisive separating triples τ and τ'. We define $S_\tau \leq_F T_{\tau'}$ if one of the following holds:

1. $\mathsf{size}(S_\tau) < \mathsf{size}(T_{\tau'})$ or

2. $\mathsf{size}(S_\tau) = \mathsf{size}(T_{\tau'})$, but $\#\tau < \#\tau'$ or

3. $\mathsf{size}(S_\tau) = \mathsf{size}(T_{\tau'})$, $\#\tau = \#\tau' = k$, but $(S_{F_1}, \ldots, S_{F_k}) < (T_{F_1'}, \ldots, T_{F_k'})$ lexicographically (with respect to $<_F$), where we assume that $S_{F_1} \leq_F \cdots \leq_F S_{F_k}$ and $T_{F_1'} \leq_F \cdots \leq_F T_{F_k'}$ are the ordered subtrees of S_τ and $T_{\tau'}$, respectively. For the isomorphism order between the subtrees S_{F_i} and $T_{F_i'}$ we compare lexicographically the codes of F_i and F_i' and *recursively* the subtrees rooted at the children of F_i and F_i'. These children are again separating triple nodes, say τ_j and τ_j', and the comparison is done together with an induced order on their edges: i.e. we compare S_{τ_j} with $T_{\tau_j'}$ and check whether τ_j is mapped onto τ_j' properly. This induced order comes from the arrangement of the virtual edges in the codes of F_i and F_i' which are compared currently. We describe this in more detail below (see Steps $(i), (ii)$ and (iii) on Page 134).

4. $\mathsf{size}(S_\tau) = \mathsf{size}(T_{\tau'})$, $\#\tau = \#\tau' = k$, $(S_{F_1}, \ldots, S_{F_k}) = (T_{F_1'}, \ldots, T_{F_k'})$ lexicographically (with respect to $<_F$), but $\mathsf{reforient}(\tau) < \mathsf{reforient}(\tau')$, where $\mathsf{reforient}(\tau)$ is the *reference orientation of* τ which is defined below on Page 136.

The reference orientation of a separating triple τ is a sequence of counters which consider each of the 6 directed edges that connect the vertices of τ. This is an extension of the orientation counters for separating pairs.

We say that two four-connected component trees S_τ and $T_{\tau'}$ are *equal according to the isomorphism order*, denoted by $S_\tau =_F T_{\tau'}$, if neither $S_\tau <_F T_{\tau'}$ nor $T_{\tau'} <_F S_\tau$ holds.

We define the isomorphism order on four-connected component trees and distinguish the cases when the trees are rooted at four-connected component nodes or separating triple nodes.

Isomorphism Order of two Subtrees Rooted at Four-Connected Component Nodes

We consider the isomorphism order of two subtrees S_{F_1} and $T_{F_1'}$ rooted at four-connected component nodes F_1 and F_1', respectively, see Figure 7.7. To canonize a four-connected component F_1, we use the logspace algorithm from [DLN08]. Besides F_1, the algorithm gets as input a starting edge and a combinatorial embedding ρ of F_1. Let $\tau = \{a, b, c\}$ be the parent 3-divisive separating triple of F_1. There are three choices of selecting a starting edge, namely $\{a, b\}$, $\{b, c\}$, or $\{a, c\}$. Then there are two choices for the direction of each edge. Further, a 3-connected planar graph has two planar combinatorial embeddings [Whi33]. Hence, there are 12 possible ways to canonize F_1.

7. K_5-MINOR FREE GI

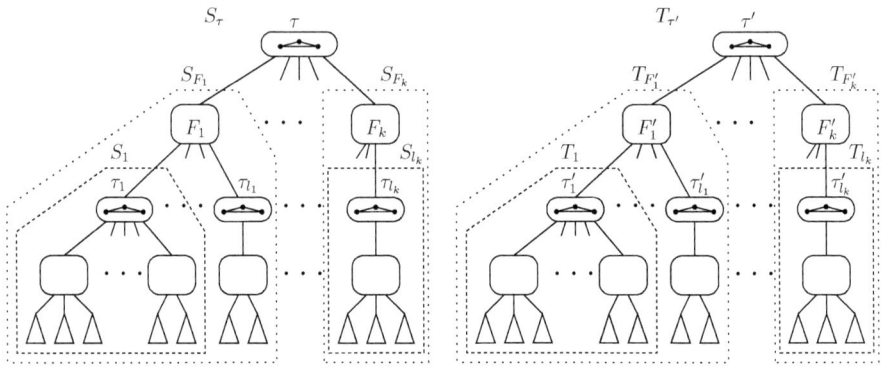

Figure 7.7: The four-connected component trees.

Let C and C' be two codes of F_1 and F_1', respectively, to be compared. The base case is that F_1 and F_1' are leaf nodes and therefore contain no further virtual edges. In this case we use the lexicographic order between C and C'.

Assume now, F_1 and F_1' contain further virtual edges. The vertices of virtual edges belong to a child separating triple. These edges are specially treated in the bitwise comparison of C and C':

(i) If a virtual edge is traversed in the construction of one of the codes C or C' but not in the other, then we define the one without the virtual edge to be the smaller code.

(ii) If C and C' encounter all virtual edges at the same positions then we do the following. We order the child separating triples according to the positions of their virtual edges in the codes. Since a virtual edge of a separating triple τ might occur several times, we consider only the position of its first occurrence. This order is called the *edge position order of τ with respect to C*, denoted by edge-pos$_C(\tau)$. That is, edge-pos$_C(\tau)$ consists of the positions of the 6 directed virtual edges between the vertices of τ in the code C. We compare two such edge position orders lexicographically.

We sort the separating triples for C and C' according to their edge position order. Let edge-pos$_C(\tau_1) < \cdots <$ edge-pos$_C(\tau_{l_1})$ be all the separating triples of C and edge-pos$_{C'}(\tau_1') < \cdots <$ edge-pos$_{C'}(\tau_{l_1}')$ those of C'. Then we compare (edge-pos$_C(\tau_1), \ldots,$ edge-pos$_C(\tau_{l_1})$) and (edge-pos$_{C'}(\tau_1'), \ldots,$ edge-pos$_{C'}(\tau_{l_1}')$). If they are not equal, then their lexicographic order defines the order of C and C'.

(iii) If in the comparison of the code C with the code C' we find that
(edge-pos$_C(\tau_1), \ldots,$ edge-pos$_C(\tau_{l_1})$) = (edge-pos$_{C'}(\tau_1'), \ldots,$ edge-pos$_{C'}(\tau_{l_1}')$), then we go

into recursion and compare the corresponding subtrees rooted at the child separating triples. That is, we compare $(S_{\tau_1}, \ldots, S_{\tau_{l_1}})$ with $(T_{\tau'_1}, \ldots, T_{\tau'_{l_1}})$. If we encounter an inequality the first time, then this defines the order of C and C'.

We eliminate the codes which were found to be the larger codes in at least one of the comparisons. In the end, the codes that are not eliminated are the *minimum codes*. In general, if we have the same minimum code for both F_i and F'_j then we define $S_{F_i} =_{\mathsf{F}} T_{F'_j}$. The construction of the codes also defines an isomorphism between the subgraphs associated to S_{F_i} and $T_{F'_j}$, i.e. graph(S_{F_i}) $\cong$ graph($T_{F'_j}$). For a single four-connected component this follows from [DLN08]. If the trees contain several components, then our definition of $S_{F_i} =_{\mathsf{F}} T_{F'_j}$ guarantees that we can combine the isomorphisms of the components to an isomorphism between graph(S_{F_i}) and graph($T_{F'_j}$).

Definition 7.3.2 *The orientation given to the parent separating triple τ of F_i is an* orientation graph X_i, *a complete graph with vertices* $V(X_i) = \tau$. *Accordingly, we define X'_j for τ' and F'_j. The 6 directed edges of X_i get colors as follows: we take each of the edges as starting edge for the isomorphism order on S_{F_i} and $T_{F'_j}$. This is done via cross comparisons, i.e. the isomorphism order starts with the edges in X_i and the corresponding edges in the orientation graph X'_j of $T_{F'_j}$. That is, we start with comparing and sorting the 6 codes in F_i and F'_j. If the edge e as root leads to the r-th smallest code for some $1 \leq r \leq 6$, then e gets color r. Note that edges which lead to the same code will have the same color.*

Every subtree rooted at a four-connected component node gives an orientation graph to the parent separating triple. If the orientation is consistent, then we define $S_\tau =_{\mathsf{F}} T_{\tau'}$ and we will show that the corresponding graphs are isomorphic in this case.

For a single child subtree F_i of S_τ and F'_i of $T_{\tau'}$ this is true: an isomorphism ϕ that maps τ onto τ' can be extended to the whole of F_i which is mapped onto F'_i if and only if ϕ maps a directed edge e in τ onto an edge e' in τ' such that the code of F_i starting with e is the same as the code of F'_i starting with e'. When comparing the codes then we go into recursion at child separating triples (say τ_{i_0} of F_i and τ'_{j_0} of F'_j). This means that we also check whether ϕ can be extended to the corresponding subgraphs graph($S_{\tau_{i_0}}$) and graph($T_{\tau'_{j_0}}$). By induction we know whether graph($S_{\tau_{i_0}}$) $\cong$ graph($T_{\tau'_{j_0}}$) such that τ_{i_0} is mapped onto τ'_{j_0}. By induction hypothesis, the reference orientation tells us all such possibilities to map τ_{i_0} onto τ'_{j_0}.

We consider next the situation where τ and τ' have more than one subtree.

Isomorphism Order of Subtrees Rooted at Separating Triple Nodes

Let τ and τ' be the roots of S_τ and $T_{\tau'}$ with the subtrees $S_{F_1}, \ldots, S_{F_k}$ and $T_{F'_1}, \ldots, T_{F'_k}$. We partition the subtrees into isomorphism classes. The isomorphism order involves the comparison of the *orientations* given by the corresponding isomorphism classes defined as follows:

7. K_5-MINOR FREE GI

We first order the subtrees, say $S_{F_1} \leq_\mathsf{F} \cdots \leq_\mathsf{F} S_{F_k}$ and $T_{F_1'} \leq_\mathsf{F} \cdots \leq_\mathsf{F} T_{F_k'}$, and verify that $S_{F_i} =_\mathsf{F} T_{F_i'}$ for all i. If we find an inequality then the one at the smallest index i defines the isomorphism order between S_τ and $T_{\tau'}$. Now assume that $S_{F_i} =_\mathsf{F} T_{F_i'}$ for all i. Inductively, the corresponding split components are isomorphic, i.e. $\mathsf{graph}(S_{F_i}) \cong \mathsf{graph}(T_{F_i'})$ for all i.

The next comparison concerns the orientation of τ and τ'. Assume that S_τ and $T_{\tau'}$ are not large children of their parent nodes. The case of large children is treated separately below.

We already explained above the orientation graph X_i for τ defined by each of the S_{F_i}'s. We define a reference orientation for τ from all these orientations as a sequence of counters as follows: we partition $(S_{F_1}, \ldots, S_{F_k})$ into classes of isomorphic subtrees, say $I_1, \ldots, I_p$ for some $p \leq k$ and where the classes are ordered according to $<_\mathsf{F}$. For each directed edge e in τ, each isomorphism class I_j and each color r we define a counter $c_{e,j,r}$ as the number of times that e has color r in an orientation graph in the class I_j:

$$c_{e,j,r} = |\{i \mid e \text{ has color } r \text{ in } X_i, \text{ for } S_{F_i} \in I_j\}|.$$

The *reference orientation of* τ is defined as the sequence of all these counters in a fixed order. To define this order, we have to define an order $(e_1, \ldots, e_6)$ on the edges of τ.

(i) If τ is not the root of the overall tree, then τ has a parent component with a current code C. We enumerate the edges of τ according to the edge position order $\mathsf{edge\text{-}pos}_C(\tau)$.

(ii) If τ is the root of the overall tree $\mathcal{T}^\mathsf{F}(G_i)$, then we have a current order of the vertices of τ, because the algorithm that compares two such trees cycles through all permutations of the vertices of τ as possible orders of these vertices. Any order of the vertices of τ induces a lexicographical order on the edges of τ. For example for $\tau = \{a, b, c\}$, the order $a < b < c$ induces the lexicographic enumeration of the edges $(e_1, \ldots, e_6) = ((a, b), (a, c), (b, a), (b, c), (c, a), (c, b))$.

Now the reference orientation of τ is defined as

$$\mathsf{reforient}(\tau) = (c_{e_i, j, r})_{i=1,\ldots,6,\ j=1,\ldots,p,\ r=1,\ldots,6}.$$

Let $\mathsf{reforient}(\tau')$ be the corresponding reference orientation of τ'. Clearly, for isomorphic graphs, τ and τ' must have the same reference orientation.

We argue that the counters of S_τ are equal to the counters of $T_{\tau'}$ if and only if the underlying graphs are isomorphic, i.e. $\mathsf{graph}(S_\tau) \cong \mathsf{graph}(T_{\tau'})$. That is, we are interested in an isomorphism which maps τ onto τ'. We already showed that this is the case if we have one child of τ and τ'. First, the counters $c_{e,j,r}$ distinguish between subtrees of different isomorphism classes. Second, since the isomorphism classes already are of the same cardinality, it is possible that F_i is isomorphic to F_i' but up to a certain mapping of τ onto τ'. Hence, an isomorphism that maps F_i onto F'_i guarantees to map all directed edges of τ onto directed edges of τ' which have the same color. When combining both arguments, counting the edges of the same color gives information about how many isomorphic subtrees can be mapped onto each other such that they induce an isomorphism.

Large Children. In the case that τ is a large child of its parent node F_0, we go into recursion at τ *a priori*, i.e. before computing a code C for F_0. Note that the definition of the reference orientation of τ relies on C. Hence we have to deviate from the algorithm described above in this case.

Another point is, that we want to store the result of the recursion of a large child in $O(1)$ bits. However, the reference orientation cannot be stored within $O(1)$ bits. We solve these issues as follows.

Let $\tau = \{a, b, c\}$. We cycle though all the orders of the vertices of τ, and consider reforient(τ) for all induced lexicographical orders on the edges of τ. Let M be the set of those orders of τ, where reforient(τ) becomes minimal. The set M has size $O(1)$ and is stored on the work tape when we return from the recursion of the large child.

Then we start computing the codes of the parent node F_0, where we try all orders in M for τ. The minimum ones are used for the definition of the isomorphism order.

We summarize the correctness of the isomorphism order.

Theorem 7.3.3 *Let G and H be 3-connected non-planar graphs which contain 3-divisive separating triples. Then $G \cong H \iff S_\tau =_\mathsf{F} T_{\tau'}$ for some separating triples τ in G and τ' in H.*

Proof. The direction from left to right is clearly true. So let $S_\tau =_\mathsf{F} T_{\tau'}$. The argument is an induction on the depth of the trees which follows the inductive definition of the isomorphism order.

We already considered the case for trees of depth ≤ 1. For trees of depth $d > 1$ we consider first the subtrees rooted at four-connected component nodes at depth 1, say F_i and F'_j. The comparison states equality if the components have the same canon, i.e. are isomorphic. Let τ_0 and τ'_0 be children of F_i and F'_j. Let S_{τ_0} and $T_{\tau'_0}$ be the corresponding subtrees. By the induction hypothesis we know that graph(S_{τ_0}) is isomorphic to graph($T_{\tau'_0}$). For each such isomorphism consider the mapping ϕ of τ_0 to τ'_0. If we can find a code for F_i and one for F'_j such that virtual edges of τ_0 and τ'_0 appear at the same places in the canons (in such a way that ϕ describes the mapping which brings the order of edges from τ_0 into the order of edges from τ'_0), then ϕ can be extended to an isomorphism of F_i to F'_j. The $=_\mathsf{F}$-equality between child separating triples (together with their subtrees) inductively describes an isomorphism between the corresponding subgraphs. In the preceding discussion we argued how ϕ can be extended to an isomorphism of

7. K_5-MINOR FREE GI

graph(S_τ) onto graph($T_{\tau'}$). This is done with the help of the counters which form the reference orientation of τ and τ'. We argued that the counters are equal exactly if the corresponding subgraphs (rooted at the children of τ and τ') are isomorphic.

Finally, we consider the whole trees rooted at separating triple nodes. The comparison describes an order on the subtrees which corresponds to the split components of the separating triples. The order describes an isomorphism among the split components.

Hence, the isomorphism between the children at any level can be extended to an isomorphism between the corresponding subgraphs in G and H and therefore to G and H itself. □

7.3.2 Limiting the Number of Choices for the Roots of the Component Trees

The isomorphism order algorithm explores for a K_5-free graph G the biconnected, triconnected and four-connected component trees. There are usually several candidates for the root of these trees. In order to maintain the logspace bound, we cannot afford to cycle through all of them in case we have to go into recursion on more than one subtree. We describe how the algorithm chooses a small set of root candidates if necessary. We consider first the case of triconnected component trees and then the four-connected component trees.

As we will see below, the sub-routine to choose a small set of roots makes itself calls to the isomorphism test in some cases. This is similar to the case of a large child, where we deviate from the main algorithm and explore the large child a priori. Here we also have in some cases a single child to be explored and deviate to an isomorphism test for it. When we return, we store the result and continue with the root finding procedure.

Limiting the Number of Choices for the Root of a Triconnected Component Tree

We extend the algorithm of Datta et.al. [DLN+09] where they showed for given planar graphs that the number of possible choices for the root of a triconnected component tree can be bounded by a sufficiently small number of separating pair nodes.

Let G be a K_5-free graph. An easy case is when G has no articulation points, i.e. G is 2-connected. Then the isomorphism order algorithm runs through all possibilities of separating pairs $\{a, b\}$ as root and explores $S_{\{a,b\}}$, the triconnected component tree rooted at $\{a, b\}$. If there is no separating pair in G, then G is even triconnected. If G is additionally planar then we are done, because isomorphism testing is in logspace [DLN08]. If G is not planar, it can be the V_8. In this case G is of constant size and isomorphism testing requires constant effort. Otherwise G contains 3-divisive separating triples. The isomorphism order algorithm runs through all possibilities of separating triples τ as roots and explores S_τ, the four-connected component tree rooted at τ.

The more interesting case is when G has articulation points. Then the isomorphism order algorithm runs through all articulation points as roots. Let S_a be a biconnected component tree of G rooted at articulation point a. Let B be a biconnected component which is a child of a in S_a. Let $\mathcal{T}^{\mathsf{T}}(B)$ be the triconnected component tree of B, see Figure 7.8.

We want to determine a small set of root candidates for $\mathcal{T}^{\mathsf{T}}(B)$. Let C_0 be the center of $\mathcal{T}^{\mathsf{T}}(B)$. If C_0 is a separating pair node then we take this pair as the unique root. If C_0 is a triconnected planar component node, then we can find roots in logspace due to Datta et.al. [DLN+09]. If C_0 is the V_8, then we can run through all edges as roots for $\mathcal{T}^{\mathsf{T}}(B)$, because there are only constantly many.

The interesting case is when C_0 is non-planar and contains 3-divisive separating triples. Then we consider $\mathcal{T}^{\mathsf{F}}(C_0)$, the four-connected component tree of C_0 and invoke the computation of the parent separating triples for C_0 which is described below. This algorithm either directly returns a small set of separating pairs as root candidates for $\mathcal{T}^{\mathsf{T}}(B)$, or a small set of separating triples as root candidates for $\mathcal{T}^{\mathsf{F}}(C_0)$, say k triples. We use each of the three edges which are part of a 3-divisive separating triple as a root candidate for $\mathcal{T}^{\mathsf{T}}(B)$. Note that an edge e of such a separating triple may not be a separating pair in $\mathcal{T}^{\mathsf{T}}(B)$, and hence may not be a node in $\mathcal{T}^{\mathsf{T}}(B)$, Therefore, we extend $\mathcal{T}^{\mathsf{T}}(B)$ in this case by a node for e and connect it with the component where its separating triple is contained. Now we take the new node as one of the root candidates. Hence, we get $\leq 3k$ root separating pairs. We will see, that this is good enough.

This means that we invoke the computation of the parent separating triples for C_0 *twice*: the first time to get roots for $\mathcal{T}^{\mathsf{T}}(B)$, and the second time when we actually compute roots for $\mathcal{T}^{\mathsf{F}}(C_0)$. The result can be different, because we start the second pass with a *rooted* tree $\mathcal{T}^{\mathsf{T}}(B)$ and hence C_0 will have a parent separating pair.

Limiting the Number of Choices for the Root of a Four-Connected Component Tree

Let G be a K_5-free graph, B a biconnected component of G with parent articulation point a. Let C a triconnected component in B and C_0 the center node in $\mathcal{T}^{\mathsf{T}}(B)$. We describe how to determine a small number of separating triples as root candidates for C. We may assume that C is non-planar, otherwise isomorphism testing is in logspace.

We cannot take all the separating triples as possible roots, because then we would need $O(\log n)$ bits on the work-tape to remember the current out of $O(n)$ possible roots. If we do this recursively then we end up in a polynomial amount of space on the work-tape.

If C is the $K_{3,3}$, then we have exactly two choices of selecting a root separating triple in the decomposition of C. Figure 7.8 shows an example. Because these two separating triples are conflicting, we obtain two trees which contain one separating triple node each.

It remains the case that C is non-planar and contains 3-divisive non-conflicting separating

7. K_5-MINOR FREE GI

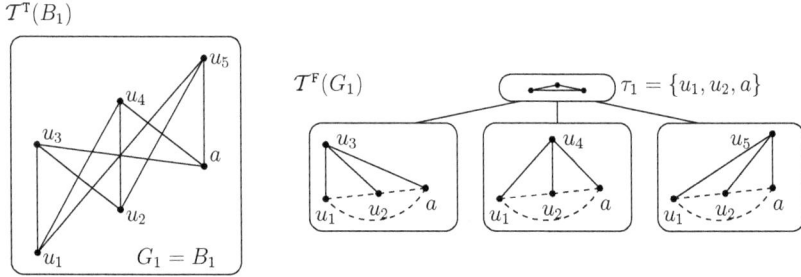

Figure 7.8: The biconnected component B_1 contains no separating pairs and is therefore trivially triconnected such that the corresponding triconnected component tree $\mathcal{T}^\mathsf{T}(B_1)$ contains only one node, i.e. $G_1 = B_1$. G_1 is further decomposed into four-connected components as illustrated by the four-connected component tree $\mathcal{T}^\mathsf{F}(G_1)$.

triples. We distinguish the cases whether there is a parent separating pair for C in B or not. If C has a parent separating pair we show that we can determine ≤ 4 separating triples as root candidates for $\mathcal{T}^\mathsf{F}(C)$. The case that C has no parent separating pair can occur in two situations:

- There is no separating pair in B. Then C is the single triconnected component in B.
- There are separating pairs in B and $C = C_0$, the center of $\mathcal{T}^\mathsf{T}(B)$.

C has a Parent Separating Pair. Let $\{a, b\}$ be the parent separating pair of C. We consider the four-connected component tree $\mathcal{T}^\mathsf{F}(C)$. Let D_0 be the center of $\mathcal{T}^\mathsf{F}(C)$. If D_0 is a separating triple node then we choose it as root and are done. Otherwise, D_0 corresponds to a four-connected planar component.

To each separating pair we can associate a unique component in $\mathcal{T}^\mathsf{F}(C)$.

Definition 7.3.4 *Let D be the node closest to the center D_0 in $\mathcal{T}^\mathsf{F}(C)$, whose associated four-connected component or separating triple contains the edge $\{a, b\}$. We define $\{a, b\}$ to be associated with D.*

To define the root candidates, we distinguish two cases:

1. $\{a, b\} \notin D_0$. Let $\{a, b\}$ be associated with D. We choose the separating triple as root that is nearest to D_0 on the unique simple path between D_0 and D.

2. $\{a, b\} \in D_0$. We canonize D_0 with $\{a, b\}$ as the starting edge. This gives four codes. In the smallest code among these, choose the separating triple in D_0 which gets the lexicographically smallest label. Thus, we have at most four choices for the root.

C **has no Parent Separating Pair.** We start with some definitions. We associate each articulation point in B to a unique component in $\mathcal{T}^\mathsf{T}(B)$ (unique with respect to C). The nodes of $\mathcal{T}^\mathsf{T}(B)$ which contain an articulation point a form a subtree of $\mathcal{T}^\mathsf{T}(B)$. Therefore there is a unique node in this subtree which is closest to C. We associate a to this node.

Definition 7.3.5 *Let C' be the node in $\mathcal{T}^\mathsf{T}(B)$ which contains a and is closest to C in $\mathcal{T}^\mathsf{T}(B)$. We define a to be* associated with C'.

We define colors for child articulation points which occur in the biconnected component B and for the adjacent separating pairs of C in $\mathcal{T}^\mathsf{T}(B)$. Let a be the parent articulation point of B.

- Let $a_1, \ldots, a_l$ be the child articulation points of C in $\mathcal{T}^\mathsf{T}(B)$. Let a_j be the root node of the biconnected subtree S_{a_j} of S_a. We partition the subtrees $S_{a_1}, \ldots, S_{a_l}$ into classes $E_1, \ldots, E_p$ of equal size subtrees. Let k_j be the number of subtrees in E_j. Let the order of the size classes be such that $k_1 \leq k_2 \leq \cdots \leq k_p$. All articulation points with their subtrees in size class E_j are colored with color j.

- Let $s_1, \ldots, s_m$ be the separating pairs which are connected to C in $\mathcal{T}^\mathsf{T}(B)$. Let S_{s_j} be the subtree of $\mathcal{T}^\mathsf{T}(B)$ rooted at s_j. We partition the subtrees $S_{s_1}, \ldots, S_{s_m}$ into classes $\widehat{E}_1, \ldots, \widehat{E}_{\hat{p}}$ of equal size subtrees. Let $\widehat{k}_j$ be the number of subtrees in $\widehat{E}_j$. Let the order of the size classes be such that $\widehat{k}_1 \leq \widehat{k}_2 \leq \cdots \leq \widehat{k}_{\hat{p}}$. All virtual edges of separating pairs with their subtrees in size class $\widehat{E}_j$ are colored with color j.

Let n_a be the size of S_a and n_B be the size of S_B. The subtrees in E_j have size $\leq n_a/k_i$, for $j \geq i$, and similar, the subtrees in $\widehat{E}_j$ have size $\leq n_B/\widehat{k}_i$, for $j \geq i$. Let

$$k_0 = \begin{cases} k_1, & \text{if } k_1 > 1, \\ \min\{k_2, \widehat{k}_1\}, & \text{if } k_1 = 1. \end{cases}$$

We will show that in the cases where we have to bound the number of root candidates, we either have a constant number of candidates, if $k_0 = 1$, or $\leq 8k_0$ candidates, if $k_0 \geq 2$. In the latter case we go into recursion on trees of size $\leq n_a/k_0$, respectively n_B/k_0. This is good enough to maintain the space bound.

To limit the number of potential root nodes for $\mathcal{T}^\mathsf{F}(C)$, we distinguish several cases below. The center D_0 of $\mathcal{T}^\mathsf{F}(C)$ will play an important role thereby. In some of the cases we will show that the number of automorphisms of D_0 is small. This already suffices for our purpose: in this case, we cycle through every edge of D_0 as starting edge, and canonize the component D_0 separately. Let A be the set of separating triples that lead to the minimum code. Although there can be polynomially many possible candidates for the canon, the minimum ones are bounded

7. K_5-MINOR FREE GI

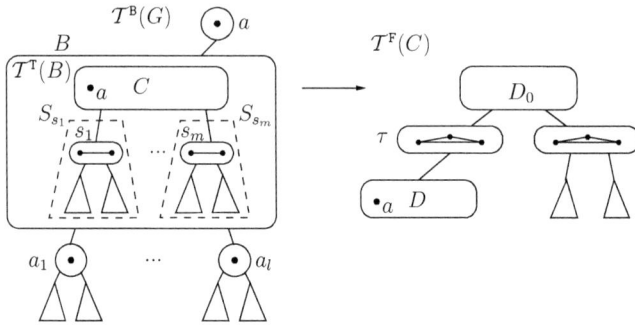

Figure 7.9: (a) The decomposition of a graph G into biconnected and triconnected components. In $T^B(G)$ we have a biconnected component B with its parent articulation point a. B is decomposed into its triconnected component tree $T^T(B)$. C is a triconnected component in $T^T(B)$, where $a_1, \ldots, a_l$ are child articulation points and $s_1, \ldots, s_m$ are adjacent separating pairs of C in $T^T(B)$. (b) The decomposition of C into its four-connected component tree $T^F(C)$. The parent articulation point is contained in C and hence in $T^F(C)$. The situation is shown where a occurs not in the center D_0.

by the number of automorphisms of D_0, which is small. We take the separating triples as root candidates for $T^F(C)$ which come first in the position order encountered in each of these minimum codes. Hence the number of roots is bounded by the number of automorphisms of D_0.

Consider the case where the parent articulation point a is associated with some component $D \neq D_0$. We find the path from D to D_0 in $T^F(C)$ and find the separating triple closest to D_0 on this path. This serves as the unique choice for the root of $T^F(C)$, see Figure 7.9.

For the following cases, we assume that a is associated with D_0. We proceed with the case analysis according to the number $l \geq 0$ of child articulation points and the number $m \geq 0$ of separating pairs adjacent to C in $T^F(C)$.

Case I: $l = 0$. There are no articulation points associated with C and hence, C is a leaf node in S_a.

1) $m = 0$. There are no separating pairs in C and hence, C is also a leaf node in $T^T(B)$. There is no recursion on biconnected or triconnected subtrees of C. In this case we can cycle through all separating triples as root for $T^F(C)$. We also color a with a distinct color.

2) $m \geq 1$. We return the $\widehat{k}_1$ separating pairs which are the roots of the subtrees in $\widehat{E}_1$ as root candidates for $T^T(B)$.

Case II: $l = 1$. We do the isomorphism test for the single child articulation point associated with C a priori and store the result. We color the parent and the unique child with distinct colors and proceed with C as in Case I.

Case III: $l \geq 2$. We distinguish the following sub-cases.

1) $1 \leq \widehat{k}_1 < k_1$. We return the $\widehat{k}_1$ separating pairs which are the roots of the subtrees in $\widehat{E}_1$ as root candidates for $\mathcal{T}^\mathsf{T}(B)$.

2) $1 \leq k_1 \leq \widehat{k}_1$ or $m = 0$, i.e. $\widehat{k}_1 = 0$. We consider the following sub-cases.

   a) **Some articulation point a_j from E_1 is not associated with C.** Note that we must have $m > 0$ in this case, i.e. there are separating pairs in B. Let a_j be associated with component $C' \neq C$ in $\mathcal{T}^\mathsf{T}(B)$. Find the path from C' to C in $\mathcal{T}^\mathsf{T}(B)$ and select the separating pair node closest to C on this path. Thus a_j uniquely defines a separating pair. In the worst case, this may happen for every articulation point from E_1. Therefore, we get up to k_1 separating pairs as candidates for the root.

   b) **All articulation points from E_1 are associated with C.** In this case we consider the four-connected component tree of C, $\mathcal{T}^\mathsf{F}(C)$, and its center D_0.

      (i) **Some articulation point a_j from E_1 is not associated with D_0.** Let a_j be associated with a four-connected component $D \neq D_0$. Find the path from D to D_0 in $\mathcal{T}^\mathsf{F}(C)$ and select the separating triple node closest to D_0 on this path. Thus a_j uniquely defines a separating triple. In the worst case, this may happen for every articulation point from E_1. Therefore, we get up to k_1 separating triples as candidates for the root.

      (ii) **All articulation points from E_1 are associated with D_0.**
      - $k_1 \geq 2$. Every automorphism of D_0 fixes the parent articulation point a and setwise fixes the k_1 articulation points from E_1. By Lemma 7.3.6 below, there are at most $4k_1$ automorphisms of D_0.
      - $k_1 = k_2 = 1$. Every automorphism of D_0 fixes the parent articulation point a and the two articulation points from E_1 and E_2. By Corollary 7.3.7 below, D_0 has at most one non-trivial automorphism in this case.
      - $k_1 = 1 < k_2$ and $(k_2 \leq \widehat{k}_1$ or $\widehat{k}_1 = 0)$. We do the isomorphism test for the single child articulation point from E_1 a priori and store the result. By an analogous argument as in the case where $k_1 \geq 2$, D_0 has at most $4k_2$ automorphisms.
      - $k_1 = 1 \leq \widehat{k}_1 < k_2$. Again we do the isomorphism test for the single child articulation point from E_1 a priori and store the result. We distinguish two sub-cases.

7. K_5-MINOR FREE GI

- Some separating pair s_j from $\widehat{E}_1$ is not associated with D_0. Choose the separating triple nearest to D_0 which is on the unique path between D_0 and the 4-connected component associated with s_j. Hence, we get up to $\widehat{k}_1$ separating triples as candidates for the root.
- All separating pairs in $\widehat{E}_1$ are associated with D_0. Every automorphism of D_0 fixes the parent articulation point a and setwise fixes the $2\widehat{k}_1$ separating pairs from $\widehat{E}_1$. By Lemma 7.3.6 below, there are at most $4 \cdot 2\widehat{k}_1$ automorphisms for D_0.

As already mentioned before the case analysis, we have shown that for

$$k_0 = \begin{cases} k_1, & \text{if } k_1 > 1, \\ \min\{k_2, \widehat{k}_1\}, & \text{if } k_1 = 1, \end{cases}$$

we have $\leq 8k_0$ root candidates, if $k_0 \geq 2$, and a constant number otherwise.

The following lemma bounds the number of automorphisms of a 3-connected planar component.

Lemma 7.3.6 [DLN+09] *Let G be a 3-connected planar graph with colors on its vertices such that one vertex a is colored distinctly, and let $k \geq 2$ be the size of the smallest color class apart from the one which contains a. G has $\leq 4k$ automorphisms.*

Corollary 7.3.7 [DLN+09] *Let G be a 3-connected planar graph with at least 3 colored vertices, each having a distinct color. Then G has at most one non-trivial automorphism.*

Note that Lemma 7.3.6 holds for all 3-connected planar graphs, except for some special cases which are of constant size. For these special cases, we do not have to limit the number of possible minimum codes.

The preceding discussion implies that if two biconnected component trees have equal isomorphism order for some choice of the root, then the corresponding graphs are isomorphic. The reverse direction clearly holds as well.

Theorem 7.3.8 *Given two biconnected graphs B and B' and their triconnected component trees S and T, then $B \cong B'$ if and only if there is a choice of separating pairs $\{a,b\}, \{a',b'\}$ in B and B' such that $S_{\{a,b\}} =_T T_{\{a',b'\}}$.*

Proof. We refer to Theorem 7.3.3 for the correctness of isomorphism order of four-connected component trees, and assume the correctness of the isomorphism order on four-connected component trees.

We prove the right to left implication first. Assume $S_{\{a,b\}} =_T T_{\{a',b'\}}$. Then an inductive argument on the depth of the trees that follows the definition of the isomorphism order implies that B and B' are isomorphic. If the grandchildren of $\{a,b\}$ and $\{a',b'\}$, are equal up to step 4 of the isomorphism order, then the corresponding subgraphs are isomorphic by induction hypothesis. We compare the children of $\{a,b\}$ and $\{a',b'\}$. If they are equal then we can extend the $=_T$-equality to the separating pairs s and t.

When subtrees are rooted at separating pair nodes, the comparison describes an order on the subtrees which correspond to split components of the separating pairs. The order describes an isomorphism among the split components.

When subtrees are rooted at triconnected component nodes, say C and H_j, the comparison states equality if the components are isomorphic. If C and H_j are 3-connected non-planar components, then their isomorphism is checked from the isomorphism order of their four-connected component trees. This algorithm not only gives an isomorphism between C and H_j, but also checks whether the children of C and H_j mapped to each other are indeed isomorphic, and also ensures that parents of C and H_j are mapped to each other.

Hence, the isomorphism between the children of $\{a,b\}$ and $\{a',b'\}$ can be extended to an isomorphism between B and B'.

The reverse direction holds obviously as well. Namely, if B and B' are isomorphic and there is an isomorphism that maps the separating pair $\{a,b\}$ of B to the separating pair $\{a',b'\}$ of B', then the triconnected component trees $S_{\{a,b\}}$ and $T_{\{a',b'\}}$ rooted respectively at $\{a,b\}$ and $\{a',b'\}$ are clearly equal. Hence, such an isomorphism maps separating pairs of B onto separating pairs of B'. This isomorphism describes a permutation on the split components of separating pairs, which means we have a permutation on triconnected components, the children of the separating pairs. By induction hypothesis, the children (at depth $d+2$) of two such triconnected components are isomorphic and equal according to $=_T$. More formally, one can argue inductively on the depth of $S_{\{a,b\}}$ and $T_{\{a',b'\}}$. □

7.3.3 Limiting the Number of Recursive Calls for Articulation Points and Separating Pairs

When we explore the triconnected component tree $\mathcal{T}^T(B)$, we might find several copies of articulation point a. That is, a may occur in several components in $\mathcal{T}^T(B)$ if a is part of a separating pair. We want to go into recursion on a to the subtree S_a only once. Datta et.al. [DLN+09] defined the *reference copy* of articulation point a as the unique copy of a in the node C in $\mathcal{T}^T(B)$ which is closest to the root in $\mathcal{T}^T(B)$. Their algorithm goes into recursion to S_a only once, when it reaches a in node C.

If C is a component node which is not further decomposed, then we can directly take the algorithm of [DLN+09]. If C is decomposed into its four-connected component tree $\mathcal{T}^F(C)$, then

7. K_5-MINOR FREE GI

we define the *reference copy of a* as follows. This is the unique copy of a in the component or separating triple which is associated to the node D, which is closest to the root in $\mathcal{T}^{\text{F}}(C)$.

We have an analog situation for child separating pairs of a triconnected component C in $\mathcal{T}^{\text{F}}(C)$. For a child separating pair $\{a,b\}$ of C we define a *reference copy of $\{a,b\}$* in $\mathcal{T}^{\text{F}}(C)$ as as the unique copy of $\{a,b\}$ as follows. This is the unique copy of $\{a,b\}$ in the component or separating triple which is associated to the node D, which is closest to the root in $\mathcal{T}^{\text{F}}(C)$.

If D is a component node, then we compute codes and explore all edges of D. The algorithm goes into recursion at S_a or $S_{\{a,b\}}$ only when it reaches a or $\{a,b\}$ for the first time in a code of D.

Lemma 7.3.9 *Let C be a triconnected component. The reference copy of an articulation point a or a separating pair $\{a,b\}$ in $\mathcal{T}^{\text{F}}(C)$ can be found in log-space.*

Proof. The proof is similar to the proof of the corresponding lemma in [DLN+09]. We distinguish three cases for a and $\{a,b\}$ in $\mathcal{T}^{\text{F}}(C)$. We define a unique component D, where a or $\{a,b\}$ is contained. We distinguish the following cases. Let P be one of a or $\{a,b\}$.

- P occurs in the root separating triples of $\mathcal{T}^{\text{F}}(C)$. That is, P occurs already at the beginning of the comparisons for $\mathcal{T}^{\text{F}}(C)$. Then we define D as the root separating triple.

- P occurs in separating triples other than the root of $\mathcal{T}^{\text{F}}(C)$. Then P occurs in all the component nodes, which contain such a separating triple. These nodes form a connected subtree of $\mathcal{T}^{\text{F}}(C)$. Hence, one of these component nodes is the closest to the root of $\mathcal{T}^{\text{F}}(C)$. This component is always a four-connected component node. Let D be this component. Note, that the comparison first compares P with P' before comparing the biconnected, triconnected or four-connected subtrees, so we reach these copies first in the comparison.

- P does not occur in a separating triple. Then, P occurs in only one four-connected component node in $\mathcal{T}^{\text{F}}(C)$. Let D be this component node.

Clearly, the cases can be detected in logspace. □

As in [DLN+09], we define trees which are based on the actual recursive structure of the algorithm described above. We distinguish the case of triconnected and four-connected component trees. Recall that a *large child* of a tree of size N is a child of size $> N/2$. A large child is visited a priori.

Definition 7.3.10 *Let B be a biconnected component and $\mathcal{T}^{\text{T}}(B)$ its triconnected component tree. Let C be a node in $\mathcal{T}^{\text{T}}(B)$, i.e. a triconnected component node or a separating pair node. The tree S_C^* rooted at C is defined as*

- *the subtree of $\mathcal{T}^{\text{T}}(B)$ rooted at C (with respect to the root of $\mathcal{T}^{\text{T}}(B)$) and*

- the subtrees S_a for all articulation points a that have a reference copy in the subtree of $T^T(B)$ rooted at C, except those S_a that are a large child of S_B.

Let $T^F(C)$ be the four-connected component tree of C. Let D be a node in $T^F(C)$, i.e. a four-connected component node or a separating triple node. The tree S_D^* rooted at D is defined as

- the subtree of $T^F(C)$ rooted at D (with respect to the root of $T^F(C)$) and
- the subtrees S_a for all articulation points a that have a reference copy in the subtree of $T^F(C)$ rooted at D, except those S_a that are a large child of B in S_B or a large child of C in S_C, and
- the subtrees $S_{\{u,v\}}$ for all separating pairs $\{u,v\}$ that have a reference copy in the subtree of $T^F(C)$, except those $S_{\{u,v\}}$ that are a large child of C in S_C.

Figure 7.10 illustrates the definition.

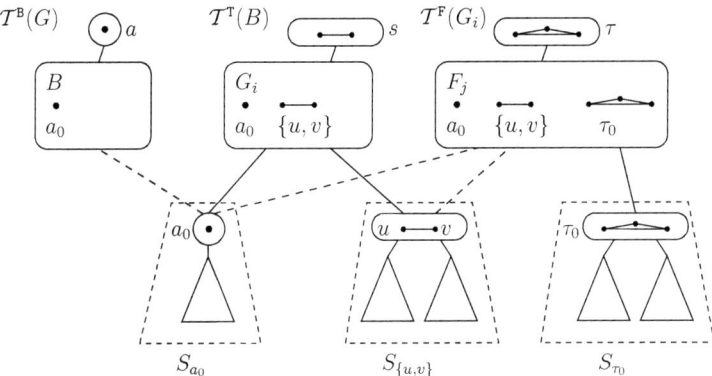

Figure 7.10: The figure shows a series of decompositions upto four-connected components. The situation is shown where a_0 is a child articulation point of B and which has reference copies in C and D. From left to right, if it is a large child of B, C or D then it is treated at the corresponding position as large child a priori. Here, a_0 is no large child of B but a large child of C. The situation is similar for the separating pair $\{u,v\}$, which is a child of C and has a reference copy in D. Here, $\{u,v\}$ is a large child of C. The dashed lines summarize all possible connections for subtrees S_{a_0} and $S_{\{u,v\}}$. The algorithm selects only one connection for each subtree.

7. K_5-MINOR FREE GI

Separating Triples or Four-Connected Components

We go into recursion at separating triples and four-connected components in $\mathcal{T}^F(G_i)$ and $\mathcal{T}^F(H_j)$. When we reach a reference copy of an articulation point or a separating pair in both trees, then we interrupt the comparison of G_i with H_j and go into recursion as described before, i.e. we compare the corresponding nodes, the children of B and B' or the children of G_i and H_j, respectively. When we return from recursion, we proceed with the comparison of $\mathcal{T}^F(G_i)$ and $\mathcal{T}^F(H_j)$.

In this part we concentrate on the comparison of $\mathcal{T}^F(G_i)$ and $\mathcal{T}^F(H_j)$. We give an overview of what is stored on the work-tape when we go into recursion at separating triples and four-connected components. Basically, the comparison is similar to that for biconnected and triconnected component trees in [DLN+09].

- For a root separating triple node, we store at most $O(\log k)$ bits on the work-tape, when we have k candidates as root separating triples for $\mathcal{T}^F(G_i)$. Hence, whenever we make recomputations in $\mathcal{T}^F(G_i)$, we have to find the following in advance: first, recompute the root separating pair node, then we can determine the parent separating pair node. Then we can recompute the root separating triple node. For this, we compute $\mathcal{T}^F(G_i)$ in log-space and with the rules described above, we find the candidate edges in log-space. With the bits on the work-tape, we know which of these candidate edges is the current root separating triple. We proceed as in the case of non-root separating triple nodes described next.

- For a non-root separating triple node and four-connected component nodes, we store the following. For separating triple nodes, we have some information of the orientation graphs on the work-tape. More precisely, for the i-th isomorphism class we compute the number of edges with color i. For these counters we need $O(\log k)$ bits if k is the number of subtrees in this isomorphism class.

For four-connected component nodes we cannot afford to store the entire work-tape content when we go into recursion at a child separating triple node τ. It suffices to store the information of

- the codes which are not eliminated,
- the codes which encounter a virtual edge of τ for the first time
- the direction in which the virtual edge of τ is encountered.

This takes altogether $O(1)$ space.

When we return from recursion we do the following. First, recompute the root separating pair node, then we can determine the parent separating pair node. Then we can recompute the root separating triple node of the triconnected component where we are. With this, we can determine the triconnected node which is the parent. With the information on the work-tape, we can proceed with the computations. That is, for separating triple nodes we proceed with the next comparison of children and for four-connected component nodes, we look at the work-tape which the active codes are and proceed with the next edges in the bit-by-bit comparisons of the codes.

V_8-Components

The tasks are similar to that for triconnected planar components. We compare the codes of the V_8-nodes and when we reach child articulation points associated to these V_8-components, then we go into recursion.

When we return from recursion we recompute the root for the triconnected component tree. Then, we can determine the parent of the V_8 and obtain this way the starting edge of the codes which we compare bit-by-bit. There are $O(1)$ many codes, so we can store in constant size which the current codes are. We proceed at the first occurrence of an edge with the child articulation point node where we went into recursion. Hence, we need $O(1)$ bits on the work-tape.

Analysis of the Space Requirement for the Component Trees

We analyze the comparison algorithm when it compares subtrees rooted at separating triples, subtrees rooted at separating pairs and subtrees rooted at articulation points. For the analysis, the recursion goes here from depth d to $d+2$ of the trees. Observe, that large children are handled a priori at any level of the trees. We set up the following recursion equation for the space requirement of our algorithm.

$$\mathcal{S}(N) = \max_j \left\{ \mathcal{S}\left(\frac{N}{k_j}\right) + O(\log k_j) \right\},$$

where $k_j \geq 2$ (for all j) is the number of subtrees of the same size. Hence, $\mathcal{S}(N) = O(\log N)$.

For the explanation of the recursion equation it is helpful to imagine that we have three work-tapes. We use the first work-tape when we go into recursion at articulation point nodes, we use the second work-tape when we go into recursion at separating pair nodes and we use the third work-tape when we go into recursion at separating triple nodes. The total space needed is the sum of the space of the three work-tapes.

- At an articulation point node, the value k_j is the number of elements in the j-th size class among the children $B_1, \ldots, B_k$ of the articulation point node. We store $O(\log k_j)$ bits and recursively consider subtrees of size $\leq N/k_j$.

- At a separating pair node the value k_j is the number of elements in the j-th isomorphism class among the children $G_1, \ldots, G_k$ of the separating pair node. We store $O(\log k_j)$ bits and we consider recursively subtrees of size $\leq N/k_j$.

7. K_5-MINOR FREE GI

- At a separating triple node the value k_j is the number of elements in the j-th isomorphism class among the children $F_1, \ldots, F_k$ of the separating triple node. We store $O(\log k_j)$ bits and we consider recursively subtrees of size $\leq N/k_j$.

This finishes the complexity analysis. We get the following theorem.

Theorem 7.3.11 *The isomorphism order between two K_5-free graphs can be computed in logspace.*

7.3.4 The Canon of K_5-Minor Free Graphs.

Using this algorithm for isomorphism order, we show that the canon of a planar graph can be output in log-space. The canonization of K_5-free graphs proceeds exactly as in the case of planar graphs. We extend the canonization procedure for the non-planar components.

The Canon for a V_8-Component

We already described, how to compute a canon for a single V_8-component. It consists of a list of all directed edges in the V_8. For a V_8-component node C and a parent separating pair $\{a, b\}$ we define the tree-code $l(C, a, b)$ exactly as if C is a 3-connected component. That is, (a, b) followed by the code of C and the starting edge and then the tree-codes for the child separating pairs of C in that order in which the child separating pairs appear in the code of C.

The Canon for a Four-Connected Component Tree

Let G_i be a 3-connected K_5-free component with 3-divisive separating triples. We describe now the canon of $\mathcal{T}^\mathsf{F}(G_i)$.

A log-space procedure traverses the four-connected component tree and makes oracle queries to the isomorphism order algorithm and outputs the code, i.e. a canonical list of edges, along with delimiters to separate the lists for siblings.

For an example, consider the tree-code $l(S, \tau)$ for the tree S_τ of Figure 7.7. Let $\tau = \{a, b, c\}$. Let $l(F_i, a, b, c)$ be the tree code of the four-connected component F_i and a given order on the vertices of τ (i.e. the code of F_i with τ the parent separating triple). Since F_i is planar and at least 3-connected, we invoke the algorithm of [DLN08] for canonization. Let $\tau_1, \ldots, \tau_{l_1}$ be the order of the separating triples as they occur in the canon of F_i. We also write for short $l'(S_{\tau_i}, \tau_i)$ which is one of $l(S_{\tau_i}, \varphi(\tau_i))$ where $\varphi(\tau_i)$ is a permutation of separating triple τ_i. Then we get the following tree-code for S_τ.

$$l(S,a,b,c) = [\,(a,b,c)\,l(S_{F_1},a,b,c)\,\ldots\,l(S_{F_k},a,b,c)\,],\text{ where}$$
$$l(S_{F_1},a,b,c) = [\,l(F_1,a,b,c)\,l'(S_{\tau_1},\tau_1)\,\ldots\,l'(S_{\tau_{l_1}},\tau_{l_1})\,]$$
$$\vdots$$
$$l(S_{F_k},a,b,c) = [\,l(F_k,a,b,c)\,l'(S_{\tau_{l_k}},\tau_{l_k})\,]$$

If a triconnected non-planar component is a $K_{3,3}$, say G_i, then for the code of $l(G_i,a,b)$ (if a,b is the parent separating pair) we have to fix one separating triple. To select the canonical smaller separating triple, we query the isomorphism order algorithm. We have a similar situation if the $K_{3,3}$ forms a biconnected component, say B_i, for the tree-code of $l(B_i,a)$ (if a is a parent articulation point). The canonical smaller separating triple is those which contains a.

For the planar 3-connected components and for the canonization of biconnected components we use the algorithm from Datta et.al. [DLN+09].

A logspace transducer renames then the vertices according to their first occurrence in this tree-code. Further logspace transducers cycle through all the articulation points as roots to find the minimum tree-code among them, then rename the vertices according to their first occurrence and finally, remove the virtual edges and delimiters to obtain a canon for the K_5-free graph. We get

Theorem 7.3.12 *A K_5-free graph can be canonized in log-space.*

8 Isomorphism for Graphs of Bounded Treewidth

8.1 Introduction

In this chapter we address the question of whether the isomorphism problem restricted to graphs of bounded treewidth and bounded tree distance width can be solved in logarithmic space. Intuitively speaking, the treewidth of a graph measures how much it differs from a tree. This concept has been used very successfully in algorithmics and fixed-parameter tractability (see e.g. [Bod98, BK08]). For many complex problems, efficient algorithms have been found for the cases when the input structures have bounded treewidth. Bodlaender showed in [Bod90] that Graph Isomorphism can be solved in polynomial time when restricted to graphs of bounded treewidth. More recently Grohe and Verbitsky [GV06] improved this upper bound showing that the isomorphism problem for this kind of graphs can be solved by a uniform family of threshold circuits of logarithmic depth and polynomial size and lies therefore in the class TC^1.

In this paper we improve this result showing that the isomorphism problem for bounded treewidth graphs lies in LogCFL, the class of problems logarithmic space reducible to a context free language. LogCFL can be alternatively characterized as the class of problems computable by a uniform family of polynomial size and logarithmic depth circuits with fanin 2 *and*-gates and unbounded fanin *or*-gates, and is therefore a subclass of TC^1. In our isomorphism algorithm, we use the fact that a tree decomposition of a graph of bounded treewidth can be computed in LogCFL [Wan94, GLS02]. We prove that if tree decompositions of both graphs are given as part of the input, the question of whether there is an isomorphism respecting the vertex partition defined by the decompositions can be solved in logarithmic space. Our proof techniques are based on methods from recent isomorphism results [DLN+09, DNTW09] and are very different from those in [GV06].

Graphs of treewidth k are also known as partial k-trees. There is a subclass of bounded treewidth graphs, the class of k-trees. Clearly, 1-trees are trees. Lindell proved that Tree Canonization is in L [Lin92]. Completeness follows from Jenner et.al. who proved that tree isomorphism is also hard for L [JKMT03] if the trees are given as a list of edges. Köbler and Kuhnert showed that Isomorphism testing for k-trees is in L [KK09]. Elberfeld, Jakoby and

8. BOUNDED TREEWIDTH GI

Tantau [EJT10] showed very recently, that a tree decomposition can be computed in logspace.

The notion of tree distance width, a stronger version of the treewidth concept, was introduced in [YBdFT99]. There it is shown that for graphs with bounded tree distance width the isomorphism problem is fixed parameter tractable, something that is not known to hold for the more general class of bounded treewidth graphs. We prove that for graphs of bounded tree distance width it is possible to obtain a tree distance decomposition within logspace. Using this result we show that graph isomorphism for bounded tree distance width graphs can also be solved in logarithmic space. Since it is known that the question is also hard for the class L under AC^0 reductions [JKMT03], this exactly characterizes the complexity of the problem. We show that in fact a canon for graphs of bounded tree distance width, i.e. a fixed representative of the isomorphism equivalence class, can be computed in logspace.

8.2 Graphs of Bounded Tree Distance Width

8.2.1 Tree Distance Decomposition in L

We describe an algorithm that on input a graph G and a subset $S \subset V$ produces the minimal tree distance decomposition $D = (\{X_i \mid i \in I\}, T = (I, F), r)$ of G with root set $X_r = S$. The algorithm works within space $c \cdot k \log n$ for some constant c, where k is the width of the minimal tree distance decomposition of G with root set S. The output of the algorithm is a sequence of strings of the form (bag label, bag depth, $v_{i_1}, v_{i_2}, \ldots, v_{i_l}$), indicating the number of the bag, the distance of its elements to S and the list of the elements in the bag.

The algorithm basically performs a depth first traversal of the tree T in the decomposition while constructing it. We refine tree traversal algorithm from Section 2.6.2 on page 34. Starting at S the algorithm uses three functions for traversing T. These functions perform queries to a logspace sub-routine computing reachability [Rei08].

Parent(X_i): On input the elements of a bag X_i the function returns the elements of the parent bag in T. These are the vertices $v \in V$ with the following two properties: $v \in \Gamma(X_i) \setminus X_i$ and v is reachable from S in $G \setminus X_i$. For a vertex v these two properties can be tested in space $O(\log n)$ by an algorithm with input G, S and X_i. In order to find all the vertices in the parent set, the algorithm searches through all the vertices in V.

First Child(X_i, order): This function returns the elements of the first child of i in T, where order specifies the first child as follows. This is the child with the vertex $v_j \in V$ with the smallest index j. v_j satisfies that $v_j \in \Gamma(X_i) \setminus X_i$ and that v_j is not reachable from S in $G \setminus X_i$. It can be found cycling through the vertices of G (in order as they are given on the input-tape) until the first one satisfying the properties is found. The other elements $w \in X_i$ must satisfy the same two properties as v_j and additionally, they must be in the same connected component in $G \setminus X_i$ where v_j is contained. In case X_i does not have any children, the function outputs some special symbol.

Next Sibling(X_i, order): This function first computes $X_p := \mathsf{Parent}(X_i)$ and then order searches for the child of p in T next to X_i. Let v_i be the vertex with the smallest label in X_i. This is done similarly as the computation of First Child. The next sibling is the bag containing the unique vertex v_j with the following properties: v_j is the vertex with the smallest label in this bag, $label(v_j) > label(v_i)$ and there is no other bag which has a vertex with a label between v_i and v_j. The vertex v_j is not reachable from S in $G \setminus X_p$. The other elements in the bag are the vertices satisfying these properties and which are in the same connected component of $G \setminus X_p$ where v_j is contained.

With these three functions the algorithm performs a depth-first traversal of T. It only needs to remember the initial bag $X_0 = S$ which is part of the input, and the elements of the current bag. On a bag X_i it searches for its first child. If it does not exist then it searches for the next sibling. When there are no further siblings, the next move goes up in the tree T to the parent. The algorithm finishes when it returns to S. It also keeps two counters in order to be able to output the number and depth of the bags. The three mentioned functions only need to keep at most two bags (X_i and the root S) in memory and work in logarithmic space. On input a graph G with n vertices and a root set S, the space used by the algorithm is therefore bounded by $c \cdot k \log n$, for a constant c, and k being the minimum width of a tree distance decomposition of G with root set S. When considering how the three functions are defined it is clear that the algorithm constructs a tree distance decomposition with root set S. Also they make sure that for each i the subgraph corresponding to the subtree of T rooted at i (i.e. the subgraph induced by the vertices of the bags in this subtree) is connected, thus producing a minimal decomposition. As observed in [YBdFT99], this is the unique minimal tree distance decomposition of G with root set S.

8.2.2 Isomorphism Algorithm for Bounded Tree Distance Width Graphs

For our isomorphism algorithm we use a structure called the *augmented tree* which is based on the underlying tree of a minimal tree distance decomposition. This augmented tree, apart from the bags, contains information about the separating sets which separate bags.

Definition 8.2.1 *Let G be a graph with a minimal tree distance decomposition $D = (\{X_i \mid i \in I\}, T = (I, F), r)$. The augmented tree $T_{(G,D)} = (I_{(G,D)}, F_{(G,D)}, r)$ corresponding to G and D is a tree defined as follows:*

8. BOUNDED TREEWIDTH GI

- The set of nodes of $T_{(G,D)}$ is $I_{(G,D)}$ which contains two kinds of nodes, namely $I_{(G,D)} = I \cup J$. Those in I form the set of bag nodes in D, and those in J the separating set nodes. For each bag node $a \in I$ and each child b of a in T we consider the set $X_a \cap \Gamma(X_b)$, i.e. the minimum separating set in X_a which separates X_b from the root bag X_r in G. Let $M_{s_1^a}, \ldots, M_{s_{l(a)}^a}$ be the set of all minimum separating sets in X_a, free of duplicates. There are nodes for these sets $s_1^a, \ldots, s_{l(a)}^a$, the separating set nodes. We define $J = \bigcup_{a \in I} \{s_1^a, \ldots, s_{l(a)}^a\}$. The node $r \in I$ is the root in $T_{(G,D)}$.

- The set of edges $F_{(G,D)}$ contains edges between bag nodes $a \in I$ and the separating set nodes $s_1^a, \ldots, s_{l(a)}^a \in J$ (edges between bag nodes and their children in the augmented tree). It also contains edges between nodes $b \in I$ and s_j^a if a is the parent node of b in I and $M_{s_j^a}$ is the minimum separating set in X_a which separates X_b from X_r (edges between bag nodes and their parents).

To simplify notation, we will say for example that $s_1, \ldots, s_l$ are the children of a bag node a if the context is clear. To each separating set node s_i, we will address the set of vertices by X_{s_i}. The odd levels of the augmented tree correspond to bag nodes and the even levels correspond to separating set nodes.

Observe that for each node in the augmented tree, we associate a bag to a bag node and a minimum separating set to a separating set node. Hence, every vertex v in the original graph occurs in at least one associated component and it might occur in more than one, e.g. if v is contained in a bag and in a minimum separating set.

Let $T_{(G,D)}$ be an augmented tree of some minimal tree distance decomposition D of a graph G. Let a be a node of $T_{(G,D)}$. The subtree of $T_{(G,D)}$ rooted at a is denoted by T_a. Note that $T_{(G,D)} = T_r$ where X_r is the bag corresponding to the root of the tree distance decomposition D. Recall, that $\mathsf{graph}(T_a)$ is the subgraph of G induced by all the vertices associated to at least one of the nodes in T_a. We define $\mathsf{size}(T_a)$ as sum of the sizes of the components (bags and separating sets) associated to the nodes of T_a. We also define $\mathsf{graph}(T_a)$ as the induced graph in G of the vertices associated to nodes in T_a.

When given a tree distance decomposition, the augmented tree can be computed in logspace. Using the result in Section 8.2.1 we immediately get:

Lemma 8.2.2 *There is a function f and an algorithm that on input of a graph G with n vertices and of tree distance width k, computes an augmented tree for G in space $O(f(k) \log n)$.*

Isomorphism Order of Augmented Trees. We describe an isomorphism order procedure for comparing two augmented trees $S_{(G,D)}$ and $T_{(H,D')}$ corresponding to the graphs G and H and their minimal tree distance decompositions D and D', respectively. This isomorphism order is an extension of the one for trees given by Lindell [Lin92]. The trees $S_{(G,D)}$ and $T_{(H,D')}$

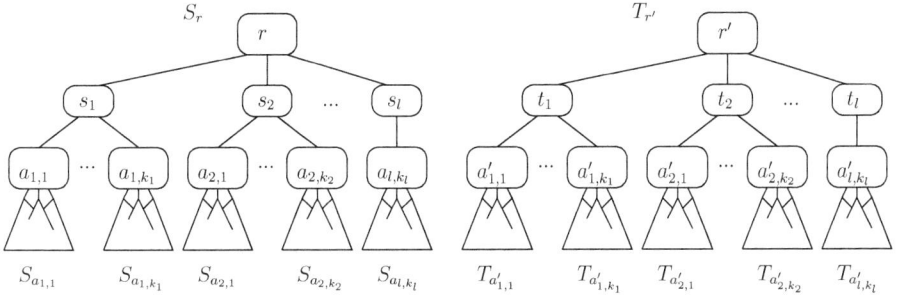

Figure 8.1: The augmented trees S_r and $T_{r'}$ rooted at bag nodes r and r'. Node r has separating set nodes $s_1, \ldots, s_l$ as children. The children of s_1 are again bag nodes $a_{1,1}, \ldots, a_{1,k_1}$. $S_{a_{i,j}}$ is the subtree rooted at $a_{i,j}$. Bag nodes and separating set nodes alternate in the tree.

are rooted at bag nodes r and r'. The rooted trees are denoted then S_r and $T_{r'}$ as shown in Figure 8.1. We will show that two graphs of bounded tree distance width are isomorphic if and only if for some root nodes r and r' the augmented trees corresponding to the minimal tree distance decompositions have the same isomorphism order.

The isomorphism order is defined recursively based on the two order procedures $<_A$ and $\prec_A$. The first one $<_A$ will be used for comparing augmented subtrees rooted at bag nodes, while $\prec_A$ compares augmented subtrees rooted at separating set nodes.

We introduce some notation needed for the definition of the isomorphism order. For sets of structures $\{A_1, \ldots, A_k\}$ and $\{B_1, \ldots, B_k\}$ and a total order $<$ between such structures the notation $(A_1, \ldots, A_k) < (B_1, \ldots, B_k)$ represents that the structures can be ordered within the tuples according to $\leq$ and that for some $i \in \{1, \ldots, k\} : A_i < B_i$ and for all $j \in \{1, \ldots, i-1\} : A_j = B_j$. To simplify notation, we assume that the structures $\{A_1, \ldots, A_k\}$ and $\{B_1, \ldots, B_k\}$ are already given in ascending order according to $\leq$. In general, the elements have to be reordered.

The isomorphism order procedure compares first the set of vertices X_r and $X'_{r'}$ where r and r' are the root nodes in the decompositions D and D'. For this we consider pairs of permutations $(\sigma, \sigma') \in Sym(X_r) \times Sym(X'_{r'})$. The notation $\sigma(G[X_r])$ and $\sigma'(H[X'_{r'}])$ describes a fixed labeling of the vertices of the corresponding induced subgraphs, given by the permutations. We say $\sigma(G[X_r]) < \sigma'(H[X'_{r'}])$ if $|X_r| < |X'_{r'}|$ or if the adjacency matrix of the induced subgraph $G[X_r]$ with its vertices ordered according to σ is lexicographically smaller than that of the induced subgraph $H[X'_{r'}]$ ordered according to σ'.

Furthermore, we need a function $\mathsf{pos}_r : X_r \to \{1, \ldots, |X_r|\}$ which gives labels to vertices

157

8. BOUNDED TREEWIDTH GI

according to their order in V. For example if $X_r = \{v_1, v_5, v_7\}$ then $\mathsf{pos}_r(v_1) = 1, \mathsf{pos}_r(v_5) = 2$ and $\mathsf{pos}_r(v_7) = 3$. Accordingly, we define $\mathsf{pos}'_{r'} : X'_{r'} \to \{1, \ldots, |X'_{r'}|\}$.

Recall that for a graph $G = (V, E)$ and two disjoint vertex sets $U, W \subseteq V$, $B_G[U, W]$ denotes the bipartite graph with vertices $U \cup W$ and edge set $\{\{u, w\} \in E(G) \mid u \in U, w \in W\}$. For $\sigma \in Sym(U)$ and $\phi \in Sym(W)$, $\sigma\phi(B_G[U, W])$ describes the adjacency matrix of $B_G[U, W]$ with the vertices in U ordered according to σ and those in W ordered according to ϕ.

For two permutations $(\sigma, \sigma') \in Sym(X_r) \times Sym(X_{r'})$ we define now the isomorphism order for two augmented trees $S_r^\sigma <_\mathsf{A} T_{r'}^{\sigma'}$.

Definition 8.2.3 *For two augmented trees rooted at bag nodes r and r' we will say $S_r <_\mathsf{A} T_{r'}$ if there exists a permutation $\sigma \in Sym(X_r)$ such that for all $\sigma' \in Sym(X_{r'})$: $S_r^\sigma <_\mathsf{A} T_{r'}^{\sigma'}$.*
We say, $S_r^\sigma <_\mathsf{A} T_{r'}^{\sigma'}$ is true if one of the following holds:

1) $\sigma(G[X_r]) < \sigma'(H[X'_{r'}])$ or

2) $\sigma(G[X_r]) = \sigma'(H[X'_{r'}])$ but $\mathsf{size}(S_r) < \mathsf{size}(T_{r'})$ or

3) $\sigma(G[X_r]) = \sigma'(H[X'_{r'}])$ and $\mathsf{size}(S_r) = \mathsf{size}(T_{r'})$ but $\#r < \#r'$ where $\#r, \#r'$ is the number of children of r and r', respectively, or

4) $\sigma(G[X_r]) = \sigma'(H[X'_{r'}])$, $\mathsf{size}(S_r) = \mathsf{size}(T_{r'})$ and $\#r = \#r' = l$ but $(S_{s_1}^\sigma, \ldots, S_{s_l}^\sigma) \prec_\mathsf{A} (T_{t_1}^{\sigma'}, \ldots, T_{t_l}^{\sigma'})$. The order $\prec_\mathsf{A}$ for subtrees rooted at separating set nodes is defined as in the following way, $S_{s_i}^\sigma \prec_\mathsf{A} T_{t_j}^{\sigma'}$ if:

  i) $\sigma(X_{s_i}) < \sigma'(X'_{t_j})$, i.e. for $X_{s_i} = \{v_{i_1}, \ldots, v_{i_h}\}, X'_{t_j} = \{v'_{j_1}, \ldots, v'_{j_{h'}}\}$:
  $(\mathsf{pos}_r\sigma(v_{i_1}), \ldots, \mathsf{pos}_r\sigma(v_{i_h})) < (\mathsf{pos}'_{r'}\sigma'(v'_{j_1}), \ldots, \mathsf{pos}'_{r'}\sigma'(v'_{j_{h'}}))$, *or*

  ii) $\sigma(X_{s_i}) = \sigma'(X'_{t_j})$ but $k_i < k'_j$, where k_i and k'_j are the number of children of s_i and t_j, respectively, or

  iii) $\sigma(X_{s_i}) = \sigma'(X'_{t_j})$, $k_i = k'_j = m$ but
  $(B_G[X_{s_i}, X_{a_{i,1}}]^\sigma, \ldots, B_G[X_{s_i}, X_{a_{i,m}}]^\sigma) < (B_H[X'_{t_j}, X'_{a'_{j,1}}]^{\sigma'}, \ldots, B_H[X'_{t_j}, X'_{a'_{j,m}}]^{\sigma'})$
  where $B_G[X_{s_i}, X_{a_{i,i'}}]^\sigma < B_H[X'_{t_j}, X'_{a'_{j,j'}}]^{\sigma'}$ if there exists $\phi \in Sym(X_{a_{i,i'}})$ such that for all $\phi' \in Sym(X'_{a'_{j,j'}})$, $\sigma\phi(B_G[X_{s_i}, X_{a_{i,i'}}]) < \sigma'\phi'(B_H[X'_{t_j}, X'_{a'_{j,j'}}])$ via lexicographical comparison of the adjacency matrices of both induced bipartite subgraphs where all vertices are ordered according to σ, ϕ and σ', ϕ' respectively, or

  iv) $\sigma(X_{s_i}) = \sigma'(X'_{t_j})$, $k_i = k'_j = m$,
  $(B_G[X_{s_i}, X_{a_{i,1}}]^\sigma, \ldots, B_G[X_{s_i}, X_{a_{i,m}}]^\sigma) = (B_H[X'_{t_j}, X'_{a'_{j,1}}]^{\sigma'}, \ldots, B_H[X'_{t_j}, X'_{a'_{j,m}}]^{\sigma'})$,
  but there exists $q \in \{1, \ldots, m\}$ such that for every $p \in \{1, \ldots, q-1\}$:
  $[\forall \phi_p \in Sym(X_{a_{i,p}}) \quad \exists \phi'_p \in Sym(X'_{a'_{j,p}}):$
  $\sigma\phi_p(B_G[X_{s_i}, X_{a_{i,p}}]) = \sigma'\phi'_p(B_H[X'_{t_j}, X'_{a'_{j,p}}])$ *and* $S_{a_{i,p}}^{\phi_p} =_\mathsf{A} T_{a'_{j,p}}^{\phi'_p}]$
  and $[\exists \phi_q \in Sym(X_{a_{i,q}}) \forall \phi'_q \in Sym(X'_{a'_{j,q}}):$
  if $\sigma\phi_q(B_G[X_{s_i}, X_{a_{i,q}}]) = \sigma'\phi'_q(B_H[X'_{t_j}, X'_{a'_{j,q}}])$ *then* $S_{a_{i,q}}^{\phi_q} <_\mathsf{A} T_{a'_{j,q}}^{\phi'_q}]$.

We say that two augmented trees S_r and $T_{r'}$ are *equal according to the isomorphism order*, denoted $S_r =_A T_{r'}$, if neither $S_r \prec_A T_{r'}$ nor $T_{r'} \prec_A S_r$ holds.

Correctness of the Isomorphism Order. It is not hard to see that the isomorphism order defines a total order on augmented trees. We show now that it is a good tool for testing graph isomorphism since two graph are isomorphic if and only if for some choice of the root bags, the augmented trees associated with the corresponding minimal tree distance decompositions have the same order under $=_A$.

Theorem 8.2.4 *Let $G = (V_1, E_1)$ and $H = (V_2, E_2)$ be two graphs and $X_r \subseteq V_1$ and $X'_{r'} \subseteq V_2$ root bags producing minimal tree distance decompositions of the graphs G and H with augmented trees S_r and $T_{r'}$ respectively.*

There is an isomorphism between G and H mapping setwise X_r to $X'_{r'}$ if and only if for some permutations $\sigma, \sigma' \in Sym(X_r) \times Sym(X'_{r'})$, $S_r^\sigma =_A T_{r'}^{\sigma'}$.

Proof. From left to right, let G and H be isomorphic graphs with an isomorphism Π mapping X_r to $X'_{r'}$. Let us denote by π the restriction from Π to the domain X_r and let $\sigma \in Sym(X_r)$ be a permutation minimizing $\sigma(G[X_r])$. Define $\sigma' = \pi\sigma\pi^{-1}$. σ' is a permutation in $Sym(X'_{r'})$ and $\sigma(G[X_r]) = \sigma'(H[X'_{r'}])$. Since G and H are isomorphic with an isomorphism mapping X_r to $X'_{r'}$ and since the minimal tree distance decomposition is unique, the augmented trees of G and H with respect to the root bags X_r and $X'_{r'}$ are also isomorphic and we have $\sigma(G[X_r]) = \sigma'(H[X'_{r'}])$, $\text{size}(S_r) = \text{size}(T_{r'})$ and $\#r = \#r' = l$ for some l. The isomorphism also implies $(S^\sigma_{s_1}, \ldots, S^\sigma_{s_l}) =_A (T^{\sigma'}_{t_1}, \ldots, T^{\sigma'}_{t_l})$ (where the equality refers here to the order $\preceq_A$ defined between subtrees rooted at separating set nodes) and for all $i \in \{1, \ldots, l\}$, $\sigma(X_{s_i}) = \sigma'(X'_{t_i})$, the number of children of S_{s_i}, k_i, coincide with that of T_{t_i}, and for all $j \in \{1, \ldots, k_i\}$, $B_G[X_{s_i}, X_{a_{i,j}}]^\sigma = B_H[X'_{t_i}, X'_{a'_{i,j}}]^{\sigma'}$ and the subtree $S_{a_{i,j}}$ is isomorphic to $T_{a'_{i,j}}$ via an isomorphism $\varphi_{i,j}$ mapping $X_{a_{i,j}}$ to $X'_{a'_{i,j}}$. For any permutation $\phi_{i,j} \in Sym(X_{a_{i,j}})$ consider $\phi'_{i,j} = \varphi_{i,j}\phi_{i,j}\varphi_{i,j}^{-1}$. $\phi'_{i,j} \in Sym(X'_{a'_{i,j}})$ and $\phi'_{i,j}(H[X'_{a'_{i,j}}]) = \phi_{i,j}(G[X_{a_{i,j}}])$ which implies $S^{\phi_{i,j}}_{a_{i,j}} =_A T^{\phi'_{i,j}}_{a'_{i,j}}$. Since this is true for every i and j, by the definition of the isomorphism order we have $S^\sigma_r =_A T^{\sigma'}_{r'}$.

The direction from right to left is proven by induction on the number of levels with bag nodes in the augmented tree. The base case is when there is only one bag node in each of the augmented trees, i.e. all vertices in G and H are associated to the single bags X_r and $X'_{r'}$ respectively.

By hypothesis there exists a pair of permutations $(\sigma, \sigma') \in Sym(X_r) \times Sym(X'_{r'})$ with $S^\sigma_r = T^{\sigma'}_{r'}$. This means $\sigma(G[X_r]) = \sigma'(H[X'_{r'}])$ and since $G = G[X_r]$ and $H = H[X'_{r'}]$, both graphs are isomorphic, with isomorphism $\sigma'^{-1}\sigma$.

For the induction step, since $S^\sigma_r =_A T^{\sigma'}_{r'}$, it holds $\sigma(G[X_r]) = \sigma'(H[X'_{r'}])$, $\text{size}(S_r) = \text{size}(T_{r'})$ and $\#r = \#r' = l$ for some l. Moreover $(S^\sigma_{s_1}, \ldots, S^\sigma_{s_l}) =_A (T^{\sigma'}_{t_1}, \ldots, T^{\sigma'}_{t_l})$. This means that for

8. BOUNDED TREEWIDTH GI

all $i \in \{1,\ldots,l\}$, $\sigma(X_{s_i}) = \sigma'(X'_{t_i})$, the number of children of S_{s_i}, k_i, coincide with that of T_{t_i}, and for all $j \in \{1,\ldots,k_i\}$, $B_G[X_{s_i}, X_{a_{i,j}}]^\sigma = B_H[X'_{t_i}, X'_{a'_{i,j}}]^{\sigma'}$. Let ϕ_j be any permutation in $Sym(X_{a_{i,j}})$ and let $\phi'_j \in Sym(X'_{a'_{i,j}})$ satisfying $\sigma\phi_j(B_G[X_{s_i}, X_{a_{i,j}}]) = \sigma'\phi_j(B_H[X'_{t_i}, X'_{a'_{i,j}}])$. Such a permutation ϕ'_j always exists since $B_G[X_{s_i}, X_{a_{i,j}}]^\sigma = B_H[X'_{t_i}, X'_{a'_{i,j}}]^{\sigma'}$. For all $j \in \{1,\ldots,k_i\}$, we have $S_{a_{i,j}}^{\phi_j} =_\mathsf{A} T_{a'_{i,j}}^{\phi'_j}$ and by induction hypothesis for all $j \in \{1,\ldots,k_i\}$, $\mathsf{graph}(S_{a_{i,j}})$ is isomorphic to $\mathsf{graph}(T_{a'_{i,j}})$ with an isomorphism that maps $X_{a_{i,j}}$ to $X'_{a'_{i,j}}$. Observe that since the nodes $a_{i,j}$ are bag nodes, for $j \neq j'$ the graph vertices associated to $S_{a_{i,j}}$ are disjoint from those associated to $S_{a_{i,j'}}$. All these isomorphisms between subgraphs of G and H are consistent among each other and also with $\sigma'^{-1}\sigma$ and can therefore be extended to an isomorphism between G and H mapping X_r to $X'_{r'}$ via $\sigma\sigma'^{-1}$. □

Corollary 8.2.5 *Two graphs G and H are isomorphic if and only if there is a pair of root sets producing minimal tree distance decompositions of the graphs with augmented trees S_r and $T_{r'}$ with $S_r =_\mathsf{A} T_{r'}$.*

We describe now an algorithm for computing the isomorphism order. After this, we analyze the complexity of the algorithm showing that if the tree distance width is constant then the isomorphism order of the corresponding augmented trees can be computed in logarithmic space.

Isomorphism of two Subtrees Rooted at Bag Nodes r and r'. We are interested in finding the mappings σ and σ' which lead to the minimum isomorphism order of the trees S_r and $T_{r'}$. For this we define a set of permutation pairs $\Theta_{(r,r')} \subseteq Sym(X_r) \times Sym(X'_{r'})$ related to the pair of nodes (r,r'). The order procedure cycles through all permutation pairs contained in $\Theta_{(r,r')}$. Initially $\Theta_{(r,r')} = Sym(X_r) \times Sym(X'_{r'})$. We will see, if r and r' are not the root of the overall tree, the set $\Theta_{(r,r')}$ may be restricted to a subset. The algorithm sets up a table for $\Theta_{r,r'}$ which contains at most $(k!)^2$ entries. The algorithm records for each entry $(\sigma,\sigma') \in \Theta_{r,r'}$ the result of the comparison of S_r^σ with $T_{r'}^{\sigma'}$.

In Step 1, we have constant size components associated to the bag nodes. We simply compare the adjacency matrices of $G[X_r]$ and $H[X'_{r'}]$ bitwise, where the elements are arranged in rows and columns in increasing order according to the permutations σ and σ'.

The Steps 2 and 3 can be done in logspace by comparing the tree size and the number of children of r and r'. In Step 4 the subtrees rooted at separating set nodes are compared. This requires similar arguments as in [Lin92]. We run through the children of r and r' in a fixed order using the functions **FirstChild** and **Next Sibling**. First, we find the minimum subtrees S_{s_i} and T_{t_j} according to $\prec_\mathsf{A}$. If they are $\prec_\mathsf{A}$-equal then we compute the number of $\prec_\mathsf{A}$-equal siblings for s_i and t_j, by running through all children of S_r and $T_{r'}$. If the numbers are equal, then we proceed with the minimum subtrees larger than S_{s_i} and T_{t_j} according to $\prec_\mathsf{A}$. If they are not equal, then we know that $S_r^\sigma <_\mathsf{A} T_{r'}^{\sigma'}$ (or $T_{r'}^{\sigma'} <_\mathsf{A} S_r^\sigma$). If all the tests are equal then we know that $S_r^\sigma =_A T_{r'}^{\sigma'}$ and proceed with the next entry in $\Theta_{r,r'}$. In $\Theta_{r,r'}$, the permutation σ is the smallest if $S_r^\sigma \leq_A T_{r'}^{\sigma'}$ for all σ'.

In the next paragraph we consider one such comparison of two subtrees rooted at two separating set nodes.

Isomorphism of two Subtrees Rooted at Separating Set Nodes s_i and t_j. In Step $4i$), we compare s_i with t_j only if the vertices of X_{s_i} can be mapped onto X'_{t_j} blockwise. In order to compute the relation $\prec_A$, we have to decide whether $\sigma(X_{s_i}) < \sigma'(X'_{t_j})$ for pairs X_{s_i} and X'_{t_j}. We explain the definition of the ordering $\sigma(X_{s_i}) < \sigma'(X'_{t_j})$ here in more detail with an example. Let $X_r = \{v_1, v_3, v_5, v_7\}$ and $\sigma \in Sym(X_r)$ the permutation (v_3, v_5, v_7, v_1) (written in cyclic notation). For $X_{s_i} = \{v_3, v_7\} \subseteq X_r$, $\sigma(X_{s_i})$ is defined as $\sigma(X_{s_i}) = \{\mathsf{pos}_r\sigma(v_3), \mathsf{pos}_r\sigma(v_7)\} = \{1,3\}$. Analogously, let $X'_{r'} = \{v'_6, v'_7, v'_8, v'_9\}$ and $X_{t_j} = \{v'_6, v'_7\} \subseteq X'_{r'}$ and $\sigma' \in Sym(X'_{r'})$ be the identity permutation. $\sigma'(X'_{t_j}) = \{\mathsf{pos}_{r'}\sigma'(v'_6), \mathsf{pos}_{r'}\sigma'(v'_7)\} = \{1,2\}$. Since $(1,2) < (1,3)$ (lexicographical comparison of the sets with the entries arranged in increasing order) we have $\sigma(X'_{t_j}) < \sigma(X_{s_i})$.

In Step $4ii$), we compare k_i with k_j, the number of children of s_i and of t_j. To compute k_i, we use the functions FirstChild(s_i) and count how often NextSibling returns a further child of s_i and increment this number at the end.

In Step $4iii$), assume $k_i = k_j = m$. We consider the induced bipartite subgraphs $B_G[X_{s_i}, X_{a_{i,1}}], \ldots, B_G[X_{s_i}, X_{a_{i,m}}]$ and $B_H[X'_{t_j}, X'_{a'_{j,1}}], \ldots, B_H[X'_{t_j}, X'_{a'_{j,m}}]$. Intuitively, we partition the children of s_i and t_j into classes where the bipartite subgraphs are isomorphic. Again we use similar arguments as in [Lin92]. We run through the children of s_i and t_j in a fixed order, using the functions FirstChild and Next Sibling. We find the bipartite subgraph, say $B_G[X_{s_i}, X_{a_{i,1}}]^\sigma$ which is the smallest, i.e. for which there exists a mapping $\phi \in Sym(X_{a_{i,1}})$ such that for all $j' \in \{1, \ldots, m\}$ and $\phi' \in Sym(X'_{a'_{j,j'}})$ it holds $\sigma\phi(B_G[X_{s_i}, X_{a_{i,1}}]) \leq \sigma'\phi'(B_H[X'_{t_j}, X'_{a'_{j,j'}}])$. Via cross comparisons, the algorithm runs through all bipartite subgraphs (of s_i with all siblings of $a_{i,1}$) in increasing order (and also through all bipartite subgraphs of t_j and all its children $a_{j,j'}$).

This is done as follows: When comparing $B_G[X_{s_i}, X_{a_{i,1}}]$ and $B_H[X'_{t_j}, X'_{a'_{j,j'}}]$ for some j', the algorithm records all that mappings ϕ and ϕ', where $\sigma\phi(B_G[X_{s_i}, X_{a_{i,1}}])$ and $\sigma'\phi'(B_H[X'_{t_j}, X'_{a'_{j,j'}}])$ become minimal. This builds the set $\Theta_{a_{i,1}, a'_{j,j'}}$. If the set is empty, then both bipartite subgraphs are not isomorphic and we proceed with the next pair of bipartite subgraphs in the cross comparison procedure. Thereby, the algorithm compares the number of bipartite subgraphs which are found to be isomorphic to the current one. For example, if $B_G[X_{s_i}, X_{a_{i,1}}]$ has less isomorphic siblings than the isomorphic bipartite subgraph $B_H[X'_{t_j}, X'_{a'_{j,j'}}]$, then we return $S_{s_i} \prec_A T_{t_j}$. If the numbers are equal then we invoke Step $4iv$) for all these isomorphic siblings. After this, we proceed with the next class of isomorphic bipartite subgraphs larger than $B_G[X_{s_i}, X_{a_{i,1}}]^\sigma$.

In Step $4iv$), we start with two isomorphic bipartite subgraphs $B_G[X_{s_i}, X_{a_{i,1}}]$ and

8. BOUNDED TREEWIDTH GI

$B_H[X'_{t_j}, X'_{a'_{j,j'}}]$. For both of them, we consider all the siblings which have an isomorphic bipartite subgraph. Thereby, we traverse the children of node s_i in a fixed order. Namely, we can reach all these siblings of $a_{i,1}$ with the function NextSibling. Again, this is done via cross comparisons. Consider one such pair, say $a_{i,1}$ and $a'_{j,j'}$. We recompute the set $\Theta_{a_{i,1}, a'_{j,j'}}$ and go into recursion at the corresponding subtrees $S_{a_{i,1}}$ and $T_{a'_{j,j'}}$ with the set $\Theta_{a_{i,1}, a'_{j,j'}}$. We compute the number of siblings of $a_{i,1}$ which are equal up to Step $4iv$) and if this number is equal to the number of siblings of $a'_{j,j'}$ then we proceed with the next test. We run through all the siblings and we do this test for all classes of isomorphic bipartite subgraphs and return $S_{s_i} =_\mathbf{A} T_{t_j}$.

Complexity of the Isomorphism Order Algorithm. We analyze the complexity of the isomorphism order algorithm. We show that the isomorphism order between two augmented trees of bounded tree distance width graphs can be computed in logspace.

Steps 1, 2 and 3 of the isomorphism order can be done in logspace, as we compute the size of subgraphs, the number of children and check the correctness of a partial isomorphism. Because we have a tree distance decomposition where bags have constant size, the whole graph is partitioned into separating sets of constant size. Hence, for a partial isomorphism from bag X_r onto bag $X'_{r'}$ we store the current mappings σ and σ' with $O(1)$ bits on the work-tape. We also store $\Theta_{(r,r')}$ in $O(1)$ bits. Thereby, we rename the vertices according to the lexicographical order of their labels from the input. The mapping from X_r onto $X'_{r'}$ is given by $\sigma \sigma'^{-1}$. Whether this is a partial isomorphism which fits to the partial isomorphism of the parents of X_r and $X'_{r'}$ (if we are in recursion, having a look at the work-tape contents stored one level up in recursion) can be checked with constant effort.

For this task, in Step 4 we have counters on the work-tape. For the partitioning in Step $4i$, we need $O(1)$ bits on the work-tape, because there are at most $O(1)$ different separating sets only. For the partitioning in Step $4ii$, we need $O(\log k)$ bits when considering nodes like s_i with $\geq k$ children. We can recompute these numbers and do not keep them after the comparison. For the partitioning in Step $4iii$, we need $O(1)$ bits, because the bipartite graphs (like e.g. $B[s_i, a_{i,i'}]$) are of constant size and therefore there are at most $O(1)$ different bipartite graphs only. For the partitioning in Step $4iv$, we need $O(\log k)$ bits when considering an isomorphism class with members, say like $a_{i,i'}$, of size $|S_{a_{i,i'}}| = n/k$. Note, there are $\leq k$ such members in that class.

In order to have only a logarithmic number of recursive calls there is one special situation in which we have to diverge from the isomorphism order procedure.

Definition 8.2.6 *In an augmented tree of size n, a large child of a node is a subtree rooted at a child, which is of size $\geq n/2$.*

It is important for the logspace bound not to store bits on the work-tape before going into recursion on such a large child. Each node can have only one large child. Say s_1 and t_1 are large children of r and r', respectively (accordingly, we can have a and a' as large children of s_1 and t_1). Before doing any computation we directly go into recursion. When returning from the recursion we return a constant size table Θ_0 of all the partial isomorphisms from X_{s_1} onto X'_{t_1} which correspond to the minimal isomorphism order. If the table is not empty then we recompute $\Theta_{(r,r')}$ and update it, i.e. $\Theta_{(r,r')} \leftarrow \Theta_{(r,r')} \cap \Theta_0$. If there is no partial isomorphism from X_{s_1} onto X'_{t_1} then there is no isomorphism from X_a onto $X'_{a'}$ and we return one further level up in recursion.

We summarize, when going into recursion at bag nodes we only store $O(1)$ bits, i.e. the current mapping σ (or a table of mappings of the large child) of the bag node r. This order also gives an order on the children of r. Note, r can have only $O(1)$ children because the children correspond to minimum separating sets, i.e. different subgraphs of X_r and there are only $O(1)$ possibilities for this.

When going into recursion at a separating set node, say s_1, there can be many children. Let $|T_{s_1}| = n$. To partition these children into isomorphism classes we keep counters on the worktape. First, we distinguish them by the fixed order of the parent bag node, we can recompute this primary order. Second, we distinguish them by the size of their subtrees. Hence, in one isomorphism class are only children of equal size. Therefore we keep counters on the work-tape to distinguish the children in the current isomorphism class. With cross comparisons, as done by Lindell in [Lin92], we can compute and check the number of isomorphic children in each class. For these counters we need $O(\log k_j)$ bits if the j-th isomorphism class has k_j members. Since in an isomorphism class the members have equal size, the subtrees have size $\leq N/k_j$, where N be the size of the augmented tree. We conclude that we get the same recurrence for the space $\mathcal{S}(N)$ as Lindell:

$$\mathcal{S}(N) \leq \max_j \left\{ \mathcal{S}\left(\frac{N}{k_j}\right) + O(\log k_j) \right\},$$

where $k_j \geq 2$ for all j. Thus $\mathcal{S}(N) = O(\log N)$. Note that the number n of vertices of G is in general smaller than N, because the vertices of the separating sets (of a separating set node) occur also in the bag associated to the parent node in the augmented tree. Since there are only a constant number of children for a bag node, the size of the augmented tree is polynomial in the size of the associated graph. This proves the theorem.

Theorem 8.2.7 *The isomorphism problem for graphs of bounded tree distance width is in* L.

Canonization of Bounded Tree Distance Width Graphs. We use the isomorphism order algorithm as a sub-routine for the canonization of the augmented tree S. We traverse S while computing the tree isomorphism order as in Lindell [Lin92] to output the canon of each

8. BOUNDED TREEWIDTH GI

of the nodes along with delimiters. That is, we output a '[' while going down a subtree, and ']' while going up a subtree.

We need to choose a bag node as root for the tree. Since there is no distinguished bag, we simply cycle through all of them in logspace, determining the set which, when chosen as the root, leads to the lexicographically minimum tree-code of the augmented tree S, i.e. the tree-canon of S. We describe the canonization procedure for a fixed root r.

The canonization procedure has two steps. In the first step we compute what we call a *tree-code* for S_r. Assume, that we can pre-compute a table where we have for each graph of size $\leq k$ its canon. We can use this for example, if the isomorphism order algorithm reaches a leaf in the augmented tree. This canon is given by arranging the edges of the graphs in a unique order. In the second step we compute the final canon from the lexicographical smallest tree-code.

For the tree-code of a subtree rooted at a bag node r, we compute the minimal mapping σ for r, invoking the isomorphism order algorithm. The tree-code begins with σ. According to the order of σ we order the children and output their canons in increasing isomorphism order.

For the tree-code of a subtree rooted at a separating set node s_1, we invoke the isomorphism order algorithm to arrange the children of s_1. This is done via cross comparisons of the subtrees rooted at these children. The tree-code begins with $\sigma|_{s_1}$ (i.e. the order of σ restricted to the vertices of s_1), followed by the tree-codes of the subtrees in increasing isomorphism order.

We give an example: Consider the tree-canon $l(S, r)$, a list of edges corresponding to the tree S_r of Figure 8.1 along with delimiters. Let $\sigma_{i,j}$ be the minimum mapping of the subtree rooted at bag node $a_{i,j}$.

$$\begin{aligned}
l(S, r) &= [\, (\sigma)\, l(S_{s_1}, s_1) \ldots l(S_{s_l}, s_l)\,], \text{ where} \\
l(S_{s_1}, s_1) &= [\, (\sigma|_{s_1})\, l(\sigma_{1,1}, a_{1,1}) \ldots l(\sigma_{1,k_1}, a_{1,k_1})\,] \\
&\vdots \\
l(S_{s_l}, s_l) &= [\, (\sigma|_{s_l})\, l(\sigma_{l,k_l}, a_{l,k_l})\,]
\end{aligned}$$

Canon for the Original Graph of Bounded Tree Distance Width. This list is now almost the canon, except that the names of the nodes are still the ones they have in G and the tree-canon has delimiters.

Clearly, a canon must be independent of the original names of the vertices. The final tree-canon for S_r can be obtained by a logspace transducer which relabels the vertices in the order of their first occurrence in this list of edges and outputs the list using these new labels. Also see the routine on Page 5.4.

To get the canon for G, remove the delimiters '[' and ']' in the tree-canon for S_r and order the edges of G in lexicographical order using the new labels. This is sufficient, because we describe here a bijective function f which transforms an automorphism ϕ of S_r into an automorphism $f(\phi)$ for G with X_r fixed. This proves the theorem.

Theorem 8.2.8 *A graph of bounded tree distance width can be canonized in logspace.*

8.3 Graphs of Bounded Treewidth

In this section we consider several isomorphism problems for graphs of bounded treewidth. We are interested in isomorphisms *respecting* the decompositions (i.e. vertices are mapped blockwise from a bag to another bag). We show first that if the tree decomposition of both input graphs is part of the input then the decomposition respecting isomorphism problem can be decided in L. We show then that if a tree decomposition of only one of the two given graphs is part of the input, then the isomorphism problem is in LogCFL. It follows that the isomorphism problem for graphs of bounded treewidth is also in LogCFL.

Assume first the decompositions of both input graphs are given. In order to prove that this problem is in L, we show that given tree decompositions together with designated bags as roots for G and H the question of whether there is an isomorphism between the graphs mapping root to root and respecting the decompositions (i.e. mapping bags in G blockwise onto bags in H) can be reduced to the isomorphism problem for graphs of bounded tree distance width. We argued in the previous section that this problem belongs to L.

Theorem 8.3.1 *The isomorphism problem for bounded treewidth graphs with given tree decompositions reduces to isomorphism for bounded tree distance width graphs under AC^0 many-one reductions.*

Proof. Let $(G, D, r), (H, D', r')$ be two graphs together with tree decompositions D and D' of width k and root bags X_r and $X'_{r'}$. We describe a function which transforms (G, D, r) into $(\widehat{G}, S)$ where $\widehat{G}$ is a graph of bounded tree distance width k and S is a root set for a minimum tree distance decomposition of $\widehat{G}$. This function also transforms (H, D', r') into $(\widehat{H}, S')$. We will show that this happens in such a way that $(\widehat{G}, S)$ is isomorphic to $(\widehat{H}, S')$ if and only if there is an isomorphism between G and H respecting the decompositions D and D' and mapping the vertices in the root bag r to vertices in the root bag r'.

Let $D = (\{X_i \mid i \in I\}, T = (I, F), r)$ be the given tree decomposition of G. W.l.o.g. we can assume that every bag in D contains at least two vertices. We define $S := X_r$. $\widehat{G}$ is defined as follows:

1. For each bag X_i in D and each vertex v in X_i, we define the vertex (v, i) in $\widehat{G}$. If $u, v \in X_i$ and there is an edge $\{u, v\} \in E(G)$ then we define the edge $\{(u, i), (v, i)\} \in E(\widehat{G})$.

8. BOUNDED TREEWIDTH GI

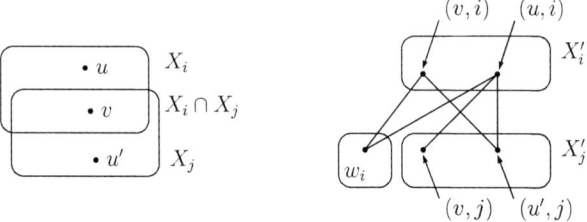

Figure 8.2: The figure shows the situation where X_i and X_j are copied. For the vertices u, u', v and w_i the new edges from Step 2 and Step 3 are drawn.

2. For all $\{i,j\} \in F$, $u \in X_i$ and $v \in X_j$ with $u \neq v$, we define an edge between (u,i) and (v,j).

3. For all i, we define a vertex $w_i \in \widehat{G}$ which is connected to (v,i), for all $v \in X_i$.

From H, the graph $\widehat{H}$ is defined the same way. We consider the minimal tree distance decomposition $\widehat{D}$ of $\widehat{G}$ with root set S. For each bag X_i in D, in Step 1 the vertices of this bag are copied in $\widehat{G}$. By considering these bags as a tree distance decomposition of $\widehat{G}$, the distance from the root set S to such a bag is equal to the distance of r to i in T. This is, because if (i,j) is an edge in T then for every vertex (u,i) in $\widehat{G}$ there is an edge to at least one vertex (v,j). It also holds that the minimal tree distance decomposition of $\widehat{G}$ with root S has width k.

If G is isomorphic to H with an isomorphism respecting the decompositions and mapping the vertices from the root bag X_r of G to the root bag of H, then clearly $\widehat{G}$ is isomorphic to $\widehat{H}$. For the other direction, observe that the edges connecting the vertices inside each bag are kept by Step 1 in the definition of $\widehat{G}$ and $\widehat{H}$. By Step 3, we guarantee, that in an isomorphism between $\widehat{G}$ and $\widehat{H}$ the vertices in one bag are all mapped blockwise to vertices in some bag, i.e. they are not split and mapped onto vertices of two or more bags. In Step 2, we distinguish between vertices in $X_i \cap X_j$ and the other vertices. That is, for an edge $(i,j) \in T$, every vertex (u,i) is connected to every vertex (v,j) except to (u,j) (in case u belongs to $X_i \cap X_j$ in D). Since all the copies of vertex u (all the vertices (u,i) for some i in $\widehat{G}$) belong to a connected subtree, this implies that in a possible isomorphism between $\widehat{G}$ and $\widehat{H}$ all copies of vertex u in $\widehat{G}$ have to be mapped blockwise to copies of the same vertex in $\widehat{H}$.

It follows that there is an isomorphism between $\widehat{G}$ and $\widehat{H}$ if and only if there is an isomorphism between G and H which respects the bags in the decompositions D and D' together with r and r', accordingly. □

From Theorem 8.3.1 we get the following corollary.

Corollary 8.3.2 *For every $k \geq 1$ there is a logarithmic space algorithm that, on input a pair of graphs together with a tree decompositions of width k for each of them, decides whether there is an isomorphism between the graphs, respecting the decompositions.*

Proof. The result follows from the previous reduction and Theorem 8.3.1. Thereby we fix a root in D and run through all possibilities for bags as roots in D'. As there are only polynomially many bags in D' this can be done by a logspace machine. □

In the previous reduction, we transformed a graph G given together with a tree decomposition D of width k and with root bag r into a new graph $\widehat{G}$ and a root set S such that the minimal tree distance decomposition of $\widehat{G}$ has width k. As done in Section 8.2 we can compute within logspace an augmented tree for $\widehat{G}$. Moreover we can use the defined total isomorphism order on augmented trees to compare in this way graphs of bounded treewidth given together with tree decompositions.

Corollary 8.3.3 *For any $k > 1$ there is a total order $<_A$ defined on the set of tuples (G, D, r) where G is a graph of treewidth k, and D a tree decomposition of G with root set r. $<_A$ can be computed in logarithmic space and $(G, D, r) =_A (H, D', r')$ if and only if there is an isomorphism between G and H respecting the decompositions and mapping the root set of r to that of r' (i.e. X_r to $X'_{r'}$ blockwise).*

We use this result in the next section for computing an isomorphism when just one of the decompositions is given.

8.3.1 A LogCFL Algorithm for Isomorphism

We consider now the more difficult situation in which only one of the input graphs is given together with a tree decomposition.

Theorem 8.3.4 *Isomorphism testing for two graphs of bounded treewidth, when a tree decomposition for one of them is given, can be done in LogCFL.*

Proof. We describe an algorithm which runs on a non-deterministic auxiliary pushdown automaton (NAuxPDA). Besides a read-only input tape and a finite control, this machine has access to a stack of polynomial size and a $O(\log n)$ space bounded work-tape. On the input tape we have two graphs G, H of treewidth k and a tree decomposition $D = (\{X_i \mid i \in I\}, T = (I, F), r)$ for G. For $j \in I$ we define G_j to be the subgraph of G induced on the vertex set $\{v \mid v \in X_i, i \in I$ and $i = j$ or i a descendant of j in $T\}$. That is, G_j contains the vertices which are separated by the bag X_j from X_r and those in X_j. We define $D_j = (\{X_i, | , i \in I_j\}, T_j = (I_j, F_j), j)$ as the tree decomposition of G_j corresponding to T_j, the

167

8. BOUNDED TREEWIDTH GI

subtree of T rooted at j. We also consider a way to order the children of a node in the tree decomposition:

Definition 8.3.5 *Given a graph G together with a tree decomposition D, let $1, \ldots, l$ be the children of a node r in the decomposition tree T. We define the* lexicographical subgraph order, *as the order among the subgraphs $G_1, \ldots, G_l$ which is given by: $G_i < G_j$ iff there is a vertex $w \in V(G_i) \setminus X_r$ which has a smaller label than every vertex in $V(G_j) \setminus X_r$.*

The algorithm non-deterministically guesses two main structures. On the one hand it guesses a tree decomposition of width k for H. This is done in a similar way as in the LogCFL algorithm from Wanke [Wan94] for testing that a graph has bounded treewidth. We briefly sketch this method which is the basis of our algorithm. Second, we guess an isomorphism ϕ from G to H by extending partial mappings from bag to bag.

Algorithm for Tree Decomposition Testing. For completeness we include here a sketch of Wanke's algorithm [Wan94] for testing whether a graph has treewidth k. On input a graph G the algorithm guesses non-deterministically the bags in the decomposition using the pushdown to test that these bags fulfill the properties of a tree decomposition and that every edge in G is included in some bag. If the guessed bags determine a tree decomposition of width k, the algorithms accepts.

Let G be the connected input graph. P and Q denote vertex sets of size $\leq k+1$ in G which are additionally separating sets and play the role of bags in the tree decomposition. For a separating set P in G and a vertex $v \notin P$, let $\Phi_G(P, v)$ be the split component of P in G containing v. For technical reasons we extend G defining an extra vertex v_0 and connecting it arbitrarily to a vertex u with the property that $\{u\}$ is not an articulation point in G. We will assume that v_0 has a label with a smaller number than all the original vertices in G. We also consider arbitrarily some other vertex $w \neq u$ in G. The algorithm is started with the initial bag $P = \{v_0, u\}$ and the initial vertex w, representant of the unique split component of P. The initial call is thus Decompose($G, v_0, \{v_0, u\}, w$). P and the sequence of bags Q defined in an accepting non-deterministic computation define a tree decomposition of G (once the vertex v_0 is deleted from them). Then it guesses non-deterministically a new bag Q in the decomposition and goes in recursion with each of the split components defined by Q. This is done with the procedure Decompose(G, v_0, P, v) where G is the original graph, v_0 the extra vertex, P the actual separating set (bag) and v a representant of a split component of P. The initial call is Decompose($G, v_0, \{v_0, u\}, w$) where u and w are chosen arbitrarily, where u is not an articulation point in G and $w \neq u$.

P and the sequence of bags Q defined in an accepting non-deterministic computation define a tree decomposition of G (once the vertex v_0 is deleted from them).

Algorithm 1 Tree decomposition testing Decompose(G, v_0, P, v)
Input: graph G, vertex v_0, separating set P with $|P| \leq k+1$,
vertex v in a split component of P
Output: accept iff the graph induced by $P \cup \Phi_G(P,v)$ has a tree decomposition of width k

1: non-deterministically choose Q of size $\leq k+1$ in $\Phi_G(P,v) \cup P$
2: **if** $Q \subseteq P$ or $P \subseteq Q$ or
   $\exists \{u_1, u_2\} \in E(G) : u_1 \in \Phi_G(P,v) \wedge u_2 \notin \Phi_G(P,v) \cup Q$
   then halt and reject
3: **for all** $w \neq v_0$ having label with smallest number in a split component of Q
4:     go into recursion with Decompose(G, v_0, Q, w)
5: **if** the stack is not empty **then** go one level up in recursion
6: halt and accept

In every iteration the algorithm chooses Q, a neighbor bag of P in a tree decomposition of G. In Line 2 it is required that Q is not contained in P nor P in Q and Q must separate its split components in the subgraph $\Phi_G(P,v)$ from the vertices in $P \setminus Q$. In Line 3 the algorithm goes into recursion at each split component of Q, except the one which contains v_0. The algorithm recursively chooses separating sets this way from the root through the whole graph.

Algorithm for Isomorphism Testing. We modify the algorithm of Wanke in a way that we can test isomorphism in parallel. Namely, our algorithm simulates Wanke's algorithm as a subroutine. In the description of the new algorithm we concentrate on the isomorphism testing part and hide the details of how to choose the bags. For simplicity the sentence "guess a bag X_j in H according to Wanke's algorithm" means that we simulate the guessing steps from Wanke, checking at the same time that the constructed structure is in fact a tree decomposition. Note, if the bags were not chosen appropriately, then the algorithm would halt and reject.

The algorithm starts guessing a root bag $X'_{r'}$ of size $\leq k+1$ for a decomposition of H. With $X'_{r'}$ as root bag it guesses step by step the tree decomposition D' of H which corresponds to D and its root r. It also constructs a mapping ϕ describing a partial isomorphism from the vertices of G onto the vertices of H. At the beginning, ϕ is the empty mapping and the algorithm guesses an extension of ϕ from X_r onto $X'_{r'}$ that is stored on the top of the stack. In general when dealing with a set of vertices from a bag X_a in D, the algorithm cycles through all possible subsets S of X_a and considers the children i of a in D with $X_a \cap X_i = S$. Note, S is the separating set of minimum size which separates $X_i \setminus X_a$ from the root bag X_r. The corresponding subgraphs G_i of G are then partitioned in isomorphism classes respecting the decomposition D_i given in the input. This is done considering the total isomorphism order

8. BOUNDED TREEWIDTH GI

of (G_i, D_i, X_i) as defined in Corollary 8.3.3. The algorithm compares the children of a with separating set S with guessed children of a' (with separating set $\phi(S)$) testing that for each isomorphism class there is the same number of isomorphic subgraphs with root a' in H. For this the algorithm uses the lexicographical subgraph order (Definition 8.3.5) to go through the isomorphic siblings from left to right, just keeping a pointer to the current child on the worktape, so that no child is counted twice. For two such children, say s_1 of a and t_1 of a', the algorithm checks then recursively that (G_1, D_1) is isomorphic to the corresponding subgraph of t_1 in H, by an extension of ϕ. Inside an isomorphism class the subgraphs have the same intersection with X_a and are isomorphic to each other. Because of this, they are interchangeable and could be mapped to subgraphs in the corresponding isomorphism class from $X'_{a'}$ in any order. The isomorphism computed by the algorithm maps these subgraphs to subgraphs in the isomorphism class from $X'_{a'}$ in lexicographical subgraph order.

When the algorithm goes into recursion, it pushes on the stack $O(\log n)$ bits for a description of X_a and $X'_{a'}$ as well as a description of the partial mapping ϕ from X_a onto $X'_{a'}$ and the description of S.

In general, not all the information about ϕ is kept on the stack. We only have the partial isomorphism $\phi : \{v \mid v \in X_r \cup \cdots \cup X_a\} \to \{v \mid v \in X'_{r'} \cup \cdots \cup X'_{a'}\}$, where $r, \ldots, a$ ($r', \ldots, a'$, respectively) is a simple path in T from the root to the node at the current level of recursion. After the algorithm runs through all children of some node (going through all its subsets S) it goes one level up in recursion and recomputes all the other information which is given implicitly by the subtrees from which it returned. Suppose the control of the algorithm returned to the bag X_a, from a child X_i with $X_a \cap X_i = S$ after checking that the partial isomorphism can be extended to map X_i to $X'_{i'}$. It then has to do the following:

- Copy from the top of the stack into the work-tape the partial isomorphism ϕ of the bags X_a onto $X'_{a'}$.

- Compute the lexicographical next isomorphic sibling of X_i with separating set S and guess the lexicographical next isomorphic sibling of $X'_{i'}$ with separating set $\phi(S)$. Check that the guessed sibling satisfies the decomposition properties that the isomorphism can be extended to include the new subgraphs.

- If there is no such sibling then look for the next isomorphism class (Corollary 8.3.3) of a subtree with minimum sized separating set S and look for the lexicographical first child of X_a inside this class.

- If there is no higher isomorphism class of subtrees with minimum sized separating set S then go to the next subset $S' \subseteq X_a$.

- If there is no further subset S' then the algorithm has visited all children of X_a and it is ready to further return one level up in the recursion.

Algorithm 2 Isomorphism testing $\mathsf{TWIso}(G, H, D, X_a, X'_{a'})$

Input: Graphs G, H, tree decomposition D for G, bags X_a in G and $X'_{a'}$ in H
Top of Stack: Partial isomorphism ϕ mapping the vertices in the parent bag of X_a onto the vertices in the parent bag of $X'_{a'}$
Output: Accept, iff G_a is isomorphic to H_a by an extension of ϕ

1: Guess an extension of ϕ to a partial isomorphism from X_a onto $X'_{a'}$
2: **if** ϕ cannot be extended to a partial isomorphism which maps X_a onto $X'_{a'}$
    then halt and reject
3: **for** each subset $S \subseteq X_a$
4:     Let $1, \ldots, l$ be the children of a in T with $X_a \cap X_i = S$. Partition the
        subgraphs corresponding to the subtrees of T rooted at $1, \ldots, l$
        into (decomposition respecting) isomorphism classes $E_1, \ldots, E_p$
5:     **for** each class E_j from $j = 1$ to p
6:         **for** each subtree $T_i \in E_j$ (in lexicographical subgraph order)
7:             guess a bag $X'_{i'}$ in H in increasing lexicographical subgraph order of $H_{i'}$
8:             **if** $X'_{i'}$ is not a correct child bag of $X'_{a'}$ (see Wanke's algorithm)
                then halt and reject
9:             Invoke $\mathsf{TWIso}(G_i, H_{i'}, D_i, X_i, X'_{i'})$ recursively and push X_a, $X'_{a'}$
                and the partial isomorphism ϕ on the stack
10:            After recursion pop these informations from the stack
11: **if** the stack is not empty **then** go one level up in recursion
12: halt and accept

Algorithm 2 summarizes the above considerations. In Line 1, it guesses an extension of the partial isomorphism ϕ to include a mapping from X_a onto $X'_{a'}$. We the partial isomorphism of their parent bags can be found on the top of the stack.

In Line 3 the algorithm cycles through all the subsets of X_a. The partition in Line 4 can be obtained in logspace by decomposition respecting isomorphism tests of the tree structures. Two subtrees rooted at X_i and X_j are in the same isomorphism class if and only if $(G_i, D_i, S) =_\mathsf{A} (G_j, D_j, S)$.

In Lines 7 to 10, the algorithm guesses the bag $X'_{i'}$ in H which corresponds to X_i and tests recursively whether the corresponding subgraphs G_i and $H_{i'}$ are isomorphic with an extension of the partial isomorphism ϕ. Observe that the algorithm cannot guess the same bag $X'_{i'}$ in H for two different bags X_i and X_j in G. This is because if the corresponding subgraphs G_i and G_j are isomorphic the bags in H are chosen in increasing lexicographical order (Line 7) and must be different. On the other hand if G_i and G_j are not isomorphic then the subgraph of H defined by $X'_{i'}$ cannot be isomorphic to both of them.

8. BOUNDED TREEWIDTH GI

In Line 8, the algorithm checks whether $X'_{i'}$ fulfills the properties of a correct tree-decomposition as in Wanke's algorithm (i.e. $X'_{i'}$ must be a separating set which separates its split components from the vertices in $X'_{a'} \setminus X'_{i'}$).

To show that the algorithm correctly computes an isomorphism, we make the following observation. A bag X_a and a subset $S \subseteq X_a$ constitute a separating set defining the connected subgraphs $G_1, \ldots, G_l$. These subgraphs do not contain the root X_r and $V(G_i) \cap V(G_j) = S$ since we have a tree decomposition D. The algorithm guesses and keeps from the partial isomorphism ϕ exactly those parts which correspond to the path from the roots X_r and $X'_{r'}$ to the current bags X_a and $X'_{a'}$. Once it verified a partial isomorphism from one child component (e.g. G_i) of X_a onto a child component (e.g. $H_{i'}$) of $X'_{a'}$, for the other child components it suffices to know the partial mapping of ϕ from X_a onto $X'_{a'}$.

Observe that for each v in G in a computation path from the algorithm there can only be a value for $\phi(v)$, since in the decomposition all the appearances of vertex v belong to bags from a connected subtree in D. Clearly, if G and H are isomorphic then the algorithm can guess the decomposition of H which fits to D, and the extensions of ϕ correctly. In this case the NAuxPDA has some accepting computation. On the other hand, if the input graphs are non-isomorphic then in every non-deterministic computation either the guessed tree decomposition of H does not fulfill the conditions of a tree decomposition (and would be detected) or the partial isomorphism ϕ cannot be extended at some point. □

Wanke's algorithm decides in LogCFL whether the treewidth of a graph is at most k by guessing all possible tree decompositions. Using a result from [GLS02] it follows that there is also a (functional) LogCFL algorithm that, on input of a bounded treewidth graph, computes a *certificate*, i.e. a particular tree decomposition, for it. Since LogCFL is closed under composition, from this result and Theorem 8.3.4 we get:

Theorem 8.3.6 *([GLS02]) Computing a* LogCFL *certificate can be done in (functional)* L^{LogCFL}.

The functional version of L^{LogCFL} has exactly the same parallel complexity as LogCFL. Hence, computing bits which encode a unique tree decomposition can be done in LogCFL. To see this, we can query the co-LogCFL machine the following: Given a graph G, a bag P and an extension Q (i.e. a child bag of P in a tree decomposition), and a root node r, we can query, whether there is *no* extension Q' of P in the tree decomposition, which has bitwise a lexicographically smaller representation than Q. This is done inductively to produce a unique tree decomposition for G. Since LogCFL is closed under composition, from this result and Theorem 8.3.4 we get:

Corollary 8.3.7 *The isomorphism problem for bounded treewidth graphs is in* LogCFL.

Reachability on Bounded Tree Distance Width Graphs

In [DDN10], the reachability problem on k-trees is considered with k a constant, as well as the distance and the long-path problem when given as acyclic graphs. They also give a logspace algorithm for Distance and LongPath on directed acyclic k-trees. These results are also applicable for bounded tree width graphs when a tree decomposition is given.

In Section 8.2.1 on Page 154 we argued that a tree distance decomposition can be computed in logspace.

Claim 8.3.8 *There is an AC^0-computable function which computes for a tree distance decomposition of width k a tree decomposition of width $\leq 2k$.*

To see this, simply define bags for all pairs of adjacent bags in the tree distance decomposition. We bring these facts together and state the following corollary.

Corollary 8.3.9 *The reachability problem on directed bounded tree-distance width graphs is in L. The distance problem and the long-path problem on directed acyclic graphs of bounded tree distance width is in L.*

Conclusions and Open Problems

We have shown that the isomorphism problem for graphs of bounded treewidth is in the class LogCFL and that for the more restricted case of bounded tree distance width graphs the problem is complete for L. Moreover for this second class of graphs we also give a logspace algorithm for the canonization problem. By using standard techniques in the area it can be shown that the same upper bounds apply for other problems related to isomorphism on these graph classes. For example the problem of deciding whether a given graph has a non-trivial automorphism or the functional versions of automorphism and isomorphism can be done within the same complexity classes. The main question remaining is whether the LogCFL upper bound for isomorphism of bounded treewidth graphs can be improved. On the one hand, no LogCFL-hardness result for the isomorphism problem is known, so maybe the result can be improved.

We believe that proving a logspace upper bound for the isomorphism problem of bounded treewidth graphs would require to compute tree decompositions within logarithmic space, which is a long standing open question. Elberfeld, Jakoby and Tantau [EJT10] showed very recently, that in fact, a tree decomposition can be computed within logarithmic space. Another interesting open question is whether bounded treewidth graphs can be canonized in LogCFL.

9 Reachability in $K_{3,3}$-Minor Free and K_5-Minor Free Graphs

9.1 Introduction

We consider the reachability problem on restricted classes of directed graphs. It is a widely studied problem in complexity theory, especially in the space setting. It also has its importance in graph theory where it is of interest to consider variants of reachability, i.e. computing shortest and longest simple paths in graphs.

For undirected graphs, the reachability problem is L-complete [Rei08]. For general graphs, reachability is NL-complete. Bourke, Tewari and Vinodchandran [BTV07] proved that reachability on planar graphs is in UL ∩ coUL and is hard for L. They built on work of Reinhard and Allender [RA00] and Allender, Datta and Roy [ADR05]. A more direct proof is given by Kulkarni [Kul09]. In Section 5.3 we prove that the distance problem for planar graphs is in UL ∩ coUL. For general graphs and even undirected planar graphs, the longest path problem is complete for NP. It is NL-complete for directed acyclic graphs (DAG). Limaye, Mahajan and Nimbhorkar [LMN09] prove that longest paths in planar DAGs can be computed in UL ∩ coUL.

We study reachability on extensions of planar graphs. Our main result is that reachability for directed $K_{3,3}$-free graphs and directed K_5-free graphs logspace-reduces to planar reachability. Thus, the current upper bound for planar reachability, UL ∩ coUL, carries over to reachability for directed $K_{3,3}$-free graphs and directed K_5-free graphs. One motivation for our results clearly is to improve the complexity upper bounds of certain reachability problems, from NL to UL in this case. Another aspect is that thereby we also consider the relationship of complexity classes, namely of UL vs. NL. The major open question is whether one can extend our results further such that we finally get a collapse of NL to UL.

In the case of a $K_{3,3}$-free graph G, our technique is to decompose G into biconnected components. Then these biconnected components are decomposed further into planar triconnected components and K_5-components (cf. [Vaz89]). We construct a similar tree where the nodes are associated with planar components (which are not further decomposed) and K_5-components, the PlaK$_5$-*component tree*.

For the reachability problem from vertex s to t in graph G we consider the simple path P

9. $K_{3,3}$-FREE AND K_5-FREE REACHABILITY

in the PlaK$_5$-component tree from component nodes S to T, where s and t are contained, respectively. We split the graph into components along the separating pairs associated to nodes which we have on path P. A path from s to t in G must contain vertices of all these separating pairs. We make the reachability test for all these components. The difficulty is to handle the non-planar components. The crucial step is to replace all the K_5-components in the tree by planar components such that the reachability conditions are not changed. Then we recombine the planar components into a planar graph H such that there is a path from s to t in G if and only if this holds in H, too. The construction can be carried out in logspace.

There also exists a decomposition of K_5-free graphs (cf. Khuller [Khu88]). This is obtained by decomposing the graph into triconnected components. Each triconnected component is either planar, isomorphic to the four-rung Möbius ladder (also called V_8) or it is constructed by taking 3-clique sums of planar 4-connected components [Wag37]. We replace the V_8-components by planar components such that the reachability conditions are not changed. Then we recombine the planar components into a planar graph. A difficulty which arises here is, that we cannot use the 3-clique sum to recombine the components, because this would result again in a non-planar graph. Instead, we carefully add copies of the components which can be arranged in a planar way such that the reachability conditions are not altered. All the steps can be accomplished in logspace.

It is easy to see that our transformations from $K_{3,3}$-free or K_5-free graphs to planar graphs maintain not just reachability, but also the distances of the vertices. Therefore it follows from our results that distances in $K_{3,3}$-free or K_5-free graphs can be computed UL ∩ coUL.

The same is true with respect to the longest path problem, when considering DAGs instead. This is easy to see in the case of $K_{3,3}$-free DAGs and requires some extra arguments in the case of K_5-free DAGs. Hence, longest paths in $K_{3,3}$-free or K_5-free DAGs can be computed in UL ∩ coUL.

In Section 9.2 we prove that Reachability on $K_{3,3}$-free graphs reduces to planar Reachability. In Section 9.3 we prove that Reachability on K_5-free graphs reduces to planar Reachability.

9.2 Reachability in $K_{3,3}$-Minor Free Graphs

We give a logspace reduction from the reachability problem for directed $K_{3,3}$-free graphs to the reachability problem for directed planar graphs. The latter problem is known to be in UL ∩ coUL [BTV07].

For the reduction, consider the decomposition of a given graph G into triconnected components. Moreover, Asano [Asa85] proved that the decomposition has the following form.

Lemma 9.2.1 *[Asa85] Each triconnected component of a $K_{3,3}$-free graph is either planar or exactly the graph K_5.*

For the decomposition, we consider G as *undirected*. That is, each directed edge of G is considered as an undirected edge. After the decomposition we consider the components again as directed graphs.

9.2.1 The PlaK$_5$-Component Tree

We define a tree based on planar and K_5-components. We deviate here from the triconnected component tree. Vazirani [Vaz89] recombines the *planar* triconnected components which are neighbors in the tree into one planar component. This defines a new tree with alternating planar and K_5-component nodes which we call the PlaK$_5$-*component tree*. Miller and Ramachandran [MR87] showed that the PlaK$_5$-component tree can be computed in NC^2. Thierauf and Wagner [TW09] describe a simpler and more direct construction that works in logspace. Here, for the following lemma we refer to Lemma 2.2.2 where we proved that 3-connected components can be obtained in logspace.

Lemma 9.2.2 *The decomposition of an undirected $K_{3,3}$-free biconnected graph into planar and K_5-components can be computed in logspace.*

In Lemma 2.2.2 we proved that the triconnected components of a biconnected graph can be computed in logspace. Because G is $K_{3,3}$-free and biconnected, a further logspace machine records the separating pairs which have both ends in a K_5 component. We call these the K_5-*separating pairs*. We also record the components in logspace.

We show now how to compute the planar components. Two vertices u and v are in the same planar component, if there is a path p from u to v in G such that p contains ≤ 2 vertices a, b from any K_5-component D and a, b separates u and v from the other three vertices in D. In addition, we require that the components have ≥ 3 vertices. That is, if both $u, v \in D$ and $\{u, v\}$ is no K_5-separating pair in D then there is no planar component that consists of u and v only.

Note, that path p can go through at most two vertices of a K_5-component. Intuitively, this allows p to touch a K_5-component, but not to go through the other components connected to the K_5-component.

The PlaK$_5$-component tree of G consists of

- K_5-*component nodes*,
- *planar component nodes* and
- K_5-*separating pair nodes*.

9. $K_{3,3}$-FREE AND K_5-FREE REACHABILITY

The tree has K_5-component nodes and planar component nodes and between two such nodes a K_5-separating pair node. That is, there is an edge between a K_5- or planar component node and a K_5-separating pair node if the corresponding component contains both vertices of the separating pair. Figure 9.1 shows an example.

We navigate in the tree in depth-first manner according to Theorem 2.6.1. Let the tree be rooted at node R and let C be a component node in the tree. The function Parent(C), i.e. the parent node of C, is computed as follows. The parent is a K_5-separating pair node, say $\{u, v\}$, if there is no path from vertices in C to vertices of R in $G \setminus \{u, v\}$. All the other K_5-separating pairs do not satisfy this condition, they are children of C. We define an order-function on these children of C, according to the minimum labels of vertices which belong to the children of C (and not to C). This provides a logspace computation of FirstChild(C, order) and NextSibling(C, order). Hence, we can navigate in logspace through the tree. We summarize.

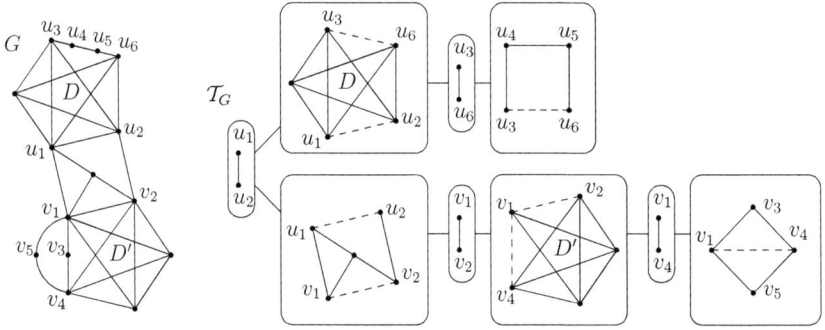

Figure 9.1: The $K_{3,3}$-minor free graph G contains two K_5-components D and D' which appear as nodes in the PlaK$_5$-component tree together with planar component nodes. The planar components are not further decomposed into triconnected components.

Theorem 9.2.3 *The decomposition of a $K_{3,3}$-free biconnected graph into a* PlaK$_5$*-component tree can be computed in logspace.*

9.2.2 Reduction to Planar Reachability

We describe a reduction from the reachability problem on directed $K_{3,3}$-free graphs to the reachability problem on directed planar graphs. We prove the following theorem.

Theorem 9.2.4 $K_{3,3}$-*free* Reachability $\leq_m^{log}$ *planar* Reachability.

We start with the simple observation that it suffices to consider *biconnected* directed $K_{3,3}$-free graphs.

Lemma 9.2.5 Reachability $\leq_m^{log}$ biconnected Reachability.

Proof. Let G be a directed and connected graph. In Lemma 2.2.1 we argued, that we can compute articulation points in logspace. Add a new vertex v to G and connect each articulation point to v, such that the out-degree of v is zero. This does not alter the reachability properties. Clearly, the resulting graph is still $K_{3,3}$-free or K_5-free and it is biconnected when considering edges to be undirected. □

Let $G = (V, E)$ be a biconnected directed $K_{3,3}$-free graph and s,t be two vertices in G. The problem is to find a path from s to t in G. Let $\mathcal{T}_G$ be the PlaK$_5$-component tree of G. Let S be the biconnected component that contains s and T the one that contains t.

We partition the tree into subtrees and consider the reachability problem for these subtrees. Then we replace *non-planar* components of $\mathcal{T}_G$ by *planar* components such that the reachability condition remains unchanged.

Partitioning of G into Subgraphs. Consider the simple path from S to T in $\mathcal{T}_G$, say $S = C_1, C_2, \ldots, C_l = T$. Let C_i be a separating pair node and C_{i-1} and C_{i+1} component nodes. A path from s to t always contains vertices of such separating pairs, say $\{u_i, v_i\}$. Here, $\{u_i, v_i\}$ separates the components associated to C_{i-1} and C_{i+1}. For an example see Figure 9.2.

Observe, that a simple path p from s to t must visit at least one vertex of each of these separating pairs. Once we have reached C_i, then p will not go back to C_{i-1}, because otherwise p would not be simple.

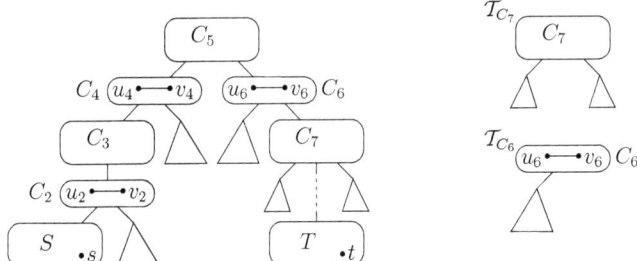

Figure 9.2: The PlaK$_5$-component tree $\mathcal{T}_G$ partitioned into pieces $\mathcal{T}_{C_i}$. The boxes indicate component nodes and the triangles indicate subtrees.

We partition the reachability problem into sub-problems. For a component node C_i define the tree $\mathcal{T}_{C_i}$ as the subtree of $\mathcal{T}_G$ rooted at C_i, where the branches to C_{i-1} and C_{i+1} are cut

9. $K_{3,3}$-FREE AND K_5-FREE REACHABILITY

off. Let G_i be the graph corresponding to $\mathcal{T}_{C_i}$. If C_i is a component node then $\{u_{i-1}, v_{i-1}\}$ and $\{u_{i+1}, v_{i+1}\}$ are separating pairs of C_i. In the case, when C_i is a separating pair node then instead of $\{u_{i-1}, v_{i-1}\}$ and $\{u_{i+1}, v_{i+1}\}$ we consider only one separating pair $\{u_i, v_i\}$ in C_i.

The following lemma states that the reachability problem in G can be partitioned into reachability problems in G_i.

Lemma 9.2.6 *Any simple path p from s to t in G can be written as a concatenation of paths, $p = p_1, \ldots, p_l$, such that*

- *path p_1 goes from s to u_2 or v_2 in G_1,*
- *path p_i is a path from one of u_{i-1} or v_{i-1} to one of u_{i+1} or v_{i+1} in G_i, if $i \in \{3, 5, \ldots, l-2\}$ (i.e. when C_i is a component node),*
- *path p_i is a path from u_i to v_i or from v_i to u_i or is of length zero in G_i, if $i \in \{2, 4, \ldots, l-1\}$ (i.e. when C_i is a separating pair node),*
- *path p_l is a path from u_{l-1} or v_{l-1} to t in G_l.*

Note, if s and t are in the same component C_1 then $S = C_1 = T$ and $\mathcal{T}_G = \mathcal{T}_{C_1}$. In the reachability problems for G_i, we search for a path from u_{i-1} (or v_{i-1}) to u_{i+1} (or v_{i+1}). Each separating pair is connected by a virtual edge. If we have the virtual edge $\{a, b\}$ in C_i on our path, then we have to check whether there is a path from a to b in G_i, i.e. traversing a child of C_i in $\mathcal{T}_{C_i}$. Note, at the child component the same situation can occur, recursively. If e.g. (a, b) is also a directed edge in G then there is a child component, a leaf node in the tree which corresponds to a 3-bond. This node indicates the directed edge (a, b).

Lemma 9.2.7 *There is a path from u_{i-1} or v_{i-1} to u_{i+1} or v_{i+1} in G_i for i even (or from u_i to v_i or v_i to u_i in G_i for i odd, respectively) if and only if there exists a path in C_i such that for virtual edges $\{a, b\}$ on this path there exists a path from a to b in the child component of C_i, recursively.*

Because we have K_5-component nodes, it is not clear yet, how we can test reachability in UL $\cap$ coUL. We transform the $K_{3,3}$-free graph into a planar graph.

Transforming a K_5-Component into a Planar Component. Let $\mathcal{T}_{C_i}$ be a PlaK$_5$-component tree rooted at C_i as described above. We start with the root C_i and traverse the tree in depth first manner. When we reach a K_5-component node D, then we replace it by a planar component D' as described next such that the reachability problem does not change. This results in a new component tree of a planar graph G'.

Lemma 9.2.8 *There is a logspace algorithm that transforms G into a planar graph G' such that there is a path from s to t in G if and only if there is such a path in G'.*

Let D be a K_5-component node with vertices $v_1, \ldots, v_5$. Let $\mathcal{T}_{C_i}$ be the subtree that contains D. Let N be the size of the subtree rooted at D in $\mathcal{T}_{C_i}$. Since our algorithm works recursively and in order to have a logspace bound, we would like to have recursive calls only on subtrees of small size, i.e. a fraction of N. Recall that there can be at most one large child of node D in $\mathcal{T}_{C_i}$. In the following, we consider the situation that we search a path from v_1 to v_2 in D and we have a large child at v_3, v_4. The same construction works if there is no large child, and it can be easily adapted to the case that the large child is at another pair (e.g. $\{v_2, v_4\}$). The graph D' is defined as shown in Figure 9.3.

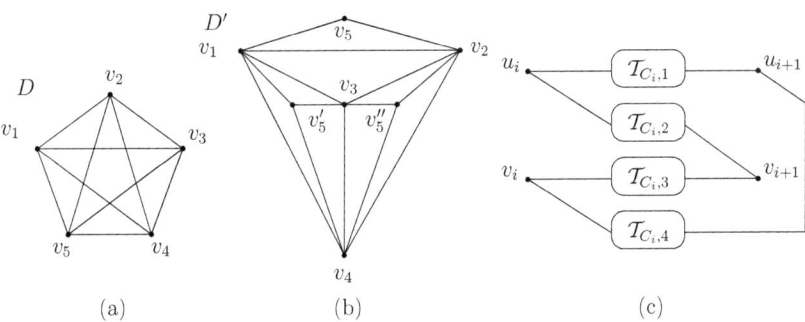

(a)   (b)   (c)

Figure 9.3: (a) A K_5-component node D and (b) the planar component node D'. The two vertices v_5' and v_5'' are copies of v_5. For example, an edge (v_1, v_5) in D occurs twice in D', as (v_1, v_5) and (v_1, v_5'). The edges of D and D' are drawn undirected to not overload the picture. But note that only the virtual edges are undirected. The edges that come from graph G have the same direction as in G. (c) The construction if D is the root of $\mathcal{T}_{C_i}$. Because there are four reachability problems, we have four versions of D, say $D_1, \ldots, D_4$ which replace the root in $\mathcal{T}_{C_i}$. This leads to four trees $\mathcal{T}_{C_i,1}, \ldots, \mathcal{T}_{C_i,4}$. The resulting graph is planar.

The new component D' has the following properties:

1. D' is planar.

2. Every path from v_1 to v_2 in D exists as well in D', possibly going through one of the copies v_5' or v_5'' instead of v_5.

3. D' contains the edge $\{v_3, v_4\}$ only once. This edge corresponds to a large child if there is one.

4. Vertices v_1 and v_2 are on the outer face of D'.

9. $K_{3,3}$-FREE AND K_5-FREE REACHABILITY

The last property is important for the special case when D is the root of the subtree, i.e. $D = C_i$. Then we have two vertices u_i, v_i and ask whether we can reach two other vertices u_{i+1} and v_{i+1} and all these vertices belong to D. For a planar arrangement, we make the construction as shown in Figure 9.3 (c). For example, D_1 is a copy of D where v_1 is identified with u_i and v_2 with u_{i+1}. In total, this gives four combinations of reachability questions. Hence, we make four copies of the whole planar graph corresponding to $\mathcal{T}_{C_i}$, one for each path from a vertex of the incoming separating pair to a vertex of the outgoing separating pair. Note, that this case can occur only at the root, and not in the recursion in the tree $\mathcal{T}_{C_i}$. Therefore, we can afford to make the four copies.

The replacement of the K_5-components is done recursively in depth-first manner with all the copies of children (i.e. the subtrees rooted at separating pairs) which we have in the new components D'. Consequently, we give new names to vertices in the copies of the subtrees.

We do this for all edges on all paths in D'. The order of the edges is given by the order they appear on the input tape. We can always recompute the new planar component D', because we can recompute the sizes of the subtrees of D. We can always refer to which copy of a separating pair we went into recursion by storing $O(1)$ bits on the work-tape when we go into recursion. Hence, whenever we have to change vertex names, we can recompute the new vertex names of the copy of a separating pair. We need such bits at each level of recursion. At each stage in the tree, say at sub-tree $\mathcal{T}_D$, the sizes of the copied immediate subtrees are at most $1/2$ the size of $\mathcal{T}_D$. Hence, there are at most $O(\log n)$ levels of recursion and the algorithm runs in logspace.

Lemma 9.2.9 *The resulting graph G' after the transformation of K_5 components has the following properties for all i.*

- G'_i *is a planar graph.*
- *There are simple paths from u_i or v_i to u_{i+1} or v_{i+1} in G_i if and only if there are such simple paths in G'.*
- *The size of the resulting graph G'_i remains polynomial.*

Proof. The planarity and the reachability test on G'_i can be proven by induction on the number of K_5-components, when replaced one by one. The same way as in a K_5-component node D, G' contains the same copies of vertices we have in D' and for each copied edge in D' we have a copy of the according split component in G'.

The resulting graph is of polynomial size $\mathcal{S}(N)$, because we recursively copy subgraphs of size smaller than $N/2$. For some constant k we get the following recurrence:

$$\mathcal{S}(N) = k\mathcal{S}(N/2) + O(N)$$

□

This finishes the proof of Theorem 9.2.4 and we get the following corollary.

Corollary 9.2.10 $K_{3,3}$-*free* Reachability *is in* UL ∩ coUL.

Distance and Longest Paths in $K_{3,3}$-Free Graphs. For the distance problem and the longest path problem it suffices again to consider biconnected graphs, because we can pass only once through every articulation point on a simple path from s to t. Hence we can consider longest paths or distances in the biconnected components, and then sum up these lengths appropriately.

For biconnected graphs we use the transformation from Lemma 9.2.8. It suffices to say that simple paths in a K_5-component D of graph G have the same length as the corresponding paths in the planar component D' in graph G'. Hence, the following lemma holds.

Lemma 9.2.11 $K_{3,3}$-*free* Distance $\leq_m^{log}$ *planar* Distance.
$K_{3,3}$-*free* LongPath $\leq_m^{log}$ *planar* LongPath.

By Theorem 5.3.1 (also see [TW08]) we proved that computing the distance in planar directed graphs is in UL ∩ coUL. Limaye, Mahajan and Nimbhorkar [LMN09] proved that computing a longest path in planar DAGs is in UL ∩ coUL. As a consequence we get the following corollary.

Corollary 9.2.12 $K_{3,3}$-*free* Distance ∈ UL ∩ coUL.
$K_{3,3}$-*free* LongPath ∈ UL ∩ coUL.

9.3 Reachability in K_5-Minor Free Graphs

We give a logspace reduction from the reachability problem for directed K_5-free graphs to the reachability problem for directed planar graphs.

For the reduction, we decompose the given graph G into 3-connected and 4-connected components. For the decomposition we consider G as undirected. It follows from a theorem of Wagner [Wag37] that besides planar components we obtain the following non-planar components that way:

- the four-rung Möbius ladder, also called V_8 (see Figure 9.4), a 3-connected graph on 8 vertices, which is non-planar because it contains a $K_{3,3}$.

- The remaining 3-connected non-planar components are further decomposed into 4-connected components which are all planar.

We define trees based on these components. There are nodes for the triconnected components and the V_8-components which are connected via separating pair nodes. This is the triconnected component tree of a K_5-free graph. The non-planar 3-connected components are further decomposed into 4-connected components for which we define a 4-connected component tree. We will show, that this can be done in logspace.

183

9. $K_{3,3}$-FREE AND K_5-FREE REACHABILITY

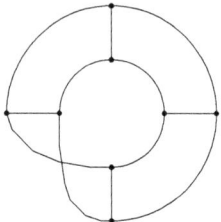

Figure 9.4: The four-rung Möbius ladder, also called V_8.

The key step in the reduction is to replace the V_8-components by planar components such that the reachability properties are not altered.

9.3.1 The Tree Decomposition

The decomposition of K_5-minor free graphs into planar components is the same as in Section 7.2.
    According to Lemma 2.2.1 the decomposition into biconnected components can be done in logspace.

The Triconnected Component Tree for Biconnected K_5-Free Graphs. Datta et.al. [DLN+09] show how to construct the triconnected component tree for a planar biconnected graph in logspace. Thierauf and Wagner [TW09] give a different construction which is suitable for K_5-free biconnected graphs. The difference is, that the 3-connected components must not be planar. Due to the work of [DNTW09] a construction is shown which works for all graphs. Also see the proof of Lemma 2.2.2, saying that any graph can be decomposed into triconnected components in logspace. We obtain in logspace a *triconnected component tree* $\mathcal{T}^\intercal(G)$ for a K_5-free biconnected graph G. $\mathcal{T}^\intercal(G)$ contains nodes for planar and non-planar triconnected components.

Decomposition into 4-Connected Components. It remains to further decompose the 3-connected components which are non-planar and not isomorphic to the V_8. We describe a special decomposition which can be computed in logspace. For this, we need the notion of maximum separating triples.

Definition 9.3.1 *Let τ be a separating triple and G a split component of τ. A separating triple $\tau_{\max} \neq \tau$ is a* candidate separating triple *in G with respect to τ if for any separating triple $\tau' \notin \{\tau, \tau_{\max}\}$ there is a path from a vertex of $\tau_{\max}$ to a vertex of τ in $G \setminus \tau'$.*

Two candidate separating triples τ_1, τ_2 are crossing if $\tau_1 \cap \tau_2 \neq \emptyset$ and τ_1 and τ_2 have a split component in common (i.e. if there is a vertex v in $G \setminus (\tau \cup \tau_1 \cup \tau_2)$ which belongs to a split component G_1 of τ_1 and a split component G_2 of τ_2). Note, if τ_1, τ_2 are crossing then there is no τ_3 which is also crossing τ_1 or τ_2. See Figure 9.5 for an example.

A maximum separating triple with respect to τ is either a candidate separating triple which is not crossing with any other candidate separating triple or the lexicographical smaller one of two crossing candidate separating triples.

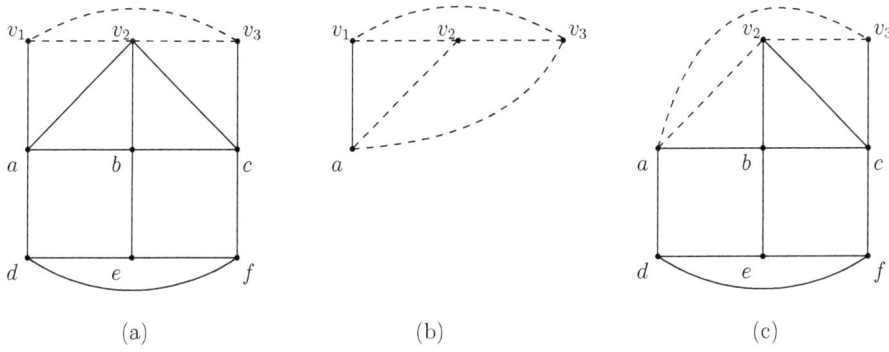

Figure 9.5: (a) The parent separating triple $\tau = \{v_1, v_2, v_3\}$ and two pairwise crossing candidate separating triples $\{a, v_2, v_3\}$ and $\{v_1, v_2, c\}$.
(b) The 4-connected component split by τ and $\{a, v_2, v_3\}$.
(c) The split component split by $\{a, v_2, v_3\}$ which has to be further decomposed recursively.

We use the following claim to argue, that the logspace machine can select simply one of the crossing separating triples arbitrarily. Note, this kind of decomposition is not entirely canonical, but this does not affect the reachability tests.

Claim 9.3.2 *In a triconnected, non-planar graph, not the V_8, let τ be a separating triple. If candidate separating triples τ_1 and τ_2 with respect to τ are crossing then there is no candidate separating triple τ_3 which is also crossing τ_1 or τ_2.*

Proof. Let $\tau = \{a, b, c\}$ be a separating triple with G a split component of τ where $\tau_i = \{a_i, b_i, c_i\}$ (for $i \in \{1, 2, 3\}$) are contained. First, τ_1 and τ_2 cannot share two vertices, since then one of them is no candidate separating triple. Hence, they share only one vertex and we can assume that $a_1, c_1 \notin \tau_2$ and vice versa $a_2, c_2 \notin \tau_1$. We assume, that τ_2 separates a_1 from c_1 such that one vertex, say c_1 is in the split component of τ_2 where the parent separating triple τ is

185

9. $K_{3,3}$-FREE AND K_5-FREE REACHABILITY

contained. The same holds vice versa, namely τ_1 separates a_2 from c_2 where we assume that c_2 is in the split component of τ_1 where τ is contained. Figure 9.6 (a) shows the current situation schematically.

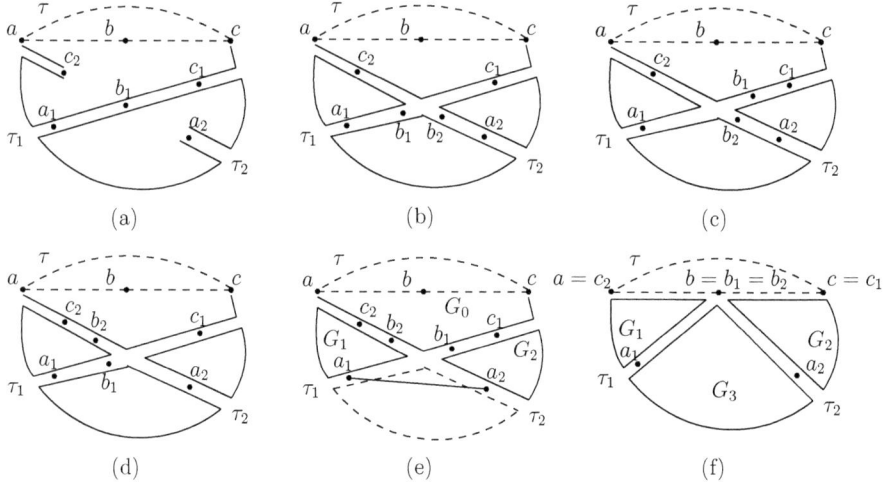

Figure 9.6: (a) Split component G of τ and candidate separating triple τ_1, where a_2 and c_2 are separated by τ_1.
(b) The candidate separating triples τ_1 and τ_2 are arranged in such a way that $\{c_1, c_2\}$ forms a separating pair.
(c) Here, $\{c_2, b_1, c_1\}$ is a candidate separating triple instead of τ_1 and τ_2.
(d) Here, $\{c_2, b_2, c_1\}$ is a candidate separating triple instead of τ_1 and τ_2.
(e) A situation is shown where τ_1 and τ_2 are crossing. The part split by a_1 and a_2 is trivially an edge, since otherwise this pair forms a separating pair.
(f) The split components when $a = c_2$, $b = b_1 = b_2$ and $c = c_1$.

First, we consider the case that $b_2 \notin \tau_1$. We distinguish some situations, namely where b_2 is located in the split components of τ_1 and τ_2 in G.

- b_2 is in the split component of τ_1 where a_2 is contained. Conversely, if b_1 is in the split component of τ_2 where a_1 is contained, then $\{c_1, c_2\}$ is a separating pair. This situation is shown in Figure 9.6 (b).
  Otherwise, if b_1 is in the split component of τ_2 where c_1 is contained, then $\{c_2, b_1, c_1\}$ would be a candidate separating triple, contradicting that τ_1, τ_2 are candidate separating triples, also see Figure 9.6 (c).

- b_2 is in the split component of τ_1 where c_2 is contained. Conversely, if b_1 is in the split component of τ_2 where a_1 is contained, then $\{c_2, b_2, c_1\}$ would be a candidate separating triple, contradicting that τ_1, τ_2 are candidate separating triples, also see Figure 9.6 (d). Otherwise, if b_1 is in the split component of τ_2 where c_1 is contained, then $\{a_1, a_2\}$ is an edge, since otherwise this pair would be a separating pair. This situation is shown in Figure 9.6 (e). We give names to the split components: G_0 where τ is contained, G_1 split by $\{c_2, b_2, a_1\}$ and G_2 split by $\{c_1, b_1, a_2\}$.
  Now to τ_3: If there is no vertex of τ_3 in $G_1 \setminus \{b_2, c_2\}$, then τ_2 would not be a candidate separating triple, because τ_3 separates τ_2 from τ. The same holds for $G_2 \setminus \{b_1, c_1\}$ instead of $G_1 \setminus \{b_2, c_2\}$ and τ_1 instead of τ_2. Assume that τ_3 and τ_1 are crossing. If there is only one vertex of τ_3 in G_1, say a_3, then $\{a_3, b_1, c_1\}$ is a candidate separating triple, contradicting that τ_1 is a candidate separating triple. If there are two vertices in G_1 then there is only one vertex in G_2, say a_3, then $\{c_2, b_2, a_3\}$ is a candidate separating triple, contradicting that τ_2 is a candidate separating triple. Hence, in this case τ_3 is not crossing τ_1 and with the same arguments, not crossing τ_2.

Now, we assume that $b_2 \in \tau_1$. Assume, $b_2 = a_1$ then G has separating pairs, namely at least one of $\{c_2, a_1\}$ and $\{a_1, a_2\}$, contradicting that G is triconnected. Conversely, if $\{c_2, a_1\}$ and $\{a_1, a_2\}$ are both edges, then τ_2 is no separating triple, because then it does not separate anything. The same argument can be applied to $b_2 = c_1$. We conclude, that $b_1 = b_2$. Assume, that at least one of $c_2, b_1, c_1 \notin \tau$, then it follows that c_2, b_1, c_1 is a candidate separating triple, contradicting that τ_1 is a candidate separating triple. We conclude that $\tau = \{c_2, b_1, c_1\}$ (i.e. $a = c_2, b = b_1 = b_2, c = c_1$). This situation is shown in Figure 9.6 (f).
Suppose now, that τ_3 is a candidate separating triple that is crossing τ_1. Following the same arguments as above, τ_1 and τ_3 share at most one vertex, say $a_3, c_3 \notin \tau_1$. If there is no vertex in G_1 or G_2 then τ_3 is no candidate separating triple, because one of τ_1, τ_2 separates τ_3 from τ entirely. If there is one vertex in G_1, say a_3, then $\{a_3, b, c\}$ is a candidate separating triple, contradicting that τ_1 is a candidate separating triple. The same holds with respect to G_2 and τ_2. There cannot be two vertices in G_1 and G_2 at the same time, unless $b = b_3$. But also in this case, $\{a_3, b, c\}$ is a candidate separating triple as we had before, a contradiction. This proves the claim. □

Let C be a 3-connected component in a K_5-free graph and let τ be a separating triple in C. We define a 4-*connected component* D *with respect to* τ as follows. Two vertices u and v are in D if there are simple paths from u and v to some vertices of τ and from u to v in $C \setminus \tau'$, for all maximum separating triples τ' with respect to τ.

9. $K_{3,3}$-FREE AND K_5-FREE REACHABILITY

Connect each pair of vertices of τ or of a maximum separating triple in D by a virtual edge. If for such a pair there is an edge in G then this is not contained in D, we define a 3-bond instead.

The resulting component D is 4-connected, because it does not contain separating triples by construction.

We define a tree $\mathcal{T}^4(C)$ as follows. There is a node for each separating triple and each 4-connected component. A *separating triple node* is connected to a *4-connected component node* if the separating triple is contained in the 4-connected component. Choose one separating triple τ_{root} in C as the root node of $\mathcal{T}^4(C)$. The resulting graph is a tree, the *4-connected component tree of* C. This tree can be computed in logspace, since the tasks are similar to those of the PlaK$_5$-component tree in the previous section.

Lemma 9.3.3 *The 4-connected component tree of a 3-connected K_5-free graph can be computed in logspace.*

9.3.2 Reachability in K_5-Minor Free Graphs

In this section, we prove the following theorem.

Theorem 9.3.4 K_5-*free* Reachability $\leq_m^{log}$ *planar* Reachability.

Let G be a connected graph and s and t be two vertices in G. By Lemma 9.2.5 and Lemma 9.2.7, we can partition the reachability problem for G into reachability problems on the triconnected components of G. If a triconnected component is planar, then we are done with it. If it is non-planar then we distinguish whether it is isomorphic to the V_8 or not.

In a triconnected component tree, a triconnected component has an incoming separating pair $\{u_i, v_i\}$ and an outgoing separating pair $\{u_{i+1}, v_{i+1}\}$. We consider four reachability tests, from u_i to u_{i+1}, from u_i to v_{i+1}, from v_i to u_{i+1} and from v_i to v_{i+1}. For each of these reachability tests, we construct a planar copy of the triconnected non-planar component and connect them as shown in Figure 9.3 (c) on Page 181.

Transforming a V_8-Component into a Planar Component. Let $\mathcal{T}_C^{\mathsf{T}}$ be a triconnected component tree rooted at some node C. Let D be a V_8-component node in $\mathcal{T}_C^{\mathsf{T}}$ and $v_1, \ldots, v_8$ the vertices in D. We transform D into a planar component D' such that the reachability conditions remain unchanged. The transformation is shown in Figure 9.7. For this, let $v_1, \ldots, v_4$ be four vertices in D such that $v_1 \neq v_2$. Assume, we search for a path from v_1 to v_2 in D and that $\{v_3, v_4\}$ is a virtual edge in D which corresponds to a large child of D.

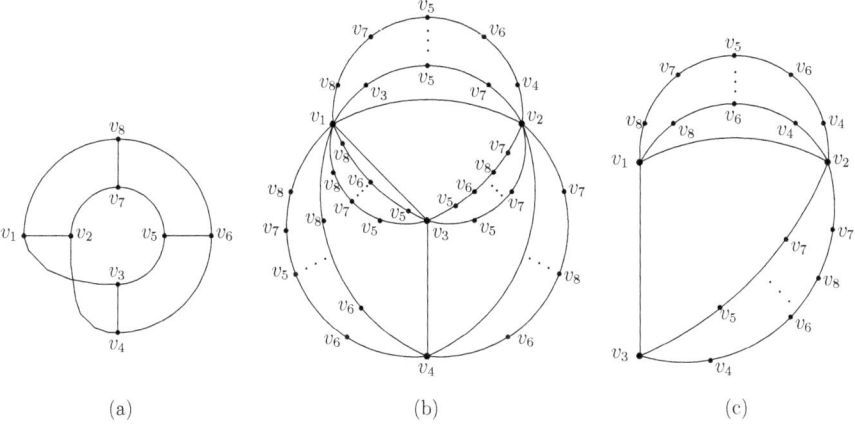

Figure 9.7: To simplify matters, all the copies of a vertex have the same label. We do not identify them as one single vertex.
(a) The V_8 component D with edges drawn undirected.
(b) The planar component D' is shown schematically. v_1 and v_2 can be any two vertices in D and v_3, v_4 correspond to a large child of D such that $\{v_1, v_2\} \cap \{v_3, v_4\} = \emptyset$. For every simple path from v_1 to v_2 *not* containing (v_3, v_4), there is a copy of the path in D', i.e. a copy of all vertices and edges on this path. This is indicated above the vertices v_1, v_2.
The remaining paths go along (v_3, v_4) or (v_4, v_3) in D. This edge should occur only once in D'. Therefore, these paths in D are subdivided into paths from v_1 to v_3 or to v_4, and from these vertices to v_2. This is indicated in the part below v_1, v_2.
(c) $\{v_1, v_2\}$ and $\{v_3, v_4\}$ must not be disjoint. The construction is essentially the same as in (b). Here, we see D' in the case that (v_1, v_3) is the large child.

By construction, D' has the following properties.

- For each path from v_1 to v_2 *not* containing $\{v_3, v_4\}$, D' contains a copy of this path, i.e. a copy of all vertices and edges on this path.
- For all paths from v_1 to v_2 containing $\{v_3, v_4\}$, D' contains a copy of the sub-path from v_1 to v_3 and v_4 to v_2 or vice versa from v_1 to v_4 and v_3 to v_2.
- D' contains the virtual edge $\{v_3, v_4\}$ exactly once.

9. $K_{3,3}$-FREE AND K_5-FREE REACHABILITY

- v_1 and v_2 are both on the outer-face of D'. This property is important in the case, that D is the root of $\mathcal{T}_C^\mathsf{T}$ (i.e. $D = C$).

- D' is planar and has $O(1)$ copies of each edge. It contains all simple paths from v_1 to v_2.

The replacement of the V_8-components is done recursively in depth-first manner. For all copies of virtual edges in D' this includes making copies of children. More precisely, making copies of the immediate subtrees, those are rooted at separating pairs. Consequently, we give new names to vertices in the copied subtrees.

We do this for all edges on all paths in D'. The order of the edges is given by the order in which they appear on the input tape. We can always recompute the new planar component D', because we can recompute the sizes of subtrees of D. We can always recompute from which copy of a separating pair we went into recursion by storing $O(1)$ bits on the work-tape when we go into recursion. So, when we have to change vertex names, then we can recompute the new vertex names of the copied separating pair. We need such bits at each level of recursion. Since the sizes of the copied subtrees are at most $1/2$ the size of the tree, there are at most $O(\log n)$ levels of recursion. We can conclude, that the algorithm runs in logspace.

Lemma 9.3.5 *Let G_i be a K_5-free biconnected graph with incoming separating pair $\{u_i, v_i\}$ and outgoing separating pair $\{u_{i+1}, v_{i+1}\}$. Let G'_i be the resulting graph when all the V_8-components D in G_i are replaced by the new gadgets D'. G'_i has the following properties:*

- *G'_i is a planar biconnected graph.*
- *There are simple paths from u_i or v_i to u_{i+1} or v_{i+1} in G_i if and only if there are such simple paths in G'_i.*
- *The size of G'_i is polynomial in the size of G_i.*

Planar Arrangement of Split Components in a 4-Connected Component Tree. It remains to consider the remaining non-planar 3-connected components which are not isomorphic to the V_8. We decompose them into planar 4-connected components. The task is to recombine all the components into one planar graph. However, we cannot simply reverse the decomposition process because the 3-clique sum of the 4-connected (planar) components could result in a non-planar 3-connected component.

To get around this problem we make copies of some of the components and arrange the copies in a planar way. This has to be done carefully such that the size of the graph constructed that way stays polynomial in the size of the input graph.

Consider a 4-connected component tree $\mathcal{T}^4$. Let S and T be the component nodes in $\mathcal{T}^4$ where vertices s and t are contained in, respectively. Consider S as the root of $\mathcal{T}^4$ i.e., let

$\mathcal{T}_S^4 = \mathcal{T}^4$ and let P be a simple path from S to T in $\mathcal{T}_S^4$. We describe how to find a planar arrangement of the components of $\mathcal{T}_S^4$.

We start by putting the component S in the new planar arrangement. Inductively assume that we have put some component C and let τ be some child separating triple node of C in $\mathcal{T}_S^4$. Furthermore, let the children of τ be the 4-connected component nodes $C_1, \ldots, C_k$. Precisely one of the children is put once in the planar arrangement, the other children are put three times, i.e. there are two additional copies, say C_i', C_i'' of C_i and $i \in \{1, \ldots, k\}$. The three components are connected to two vertices of τ in all possible ways and contain a copy of the remaining vertex from τ. Figure 9.8 shows the construction. By G' we denote the resulting planar arranged graph we obtain for G.

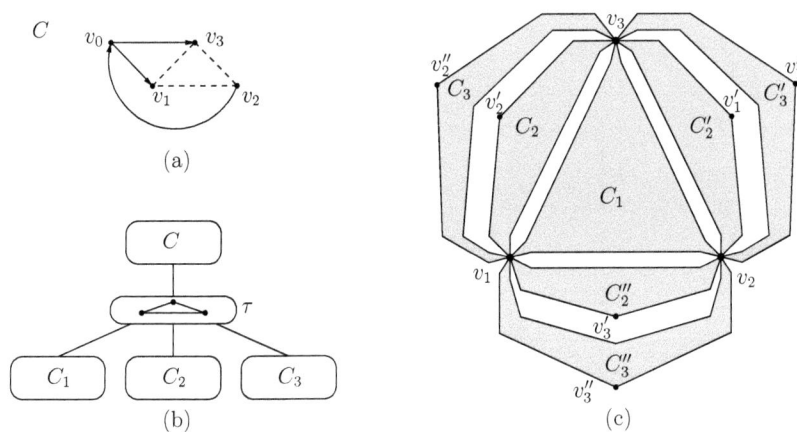

Figure 9.8: (a) A planar 4-connected component C with separating triple $\tau = \{v_1, v_2, v_3\}$. The pairwise edges among these vertices are virtual edges, indicated by dashed undirected lines. (b) The 4-connected component tree with C, separating triple τ and its children, the 4-connected component nodes C_1, C_2 and C_3. (c) The planar arrangement of C_1, C_2 and C_3 at separating triple τ is obtained by making copies of C_2 and C_3 (i.e. C_2', C_2'' and C_3', C_3'') and vertices v_i (i.e. v_i', v_i'') for $1 \leq i \leq 3$. The planar arrangement of C is obtained by connecting the vertices of τ to v_0.

Note, the construction does not change the reachability properties. For example, if there is a simple path from v_1 to v_2 in G which goes through the component C_2 and also passes vertex v_3, then there will be a simple path from v_1 to v_2 in G' which goes through the copy C_2'' of C_2 and passes the copy v_3'' instead of v_3. If there is no path from v_1 to v_2 in G then there will be no path from v_1 to v_2 in the constructed planar graph either. Recall that P is the simple path

9. $K_{3,3}$-FREE AND K_5-FREE REACHABILITY

from node S to node T in $\mathcal{T}_S^4$. The child which is put only once is selected as follows:

1. If a child C_i of τ is a vertex on path P, then we select C_i.
2. If no child of τ is a node on path P but there is a large child C_j, then we select C_j.
3. If none of the first two cases occurs then we select an arbitrary component, say C_1.

Let N be the size of the triconnected component tree rooted at node C. We emphasize that in Case 1, if a large child is copied three times because another child of τ is on path P then this situation does not occur recursively. That is, because the ancestors of the copied large child do not belong to path P. Hence, the planar arranged graph G' is of polynomial size, because we just copy recursively subgraphs of size smaller than $N/2$ even if we consider the exception of case 1. The recursion equation for the size $\mathcal{S}(N)$ of G' with some constant k is:

$$\mathcal{S}(N) = k\mathcal{S}(N/2) + O(N).$$

This finishes the proof of Theorem 9.3.4. Since reachability on planar graphs is in UL ∩ coUL [BTV07], we get the following corollary.

Corollary 9.3.6 K_5-*free* Reachability *is in* UL ∩ coUL.

Distance and Longest Paths in K_5-Free Graphs. To compute distances, we search for shortest simple paths. Again it is easy to see that the graph transformations do not change the distances between the vertices. Also for the longest path problem we can guarantee the same length of a simple path in the resulting graph, but here we have to argue more carefully. Namely, we have to make sure that we do not get longer paths by the copies of the components introduced in the planar arrangement of the 4-connected components. We use the fact that sub-paths of longest paths are again longest paths in a DAG.

Fact 9.3.7 *Let $p_{u,v}$ be a longest simple path from u to v in a DAG G. Let a, b be two vertices on path $p_{u,v}$ and let $p_{a,b}$ be the sub-path of $p_{u,v}$ from a to b. Then $p_{a,b}$ is a longest simple path from a to b in G.*

Since we make up to three copies of a component in our construction of a planar graph, we have to ensure that we do not get longer paths by using the copies. We show that it is not possible for a path to pass through a vertex and its copy.

Lemma 9.3.8 *Let v be vertex of DAG G and let v' be a copy of v in the planar graph G' constructed from G. Then there is no path from v to v' in G'.*

Proof. Let C be the 4-connected component that contains v and let $\{v_1, v_2, v_3\}$ be the separating triple that separates C from G. In G', assume that there is a path p from v in C to v' in C'. The components C and C' are connected by one vertex of v_1, v_2, v_3, say v_1. Hence p can have the form $p = (v, u_1, \ldots, u_l, v_1, u'_{l+1}, \ldots, u'_k, v')$, where $u_1, \ldots, u_l \in C$ and $u'_{l+1}, \ldots, u'_k \in C'$. But then we have the cycle $(v, u_1, \ldots, u_l, v_1, u_{l+1}, \ldots, u_k, v)$ in C which is a contradiction. Path p might also go through v_2 and v_3. Then the argument is similar. □

We argue that the length of longest paths are not changed by the transformations. Consider Figure 9.8. Let p be a longest path from v_1 to some vertex v in G. Assume that p goes through component C_2 and that $v \in C_1$. The interesting case is when p passes through v_2 and v_3 (in this order), because then we have two ways to go in the planar graph:

1. we can go through component C_2 and pass through v'_2 and then switch to C_1 via v_3.
2. we can go to v_2 through component C'''_2 and then to v_3 through component C'_2.

The first case corresponds exactly to path p in G because after passing through v'_2, the path cannot go through v_2 anymore by Lemma 9.3.8. In the second case the longest simple path from v_1 to v_2 in C'''_2 has the same length as the first part of p from v_1 to v_2 in C_2 by Fact 9.3.7. Also, the longest simple path from v_2 to v_3 in C'_2 has the same length as the second part of p from v_2 to v_3 in C_2. Hence, the second possibility does not lead to longer paths. We conclude that the lengths of longest paths are not changed by the reduction.

Theorem 9.3.9 K_5-*free* Distance $\leq_m^{log}$ *planar* Distance.
K_5-*free* LongPath $\leq_m^{log}$ *planar* LongPath.

As a consequence, we get the following corollary.

Corollary 9.3.10 K_5-*free* Distance $\in$ UL ∩ coUL.
K_5-*free* LongPath $\in$ UL ∩ coUL.

Conclusion. We gave a reduction from the reachability, the distance and the longest path problem on $K_{3,3}$-free graphs and on K_5-free graphs (DAG's in the case of the longest path problem) to the corresponding problem on planar graphs (DAG's), respectively. It would be interesting to extend the result to $K_{3,4}$-free graphs or to K_6-free graphs, or even to minor-closed graph classes.

10 The Quasigroup Isomorphism Problem

10.1 Introduction.

Quasigroups. A *quasigroup* is an algebraic structure $(\Omega, \cdot)$ where the finite set Ω is closed under the binary operation $\cdot$ which has unique left- and right inverses. In contrast to groups, a quasigroup is not necessarily associative.

The *quasigroup isomorphism problem* computes, on input of two finite quasigroups $G = (\Omega, \cdot)$, $G' = (\Omega, \circ)$ of order n in table representation, whether G is isomorphic to G'. This means, for all $i, j \in \Omega : \phi(i \cdot j) = \phi(i) \circ \phi(j)$.

Papadimitriou and Yannakakis [PY96] make the observation that the quasigroup isomorphism problem is in $\beta_2\mathsf{P}$, a restricted version of NP, where on input of length n, a polynomial time bounded Turing machine has access to $O(\log^2 n)$ non-deterministic bits. Arvind and Torán [AT06] prove that the quasigroup non-isomorphism problem is in AM and give evidence that it is not complete for $\mathsf{NP}[\log^2 n]$, answering a question from [PY96]. Wolf [Wol94] showed that the quasigroup isomorphism problem is in $\beta_2\mathsf{NC}^2$ i.e. the circuit gets $O(\log^2 n)$ non-deterministic bits together with the input. The circuit can guess the generators of both quasigroups and computes, whether there is a bijection which maps the i-th generator of G onto the i-th generator of G'. Hence, the verification can be done in NC^2. Since NC^2 is in $\mathsf{SPACE}(\log^2 n)$ and we have $O(\log^2 n)$ non-deterministic bits only, it follows that quasigroup isomorphism is in $\mathsf{SPACE}(\log^2 n)$.

We consider the complexity of the quasigroup isomorphism problem. When given two sequences of k generators, say $(g_1, \ldots, g_k)$ and $(h_1, \ldots, h_k)$ within $O(k \log n)$ bits, isomorphism can be computed in SAC^1, which maps g_i onto h_i for all $i \in \{1, \ldots, k\}$. Formally, quasigroup isomorphism is in $\beta_2\mathsf{SAC}^1$.

Groups. The group isomorphism problem is defined analogously, with the difference, that the structure $(\Omega, \circ)$ is a group. It is not hard to see, that the group axioms can be tested easily in AC^0. The *Cayley-group isomorphism problem* computes, on input of two finite groups $G = (\Omega, \cdot), G' = (\Omega, \circ)$ of order n in table representation, whether G is isomorphic to G'.

The complexity of the group isomorphism problem depends on the representation. When groups are given by their generating sets then graph isomorphism is polynomial time Turing reducible to the permutation group isomorphism problem which is known to be in

10. QUASIGROUP ISOMORPHISM

NP ∩ coAM [Luk93]. When groups are given as multiplication tables, the problem can be reduced to directed graph isomorphism [Mil79]. From now on, we consider groups in table representation. Tarjan gave a $n^{\log n + O(1)}$ time algorithm for isomorphism testing on two finite groups G, G': Compute a generating set S of size $\log n$ for G. Try all mappings from S bijectively onto each possible subset S' of G', i.e. there are $\binom{n}{|S|} \cdot |S|!$ many such ordered sets. With the multiplication table of G, check for each such map whether it extends to an isomorphism from G onto G'. This can be done, starting with S and S' as partial ordered sets, by recursively checking whether $\phi(i \cdot j) = \phi(i) \circ \phi(j)$ is consistent with the partial ordered sets and by extending the partial ordered sets whenever $\phi(i \cdot j)$ is a new element. This algorithm is attributed to Tarjan, c.f. [Mil78] and improved by Lipton, Snyder and Zalcstein [LSZ76] as a sharper $O(\log^2 n)$ space algorithm. Miller [Mil78] generalized this result to work with quasigroups in time $n^{\log n + O(1)}$.

For Cayley-groups, we can get an upper bound $\beta_2 \text{FOLL}$. The algorithm runs through all generating sequences for the groups. We test whether the sequences $(g_1, \ldots, g_k)$ and $(h_1, \ldots, h_k)$ are cube generating sequences. If so, we check whether they induce an isomorphism which maps g_i onto h_i for all $i \in \{1, \ldots, k\}$.

Abelian Groups. We also consider the Cayley-group isomorphism problem restricted to abelian groups. When abelian groups are given as generating sets, isomorphism testing is hard for ModL and contained in ZPL^{ModL} [AV04]. But when abelian groups are given as multiplication tables, then isomorphism testing is trivially in L, we can prove that it is also in $\text{TC}^0(\text{FOLL})$.

10.2 On the Complexity of Quasigroup Isomorphism

We consider the complexity of the quasigroup isomorphism problem. We improve the upper bound from $\beta_2 \text{NC}^2$ [Wol94] to $\beta_2 \text{SAC}^1$. First, we consider the verification problem, i.e. the isomorphism problem when generators for both quasigroups are given in a special form.

Theorem 10.2.1 *Let G and G' be two quasigroups of order n in table representation and let S and S' be two sequences of $k = \lceil \log_2 n \rceil$ elements each, say $S = (s_1, \ldots, s_k)$ of G and $S' = (s'_1, \ldots, s'_k)$ within $O(k \log n)$ bits. There is a function computable in DLOGTIME-uniform SAC^1, that on this input (G, G', S, S') computes whether both sequences S and S' are generating sets for G and G' and whether there is an isomorphism which maps s_i onto s'_i for all $i \in \{1, \ldots, k\}$.*

Proof. Every element of G can be expressed as a product of elements in S, if S is a generating set. Since quasigroups are not necessarily associative, a product of elements must be fully parenthesized. A product can be seen as a parse tree where internal nodes represent multiplications and leafs represent generators. Wolf proved that for every element in G there is a well parenthesized product of the generators. This product can be represented as a tree of small depth.

Theorem 10.2.2 (Wolf [Wol94]) *Let G be a quasigroup of order n and S a generating set for G. For every element in G, there is a product, where its associated parse tree has depth $\leq 2\lceil \log_2 n \rceil + 3$.*

Hence, if S is a generating set for G, then for every element in G, there is a product of size polynomial in n. Wolf proved that with this shallow tree representation of elements of G, that isomorphism testing is in NC^2 when generators are given, such that s_i is mapped onto s_i'. We sketch the isomorphism algorithm of Wolf [Wol94] first.

Isomorphism testing in NC^2 (Wolf [Wol94]). Start checking whether the generators (i.e. s_i mapped onto s_i') induce a partial isomorphism. Let T, T' be the sets of elements of both quasigroups G, G', currently known to be generated by S, S' respectively. Initially, $T = S$ and $T' = S'$. In parallel, for each pair of elements $x, y \in T$ a small circuit determines $z = x \cdot y$ by a lookup operation. Do the same with $x', y' \in T'$ where $z' = x' \circ y'$. Another small circuit z, z' is consistent with the current partial bijection. If consistent, then z, z' are added to T, T', respectively.

For each level of the parse trees, there is a level of a verification device as described above, i.e. verifying that the partial bijection is consistent with the currently new generated elements. The circuit receives at each level T and T', and the partial bijection from the previous level. It then performs the multiplications and does the indicated consistency checks on the partial bijection. Then, the circuit passes T, T' and the updated bijection to the next level. If after $2\lceil \log_2 n \rceil + 3$ levels all elements of Q, Q' have not been generated, then S, S' are no generating sets and the circuit rejects.

Wolf argues, that the multiplication at each level corresponds to adding one to the depth of the parse tree, that represents the element. Each multiplication requires an $O(\log n)$ depth polynomial-size circuit. At each level there are at most n^2 multiplications taking place in parallel. Hence this gives the $O(\log^2 n)$ depth bound.

Isomorphism testing in SAC^1. We prove that there is a SAC^1-circuit that computes the isomorphism. The difference is, that Wolf uses a circuit of depth $O(\log n)$ to perform the multiplications and the consistency checks at each level. We prove, that the new generated elements at each level, can be computed by a circuit of constant size, if we allow *or*-gates to have unbounded fanin. For the consistency checks, we use the fact that SAC^1 is closed under complementation [BCD+89]. We will see, that the construction of the SAC^1-circuit can be done in AC^0.

10. QUASIGROUP ISOMORPHISM

For each $m \in \{0, \ldots, 2\lceil \log_2 n \rceil + 3\}$ we define gates T_G^m and M_G^m. We have inputs:

$$T_G^0(s_i) = \begin{cases} 1 & \text{if } s_i \in S \\ 0 & \text{otherwise.} \end{cases}$$

For each $m \geq 1$, we have gates for each row and column in the multiplication table of G, namely fanin $n+1$ *or*-gates $T_G^m(i)$ for the i-th element (at i-th row and column), respectively. We have fanin 2 *and*-gates $M_G^m(i,j)$ for each pair of elements. For all $x, y \in \{1, \ldots, n\}$ and $m \geq 1$ we have:

$$M_G^m(x, y) = T_G^{m-1}(x) \wedge T_G^{m-1}(y),$$

and we have:

$$T_G^m(z) = T_G^{m-1}(z) \vee \bigvee_{z = x \cdot y} M_G^m(x, y).$$

This circuit has the property that $T_G^m(i) = 1$ if element i can be generated after m iterations. Accordingly, we define for G' and S' the gates $T_{G'}^m(i)$, $M_{G'}^m(i,j)$ and the connections the same way.

We define now the sub-circuits for the consistency check of the bijection. If S and S' are generating sets, then every element is generated at the end. In this case the following circuit has the property, that every element in G is mapped onto at least one element in G' and vice versa. We will see, that it suffices to check, whether there exists a generated element in G that is mapped onto *more than one* generated element in G' or vice versa. At the beginning we have a bijection among the elements in the generating sequences. We have inputs $bij^0(s_i, s_i') = 1$ for $s_i \in S$ and $s_i' \in S'$ at the same positions in the sequences and inputs $bij^0(x, x') = 0$ in all the other cases, for x in G and x' in G'. For each level of the circuit, namely for each $m \geq 1$, we have a small circuit containing fanin 2 *and*-gates and *or*-gates of fanin $n+1$ for all z, z' to compute the bijection:

$$bij^m(z, z') = bij^{m-1}(z, z') \vee \bigvee_{\{(x,y,x',y') | x \cdot y = z, x' \circ y' = z'\}} T^m(x, y, z, x', y', z') \wedge bij^{m-1}(x, x') \wedge bij^{m-1}(y, y')$$

where we consider elements only that can be generated:

$$T^m(x, y, z, x', y', z') = T_G^m(x) \wedge T_G^m(y) \wedge T_G^m(z) \wedge T_{G'}^m(x') \wedge T_{G'}^m(y') \wedge T_{G'}^m(z')$$

and we have gates for each $m \geq 0$ for the consistency check of the bijection:

$$con_G^m(x) = \bigvee_{y' \neq z'} bij^m(x, y') \wedge bij^m(x, z'),$$

$$con_{G'}^m(x') = \bigvee_{y \neq z} bij^m(y, x') \wedge bij^m(z, x').$$

For the isomorphism test, we require that all elements can be generated at the end, i.e. for $m = 2\lceil \log_2 n \rceil + 3$ we have

$$gen = \bigwedge_{x \in G, x' \in G'} (T_G^m(x) \wedge T_{G'}^m(x'))$$

and if the bijection is consistent in all the levels

$$con = \bigvee_{m \in \{0,\ldots,2\lceil \log_2 n \rceil+3\}, x \in G, x' \in G'} (con_G^m(x) \wedge con_{G'}^m(x')).$$

The gate *gen* evaluates to 1 if and only if all elements can be generated by S and S', respectively. We can compute *gen* in SAC^1, if we use an NC^1-circuit of fanin 2 *and*-gates instead of an unbounded fanin *and*-gate. The gate *con* evaluates to 0 if and only if there is *no* inconsistency, i.e. the bijection is an isomorphism. We can compute *con* in SAC^1. Since this complexity class is closed under complementation [BCD$^+$89], we can also compute $\overline{con}$ in SAC^1.
The quasigroups are isomorphic if and only if *gen* $\wedge$ $\overline{con}$ evaluates to 1. □

Miller [Mil78] proved that a quasigroup of order n has at most $\lceil \log_2 n \rceil$ generators. When giving $2 \log^2 n$ non-deterministic bits to the input of the circuit, then we can guess the generating sequences which we have in Theorem 10.2.1. Wolf proved this way, that the isomorphism problem on quasigroups is in β_2NC^2. We get the following improvement.

Corollary 10.2.3 *The isomorphism problem on quasigroups is in* β_2SAC^1.

10.3 On the Complexity of Cayley-Group Isomorphism

We conclude from Theorem 10.2.1, that the isomorphism problem for groups is in SAC^1 when given $O(\log^2 n)$ non-deterministic bits to the input. We try to do better. When groups are given by multiplication tables, we can further improve the upper bound.

Theorem 10.3.1 *The isomorphism problem for Cayley-groups is in* FOLL *and in* L *when given* $O(\log^2 n)$ *non-deterministic bits to the input.*

Proof. With the non-deterministic bits, we guess the generators for the groups, which have a special form.

Definition 10.3.2 *A sequence of k group elements $X = (g_1, \ldots, g_k)$ is a cube generating k-sequence for group $G = (\Omega, \circ)$ if*

$$G = \{g_1^{\epsilon_1} \circ \cdots \circ g_k^{\epsilon_k} \mid \epsilon_i \in \{0,1\}\}.$$

The set $\{g_1^{\epsilon_1} \circ \cdots \circ g_k^{\epsilon_k} \mid \epsilon_i \in \{0,1\}\}$ is the cube $Cube(X)$ generated by the sequence X.

10. QUASIGROUP ISOMORPHISM

In a cube generating sequence, the generators are given in a fixed order. Let $G = (\Omega, \circ), G' = (\Omega', \cdot)$ be two groups given as multiplication tables and two cube generating sequences with $g_1, \ldots, g_k \in \Omega$ and $g'_1, \ldots, g'_k \in \Omega'$, such that the following holds. If G is isomorphic to G' then there is an isomorphism which maps g_i onto g'_i for all $k \in \{1, \ldots, k\}$.

We use the following theorem which in its simplified version can be derived from [ER65] and [AT04].

Theorem 10.3.3 *[AT04] Let G be a finite group with n elements. The probability, that a sequence of size $4 \log n$ selected uniformly at random is a cube generating sequence for G, is $> 1 - 1/n$.*

For our purposes it suffices to have the following version.

Fact 10.3.4 *For a finite group G and $k = 4 \log n$, there exists a cube generating sequence.*

We assume that the generators $(g_1, \ldots, g_k)$ and $(g'_1, \ldots, g'_k)$ are cube generating sequences for both groups. The following routine uses the properties of cube generating sequences for the isomorphism test which maps g_i onto g'_i for all $i \in \{1, \ldots, k\}$.

---

input: groups G, H on elements in $\{1, \ldots, n\}$ given as multiplication tables,
cube generating sequences $X = (g_1, \ldots, g_k)$ for G and $Y = (h_1, \ldots, h_k)$ for H
computation: accept, if $G = Cube(X), H = Cube(Y)$ and there is an
isomorphism from G onto H which maps g_i onto h_i, for all $i \in \{1, \ldots, k\}$

1: { test $G = Cube(X)$ and $H = Cube(Y)$ }
2: **for all** $g, h \in \{1, \ldots, n\}$
3:   **for all** $(\epsilon_1, \ldots, \epsilon_k) \in \{0, 1\}^k$
4:     check whether $g = g_1^{\epsilon_1} \circ \cdots \circ g_k^{\epsilon_k}$ and $h = h_1^{\epsilon_1} \circ \cdots \circ h_k^{\epsilon_k}$
5:   **if** G or h was not generated then reject and halt.
6: { isomorphism test }
7: **for all** $(\epsilon_1, \ldots, \epsilon_k) \in \{0, 1\}^k$
8:   **for all** $(\eta_1, \ldots, \eta_k) \in \{0, 1\}^k$
9:     $a \leftarrow g_1^{\epsilon_1} \circ \cdots \circ g_k^{\epsilon_k}, b \leftarrow g_1^{\eta_1} \circ \cdots \circ g_k^{\eta_k}$
10:     $a' \leftarrow h_1^{\epsilon_1} \circ \cdots \circ h_k^{\epsilon_k}, b' \leftarrow h_1^{\eta_1} \circ \cdots \circ h_k^{\eta_k}$
11:     **for all** $(\nu_1, \ldots, \nu_k) \in \{0, 1\}^k$
12:       **if** $a \circ b = g_1^{\nu_1} \circ \cdots \circ g_k^{\nu_k}$ and $a' \cdot b' \neq h_1^{\nu_1} \cdots h_k^{\nu_k}$ **then** halt and reject.
13: halt and accept.

Since $k \in O(\log n)$, the number of tests are bounded by a polynomial which can be done in parallel. Check carefully, that every step can be computed in AC^0 and that the query

$g = g_1^{\epsilon_1} \circ \cdots \circ g_k^{\epsilon_k}$ can be computed by a family of circuits of depth $O(\log \log n)$, polynomial size with unbounded fanin *and*-gates and *or*-gates. To see this, we use the fact that groups are associative. Pairwise make multiplications in parallel using the multiplication table. This terminates after $\log \log n$ steps since $k \in O(\log n)$. It is also easy to see, that the query can be computed also in L, because the sequences $(\epsilon_1, \ldots, \epsilon_k)$ can be stored in $O(\log n)$ bits, and performing the multiplications sequentially from left to right. We conclude, that this proves Theorem 10.3.1. □

More formally, the complexity of the Cayley-group isomorphism problem in terms of bounded non-determinism can be expressed as follows.

Corollary 10.3.5 *The Cayley-group isomorphism problem is in* β_2FOLL *and in* β_2L.

10.4 On the Complexity of Abelian Cayley-Group Isomorphism

Let G and H be two finite groups in table representation. The abelian Cayley-group isomorphism problem accepts the input (G, H), if the groups are abelian and isomorphic.

Clearly, testing the property whether G is abelian can be done in AC^0 by simply testing whether $a \cdot b = b \cdot a$ holds for all elements a, b in parallel. The isomorphism test is based on the following fact.

Fact 10.4.1 *Two finite abelian groups G and H with $|G| = |H| = n$ are isomorphic iff the number of elements of order m in G and H is the same, for all $1 \leq m \leq n$.*

A proof can be found in [Hal59] or [Kav03]. The order of an element a is the smallest integer $i \geq 0$ such that $a^i = e$. Hence, an isomorphism test simply computes the orders for all elements using the power predicate. Barrington et.al. [BKLM00] considered the complexity of the power predicate on abelian groups.

Proposition 10.4.2 *([BKLM00]) For all elements a and b in a Cayley-group and all $i \leq n$, the predicate $b = a^i$ can be calculated in* FOLL $\cap$ L.

They introduce the complexity class FOLL, or FO$(\log \log n)$, of problems solvable by uniform polynomial size circuit families of unbounded fanin and depth $O(\log \log n)$. Since Parity is not in FOLL, no problem in FOLL can be complete for any class containing Parity, such as NC^1, L or NL. But FOLL is not known to be contained in L.

In the isomorphism test, the FOLL algorithm outputs the order of all group elements. This is a set of numbers in arbitrary order.

10. QUASIGROUP ISOMORPHISM

Given two sets of numbers, the problem of pairwise comparing them is not known to be in AC^0, since the function Majority is not contained in this class. This function outputs 1, if at least half of the inputs are 1's, and 0 otherwise. It is known that the function Sorting, i.e. arranging n n-bit numbers in ascending order, is in TC^0. This suffices for an isomorphism test. When given two sorted sets of numbers, say $e_1 \leq \cdots \leq e_n$ and $e'_1 \leq \cdots \leq e'_n$, we can test in AC^0 whether $e_i = e'_i$ for all $i \in \{1, \ldots, n\}$ in parallel. We conclude:

Theorem 10.4.3 *The abelian Cayley-group isomorphism problem is in* TC^0(FOLL), *and in* L.

11 Further Work and Conclusions

In this work we have improved many existing results concerning upper and lower bounds for the graph isomorphism and reachability problems on restricted classes of graphs. A summary of the results can be seen in Table 1.1 for isomorphism testing and in Table 1.2 for the reachability problems. We mention now the conclusions of this work, pointing to several open questions.

Isomorphism of Paths and Planar Graphs. Given two graphs where each graph consists of two paths each. Intuitively, testing isomorphism for such graphs seems to be an easier computational problem than testing isomorphism of two arbitrary planar graphs. Surprisingly, both problems Path-GI and Planar-GI have the same complexity, they are complete for L.

Graph Isomorphism, Reachability and Planarity. There is a close connection between the reachability problem for undirected graphs and the complexity class L. There is also a close connection between the reachability problem for directed graphs and the class NL. By the work of [RA00], [ADR05] and [BTV07], reachability in planar graphs is in UL ∩ coUL.

It is interesting to see that for general directed graphs, reachability (complete for NL) seems to be an easier computational problem as graph isomorphism (hard for DET), whereas for planar graphs the current situation is the other way around. Planar-GI is complete for L and planar-Reachability is just known to be in UL ∩ coUL. It would be interesting to analyze the complexity of the reachability problem on planar graphs.

When considering the more general graph classes of $K_{3,3}$-minor free and K_5-minor free graphs, isomorphism testing and reachability reduce to the planar case. Hence, it seems to be reasonable to consider more general classes of graphs than planarity for decision problems. This was earlier described under NC-reductions when computing the number of perfect matchings in $K_{3,3}$-free graphs in [Vaz89] and for graph coloring and finding a maximal independent set in [Khu88]. The same phenomenon appears now with respect to log-space reductions in isomorphism and reachability testing.

Graph Isomorphism and its Lower Bound Complexity. The use of PGI-tuples is a tool for the simulation of an *and*-function or an *or*-function with GI [Tor04]. That is, a NC^1 circuit can be simulated by a balanced DLOGTIME uniform family of circuits with fanout 1,

11. FURTHER WORK, CONCLUSIONS

logarithmic depth, polynomial size and alternating layers of *and*-gates and *or*-gates [BIS90]. The corresponding circuit graph is a tree. To see this, take an arbitrary NC^1-circuit and copy sub-circuits recursively to reduce the fanout. The size of the resulting circuit remains polynomial. We say that we *expand* the circuit and it becomes a formula. This fact is crucial for the reduction of the circuit value problem for circuits in NC^1 to Graph Isomorphism [Tor04]. We could show that the proof techniques to obtain lower bounds for GI are also applicable for tournament graphs.

However, it is an open problem whether the simulation of boolean functions with GI can be realized for computationally more powerful circuits. When increasing the depth of the circuit or the fanin of the gates, the expansion leads to formulas of exponential size. It is not clear how to reduce the circuit value problem for such circuits to GI, because of this exponential blow-up.

It is also of high interest to consider the upper bound complexity of GI restricted to certain graph classes. Grohe and Verbitsky [GV06] developed a proof technique to show that isomorphism testing for planar graphs is in AC^1 and for bounded tree width graphs is in TC^1. We improve the upper bound for planar graphs to L and for bounded tree width graphs to LogCFL. Hence, the class of bounded tree width graphs is one of the remaining classes where the complexity of isomorphism testing is sandwiched between L and NC^2 and whose complexity is not yet settled.

It remains an interesting open question to settle the complexity of bounded treewidth GI. This gives more insight, whether bounded treewidth GI is a candidate for which the known lower bounds of GI can be strengthened towards LogCFL. In this direction, we could answer this question for the class of planar graphs.

Quasigroup Isomorphism and its Lower Bound Complexity. For the quasigroup and group isomorphism problems, no lower bounds are known. One reason why this might be a difficult task is, that problems in FOLL cannot compute the parity-function [Smo87]. For this, polynomial size, unbounded fanin circuits of depth $\Omega(\log n/(\log \log n))$ are required. Therefore, these problems cannot be complete for complexity classes between AC^0 and AC^1, like, for example, the complexity classes NC^1, L, NL or LogCFL. There is a huge gap between the known lower the upper bounds, no polynomial time algorithm is known.

Index

3-bond, 127
3-bond component, 22
3-connected component, 22
3-connected graph, 21
3-connected vertex pair, 22
3-divisive separating triple node, 127
4-connected component, 187
4-connected component node, 188
4-connected component tree, 188

abelian group, 29
AC^0 many-one reduction, 17
AC^i, 14
act cyclically
    on subgraphs, 30
    on vertex set, 30
adjacent, 17
alphabet, 9
and-gate, 10
articulation point, 20
    associated with, 105
articulation point node, 21
    size, 106
augmented tree, 155
    bag node, 156
    large child, 162
    minimum separating set, 156
    separating set node, 156
automorphism, 18

act cyclically, 30
    coloring, 18
automorphism group, 30
auxiliary pushdown automaton, 12

bag, 28
biconnected component, 20
biconnected component node, 21
    size, 106
biconnected component tree, 21, 26
    size, 106
biconnected graph, 20
bipartite graph, 18
block, 36
bond, 22
Boolean function, 9
Boolean value, 9
bounded color class GI, 31

candidate separating triple, 184
    crossing, 185
canon, 30
canonical form, 30
Cartesian product
    of graphs, 19
    of sets, 19
Caylay-group isomorphism, 32
Cayley table, 29
center, 19

205

INDEX

child, 19
circuit, 10
    accept a language, 10
    assignment, 10
    basis, 10
    compute a function, 10
    depth, 10
    layer, 10
    output gate, 10
    represent a function, 10
    size, 10
    wire, 10
circuit evaluation problem (CVP), 10
circuit family, 13
    DLOGTIME uniform, 14
    compute a function, 14
circuit graph, 10
clique, 17
clique-sum, 122
code of a graph, 30
color graph automorphism problem, 31
color graph isomorphism problem, 31
coloring, 18
complement language, 9
complete bipartite graph, 18
complete graph, 17
complete invariant, 30
completeness for complexity classes, 17
complexity class, 12
component node, 26
    size, 27
configuration graph, 33
conjunctive truth table reduction, 17
connected, 19
connected component, 20
context free language (CFL), 15
cut vertex, 20

cycle, 18
    simple, 18
cycle component, 22
cycle-GI, 63
cyclic tournament, 40

decision problem, 9
degree, 18
depth first traversal, 35
det. logarithmic time (DLOGTIME), 13
det. Turing machine (DTM), 11
determinant (DET), 15
deterministic logspace (L), 13
digraph, 17
directed acyclic graph (DAG), 19
disjunctive truth table reduction, 17
distance, 19
distance problem, 33
DLOGTIME uniform, 14

eccentricity, 19
exact-counting logspace ($C_=L$), 15

face, 19
fanin, 9
    semi-unbounded, 15
finite group, 29
fix blockwise, 30
fix pointwise, 30
forest, 19
four-connected component, 126
four-connected component node, 127
four-connected component tree, 127
functional det. logspace (FL), 16
functional det. polynomial time (FP), 16

graph, 17
    d-regular, 18
    PGI-representation, 54

center, 19
coloring, 18
connected, 20
disjoint union, 19
labeling, 18
orbit, 30
regular, 18
rigid, 18
simple, 17
size, 17
valence, 18
graph automorphism problem (GA), 31
graph isomorphism problem (GI), 31
grid graph, 74
group, 29
    abelian, 29
    associativity, 29
    Cayley representation, 29
    closure, 29
    commutativity, 29
    coset, 29
    finite, 29
    generating set, 29
    identity element, 29
    inverse, 29
    inverse element, 29
    orbit, 29
    order, 29
    order of elements, 29
    table representation, 29
    word, 29

Hamiltonian cycle, 18
hardness for complexity classes, 17
hardness for languages, 17

induced subgraph, 18
integer, 28

interval, 28
isomorphism, 18
    coloring, 18
    respect a property, 18
    respect rotation schemes, 19
    respect tree (distance) decompositions, 28

K_5-component node, 177
K_5-minor free graph, 20
    decomposition, 122
K_5-separating pair, 177
K_5-separating pair node, 177
$K_{3,3}$-minor free graph, 20
k-bond, 22
k-clique-sum, 122
k-connected component, 26
k-connected component tree, 26
k-separating set, 20, 26
k-separating set node, 26
    size, 27

label, 18
label gadget, 84
labeling, 18
language, 9
large child, 27, 101, 116
line graph, 18
line-GI, 63
logic gate, 9
logspace (L), 13
logspace many-one reduction, 17
logspace Turing reduction, 17
longPath problem, 33
loop, 17

many-one reduction, 17
maximum separating triple, 185
minor, 19

INDEX

modulo addition graph gadget, 41
modulo-k addition-gate, 10
multiplication table, 29

natural number, 28
negation-gate, 10
NC^i, 14
nim-game, 69
non-det. polynomial time (NP), 13
non-det. Turing machine (NDTM), 11
    accept word, 11
    choice input, 11
non-deterministic logspace (NL), 13

oracle graph gadget, 49
oracle tape, 11
oracle tournament gadget, 49
oracle Turing machine, 11
orbit, 29, 30
order between vertices (Ord), 34, 58, 81
or-gate, 10
oriented graph, 19, 80

parallel random-access machine (PRAM), 12
    concurrent read/write (CRCW), 12
parent, 19
partial automorphism, 31
partially ordered set, 67
path, 18
    simple, 18
permutation group, 29
planar, 19
planar component node, 177
planar rotation scheme, 19
plane graph, 19
polynomial time (P), 13
poset, 67
poset game, 67

poset game problem, 68
prefix graph automorphism problem, 31
prefix-GA with fixed vertex property, 61
probabilistic logspace (PL), 15
projection function, 10
promise graph automorphism problem, 32
promise graph isomorphism problem, 32
pushdown, 12
pushdown automaton (PDA), 12

quantifier free projections, 34
quasigroup
    finite, 29
quasigroup isomorphism problem, 32

reachability problem, 32
reference copy, 113
reference orientation, 98
reflection, 19
regular, 18
rigid, 18
root, 19
rooted tree, 19
rotation, 19
rotation scheme, 19

semi-unbounded fanin AC^1 (SAC^1), 15
separating pair, 20, 21
    3-connected, 22
    orientation, 97
    symmetric, 97
separating pair node, 24
separating set, 20
    separate vertices, 20
separating triple, 20
separating triple node, 188
series parallel graph, 20
setwise stabilizer, 30
sharp-L (#L), 14

split component, 20
stack, 12
string, 9
symmetric group, 29

TC^i, 14
threshold-gate, 10
tournament, 20
tournament automorphism problem (TA), 40
tournament isomorphism problem (TI), 40
tournament modulo addition graph gadget, 43
tree, 19
    center, 19
    size, 27
tree decomposition, 27
    separate bags, 28
    width, 27
tree distance decomposition, 28
    minimal, 28
    separate bags, 28
    width, 28
tree distance width, 28
tree-canon, 30, 37
tree-code, 30
treewidth, 27
triconnected component, 22
    3-bond, 26
    3-connected component, 26
    cycle, 25
triconnected component node, 24
triconnected component tree, 24, 27
triconnected graph, 22
Turing machine, 11
    accept a language, 11
    accept word, 11
    accepting halt state, 11

blank symbol, 11
configuration, 11
control unit, 11
initial state, 11
input string, 11
oracle, 11
rejecting state, 11
running time, 11
tape alphabet, 11
tape unit, 11
transition function, 11
Turing reduction, 17

unambiguous logspace (UL), 14
unary, 9
universal exploration sequence, 90

valence, 18
vertex
    color, 18
    degree, 18
    label, 18
    valence, 18
virtual edge, 20

walk, 90
word, 9
    unary, 9

xor-gate, 10

Bibliography

[AB09] Sanjeev Arora and Boaz Barak. *Computational Complexity, A Modern Approach.* Cambridge University Press, 2009.

[ABC+09] Eric Allender, David Mix Barrington, Tanmoy Chakraborty, Samir Datta, and Sambuddha Roy. Planar and grid graph reachability problems. *Theory on Computing Systems*, 45(4):675–723, 2009.

[ABL98] V. Arvind, Richard Beigel, and Antoni Lozano. The complexity of modular graph automorphism. In *15th Annual Symposium on Theoretical Aspects of Computer Science (STACS)*, pages 172–182, 1998.

[AD04] V. Arvind and Nikhil Devanur. Symmetry breaking in trees and planar graphs by vertex coloring. In *The Nordic Combinatorial Conference (NORCOM)*, 2004.

[ADK08] V. Arvind, Bireswar Das, and Johannes Köbler. A logspace algorithm for partial 2-tree canonization. In *Computer Science Symposium in Russia (CSR)*, pages 40–51, 2008.

[ADM06] V. Arvind, Bireswar Das, and Partha Mukhopadhyay. On isomorphism and canonization of tournaments and hypertournaments. In *International Symposium on Algorithms and Computation (ISAAC)*, volume 4288 of *Lecture Notes in Computer Science*, pages 449–459, 2006.

[ADR05] Eric Allender, Samir Datta, and Sambuddha Roy. The directed planar reachability problem. In *Proceedings of the 25th annual Conference on Foundations of Software Technology and Theoretical Computer Science (FSTTCS)*, pages 238–249, 2005.

[Agr07] Manindra Agrawal. Rings and integer lattices in computer science: A Barbados workshop proposal. Lecture Notes to Annual Workshop on Computational Complexity, 2007.

[AJ93] Carme Álvarez and Birgit Jenner. A very hard log-space counting class. *Theoretical Computer Science*, 107(1):3–30, 1993.

BIBLIOGRAPHY

[AK06] V. Arvind and Piyush P. Kurur. Graph isomorphism is in SPP. *Information and Computation*, 204(5):835–852, 2006.

[AKV05] V. Arvind, Piyush P. Kurur, and T. C. Vijayaraghavan. Bounded color multiplicity graph isomorphism is in the #L hierarchy. In *Annual IEEE Conference on Computational Complexity (formerly Annual Conference on Structure in Complexity Theory)*, volume 20, 2005.

[AM00] Eric Allender and Meena Mahajan. The complexity of planarity testing. In *Proceedings of the 17th Annual Symposium on Theoretical Aspects of Computer Science (STACS)*, pages 87–98, 2000.

[AO96] Eric Allender and Mitsunori Ogihara. Relationships among PL, #L, and the determinant. *RAIRO Theoretical Informatics and Applications*, 30(1):1–21, 1996.

[Art96] M. Artin. Algebra. *Prentice Hall, India, New Delhi*, 1996.

[Asa85] Tetsuo Asano. An approach to the subgraph homeomorphism problem. *Theoretical Computer Science*, 38, 1985.

[AT04] V. Arvind and Jacobo Torán. Solvable group isomorphism is (almost) in NP ∩ coNP. In *Annual IEEE Conference on Computational Complexity (formerly Annual Conference on Structure in Complexity Theory)*, volume 19, 2004.

[AT06] V. Arvind and Jacobo Torán. The complexity of quasigroup isomorphism and the minimum generating set problem. In *International Symposium on Algorithms and Computation (ISAAC)*, volume 4288 of *Lecture Notes in Computer Science*, pages 233–242. Springer, 2006.

[AV04] V. Arvind and T. C. Vijayaraghavan. Abelian permutation group problems and logspace counting classes. In *Annual IEEE Conference on Computational Complexity (formerly Annual Conference on Structure in Complexity Theory)*, volume 19, pages 204–214, 2004.

[Bab81] László Babai. Moderately exponential bound for graph isomorphism. *Fundamentals (or Foundations) of Computation Theory (FCT)*, 3, 1981.

[Bab86] László Babai. A Las Vegas - NC algorithm for isomorphism of graphs with bounded multiplicity of eigenvalues. In *IEEE Symposium on Foundations of Computer Science (FOCS)*, pages 303–312, 1986.

[Bab95] László Babai. Automorphism groups, isomorphism, reconstruction. *Handbook of combinatorics*, 2:1447–1540, 1995.

[BCD+89] Allan Borodin, Stephen A. Cook, Patrick W. Dymond, Walter L. Ruzzo, and Martin Tompa. Two applications of inductive counting for complementation problems. *SIAM Journal on Computing*, 18:559–578, 1989.

[BDHM91] Gerhard Buntrock, Carsten Damm, Ulrich Hertrampf, and Christoph Meinel. Structure and importance of logspace-mod-classes. In *8th Annual Symposium on Theoretical Aspects of Computer Science (STACS)*, pages 360–371, 1991.

[BHZ87] Bavi B. Boppana, Johan Torkel Hastad, and S. Zachos. Does co-NP have short interactive proofs? *Information Processing Letters*, 25(2):127–132, 1987.

[BIS90] David Mix Barrington, Neil Immerman, and Howard Straubing. On uniformity within NC^1. *Journal of Computer and System Sciences*, 41(3):274–306, 1990.

[BK08] Hans L. Bodlaender and Arie M.C.A. Koster. Combinatorial optimization on graphs of bounded treewidth. *The Computer Journal*, 51(3):255–269, 2008.

[BKLM00] David Mix Barrington, Peter Kadau, Klaus-Jörn Lange, and Pierre McKenzie. On the complexity of some problems on groups input as multiplication tables. In *Proceedings of the 15th Annual IEEE Conference on Computational Complexity (COCO)*, page 62, Washington, DC, USA, 2000. IEEE Computer Society.

[BL83] László Babai and Eugene M. Luks. Canonical labeling of graphs. In *15th Annual ACM Symposium on Theory of Computing (STOC)*, pages 171–183, 1983.

[BLS87] László Babai, Eugene M. Luks, and Ákos Seress. Permutation groups in NC. In *ACM Symposium on Theory of Computing (STOC)*, pages 409–420, 1987.

[Bod90] Hans L. Bodlaender. Polynomial algorithms for graph isomorphism and chromatic index on partial k-trees. *Journal of Algorithms*, 11:631–644, 1990.

[Bod98] Hans L. Bodlaender. A partial k-arboretum of graphs with bounded treewidth. *Theoretical Computer Science*, 209:1–45, 1998.

[Boo78] Kellogg S. Booth. Isomorphism testing for graphs, semigroups, and finite automata are polynomially equivalent problems. *SIAM Journal on Computing (SICOMP)*, 7, 1978.

[Bou02] C. L. Bouton. Nim, a game with a complete mathematical theory. *The Annals of Mathematics*, 3(1/4):35–39, 1901-1902.

BIBLIOGRAPHY

[BT89]   Guiseppe Di Battista and Roberto Tamassia. Incremental planarity testing. In *IEEE Symposium on Foundations of Computer Science (FOCS)*, pages 436–441, 1989.

[BT96]   Guiseppe Di Battista and Roberto Tamassia. On-line maintenance of triconnected components with SPQR-trees. *Algorithmica*, 15, 1996.

[BTV07]   Chris Bourke, Raghunath Tewari, and N.V. Vinodchandran. Directed planar reachability is in unambiguous log-space. In *IEEE Conference on Computational Complexity*, pages 217–221, 2007.

[Bus97]   Samuel R. Buss. Alogtime algorithms for tree isomorphism, comparison, and canonization. In *5th Kurt Gödel Colloquium on Computational Logic and Proof Theory (KGC)*, volume 1289 of *Lecture Notes in Computer Science*, pages 18–33, 1997.

[Cal06]   Chris Calabro. The complexity of nim. *Essay published on website* http://cseweb.ucsd.edu/~ccalabro/essays/nim.pdf, 2006.

[CM87]   Stephen A. Cook and Pierre McKenzie. Problems complete for deterministic logarithmic space. *Journal of Algorithms*, 8(5):385–394, 1987.

[Coo85]   Stephen A. Cook. A taxonomy of problems with fast parallel algorithms. *Information and Control*, 64(1-3):2–22, 1985.

[DDN10]   Bireswar Das, Samir Datta, and Prajakta Nimbhorkar. Log-space algorithms for paths and matchings in k-trees. In *Proceedings of the 27th International Symposium on Theoretical Aspects of Computer Science*, pages 215–226, 2010.

[DLN08]   Samir Datta, Nutan Limaye, and Prajakta Nimbhorkar. 3-connected planar graph isomorphism is in log-space. In *Proceedings of the 28th annual Conference on Foundations of Software Technology and Theoretical Computer Science (FSTTCS)*, pages 153–162, 2008.

[DLN+09]   Samir Datta, Nutan Limaye, Prajakta Nimbhorkar, Thomas Thierauf, and Fabian Wagner. Planar graph isomorphism is in log-space. *Annual IEEE Conference on Computational Complexity (CCC)*, pages 203–214, 2009.

[DNTW09]   Samir Datta, Prajakta Nimbhorkar, Thomas Thierauf, and Fabian Wagner. Isomorphism for $K_{3,3}$-free and K_5-free graphs is in log-space. In *Proceedings of the 29th annual Conference on Foundations of Software Technology and Theoretical Computer Science (FSTTCS)*, pages 145–156, 2009.

[DTW10]   Bireswar Das, Jacobo Torán, and Fabian Wagner. Restricted space algorithms for isomorphism on bounded treewidth graphs. In *Proceedings of the 27th International Symposium on Theoretical Aspects of Computer Science*, pages 227–238, 2010.

[EJT10]   Michael Elberfeld, Andreas Jakoby, and Till Tantau. Logspace versions of the theorems of Bodlaender and Courcelle. In *Proceedings of the 51st Annual Symposium on Foundations of Computer Science (FOCS)*, 2010.

[ER65]   Paul Erdős and Alfred Rényi. Probabilistic methods in group theory. *Journal d'Analyse Mathématique*, 14:127–138, 1965.

[Ete97]   Kousha Etessami. Counting quantifiers, successor relations, and logarithmic space. *Journal of Computing and System Sciences*, 54(3):400–411, 1997.

[Gil77]   John Gill. Computational complexity of probabilistic turing machines. *SIAM Journal on Computing*, 6(4):675–695, 1977.

[GLM96]   Judy Goldsmith, Matthew A. Levy, and Martin Mundhenk. Limited nondeterminism. *SIGACT News (SIGACTN) (ACM Special Interest Group on Automata and Computability Theory)*, 27, 1996.

[GLS02]   Georg Gottlob, Nicola Leone, and Francesco Scarcello. Computing LOGCFL certificates. *Theoretical Computer Science (TCS)*, 270(1-2):761–777, 2002.

[GS87]   Shafi Goldwasser and Michael Sipser. Private coins versus public coins in interactive proof systems. In *Randomness and Computation*. JAI Press, Greenwich, CT, 1987.

[GV06]   Martin Grohe and Oleg Verbitsky. Testing graph isomorphism in parallel by playing a game. In *Annual International Colloquium on Automata, Languages and Programming (ICALP)*, 2006.

[GY04]   J. L. Gross and J. Yellen. *Discrete Mathematics and its Applications - Handbook of Graph Theory*. CRC Press LLC, 2004.

[Hal59]   Marshall Hall. *The theory of groups*. Macmillan, New York, 1959.

[Hof82a]   Christoph M. Hoffmann. *Group-Theoretic Algorithms and Graph Isomorphism*, volume 136 of *Lecture Notes in Computer Science*. Springer, Berlin-Heidelberg-New York, 1982.

[Hof82b]   Christoph M. Hoffmann. Subcomplete generalizations of graph isomorphism. *Journal of Computer and System Sciences (JCSS)*, 25:332–359, 1982.

BIBLIOGRAPHY

[HT73] John E. Hopcroft and Robert E. Tarjan. Dividing a graph into triconnected components. *SIAM Journal on Computing*, 2(3):135–158, 1973.

[HT74] John E. Hopcroft and Robert E. Tarjan. Efficient planarity testing. *Journal of the ACM*, 21(4):549–568, 1974.

[HW74] John E. Hopcroft and J.K. Wong. Linear time algorithm for isomorphism of planar graphs (preliminary report). In *Proceedings of the 6th annual ACM Symposium on Theory of Computing (STOC)*, pages 172–184, 1974.

[Imm88] Neil Immerman. Nondeterministic space is closed under complement. *SIAM Journal on Computing*, 17:935–938, 1988.

[JKMT03] Birgit Jenner, Johannes Köbler, Pierre McKenzie, and Jacobo Torán. Completeness results for graph isomorphism. *Journal on Computer and System Sciences*, 66(3):549–566, 2003.

[JT07] Andreas Jakoby and Till Tantau. Logspace algorithms for computing shortest and longest paths in series-parallel graphs. In *Proceedings of the 27th International Conference on Foundations of Software Technology and Theoretical Computer Science (FSTTCS)*, volume 4855 of *Lecture Notes in Computer Science*, pages 216–227. Springer, 2007.

[Kav03] Telikepalli Kavitha. Efficient algorithms for abelian group isomorphism and related problems. *Foundations of Software Technology and Theoretical Computer Science (FSTTCS)*, 23, 2003.

[KHC04] Jacek P. Kukluk, Lawrence B. Holder, and Diane J. Cook. Algorithm and experiments in testing planar graphs for isomorphism. *Journal of Graph Algorithms and Applications*, 8(2):313–356, 2004.

[Khu88] Samir Khuller. Parallel algorithms for K_5-minor free graphs. Technical Report TR88-909, Cornell University, Computer Science Department, 1988.

[KK09] Johannes Köbler and Sebastian Kuhnert. The isomorphism problem for k-trees is complete for logspace. In *Proceedings of the 34th International Symposium on Mathematical Foundations of Computer Science (MFCS)*, pages 537–548, 2009.

[KKLV10] Johannes Köbler, Sebastian Kuhnert, Bastian Laubner, and Oleg Verbitsky. Interval graphs: Canonical representation in logspace. In *37th International Colloquium on Automata, Languages and Programming (ICALP)*, pages 384–395, 2010.

[Kou02] Michal Koucký. Universal traversal sequences with backtracking. *Journal of Computing and System Sciences*, 65(4):717–726, 2002.

[Koz78] Dexter Kozen. A clique problem equivalent to graph isomorphism. *SIGACT News (SIGACTN), (ACM Special Interest Group on Automata and Computability Theory)*, 10, 1978.

[KS05] Neeraj Kayal and Nitin Saxena. On the ring isomorphism and automorphism problems. In *IEEE Conference on Computational Complexity*, pages 2–12, 2005.

[KST93] Johannes Köbler, Uwe Schöning, and Jacobo Torán. *The graph isomorphism problem: its structural complexity*. Birkhauser Verlag, 1993.

[Kul09] Raghav Kulkarni. On the power of isolation in planar structures. Technical Report TR09-024, Electronic Colloquium on Computational Complexity (ECCC), 2009.

[KV10] Jan Kynčl and Tomáš Vyskočil. Logspace reduction of directed reachability for bounded genus graphs to the planar case. *ACM Transactions on Computation Theory (TOCT)*, 1(3):1–11, 2010.

[Lee90] J.van Leeuwen, editor. *Handbook of Theoretical Computer Science: Volume A: Algorithms and Complexity*. Elsevier, Amsterdam, 1990.

[Lin92] Steven Lindell. A logspace algorithm for tree canonization (extended abstract). In *Proceedings of the 24th Annual ACM Symposium on Theory of Computing (STOC)*, pages 400–404. ACM, 1992.

[LMN09] Nutam Limaye, Meena Mahajan, and Prajakta Nimbhorkar. Longest paths in planar dags in unambiguous logspace. In *Computing: The Australian Theory Symposium (CATS)*, volume 94, 2009.

[LR98] Antoni Lozano and Vijay Raghavan. On the complexity of counting the number of vertices moved by graph automorphisms. *Foundations of Software Technology and Theoretical Computer Science (FSTTCS)*, 18, 1998.

[LSZ76] Richard J. Lipton, Lawrence Snyder, and Yechezkel Zalcstein. The complexity of word and isomorphism problems for finite groups. Technical report, John Hopkins, 1976.

[Lub81] Anna Lubiw. Some NP-complete problems similar to graph isomorphism. *SIAM Journal on Computing (SICOMP)*, 10, 1981.

BIBLIOGRAPHY

[Luk82] Eugene M. Luks. Isomorphism of graphs of bounded valence can be tested in polynomial time. *Journal of Computer and System Sciences*, 25(1):42–65, 1982.

[Luk86] Eugene M. Luks. Parallel algorithms for permutation groups and graph isomorphism. In *Proceedings of the 27th Annual Symposium on Foundations of Computer Science (SFCS)*, pages 292–302. IEEE Computer Society, 1986.

[Luk93] Eugene M. Luks. Permutation groups and polynomial-time computation. *DIMACS series in Discrete Mathematics and Theoretical Computer Science*, 11:139–175, 1993.

[Mac37] Saunders Maclane. A structural characterization of planar combinatorial graphs. *Duke Mathematical Journal*, 3:460–472, 1937.

[Mat79] Rudolf Mathon. A note on graph isomorphism counting problem. *Information Processing Letters (IPL)*, 8(3):131–132, 1979.

[Mil78] Gary L. Miller. On the $n^{log n}$ isomorphism technique. In *ACM Symposium on Theory of Computing (STOC)*, 1978.

[Mil79] Gary L. Miller. Graph isomorphism, general remarks. *Journal of Computer and System Sciences*, 18(2):128–142, 1979.

[Mil80] Gary L. Miller. Isomorphism testing for graphs of bounded genus. In *Proceedings of the 12th Annual ACM Symposium on Theory of Computing (STOC)*, pages 225–235, 1980.

[MJT98] Pierre McKenzie, Birgit Jenner, and Jacobo Torán. A note on the hardness of tree isomorphism. In *Proceedings of the 13th Annual IEEE Conference on Computational Complexity (CCC)*. IEEE Computer Society, 1998.

[Moo68] J. W. Moon. *Topics on Tournaments*. Holt, Rinehart and Winston, 1968.

[MR87] Gary L. Miller and V. Ramachandran. A new graphy triconnectivity algorithm and its parallelization. In *Proceedings of the nineteenth annual ACM Symposium on Theory of Computing, New York City, May 25-27, 1987*, pages 335–344, 1987.

[MR91] Gary L. Miller and John H. Reif. Parallel tree contraction, part 2: Further applications. *SIAM Journal on Computing*, 20(6):1128–1147, 1991.

[NTS95] Noam Nisan and Amnon Ta-Shma. Symmetric logspace is closed under complement. *Chicago Journal of Theoretical Computer Science*, 1995.

[Pon91]   Ilia N. Ponomarenko. The isomorphism problem for classes of graphs closed under contraction. *Journal of Mathematical Sciences (JSM), (formerly Journal of Soviet Mathematics)*, 55, 1991.

[Pon94]   Ilia N. Ponomarenko. Polynomial time recognition and testing of isomorphism of cyclic tournaments. *Journal of Mathematical Sciences (JSM), (formerly Journal of Soviet Mathematics)*, 70, 1994.

[PY96]   Christos H. Papadimitriou and Mihalis Yannakakis. On limited nondeterminism and the complexity of the VC dimension. *Journal of Computer and System Sciences*, 53:161–170, 1996.

[RA00]   Klaus Reinhardt and Eric Allender. Making nondeterminism unambiguous. *SIAM Journal of Computing*, 29(4):1118–1131, 2000.

[Rei08]   Omer Reingold. Undirected connectivity in log-space. *Journal of the ACM (JACM)*, 55(4):1–24, 2008.

[RR94]   Vijaya Ramachandran and John H. Reif. Planarity testing in parallel. *Journal of Computer and System Sciences*, 49:517–561, 1994.

[RST84]   Walter L. Ruzzo, Janos Simon, and Martin Tompa. Space-bounded hierarchies and probabilistic computations. *Journal of Computer and System Sciences*, 28(2):216–230, 1984.

[Sav98]   John E. Savage. *Models of Computation: Exploring the Power of Computing*. Addison Wesley Publishing Company, 1998.

[Sch78]   Thomas J. Schaefer. On the complexity of some two-person perfect-information games. *Journal of Computer System Sciences*, 16:185–225, 1978.

[Sch88]   Uwe Schöning. Graph isomorphism is in the low hierarchy. *Journal of Computer and System Sciences*, 37(3):312–323, 1988.

[Sel88]   Alan L. Selman. Promise problems complete for complexity classes. *Information and Computation (INFCTRL) (formerly Information and Control)*, 78(2):87–97, 1988.

[Smo87]   Roman Smolensky. Algebraic methods in the theory of lower bounds for boolean circuit complexity. In *STOC*, pages 77–82, 1987.

[Spi96]   Daniel A. Spielman. Faster isomorphism testing of strongly regular graphs. In *ACM Symposium on Theory of Computing (STOC)*, 1996.

BIBLIOGRAPHY

[Sud77] Ivan Hal Sudborough. Time and tape bounded auxiliary pushdown automata. In *Symposium on Mathematical Foundations of Computer Science (MFCS)*, 1977.

[SW08] Michael Soltys and Craig Wilson. On the complexity of computing winning strategies for finite poset games. In *Fourth Conference on Computability in Europe (CiE)*, pages 415–424, 2008.

[Sze88] Róbert Szelepcsényi. The method of forced enumeration for nondeterministic automata. *Acta Informatica*, 26(3):279–284, 1988.

[Tan01] Till Tantau. A note on the complexity of the reachability problem for tournaments. Technical Report TR01-092, Electronic Colloquium on Computational Complexity (ECCC), 2001.

[Tan04] Till Tantau. A logspace approximation scheme for the shortest path problem for graphs with bounded independence number. In *21st Annual Symposium on Theoretical Aspects of Computer Science (STACS)*, volume 2996 of *Lecture Notes in Computer Science*, pages 326–337. Springer, 2004.

[Tod91] Seinosuke Toda. PP is as hard as the polynomial-time hierarchy. *SIAM Journal on Computing (SICOMP)*, 20, 1991.

[Tor04] Jacobo Torán. On the hardness of graph isomorphism. *SIAM Journal on Computing*, 33(5):1093–1108, 2004.

[Tor07] Jacobo Torán. Reductions to graph isomorphism. In *Foundations of Software Technology and Theoretical Computer Science (FSTTCS)*, pages 158–167, 2007.

[Tut66] William T. Tutte. *Connectivity in graphs*. University of Toronto Press, 1966.

[TW08] Thomas Thierauf and Fabian Wagner. The isomorphism problem for planar 3-connected graphs is in unambiguous logspace. In *25th Annual Symposium on Theoretical Aspects of Computer Science (STACS)*, pages 633–644, 2008.

[TW09] Thomas Thierauf and Fabian Wagner. Reachability in $K_{3,3}$-free graphs and K_5-free graphs is in unambiguous log-space. In *17th International Symposium, Fundamentals of Computation Theory (FCT)*, LNCS 5699, 2009.

[Val82] Leslie G. Valiant. Reducibility by algebraic projections. *L'Enseignement Mathematique Revue Internationale (ENSEIGN)*, 28, 1982.

[Vaz89] Vijay V. Vazirani. NC algorithms for computing the number of perfect matchings in $K_{3,3}$-free graphs and related problems. *Information and Computation*, 80, 1989.

[Ver07]   Oleg Verbitsky. Planar graphs: Logical complexity and parallel isomorphism tests. In *24th International Symposium on Theoretical Aspects of Computer Science (STACS)*, pages 682–693, 2007.

[Wag37]   Klaus Wagner. Über eine Eigenschaft der ebenen Komplexe. In *Mathematical Annalen*, volume 114, 1937.

[Wag07]   Fabian Wagner. Hardness results for tournament isomorphism and automorphism. In *32nd International Symposium on Mathematical Foundations of Computer Science (MFCS)*, pages 572–583, 2007.

[Wag08]   Fabian Wagner. Hardness results for isomorphism and automorphism of bounded valence graphs. In *Theory and Practice of Computer Science (SOFSEM)*, volume 2 - Student Research Forum, pages 131–140, 2008.

[Wan94]   Egon Wanke. Bounded tree-width and LOGCFL. *Journal of Algorithms*, 16, 1994.

[Wei66]   Louis Weinberg. A simple and efficient algorithm for determining isomorphism of planar triply connected graphs. *Circuit Theory*, 13:142–148, 1966.

[Whi33]   Hassler Whitney. A set of topological invariants for graphs. *American Journal of Mathematics*, 55:235–321, 1933.

[Wol94]   Marty J. Wolf. Nondeterministic circuits, space complexity and quasigroups. *Theoretical Computer Science (TCS)*, 125:295–313, 1994.

[YBdFT99] Koichi Yamazaki, Hans L. Bodlaender, Babette de Fluiter, and Dimitrios M. Thilikos. Isomorphism for graphs of bounded distance width. *Algorithmica*, 24(2):105–127, 1999.

[ZKT85]   V. N. Zemlyachenko, Nickolay M. Korneenko, and R. I. Tyshkevich. Graph isomorphism problem. *JSM: Journal of Mathematical Sciences (formerly Journal of Soviet Mathematics)*, 29, 1985.

Deutsche Zusammenfassung

Ein wichtiges Ziel der Dissertation ist es, die Komplexität des Isomorphieproblems auf eingeschränkten Graphklassen näher zu untersuchen. Es zeigt sich, dass einige der Isomorphieprobleme als obere Schranke die Komplexitätsklassen L bzw. NL besitzen. In diesem Zusammenhang betrachten wir auch Erreichbarkeitsprobleme und Varianten, deren Komplexität ebenfalls zwischen L und NL liegen.

Isomorphie. Ein Isomorphismus ist eine bijektive Abbildung der Knoten eines Graphen auf die Knoten eines anderen Graphen, bei der die Kantenbeziehungen erhalten bleiben. Das Graphenisomorphieproblem (GI) besteht darin zu entscheiden, ob es einen Isomorphismus zwischen zwei gegebenen Graphen gibt. Das Problem GI ist in der Komplexitätsklasse NP. Es ist weder bekannt ob GI vollständig für diese Klasse ist [BHZ87, Sch88], noch ob es effiziente Algorithmen gibt, d.h. ob GI in der Klasse P liegt. Ob GI hart für P ist, ist ebenso eine offene Frage. Man weiß, dass GI hart für DET ist [Tor04], eine Komplexitätsklasse die in P enthalten ist.

Diese enormen Unterschiede zwischen oberen und unteren Schranken lenken das Interesse auch auf das Isomorphieproblem auf beschränkten Graphklassen, wo man bessere Schranken beweisen kann. Es zeigt sich, dass für einige Graphklassen die obere Schranke für das Isomorphieproblem sehr weit bis auf die Komplexitätsklasse L gedrückt werden kann. Man weiß beispielsweise, dass das Isomorphieproblem auf Bäumen in L liegt [Lin92].

Wir verbessern die bekannten oberen Schranken von einigen Isomorphieproblemen und betrachten dabei folgende Graphklassen:

Graphklasse	Komplexität
Graphen mit Knotengrad 2	L-vollständig [Wag08]
3-zusammenhängende planare Graphen	UL ∩ coUL [TW08], L [DLN08]
Orientierte Graphen	NL [TW08]
Planare Graphen	L [DLN+09]
$K_{3,3}$- bzw. K_5-freie Graphen	L [DNTW09]
Graphen mit beschränkter Baumweite	LogCFL [DTW10]

Graphen ohne $K_{3,3}$ bzw. K_5 als induzierten Untergraphen bezeichnen wir als $K_{3,3}$- bzw. K_5-freie Graphen. Zudem können wir zeigen, dass das Isomorphieproblem auf Turniergraphen

DEUTSCHE ZUSAMMENFASSUNG

hart für DET ist [Wag07], wobei eine superpolynomielle obere Zeitschranke bekannt ist [BL83], d.h. es gibt einen Algorithmus, der $n^{\log(n)}$ Berechnungsschritte bei Eingabelänge n benötigt. Des weiteren betrachten wir das Isomorphieproblem auf Quasigruppen und Gruppen, die in Form von Multiplikationstabellen gegeben sind. Es zeigt sich, dass diese Isomorphieprobleme nicht vollständig für einige Komplexitätsklassen, wie beispielsweise L sein können.

Erreichbarkeit. Des weiteren betrachten wir auch das Erreichbarkeitsproblem und Varianten davon. Das Erreichbarkeitsproblem ist wie folgt definiert. Gegeben ist ein gerichteter Graph und zwei Knoten s und t, das Problem ist zu entscheiden, ob es einen gerichteten Pfad von s nach t gibt. Dieses Problem ist vollständig für die Klasse NL. Ist der gegebene Graph ungerichtet, ist das Problem vollständig für die Klasse L. Beide Varianten sind zentrale Probleme in der Komplexitätstheorie. Es zeigt sich, dass viele der beschriebenen Isomorphieprobleme in L liegen. Unter Einschränkung der Graphklasse erhält man auch für die Erreichbarkeitsprobleme bessere obere Schranken. Wir verbessern die oberen Schranken für einige Varianten durch Reduktion auf das Erreichbarkeitsproblem in planaren Graphen, dessen obere Schranke UL ∩ coUL ist [BTV07], eine Klasse die zwischen L und NL liegt.

Graphklasse	Komplexität
Erreichbarkeit auf planaren Graphen	UL ∩ coUL [BTV07]
Distanzproblem auf planaren Graphen	UL ∩ coUL [TW08]
Erreichbarkeit auf $K_{3,3}$- bzw. K_5-freien Graphen	UL ∩ coUL [TW09]
Distanzproblem auf $K_{3,3}$- bzw. K_5-freien Graphen	UL ∩ coUL [TW09]
Erreichbarkeit und Distanzproblem auf Graphen mit beschränkter Baumdistanzweite	L [DDN10, DTW10]

Aus den Ergebnissen erhält man interessante Beziehungen zwischen den Erreichbarkeitsproblemen und den Isomorphieproblemen. So erscheint das Isomorphieproblem schwieriger zu sein als das Erreichbarkeitsproblem, wobei die Situation umgekehrt ist, wenn man diese Entscheidungsprobleme auf planaren Graphen betrachtet. Planar-GI ist in L, es stellt sich die Frage ob das Erreichbarkeitsproblem auf planaren Graphen ebenfalls in L liegt. Wir konnten ebenso zeigen, dass die selben Schranken auf $K_{3,3}$- bzw. K_5-freie Graphen übertragbar sind.

Die VDM Verlagsservicegesellschaft sucht für wissenschaftliche Verlage abgeschlossene und herausragende

Dissertationen, Habilitationen, Diplomarbeiten, Master Theses, Magisterarbeiten usw.

für die kostenlose Publikation als Fachbuch.

Sie verfügen über eine Arbeit, die hohen inhaltlichen und formalen Ansprüchen genügt, und haben Interesse an einer honorarvergüteten Publikation?

Dann senden Sie bitte erste Informationen über sich und Ihre Arbeit per Email an *info@vdm-vsg.de*.

Sie erhalten kurzfristig unser Feedback!

VDM Verlagsservicegesellschaft mbH
Dudweiler Landstr. 99   Telefon +49 681 3720 174
D - 66123 Saarbrücken   Fax   +49 681 3720 1749
www.vdm-vsg.de

Die VDM Verlagsservicegesellschaft mbH vertritt

Printed by Books on Demand GmbH, Norderstedt / Germany